THE LIFE OF JOAN OF ARC

BY

ANATOLE FRANCE

A TRANSLATION BY WINIFRED STEPHENS

IN TWO VOLS., VOL. II

Front cover 'Joan of Arc' by John Everett Millais

The Duke of Bedford
from The Bedford Missal

Contents

LIST OF ILLUSTRATIONS

† JOAN OF ARC †
Volume II

Chapter I
The royal army from Soissons to Compiègne – poem and prophecy

ON the 22nd of July, King Charles, marching with his army down the valley of the Aisne, in a place called Vailly, received the keys of the town of Soissons.[1]

This town constituted a part of the Duchy of Valois, held jointly by the Houses of Orléans and of Bar.[2] Of its dukes, one was a prisoner in the hands of the English; the other was connected with the French party through his brother-in-law, King Charles, and with the Burgundian party through his father-in-law, the Duke of Lorraine. No wonder the fealty of the townsfolk was somewhat vacillating; downtrodden by men-at-arms, forever taken and retaken, red caps and white caps alternately ran the danger of being cast into the river. The Burgundians set fire to the houses, pillaged the churches, chastised the most notable burgesses; then came the Armagnacs, who sacked everything, made great slaughter of men, women, and children, ravished nuns, worthy wives, and honest maids. The Saracens could not have done worse.[3] City dames had been seen making sacks in which Burgundians were to be sewn up and thrown into the Aisne.[4]

King Charles made his entry into the city on Saturday the 23rd, in the morning.[5] The red caps went into hiding. The bells pealed, the folk cried "Noël," and the burgesses proffered the King two barbels, six sheep and six gallons of "*bon suret*,"[6] begging the King to forgive its being so little, but the war had ruined them.[7] They, like the people of Troyes, refused to open their gates to the men-at-arms, by virtue of their privileges, and because they had not food enough for their support. The army encamped in the plain of Ambléný.[8]

It would seem that at that time the leaders of the royal army had the intention of marching on Compiègne. Indeed it was important to capture this town from Duke Philip, for it was the key to l'Île-de-France and ought to be taken before the Duke had time to bring up an army. But throughout this campaign the King of France was resolved to recapture his towns rather by diplomacy and persuasion than by force. Between the 22nd and the 25th of July he three times summoned the inhabitants of Compiègne to surrender. Being desirous to gain time and to have the air of being constrained, they entered into negotiations.[9]

Having quitted Soissons, the royal army reached Château-Thierry on the 29th. All day it waited for the town to open its gates. In the evening the King entered.[10] Coulommiers, Crécy-en-Brie, and Provins submitted.[11]

On Monday, the 1st of August, the King crossed the Marne, over the Château-Thierry Bridge, and that same day took up his quarters at Montmirail. On the morrow he gained Provins and came within a short distance of the passage of the Seine and the high-roads of central France.[12] The army was sore anhungered, finding nought to eat in these ravaged fields and pillaged cities. Through lack of victuals preparations were being made for retreat into Poitou. But this design was thwarted by the English. While ungarrisoned towns were being reduced, the English Regent had been gathering an army. It was now advancing on Corbeil and Melun. On its approach the French gained La Motte-Nangis, some twelve miles from Provins, where they took up their position on ground flat and level, such as was convenient for the fighting of a battle, as battles were fought in those days. For one whole day they remained in battle array. There was no sign of the English coming to attack them.[13]

Meanwhile the people of Reims received tidings that King Charles was leaving Château-Thierry and was about to cross the Seine. Believing that they had been abandoned, they were afraid lest the English and Burgundians should make them pay dearly for the coronation of the King of the Armagnacs; and in truth they stood in great danger. On the 3rd of August, they resolved to send a message to King Charles to entreat him not to forsake those cities which had submitted to him. The city's herald set out forthwith. On the morrow they sent word to their good friends of Châlons and of Laon, how they had heard that King Charles was wending towards Orléans and Bourges, and how they had sent him a message.[14]

On the 5th of August, while the King is still at Provins[15] or in the neighbourhood, Jeanne addresses to the townsfolk of Reims a letter dated from the camp, on the road to Paris. Herein she promises not to desert her friends faithful and beloved. She appears to have no suspicion of the projected retreat on the Loire. Wherefore it is clear that the magistrates of Reims have not written to her and that she is not admitted to the royal counsels. She has been instructed, however, that the King has concluded a fifteen days' truce with the Duke of Burgundy, and thereof she informs the citizens of Reims. This truce is displeasing to her; and she doubts whether she will observe it. If she does observe it, it will be solely on account of the King's honour; and even then she must be persuaded that there is no trickery in it. She will therefore keep the royal army together and in readiness to march at the end of the fifteen days. She closes her letter with a recommendation to the townsfolk to keep good guard and to send her word if they have need of her.

Here is the letter:

"Good friends and beloved, ye good and loyal French of the city of Rains, Jehanne the Maid lets you wit of her tidings and prays and requires you not to doubt the good cause she maintains for the Blood Royal; and I promise and assure you that I will never forsake you as long as I shall live. It is true that the King has made truce with the Duke of Burgundy for the space of fifteen days, by which he is to surrender peaceably the city of Paris at the end of fifteen days. Notwithstanding, marvel ye not if I do not straightway enter into it, for truces thus made are not pleasing unto me, and I know not whether I shall keep them; but if I keep them it will be solely to maintain the King's honour; and further they shall not ensnare the Royal Blood, for I will keep and maintain together the King's army that it be ready at the end of fifteen days, if they make not peace. Wherefore my beloved and perfect friends, I pray ye to be in no disquietude as long as I shall live; but I require you to keep good watch and to defend well the good city of the King; and to make known unto me if there be any traitors who would do you hurt, and, as speedily as I may, I will take them out from among you; and send me of your tidings. To God I commend you. May he have you in his keeping."

Written this Friday, 5th day of August, near Provins,[16] a camp in the country or on the Paris road. Addressed to: the loyal French of the town of Rains.[17]

It cannot be doubted that the monk who acted as scribe wrote down faithfully what was dictated to him, and reproduced the Maid's very words, even her Lorraine dialect. She had then attained to the very highest degree of heroic saintliness. Here, in this letter, she takes to herself a supernatural power, to which the King, his Councillors and his Captains must submit. She ascribes to herself alone the right of recognising or denouncing treaties; she disposes entirely of the army. And, because she commands in the name of the King of Heaven, her commands are absolute. There is happening to her what necessarily happens to all those who believe themselves entrusted with a divine mission; they constitute themselves a spiritual and temporal power superior to the established powers and inevitably hostile to them. A dangerous illusion and productive of shocks in which the illuminated are generally the worst sufferers! Every day of her life living and holding converse with saints and angels, moving in the splendour of the Church Triumphant, this young peasant girl came to believe that in her resided all strength, all prudence, all wisdom and all counsel. This does not mean that she was lacking in intelligence; on the contrary she rightly perceived that the Duke of Burgundy, with his embassies, was but playing with the King and that Charles was being tricked by a Prince, who knew how to disguise his craft in magnificence. Not that Duke Philip was an enemy of peace; on the contrary he desired it, but he was desirous not to come to an open quarrel with the English. Jeanne knew little of the affairs of Burgundy and of France, but her judgment was none the less sound. Concerning the relative positions of the Kings of France and England, between whom there could be no agreement, since the matter in dispute was the possession of the kingdom, her ideas were very simple but very correct. Equally accurate were her views of the position of the King of France with regard to his great vassal, the Duke of Burgundy, with whom an understanding was not only possible and desirable, but necessary. She pronounced thereupon in a perfectly straightforward fashion: On the one hand there is peace with the Burgundians and on the other peace with the English; concerning the peace with the Duke of Burgundy, by letters and by ambassadors have I required him to come to terms with the King; as for the English, the only way of making peace with them is for them to go back to their country, to England.[18]

This truce that so highly displeased her we know not when it was concluded, whether at Soissons or Château-Thierry, on the 30th or 31st of July, or at Provins between the 2nd and 5th of August.[19] It would appear that it was to last fifteen days, at the end of which time the Duke was to undertake to surrender Paris to the King of France. The Maid had good reason for her mistrust.

When the Regent withdrew before him, King Charles eagerly returned to his plan of retreating into Poitou. From La Motte-Nangis he sent his quartermasters to Bray-sur-Seine, which had just submitted. Situated above Montereau and ten miles south of Provins, this town had a bridge over the river, across which the royal army was to pass on the 5th of August or in the morning of the 6th; but the English came by night, overcame the quartermasters and took possession of the bridge; with its retreat cut off, the royal army had to retrace its march.[20]

Within this army, which had not fought and which was being devoured by hunger, there existed a party of zealots, led by those whom Jeanne fondly called the Royal Blood.[21] They were the Duke of Alençon, the Duke of Bourbon, the Count of Vendôme, and likewise the Duke of Bar, who had just come from the War of the Apple Baskets.[22] Before he took to painting pictures and writing moralities in rhyme, this young son of the Lady Yolande had been a warrior. Duke of Bar and heir of Lorraine, he had been forced to join the English and Burgundians. Brother-in-law of King Charles, he must needs rejoice when the latter was victorious, because, but for that victory, he would never have been able to range himself on the side of the Queen, his sister, for which he would have been very sorry.[23] Jeanne knew him; not long before, she had asked the Duke of Lorraine to send him with her into France.[24] He was said to have been one of those who of their own free will followed her to Paris. Among the others were the two sons of the Lady of Laval, Gui, the eldest to whom she had offered wine at Selles-en-Berry, promising soon to give him to drink at Paris, and André, who afterwards became Marshal of Lohéac.[25] This was the army of the Maid: a band of youths, scarcely more than children, who ranged their banners side by side with the banner of a girl younger than they, but more innocent and better.

On learning that the retreat had been cut off, it is said that these youthful princes were well content and glad.[26] This was valour and zeal; but it was a curious position and a false when the knighthood wished for war while the royal council was desiring to treat, and when the knighthood actually rejoiced at the campaign being prolonged by the enemy and at the royal army being cornered by the *Godons*. Unhappily this war party could boast of no very able adherents; and the favourable opportunity had been lost, the Regent had been allowed time to collect his forces and to cope with the most pressing dangers.[27]

Its retreat cut off, the royal army fell back on Brie. On the morning of Sunday, the 7th, it was at Coulommiers; it recrossed the Marne at Château-Thierry.[28] King Charles received a message from the inhabitants of Reims, entreating him to draw nearer to them.[29] He was at La Ferté on the 10th, on the 11th at Crépy in Valois.[30]

At one stage of the march on La Ferté and Crépy, the Maid was riding in company with the King, between the Archbishop of Reims and my Lord the Bastard. Beholding the people hastening to come before the King and crying "Noël!" she exclaimed: "Good people! Never have I seen folk so glad at the coming of the fair King...."[31]

These peasants of Valois and of l'Île de France, who cried "Noël!" on the coming of King Charles, in like manner hailed the Regent and the Duke of Burgundy when they passed. Doubtless they were not so glad as they seemed to Jeanne, and if the little Saint had listened at the doors of their poor homes, this is about what she would have heard: "What shall we do? Let us surrender our all to the devil. It matters not what shall become of us, for, through treason and bad government, we must needs forsake our wives and children and flee into the woods, like wild beasts. And it is not one year or two but fourteen or fifteen since we have been led this unhappy dance. And most of the great nobles of France have died by the sword, or unconfessed have fallen victims to poison or to treachery, or in short have perished by some manner of violent death. Better for us would it have been to serve Saracens than Christians. Whether one lives badly or well it comes to the same thing. Let us do all the evil that lieth in our power. No worse can happen to us than to be slain or taken."[32]

It was only in the neighbourhood of towns or close to fortresses and castles, within sight of the watchman's eye as he looked from the top of tower or belfry, that land was cultivated. On the approach of men-at-arms, the watchman rang his bell or sounded his horn to warn the vine-dressers or the ploughmen to flee to a place of safety. In many districts the alarm bell was so frequent that oxen, sheep, and pigs, of their own accord went into hiding, as soon as they heard it.[33]

In the plains especially, which were easy of access, the Armagnacs and the English had destroyed everything. For some distance from Beauvais, from Senlis, from Soissons, from Laon, they had caused the fields to lie fallow, and here and there shrubs and underwood were springing up over land once cultivated. – "Noël! Noël!"

Throughout the duchy of Valois, the peasants were abandoning the open country and hiding in woods, rocks, and quarries.[34]

Many, in order to gain a livelihood, did like Jean de Bonval, the tailor of Noyant near Soissons, who, despite wife and children, joined a Burgundian band, which went up and down the country thieving, pillaging, and, when occasion offered, smoking out the folk who had taken refuge in churches. On one day Jean and his comrades took two hogsheads of corn, on another six or seven cows; on another a goat and a cow, on another a silver belt, a pair of gloves and a pair of shoes; on another a bale of eighteen ells of cloth to make cloaks withal. And Jean de Bonval said that within his knowledge many a man of worship did as much.[35] – "Noël! Noël!"

The Armagnacs and Burgundians had torn the coats off the peasants' backs and seized even their pots and pans. It was not far from Crépy to Meaux. Every one in that country had heard of the Tree of Vauru.

At one of the gates of the town of Meaux was a great elm, whereon the Bastard of Vauru, a Gascon noble of the Dauphin's party, used to hang the peasants he had taken, when they could not pay their ransom. When he had no executioner at hand he used to hang them himself. With him there lived a kinsman, my Lord Denis de Vauru, who was called his cousin, not that he was so in fact, but just to show that one was no better than the other.[36] In the month of March, in the year 1420, my Lord Denis, on one of his expeditions, came across a peasant tilling the ground. He took him prisoner, held him to ransom, and, tying him to his horse's tail, dragged him back to Meaux, where, by threats and torture, he exacted from him a promise to pay three times as much as he possessed. Dragged half dead from his dungeon, the villein sent to the wife he had married that year to ask her to bring the sum demanded by the lord. She was with child, and near the time of her delivery; notwithstanding, she came because she loved her husband and hoped to soften the heart of the Lord of Vauru. She failed; and Messire Denis told her that if by a certain day he did not receive the ransom, he would hang the man from the elm-tree. The poor woman went away in tears, fondly commending her husband to God's keeping. And her husband wept for pity of her. By a great effort, she succeeded in obtaining the sum demanded, but not by the day appointed. When she returned, her husband had been hanged from the Vauru Tree without respite or mercy. With bitter sobs she asked for him, and then fell exhausted by the side of that road, which, on the point of her delivery, she had traversed on foot. Having regained consciousness, a second time she asked for her husband. She was told that she would not see him till the ransom had been paid.

While she was before the Gascon, there in sight of her were brought forth several craftsmen, held to ransom, who, unable to pay, were straightway despatched to be hanged or drowned. At this spectacle a great fear for her husband came over her; nevertheless, her love for him gave her heart of courage and she paid the ransom. As soon as the Duke's men had counted the coins, they dismissed her saying that her husband had died like the other villeins.

At those cruel words, wild with sorrow and despair, she broke forth into curses and railing. When she refused to be silent, the Bastard of Vauru had her beaten and taken to the Elm-tree.

There she was stripped to the waist and tied to the Tree, whence hung forty to fifty men, some from the higher, some from the lower branches, so that, when the wind blew, their bodies touched her head. At nightfall she uttered shrieks so piercing that they were heard in the town. But whosoever had dared to go and unloose her would have been a dead man. Fright, fatigue, and exertion brought on her delivery. The wolves, attracted by her cries, came and consumed the fruit of her womb, and then devoured alive the body of the wretched creature.

In 1422, the town of Meaux was taken by the Burgundians. Then were the Bastard of Vauru and his cousin hanged from that Tree on which they had caused so many innocent folk to die so shameful a death.[37]

For the poor peasants of these unhappy lands, whether Armagnac or Burgundian, it was all of a piece; they had nothing to gain by changing masters. Nevertheless, it is possible that, on beholding the King, the descendant of Saint Louis and Charles the Wise, they may have taken heart of courage and of hope, so great was the fame for justice and for mercy of the illustrious house of France.

Thus, riding by the side of the Archbishop of Reims, the Maid looked with a friendly eye on the peasants crying "Noël!" After saying that she had nowhere seen folk so joyful at the coming of the fair King, she sighed: "Would to God I were so fortunate as, when I die, to find burial in this land."[38]

Peradventure the Lord Archbishop was curious to know whether from her Voices she had received any revelation concerning her approaching death. She often said that she would not last long. Doubtless he was acquainted with a prophecy widely known at that time, that the maid would die in the Holy Land, after having reconquered with King Charles the sepulchre of our Lord. There were those who attributed this prophecy to the Maid herself; for she had told her Confessor that she would die in battle with the Infidel, and that after her God would send a Maid of Rome who would take her place.[39] And it is obvious that Messire Regnault knew what store to set on such things. At any rate, for that reason or for another, he asked: "Jeanne, in what place look you for to die?"

To which she made answer: "Where it shall please God. For I am sure neither of the time nor of the place, and I know no more thereof than you."

No answer could have been more devout. My Lord the Bastard, who was present at this conversation, many years later thought he remembered that Jeanne had added: "But I would it were now God's pleasure for me to retire, leaving my arms, and to go and serve my father and mother, keeping sheep with my brethren and sister."[40]

If she really spoke thus, it was doubtless because she was haunted by dark forebodings. For some time she had believed herself betrayed.[41] Possibly she suspected the Lord Archbishop of Reims of wishing her ill. But it is hard to believe that he can have thought of getting rid of her now when he had employed her with such signal success; rather his intention was to make further use of her. Nevertheless he did not like her, and she felt it. He never consulted her and never told her what had been decided in council. And she suffered cruelly from the small account made of the revelations she was always receiving so abundantly. May we not interpret as a subtle and delicate reproach the utterance in his presence of this wish, this complaint? Doubtless she longed for her absent mother. And yet she was mistaken when she thought that henceforth she could endure the tranquil life of a village maiden. In her childhood at Domremy she seldom went to tend the flocks in the field; she preferred to occupy herself in household affairs;[42] but if, after having waged war beside the King and the nobles, she had had to return to her country and keep sheep, she would not have stayed there six months. Henceforth it was impossible for her to live save with that knighthood, to whose company she believed God had called her. All her heart was there, and she had finished with the distaff.

During the march on La Ferté and Crépy, King Charles received a challenge from the Regent, then at Montereau with his baronage, calling upon him to fix a meeting at whatsoever place he should appoint.[43] "We, who with all our hearts," said the Duke of Bedford, "desire the end of the war, summon and require you, if you have pity and compassion on the poor folk, who in your cause have so long time been cruelly treated, downtrodden, and oppressed, to appoint a place suitable either in this land of Brie, where we both are, or in l'Île-de-France. There will we meet. And if you have any proposal of peace to make unto us, we will listen to it and as beseemeth a good Catholic prince we will take counsel thereon."[44]

This arrogant and insulting letter had not been penned by the Regent in any desire or hope of peace, but rather, against all reason, to throw on King Charles's shoulders the responsibility for the miseries and suffering the war was causing the commonalty.

Writing to the King crowned in Reims Cathedral, from the beginning he addresses him in this disdainful manner: "You who were accustomed to call yourself Dauphin of Viennois and who now without reason take unto yourself the title of King." He declares that he wants peace and then adds forthwith: "Not a peace hollow, corrupt, feigned, violated, perjured, like that of Montereau, on which, by your fault and your consent, there followed that terrible and detestable murder, committed contrary to all law and honour of knighthood, on the person of our late dear and greatly loved Father, Jean, Duke of Burgundy."[45]

My Lord of Bedford had married one of the daughters of that Duke Jean, who had been treacherously murdered in revenge for the assassination of the Duke of Orléans. But indeed it was not wisely to prepare the way of peace to cast the crime of Montereau in the face of Charles of Valois, who had been dragged there as a child and with whom there had remained ever after a physical trembling and a haunting fear of crossing bridges.[46]

For the moment the Duke of Bedford's most serious grievance against Charles was that he was accompanied by the Maid and Friar Richard. "You cause the ignorant folk to be seduced and deceived," he said, "for you are supported by superstitious and reprobate persons, such as this woman of ill fame and disorderly life, wearing man's attire and dissolute in manners, and likewise by that apostate and seditious mendicant friar, they both alike being, according to Holy Scripture, abominable in the sight of God."

To strike still greater shame into the heart of the enemy, the Duke of Bedford proceeds to a second attack on the maiden and the monk. And in the most eloquent passage of the letter, when he is citing Charles of Valois to appear before him, he says ironically that he expects to see him come led by this woman of ill fame and this apostate monk.[47]

Thus wrote the Regent of England; albeit he had a mind, subtle, moderate, and graceful, he was moreover a good Catholic and a believer in all manner of devilry and witchcraft.

His horror at the army of Charles of Valois being commanded by a witch and a heretic monk was certainly sincere, and he deemed it wise to publish the scandal. There were doubtless only too many, who, like him, were ready to believe that the Maid of the Armagnacs was a heretic, a worshipper of idols and given to the practice of magic. In the opinion of many worthy and wise Burgundians a prince must forfeit his honour by keeping such company. And if Jeanne were in very deed a witch, what a disgrace! What an abomination! The Flowers de Luce reinstated by the devil! The Dauphin's whole camp was tainted by it. And yet when my Lord of Bedford spread abroad those ideas he was not so adroit as he thought.

Jeanne, as we know, was good-hearted and in energy untiring. By inspiring the men of her party with the idea that she brought them good luck, she gave them courage.[48] Nevertheless King Charles's counsellors knew what she could do for them and avoided consulting her. She herself felt that she would not last long.[49] Then who represented her as a great war leader? Who exalted her as a supernatural power? The enemy.

This letter shows how the English had transformed an innocent child into a being unnatural, terrible, redoubtable, into a spectre of hell causing the bravest to grow pale. In a voice of lamentation the Regent cries: The devil! the witch! And then he marvels that his fighting men tremble before the Maid, and desert rather than face her.[50]

From Montereau, the English army had fallen back on Paris. Now it once again came forth to meet the French. On Saturday, the 13th of August, King Charles held the country between Crépy and Paris. Now the Maid from the heights of Dammartin could espy the summit of Montmartre with its windmills, and the light mists from the Seine veiling that great city of Paris, promised to her by those Voices which alas! she had heeded too well.[51] On the morrow, Sunday, the King and his army encamped in a village, by name Barron, on the River Nonnette on which, five miles lower down, stands Senlis.[52]

Senlis was subject to the English.[53] It was said that the Regent was approaching with a great company of men-at-arms, commanded by the Earl of Suffolk, the Lord Talbot and the Bastard Saint Pol. With him were the crusaders of the Cardinal of Winchester, the late King's uncle, between three thousand five hundred and four thousand men, paid with the Pope's money to go and fight against the Hussites in Bohemia. The Cardinal judged it well to use them against the King of France, a very Christian King forsooth, but one whose hosts were commanded by a witch and an apostate.[54] It was reported that, in the English camp, was a captain with fifteen hundred men-at-arms, clothed in white, bearing a white standard, on which was embroidered a distaff whence was suspended a spindle; and on the streamer of the banner was worked in fine letters of gold: "*Ores, vienne la Belle!*"[55] By these words the men-at-arms wished to proclaim that if they were to meet the Maid of the Armagnacs she would find her work cut out.

Captain Jean de Saintrailles, the Brother of Poton, observed the English first when, marching towards Senlis, they were crossing La Nonnette by a ford so narrow that two horses could barely pass abreast. But King Charles's army, which was coming down the Nonnette valley, did not arrive in time to surprise them.[56] It passed the night opposite them, near Montepilloy.

On the morrow, Monday, the 15th of August, at daybreak, the men-at-arms heard mass in camp and, as far as might be, cleared their consciences; for great plunderers and whoremongers as they were, they had not given up hope of winning Paradise when this life should be over. That day was a solemn feast, when the Church, on the authority of St. Grégoire de Tours, commemorates the physical and spiritual exaltation to heaven of the Virgin Mary. Churchmen taught that it behoves men to keep the feasts of Our Lord and the Holy Virgin, and that to wage battle on days consecrated to them is to sin grievously against the glorious Mother of God. No one in King Charles's camp could maintain a contrary opinion, since all were Christians as they were in the camp of the Regent. And yet, immediately after the *Deo Gratias*, every man took up his post ready for battle.[57]

According to the established rule, the army was in several divisions: the van-guard, the archers, the main body, the rear-guard and the three wings.[58] Further, and according to the same rule, there had been formed a skirmishing company, destined if need were to succour and reinforce the other divisions. It was commanded by Captain La Hire, my Lord the Bastard, and the Sire d'Albret, La Trémouille's half-brother. With this company was the Maid. At the Battle of Patay, despite her entreaties, she had been forced to keep with the rear-guard; now she rode with the bravest and ablest, with those skirmishers or scouts, whose duty it was, says Jean de Bueil,[59] to repulse the scouts of the opposite party and to observe the number and the ordering of the enemy.[60] At length justice was done her; at length she was assigned the place which her skill in horsemanship and her courage in battle merited; and yet she hesitated to follow her comrades. According to the report of a Burgundian knight chronicler, there she was, "swayed to and fro, at one moment wishing to fight, at another not."[61]

Her perplexity is easily comprehensible. The little Saint could not bring herself to decide whether to ride forth to battle on the day of our Lady's Feast or to fold her arms while fighting was going on around her. Her Voices intensified her indecision. They never instructed her what to do save when she knew herself. In the end she went with the men-at-arms, not one of whom appears to have shared her scruples. The two armies were but the space of a culverin shot apart.[62] She, with certain of her company, went right up to the dykes and to the carts, behind which the English were entrenched. Sundry *Godons* and men of Picardy came forth from their camp and fought, some on foot, others on horseback against an equal number of French. On both sides there were wounded, and prisoners were taken. This hand to hand fighting continued the whole day; at sunset the most serious skirmish happened, and so much dust was raised that it was impossible to see anything.[63] On that day there befell what had happened on the 17th of June, between Beaugency and Meung. With the armaments and the customs of warfare of those days, it was very difficult to force an army to come out of its entrenched camp. Generally, if a battle was to be fought, it was necessary for the two sides to be in accord, and, after the pledge of battle had been sent and accepted, for each to level his own half of the field where the engagement was to take place.

At nightfall the skirmishing ceased, and the two armies slept at a crossbow-shot from each other. Then King Charles went off to Crépy, leaving the English free to go and relieve the town of Évreux, which had agreed to surrender on the 27th of August. With this town the Regent made sure of Normandy.[64]

Their loss of the opportunity of conquering Normandy was the price the French had to pay for the royal coronation procession, for that march to Reims, which was at once military, civil and religious. If, after the victory of Patay, they had hastened at once to Rouen, Normandy would have been reconquered and the English cast into the sea; if, from Patay they had pushed on to Paris they would have entered the city without resistance. Yet we must not too hastily condemn that ceremonious promenading of the Lilies through Champagne. By the march to Reims the French party, those Armagnacs reviled for their cruelty and felony, that little King of Bourges compromised in an infamous ambuscade, may have won advantages greater and more solid than the conquest of the county of Maine and the duchy of Normandy and than a victorious assault on the first city of the realm. By retaking his towns of Champagne and of France without bloodshed, King Charles appeared to advantage as a good and pacific lord, as a prince wise and debonair, as the friend of the townsfolk, as the true king of cities. In short, by concluding that campaign of honest and successful negotiations and by the august ceremonial of the coronation, he came forth at once as the lawful and very holy King of France.

An illustrious lady, a descendant of Bolognese nobles and the widow of a knight of Picardy, well versed in the liberal arts, was the author of a number of lays, virelays,[65] and ballads. Christine de Pisan, noble and high-minded, wrote with distinction in prose and verse. Loyal to France and a champion of her sex, there was nothing she more fervently desired than to see the French prosperous and their ladies honoured. In her old age she was cloistered in the Abbey of Poissy, where her daughter was a nun. There, on the 31st of July, 1429, she completed a poem of sixty-one stanzas, each containing eight lines of eight syllables, in praise of the Maid. In halting measures and affected language, these verses expressed the thoughts of the finest, the most cultured and the most pious souls touching the angel of war sent of God to the Dauphin Charles.[66]

In this work she begins by saying that for eleven years she has spent her cloistered life in weeping. And in very truth, this noble-hearted woman wept over the misfortunes of the realm, into which she had been born, wherein she had grown up, where kings and princes had received her and learned poets had done her honour, and the language of which she spoke with the precision of a purist. After eleven years of mourning, the victories of the Dauphin were her first joy.

"At length," she says, "the sun begins to shine once more and the fine days to bloom again. That royal child so long despised and offended, behold him coming, wearing on his head a crown and accoutred with spurs of gold. Let us cry: 'Noël! Charles, the seventh of that great name, King of the French, thou hast recovered thy kingdom, with the help of a Maid.'"

Christine recalls a prophecy concerning a King, Charles, son of Charles, surnamed The Flying Hart,[67] who was to be emperor. Of this prophecy we know nothing save that the escutcheon of King Charles VII was borne by two winged stags and that a letter to an Italian merchant, written in 1429, contains an obscure announcement of the coronation of the Dauphin at Rome.[68]

"I pray God," continued Christine, "that thou mayest be that one, that God will grant thee life to see thy children grow up, that through thee and through them, France may have joy, that serving God, thou wage not war to the utterance. My hope is that thou shalt be good, upright, a friend of justice, greater than any other, that pride sully not thy prowess, that thou be gentle, favourable to thy people and fearing God who hath chosen thee to serve him.

"And thou, Maid most happy, most honoured of God, thou hast loosened the cord with which France was bound. Canst thou be praised enough, thou who hast brought peace to this land laid low by war?

"Jeanne, born in a propitious hour, blessed be thy creator! Maid, sent of God, in whom the Holy Ghost shed abroad a ray of his grace, who hast from him received and dost keep gifts in abundance; never did he refuse thy request. Who can ever be thankful enough unto thee?"

The Maid, saviour of the realm, Dame Christine compares to Moses who delivered Israel out of the Land of Egypt.

"That a Maid should proffer her breast, whence France may suck the sweet milk of peace, behold a matter which is above nature!

"Joshua was a mighty conqueror. What is there strange in that, since he was a strong man? But now behold, a woman, a shepherdess doth appear, of greater worship than any man. But with God all things are easy.

"By Esther, Judith and Deborah, women of high esteem, he delivered his oppressed people. And well I know there have been women of great worship. But Jeanne is above all. Through her God hath worked many miracles.

"By a miracle was she sent; the angel of the Lord led her to the King."

"Before she could be believed, to clerks and to scholars was she taken and thoroughly examined. She said she was come from God, and history proved her saying to be true, for Merlin, the Sibyl and Bede had seen her in the spirit. In their books they point to her as the saviour of France, and in their prophecies they let wit of her, saying: 'In the French wars she shall bear the banner.' And indeed they relate all the manner of her history."

We are not astonished that Dame Christine should have been acquainted with the Sibylline poems; for it is known that she was well versed in the writings of the ancients. But we perceive that the obviously mutilated prophecy of Merlin the Magician and the apocryphal chronogram of the Venerable Bede had come under her notice. The predictions and verses of the Armagnac ecclesiastics were spread abroad everywhere with amazing rapidity.[69]

Dame Christine's views concerning the Maid accord with those of the doctors of the French party; and the poem she wrote in her convent in many passages bears resemblance to the treatise of the Archbishop of Embrun.

There it is said:

"The goodness of her life proves that Jeanne possesses the grace of God.

"It was made manifest, when at the siege of Orléans her might revealed itself. Never was miracle plainer. God did so succour his own people, that the strength of the enemy was but as that of a dead dog. They were taken or slain.

"Honour to the feminine sex, God loves it. A damsel of sixteen, who is not weighed down by armour and weapons, even though she be bred to endure hardness, is not that a matter beyond nature? The enemy flees before her. Many eyes behold it.

"She goeth forth capturing towns and castles. She is the first captain of our host. Such power had not Hector or Achilles. But God, who leads her, does all.

"And you, ye men-at-arms, who suffer durance vile and risk your lives for the right, be ye faithful: in heaven shall ye have reward and glory, for whosoever fighteth for the just cause, winneth Paradise.

"Know ye that by her the English shall be cast down, for it is the will of God, who inclineth his ear to the voice of the good folk, whom they desired to overthrow. The blood of the slain crieth against them."

In the shadow of her convent Dame Christine shares the hope common to every noble soul; from the Maid she expects all the good things she longs for. She believes that Jeanne will restore concord to the Christian Church. The gentlest spirits of those days looked to fire and sword for the bringing in of unity and obedience; they never dreamed that Christian charity could mean charity towards the whole human race. Wherefore, on the strength of prophecy, the poetess expects the Maid to destroy the infidel and the heretic, or in other words the Turk and the Hussite.

"In her conquest of the Holy Land, she will tear up the Saracens like weeds. Thither will she lead King Charles, whom

God defend! Before he dies he shall make that journey. He it is who shall conquer the land. There shall she end her life. There shall the thing come to pass."

The good Christine would appear to have brought her poem to this conclusion when she received tidings of the King's coronation. She then added thirteen stanzas to celebrate the mystery of Reims and to foretell the taking of Paris.[70]

Thus in the gloom and silence of one of those convents where even the hushed noises of the world penetrated but seldom, this virtuous lady collected and expressed in rhyme all those dreams of church and state which centred round a child.

In a fairly good ballad written at the time of the coronation, in love and honour "of the beautiful garden of the noble flowers de luce,"[71] and for the elevation of the white cross, King Charles VII is described by that mysterious name "the noble stag," which we have first discovered in Christine's poem. The unknown author of the ballad says that the Sibyl, daughter of King Priam, prophesied the misfortunes of this royal stag; but such a prediction need not surprise us, when we remember that Charles of Valois was of Priam's royal line, wherefore Cassandra, when she revealed the destiny of the Flying Hart, did but prolong down the centuries the vicissitudes of her own family.[72]

Rhymers on the French side celebrated the unexpected victories of Charles and the Maid as best they knew how, in a commonplace fashion, by some stiff poem but scantily clothing a thin and meagre muse.

Nevertheless there is a ballad,[73] by a Dauphinois poet, beginning with this line; "Back, English *coués*, back!"[74] which is powerful through the genuine religious spirit which prevails throughout. The author, some poor ecclesiastic, points piously to the English banner cast down, "by the will of King Jesus and of Jeanne the sweet Maid."[75]

The Maid had derived her influence over the common folk from the prophecies of Merlin the Magician and the

Venerable Bede.[76] As Jeanne's deeds became known, predictions foretelling them came to be discovered. For example it was found that Engélide, daughter of an old King of Hungary,[77] had known long before of the coronation at Reims. Indeed to this royal virgin was attributed a prophecy recorded in Latin, of which the following is a literal translation:

"O Lily illustrious, watered by princes, by the sower planted in the open, in an orchard delectable, by flowers and sweet-smelling roses surrounded. But, alas! dismay of the Lily, terror of the orchard! Sundry beasts, some coming from without, others nourished within the orchard, hurtling horns against horns, have well nigh crushed the Lily, which fades for lack of water. Long do they trample upon it, destroying nearly all its roots and assaying to wither it with their poisoned breath.

"But the beasts shall be driven forth in shame from the orchard, by a virgin coming from the land whence flows the cruel venom. Behind her right ear the Virgin bears a little scarlet sign; she speaks softly, and her neck is short. To the Lily shall she give fountains of living water, and shall drive out the serpent, to all men revealing its venom. With a laurel wreath woven by no mortal hand shall she at Reims engarland happily the gardener of the Lily, named Charles, son of Charles. All around the turbulent neighbours shall submit, the waters shall surge, the folk shall cry: 'Long live the Lily! Away with the beast! Let the orchard flower!' He shall approach the fields of the Island, adding fleet to fleet, and there a multitude of beasts shall perish in the rout. Peace for many shall be established. The keys of a great number shall recognise the hand that had forged them. The citizens of a noble city shall be punished for perjury by defeat, groaning with many groans, and at the entrance [of Charles?] high walls shall fall low. Then the orchard of the Lily shall be ... (?) and long shall it flower."[78]

This prophecy attributed to the unknown daughter of a distant king would seem to us to proceed from a French ecclesiastic and an Armagnac. French royalty is portrayed in the figure of the delectable orchard, around which contend beasts nourished in the orchard as well as foreign beasts, that is Burgundians and English. King Charles of Valois is mentioned by his own name and that of his father, and the name of the coronation town occurs in full.

The reduction of certain towns by their liege lord is stated most clearly. Doubtless the prediction was made at the very time of the coronation. It explicitly mentions deeds already accomplished and dimly hints at events looked for, fulfilment of which was delayed, or happened in a manner other than what was expected, or never happened at all, such as the taking of Paris after a terrible assault, the invasion of England by the French, the conclusion of peace.

It is highly probable that when announcing that the deliverer of the orchard might be recognised by her short neck, her sweet voice and a little scarlet mark, the pseudo Engélide was carefully depicting characteristics noticeable in Jeanne herself. Moreover we know that Isabelle Romée's daughter had a sweet woman's voice.[79] That her neck was broad and firmly set on her shoulders accords with what is known concerning her robust appearance.[80] And doubtless the so-called daughter of the King of Hungary did not imagine the birth-mark behind her right ear.[81]

Chapter II
The Maid's first visit to Compiègne – the three popes – Saint Denys – Truces

FTER the English army had departed for Normandy, King Charles sent from Crépy to Senlis the Count of Vendôme, the Maréchal de Rais and the Maréchal de Boussac with their men-at-arms. The inhabitants gave them to wit that they inclined to favour the Flowers de Luce.[82] Henceforth the submission of Compiègne was sure. The King summoned the citizens to receive him; on Wednesday the 18th, the keys of the town were brought to him; on the next day he entered.[83] The Attorneys[84] (for by that name the aldermen of the town were called) presented to him Messire Guillaume de Flavy, whom they had elected governor of their town, as being their most experienced and most faithful citizen. On his being presented they asked the King, according to their privilege, to confirm and ratify his appointment. But the sire de la Trémouille took for himself the governorship of Compiègne and appointed as his lieutenant Messire Guillaume de Flavy, whom, notwithstanding, the inhabitants regarded as their captain.[85]

One by one, the King was recovering his good towns. He charged the folk of Beauvais to acknowledge him as their lord. When they saw the flowers-de-luce borne by the heralds, the citizens cried: "Long live Charles of France!" The clergy chanted a *Te Deum* and there was great rejoicing. Those who refused fealty to King Charles were put out of the town with permission to take away their possessions.[86] The Bishop and

Vidame of Beauvais, Messire Pierre Cauchon, who was Grand Almoner of France to King Henry, and a negotiator of important ecclesiastical business, grieved to see his city returning to the French;[87] it was to the city's hurt, but he could not help it. He failed not to realise that part of this disgrace he owed to the Maid of the Armagnacs, who was influential with her party and had the reputation of being all powerful. As he was a good theologian he must have suspected that the devil was leading her and he wished her all possible harm.

At this time Artois, Picardy, all the Burgundian territory in the north, was slipping away from Burgundy. Had King Charles gone there the majority of the dwellers in the strong towers and castles of Picardy would have received him as their sovereign.[88] But meanwhile his enemies would have recaptured what he had just won in Valois and the Île de France.

Having entered Compiègne with the King, Jeanne lodged at the Hôtel du Bœuf, the house of the King's proctor. She slept with the proctor's wife, Marie Le Boucher, who was a kinswoman of Jacques Boucher, Treasurer of Orléans.[89]

She longed to march on Paris, which she was sure of taking since her Voices had promised it to her. It is related that at the end of two or three days she grew impatient, and, calling the Duke of Alençon, said to him: "My fair Duke, command your men and likewise those of the other captains to equip themselves," then she is said to have cried: "By my staff! I must to Paris."[90] But this could not have happened: the Maid never gave orders to the men-at-arms. The truth of the matter is that the Duke of Alençon, with a goodly company of fighting men, took his leave of the King and that Jeanne was to accompany him. She was ready to mount her horse when on Monday the 22nd of August, a messenger from the Count of Armagnac brought her a letter which she caused to be read to her.[91] The following are the contents of the missive:

"My very dear Lady, I commend myself humbly to you, and I entreat you, for God's sake, that seeing the divisions which are at present in the holy Church Universal, concerning the question of the popes (for there are three contending for the papacy: one dwells at Rome and calls himself Martin V, whom all Christian kings obey: the other dwells at Peñiscola, in the kingdom of Valentia, and calls himself Clement VIII; the third dwells no man knows where, unless it be the Cardinal de Saint-Estienne and a few folk with him, and calls himself Pope Benedict XIV; the first, who is called Pope Martin, was elected at Constance by consent of all Christian nations; he who is called Clement was elected at Peñiscola, after the death of Pope Benedict XIII, by three of his cardinals; the third who is called Pope Benedict XIV was elected secretly at Peñiscola, by that same Cardinal Saint-Estienne himself): I pray you beseech Our Lord Jesus Christ that in his infinite mercy, he declare unto us through you, which of the three aforesaid is the true pope and whom it shall be his pleasure that henceforth we obey, him who is called Martin, or him who is called Clement or him who is called Benedict; and in whom we should believe, either in secret or under reservation or by public pronouncement: for we shall all be ready to work the will and the pleasure of Our Lord Jesus Christ.

Yours in all things,

Count d'Armagnac."[92]

He who wrote thus, calling Jeanne his very dear lady, recommending himself humbly to her, not in self-abasement, but merely, as we should say to-day, out of courtesy, was one of the greater vassals of the crown.

She had never seen this baron, and doubtless she had never heard of him. Jean IV, son of that Constable of France who had been killed in 1418, was the cruellest man in the kingdom. At that time he was between thirty-three and thirty-four years of age. He held both Armagnacs, the Black and the White, the country of the Four Valleys, the counties of Pardiac, of Fesenzac, Astarac, La Lomagne, and l'Île-Jourdain. After the Count of Foix he was the most powerful noble of Gascony.[93]

While his name was among those of the adherents of the King and while it was used to designate those who were hostile to the English and Burgundians, Jean IV himself was neither French nor English, but simply Gascon. He called himself count by the grace of God, but he was ever ready to acknowledge himself the King's vassal when it was a question of receiving gifts from that suzerain, who might not always be able to afford himself new gaiters, but who must perforce spend large sums on his great vassals. Meanwhile Jean IV showed consideration to the English, protected an adventurer in the Regent's pay, and gave appointments in his household to men wearing the red cross. He was as violent and treacherous as any of his retainers. Having unlawfully seized the Marshal de Séverac, he exacted from him the cession of all his goods and then had him strangled.[94]

This murder was quite recent. And now we have the docile son of Holy Church appearing eager to discover who is his true spiritual father. It would seem, however, that his mind was already made up on the subject and that he already knew the answer to his question. In verity the long schism, which had rent Christendom asunder, had terminated twelve years earlier. It had ended when the Conclave, which had assembled at Constance in the House of the Merchants on the 8th of November, 1417, on the 11th of that month, Saint Martin's Day, proclaimed Pope, the Cardinal Deacon Otto Colonna, who assumed the title of Martin V. In the Eternal City Martin V wore that tiara which Lorenzo Ghiberti had adorned with eight figures in gold;[95] and the wily Roman had contrived to obtain his recognition by England and even by France, who thenceforward renounced all hope of a French pontiff. While Charles VII's advisers may not have agreed with Martin V on the question of a General Council, all the rights of the Pope of Rome in the Kingdom of France had been restored to him by an edict, in 1425. Martin V was the one and only pope. Nevertheless, Alphonso of Aragon, highly incensed because Martin V supported against him the rights of Louis d'Anjou to the Kingdom of Naples, determined to oppose to the Pope of Rome a pontiff of his own making. And just ready to hand he had a canon who called himself pope, and on the following grounds: the Anti-pope, Benedict XIII, having fled to Peñiscola, had on his death-bed nominated four cardinals, three of whom appointed to succeed him a canon of Barcelona, one Gil Muñoz, who assumed the title of Clement VIII. Imprisoned in the château of Peñiscola on a barren neck of land on three sides washed by the sea, this was the Clement whom the King of Aragon had chosen to be the rival of Martin V.[96]

The Pope excommunicated the King of Aragon and then opened negotiations with him. The Count of Armagnac joined the King's party. For the baptism of his children the Count had holy water blessed by Benedict XIII brought from Peñiscola. He likewise was excommunicated. The blow had fallen upon him in this very year, 1429. Thus for some months he had been deprived of the sacraments and excluded from public worship. Hence arose all manner of secular difficulties, in addition to which he was probably afraid of the devil.

Moreover his position was becoming impossible. His powerful ally, King Alfonso, gave in, and himself called upon Clement VIII to resign. When he addressed his inquiry to the Maid of France, the Armagnac was evidently meditating the withdrawal of his allegiance from an unfortunate anti-pope, who was himself renouncing or about to renounce the tiara; for Clement VIII abdicated at Peñiscola on the 26th of July. The dictation of the Count's letter cannot have occurred long before that date and may have been after. At any rate whenever he dictated it he must have been aware of the position of the Sovereign Pontiff Clement VIII.

As for the third Pope mentioned in his missive, Benedict XIV, he had no tidings of him, and indeed he was keeping very quiet. His election to the Holy See had been singular in that it had been made by one cardinal alone. Benedict XIV's right to the papacy had been communicated to him by a cardinal created by the Anti-pope, Benedict XIII, at the time of his promotion in 1409. That Cardinal was Jean Barrère, a Frenchman, Bachelor of laws, priest and Cardinal of Saint-Étienne *in Cœlio monte*. It was not to Benedict XIV that the Armagnac was thinking of giving his allegiance; obviously he was eager to submit to Martin V.

It is not easy therefore to discover why he should have asked Jeanne to indicate the true pope. Doubtless it was customary in those days to consult on all manner of questions those holy maids to whom God vouchsafed illumination. Such an one the Maid appeared, and her fame as a prophetess had been spread abroad in a very short time. She revealed hidden things, she drew the curtain from the future. We are reminded of that *capitoul*[97] of Toulouse, who about three weeks after the deliverance of Orléans, advised her being consulted as to a remedy for the corruption of the coinage. Bona of Milan, married to a poor gentleman in the train of her cousin, Queen Ysabeau, besought the Maid's help in her endeavour to regain the duchy which she claimed through her descent from the Visconti.[98] It was just as appropriate to question the Maid concerning the Pope and the Anti-pope. But the most difficult point in this question is to discover what were the Count of Armagnac's reasons for consulting the Holy Maid on a matter concerning which he appears to have been sufficiently informed. The following seems the most probable.

Jean IV was prepared to recognise Martin V as Pope; but he desired his submission to appear honourable and reasonable. Wherefore he conceived the idea of ascribing his conduct to the command of Jesus Christ, speaking through the Holy Maid. But it was necessary for the command to be in accordance with his wishes. The letter provides for that. He is careful to indicate to Jeanne, and consequently to God, what reply would be suitable. He lays stress on the fact that Martin V, who had recently excommunicated him, was elected at Constance by the consent of all Christian nations, that he dwells at Rome and that he is obeyed by all Christian kings. He points out on the other hand the circumstances which invalidate the election of Clement VIII by only three cardinals, and the still more ridiculous election of that Benedict, who was chosen by a conclave consisting of only one cardinal.[99]

After such a setting forth could there possibly remain a single doubt as to whether Pope Martin was the true pope? But such guile was lost on Jeanne; it escaped her entirely. The Count of Armagnac's letter, which she had read to her as she was mounting her horse, must have struck her as very obscure.[100]

The names of Benedict, of Clement and of Martin she had never heard. The Saints, Catherine and Margaret, with whom she was constantly holding converse, revealed to her nothing concerning the Pope. They spoke to her of nought save of the realm of France; and Jeanne's prudence generally led her to confine her prophecies to the subject of the war. This circumstance was pointed out by a German clerk as a matter extraordinary and worthy of note.[101] But for this once she consented to reply to Jean IV, in order to maintain her reputation as a prophet and because the title of Armagnac strongly appealed to her. She told him that at that moment she was unable to instruct him concerning the true pope, but that later she would inform him in which of the three he must believe, according as God should reveal it unto her. In short, she in a measure followed the example of such soothsayers as postpone the announcement of the oracle to a future day.

Jhesus † Maria

Count of Armagnac, my good friend and beloved, Jehanne the Maid lets you to wit that your message hath come before me, the which hath told me that you have sent from where you are to know from me in which of the three popes, whom you mention in your memorial, you ought to believe. This thing in sooth I cannot tell you truly for the present, until I be in Paris or at rest elsewhere, because for the present I am too much hindered by affairs of war; but when you hear that I am in Paris send a message to me, and I will give you to understand what you shall rightfully believe, and what I shall know by the counsel of my Righteous and Sovereign Lord, the King of all the world, and what you should do, as far as I may. To God I commend you; God keep you. Written at Compiengne, the 22nd day of August.[102]

Jeanne before she made this reply can have consulted neither the good Brother Pasquerel nor the good Friar Richard nor indeed any of the churchmen of her company. They would have told her that the true pope was the Pope of Rome, Martin V. They might also have represented to her that she was belittling the authority of the Church by appealing to a revelation from God concerning popes and anti-popes. Sometimes, they would have told her, God confides the secrets of his Church to holy persons. But it would be rash to count upon so rare a privilege.

Jeanne exchanged a few words with the messenger who had brought her the missive; but the interview was brief. The messenger was not safe in the town, not that the soldiers would have made him pay for his master's crimes and treasons; but the Sire de la Trémouille was at Compiègne; and he knew that Count Jean, who for the nonce was in alliance with the Constable De Richemont, was meditating something against him. La Trémouille was not so malevolent as the Count of Armagnac: and yet the poor messenger only narrowly escaped being thrown into the Oise.[103]

On the morrow, Tuesday the 23rd of August, the Maid and the Duke of Alençon took leave of the King and set out from Compiègne with a goodly company of fighting men. Before marching on Saint-Denys in France, they went to Senlis to collect a company of men-at-arms whom the King had sent there.[104] As was her custom, the Maid rode surrounded by monks. Friar Richard, who predicted the approaching end of the world, had joined the procession. It would seem that he had superseded the others, even Brother Pasquerel, the chaplain. It was to him that the Maid confessed beneath the walls of Senlis. In that same spot, with the Dukes of Clermont and Alençon,[105] she took the communion on two consecutive days. She must have been in the hands of monks who were in the habit of making a very frequent use of the Eucharist.

The Lord Bishop of Senlis was Jean Fouquerel. Hitherto, he had been on the side of the English and entirely devoted to the Lord Bishop of Beauvais. On the approach of the royal army, Jean Fouquerel, who was a cautious person, had gone off to Paris to hide a large sum of money. He was careful of his possessions. Some one in the army took his nag and gave it to the Maid. By means of a draft on the receiver of taxes and the *gabelle* officer of the town, two hundred golden *saluts*[106] were paid for it. The Lord Bishop did not approve of this transaction and demanded his hackney. Hearing of his displeasure, the Maid caused a letter to be written to him, saying that he might have back his nag if he liked; she did not want it for she found it not sufficiently hardy for men-at-arms. The horse was sent to the Sire de La Trémouille with a request that he would deliver it to the Lord Bishop, who never received it.[107]

As for the bill on the tax receiver and *gabelle* officer, it may have been worthless; and probably the Reverend Father in God, Jean Fouquerel, never had either horse or money. Jeanne was not at fault, and yet the Lord Bishop of Beauvais and the clerks of the university were shortly to bring home to her the gravity of the sacrilege of laying hands on an ecclesiastical hackney.[108]

To the north of Paris, about five miles distant from the great city, there rose the towers of Saint-Denys. On the 26th of August, the army of the Duke of Alençon arrived there, and entered without resistance, albeit the town was strongly fortified.[109] The place was famous for its illustrious abbey very rich and very ancient. The following is the story of its foundation.

Dagobert, King of the French, had from childhood been a devout worshipper of Saint Denys. And whenever he trembled before the ire of King Clotaire his father, he would take refuge in the church of the holy martyr. When he died, a pious man dreamed that he saw Dagobert summoned before the tribunal of God; a great number of saints accused him of having despoiled their churches; and the demons were about to drag him into hell when Saint Denys appeared; and by his intercession, the soul of the King was delivered and escaped punishment. The story was held to be true, and it was thought that the King's soul returned to animate his body and that he did penance.[110]

When the Maid with the army occupied Saint-Denys, the three porches, the embattled parapets, the tower of the Abbey Church, erected by the Abbot Suger, were already three centuries old. There were buried the kings of France; and thither they came to take the *oriflamme*. Fourteen years earlier the late

King Charles had fetched it forth, but since then none had borne it.[111]

Many were the wonders told touching this royal standard. And with some of those marvels the Maid must needs have been acquainted, since on her coming into France, she was said to have given the Dauphin Charles the surname of *oriflamme*,[112] as a pledge and promise of victory.[113] At Saint-Denys was preserved the heart of the Constable Du Guesclin.[114] Jeanne had heard of his high renown; she had proffered wine to Madame de Laval's eldest son; and to his grandmother, who had been Sire Bertrand's second wife, she had sent a little ring of gold, out of respect for the widow of so valiant a man,[115] asking her to forgive the poverty of the gift.

The monks of Saint-Denys preserved precious relics, notably a piece of the wood of the true cross, the linen in which the Child Jesus had been wrapped, a fragment of the pitcher wherein the water had been changed to wine at the Cana marriage feast, a bar of Saint Lawrence's gridiron, the chin of Saint Mary Magdalen, a cup of tamarisk wood used by Saint Louis as a charm against the spleen. There likewise was to be seen the head of Saint Denys. True, at the same time one was being shown in the Cathedral church of Paris. The Chancellor, Jean Gerson, treating of Jeanne the Maid, a few days before his death, wrote that of her it might be said as of the head of Saint Denys, that belief in her was a matter of edification and not of faith, albeit in both places alike the head ought to be worshipped in order that edification should not be turned into scandal.[116]

In this abbey everything proclaimed the dignity, the prerogatives and the high worship of the house of France. Jeanne must joyously have wondered at the insignia, the symbols and signs of the royalty of the Lilies gathered together in this spot,[117] if indeed those eyes, occupied with celestial visions, had leisure to perceive the things of earth, and if her Voices, endlessly whispering in her ear, left her one moment's respite.

Saint Denys was a great saint, since there was no doubt of his being in very deed the Areopagite himself.[118] But since he had permitted his abbey to be taken he was no longer invoked as the patron saint of the Kings of France. The Dauphin's followers had replaced him by the Blessed Archangel Michael, whose abbey, near the city of Avranches, had victoriously held out against the English. It was Saint Michael not Saint Denys who had appeared to Jeanne in the garden at Domremy; but she knew that Saint Denys was the war cry of France.[119]

The monks of that rich abbey wasted by war lived there in poverty and in disorder.[120] Armagnacs and Burgundians in turn descended upon the neighbouring fields and villages, plundering and ravaging, leaving nought that it was possible to carry off. At Saint-Denys was held the Fair of Le Lendit, one of the greatest in Christendom. But now Merchants had ceased to attend it. At the Lendit of 1418, there were but three booths, and those for the selling of shoes from Brabant, in the high street of Saint-Denys, near the Convent of Les Filles-Dieu. Since 1426, there had been no fair at all.[121]

At the tidings that the Armagnacs were approaching Troyes, the peasants had cut their corn before it was ripe and brought it into Paris. On entering Saint-Denys, the Duke of Alençon's men-at-arms found the town deserted. The chief burgesses had taken refuge in Paris.[122] Only a few of the poorer families were left. The Maid held two newly born infants over the baptismal font.[123]

Hearing of these Saint-Denys baptisms, her enemies accused her of having lit candles and held them inclined over the infant's heads, in order that she might read their destinies in the melted wax. It was not the first time, it appeared, that she indulged in such practices. When she entered a town, little children were said to offer her candles kneeling, and she received them as an agreeable sacrifice. Then upon the heads of these innocents she would let fall three drops of burning wax, proclaiming that by virtue of this ceremony they could not fail to be good. In such acts Burgundian ecclesiastics discerned idolatry and witchcraft, in which was likewise involved heresy.[124]

Here again, at Saint-Denys, she distributed banners to the men-at-arms. Churchmen on the English side strongly suspected her of charming those banners. And as everyone in those days believed in magic, such a suspicion was not without its danger.[125]

The Maid and the Duke of Alençon lost no time. Immediately after their arrival at Saint-Denys they went forth to skirmish before the gates of Paris. Two or three times a day they engaged in this desultory warfare, notably by the wind-mill at the Saint-Denys Gate and in the village of La Chapelle. "Every day there was booty taken," says Messire Jean de Bueil.[126] It seems hardly credible that in a country which had been plundered and ravaged over and over again, there should have been anything left to be taken; and yet the statement is made and attested by one of the nobles in the army.

Out of respect for the seventh commandment, the Maid forbade the men of her company to commit any theft whatsoever. And she always refused victuals offered her when she knew they had been stolen. In reality she, like the others, lived on pillage, but she did not know it. One day when a Scotsman gave her to wit that she had just partaken of some stolen veal, she flew into a fury and would have beaten him: saintly women are subject to such fits of passion.[127]

Jeanne is said to have observed the walls of Paris carefully, seeking the spot most favourable for attack.[128] The truth is that in this matter as in all others she depended on her Voices. For the rest she was far superior to all the men-at-arms in courage and in good will. From Saint-Denys she sent the King message after message, urging him to come and take Paris.[129] But at Compiègne the King and his Council were negotiating with the ambassadors of the Duke of Burgundy, to wit: Jean de Luxembourg, Lord of Beaurevoir, Hugues de Cayeux, Bishop of Arras, David de Brimeu and my Lord of Charny.[130]

The fifteen days' truce had expired. Our only information concerning it is contained in Jeanne's letter to the citizens of Reims. According to Jeanne, the Duke of Burgundy had undertaken to surrender the city to the King of France on the fifteenth day.[131] If he had so agreed it was on conditions of which we know nothing; we are not therefore in a position to say whether or no those conditions had been carried out. The Maid placed no trust in this promise, and she was quite right; but she did not know everything; and on the very day when she was complaining of the truce to the citizens of Reims, Duke Philip was receiving the command of Paris at the hands of the Regent, and was henceforth in a position to dispose of the city as he liked.[132] Duke Philip could not bear the sight of Charles of Valois, who had been present at the murder on the Bridge of Montereau, but he detested the English and wished they would go to the devil or return to their island. The vineyards and the cloth looms of his dominions were too numerous and too important for him not to wish for peace. He had no desire to be King of France; therefore he could be treated with, despite his avarice and dissimulation. Nevertheless the fifteenth day had gone by and the city of Paris remained in the hands of the English and the Burgundians, who were not friends but allies.

On the 28th of August a truce was concluded. It was to last till Christmas and was to extend over the whole country north of the Seine, from Nogent to Harfleur, with the exception of such towns as were situated where there was a passage over the river. Concerning the city of Paris it was expressly stated that "Our Cousin of Burgundy, he and his men, may engage in the defence of the town and in resisting such as shall make war upon it or do it hurt."[133] The Chancellor Regnault de Chartres, the Sire de la Trémouille, Christophe d'Harcourt, the Bastard of Orléans, the Bishop of Séez, and likewise certain young nobles very eager for war, such as the Counts of Clermont and of Vendôme and the Duke of Bar, in short all the Counsellors of the King and the Princes of the Blood who signed this article, were apparently giving the enemy a weapon against them and renouncing any attempt upon Paris. But they were not all fools; the Bastard of Orléans was keen witted and the Lord Archbishop of Reims was anything but an Olibrius.[134] They doubtless knew what they were about when they recognised the Duke of

Burgundy's rights over Paris. Duke Philip, as we know, had been governor of the great town since the 13th of August. The Regent had ceded it with the idea that Burgundy would keep the Parisians in order better than England, for the English were few in number and were disliked as foreigners. What did it profit King Charles to recognise his cousin's rights over Paris? We fail to see precisely; but after all this truce was no better and no worse than others. In sooth it did not give Paris to the King, but neither did it prevent the King from taking it. Did truces ever hinder Armagnacs and Burgundians from fighting when they had a mind to fight? Was one of those frequent truces ever kept?[135] After having signed this one, the King advanced to Senlis. The Duke of Alençon came to him there twice. Charles reached Saint-Denys on Wednesday the 7th of September.[136]

Chapter III
The attack on Paris

N the days when King John was a prisoner in the hands of the English, the townsfolk of Paris, beholding the enemy in the heart of the land, feared lest their city should be besieged. In all haste therefore they proceeded to put it in a state of defence; they surrounded it with trenches and counter trenches. On the side of the University the suburbs were left defenceless; small and remote, they were burned down. But on the right bank the more extensive suburbs well nigh touched the city. One part of them was enclosed by the trenches. When peace was concluded, Charles, Regent of the Realm, undertook to surround the town on the north with an embattled wall, flanked with square towers, with terraces and parapets, with a road round and steps leading up to the ramparts.

In certain places the trench was single, in others double. The work was superintended by Hugues Aubriot, Provost of Paris, to whom was entrusted also the building of the Saint-Antoine bastion, completed under King Charles VI.[137] This new fortification began on the east, near the river, on the rising ground of Les Célestins. Within its circle it enclosed the district of Saint Paul, the Culture Sainte-Catherine, the Temple, Saint-Martin, Les Filles-Dieu, Saint Sauveur, Saint Honoré, Les Quinze Vingts, which hitherto had been in the suburbs and undefended; and it reached the river below the Louvre, which was thus united to the town. There were six gates in the circumvallation, to wit: beginning on the east, the Baudet Gate or Saint-Antoine Gate, the Saint-Avoye or Temple Gate, the

Gate of the Painters or of Saint-Denis, the Saint-Martin or Montmartre Gate, the Saint-Honoré Gate and the Gate of the Seine.[138]

The Parisians did not like the English and were sorely grieved by their occupation of the city. The folk murmured when, after the funeral of the late King, Charles VI, the Duke of Bedford had the sword of the King of France borne before him.[139] But what cannot be helped must be endured. The Parisians may have disliked the English; they admired Duke Philip, a prince of comely countenance and the richest potentate of Christendom. As for the little King of Bourges, mean-looking and sad-faced, strongly suspected of treason at Montereau, there was nothing pleasing in him; he was despised and his followers were regarded with fear and horror. For ten years they had been ranging round the town, pillaging, taking prisoners and holding them to ransom. The English and Burgundians indeed did likewise. When, in the August of 1423, Duke Philip came to Paris, his men ravaged all the neighbouring fields, albeit they belonged to friends and allies. But they were only passing through,[140] while the Armagnacs were for ever raiding, eternally stealing all they could lay hands on, setting fire to barns and churches, killing women and children, ravishing maids and nuns, hanging men by the thumbs. In 1420, like devils let loose, they descended upon the village of Champigny and burned at once oats, wheat, sheep, cows, oxen, women and children. Likewise did they and worse still at Croissy.[141] One ecclesiastic said they had caused more Christians to suffer martyrdom than Maximian and Diocletian.[142]

And yet, in the year 1429, there might have been discovered in the city of Paris not a few followers of the Dauphin. Christine de Pisan, who was very loyal to the House of Valois, said: "In Paris there are many wicked. Good are there also and faithful to their King. But they dare not lift up their voices."[143]

It was common knowledge that in the Parlement and even in the Chapter of Notre-Dame were to be found those who had dealings with the Armagnacs.[144]

On the morrow of their victory at Patay, those terrible Armagnacs had only to march straight on the town to take it. They were expected to enter it one day or the other. In the mind of the Regent it was as if they had already taken it. He went off and shut himself in the Castle of Vincennes with the few men who remained to him.[145] Three days after the discomfiture of the English there was a panic in the town. "The Armagnacs are coming to-night," they said. Meanwhile the Armagnacs were at Orléans awaiting orders to assemble at Gien and to march on Auxerre. At these tidings the Duke of Bedford must have sighed a deep sigh of relief; and straightway he set to work to provide for the defence of Paris and the safety of Normandy.[146]

When the panic was past, the heart of the great town returned to its allegiance, not to the English cause – it had never been English – but to the Burgundian. Its Provost, Messire Simon Morhier, who had made great slaughter of the French at the Battle of the Herrings, remained loyal to the Leopard.[147] The aldermen on the contrary were suspected of inclining a favourable ear to King Charles's proposals. On the 12th of July, the Parisians elected a new town council composed of the most zealous Burgundians they could find in commerce and on change. To be provost of the merchants they appointed the treasurer, Guillaume Sanguin, to whom the Duke of Burgundy owed more then seven thousand *livres tournois*[148] and who had the Regent's jewels in his keeping.[149] Such an alteration was greatly to the detriment of King Charles, who preferred to win back his good towns by peaceful means rather than by force, and who relied more on negotiations with the citizens than on cannon balls and stones.

Just in the nick of time the Regent surrendered the town to Duke Philip, not, we may be sure, without many regrets for having recently refused him Orléans. He realised that thus, by returning to its French allegiance, the chief city of the realm would make a more energetic defence against the Dauphin's men. The Parisians' old liking for the magnificent Duke would revive, and so would their old hatred of the disinherited son of Madame Ysabeau. In the Palais de Justice the Duke read the story of his father's death, punctuated with complaints of Armagnac treason and violated treaties; he caused the blood of Montereau[150] to cry to heaven; those who were present swore to be right loyal to him and to the Regent. On the following days the same oath was taken by the regular and secular clergy.[151]

But the citizens were strengthened in their resistance more by their remembrance of Armagnac cruelty than by their affection for the fair Duke. A rumour ran and was believed by them that Messire Charles of Valois had abandoned to his mercenaries the city and the citizens of all ranks, high and low, men and women, and that he intended to plough up the very ground on which Paris stood. Such a rumour represented him very falsely; on all occasions he was pitiful and debonair; his Council had prudently converted the coronation campaign into an armed and peaceful procession. But the Parisians were incapable of judging sanely when the intentions of the King of France were concerned; and they knew only too well that once their town was taken there would be nothing to prevent the Armagnacs from laying it waste with fire and sword.[152]

One other circumstance intensified their fear and their dislike. When they heard that Friar Richard, to whose sermons they had once listened so devoutly, was riding with the Dauphin's men and with his nimble tongue winning such good towns as Troyes in Champagne, they called down upon him the malediction of God and his Saints. They tore from their caps the pewter medals engraved with the holy name of Jesus, which the good Brother had given them, and in their bitter hatred towards him they returned straightway to the dice, bowls and draughts which they had renounced at his exhortation. With no less horror did the Maid inspire them. It was said that she was acting the prophetess and uttering such words as: "In very deed this or that shall come to pass." "With the Armagnacs is a creature in woman's form. What it is God only knows," they cried. They spoke of her as a woman of ill fame.[153] Among these enemies, there were those who filled them with even greater horror than pagans and Saracens – to wit: a monk and a maid. They all took the cross of Saint Andrew.[154]

While the Dauphin had been away at his coronation an army had come from England into France. The Regent intended it to overrun Normandy. In its march on Rouen he commanded it in person. The defence and ward of Paris he left to Louis of Luxembourg, Bishop of Thérouanne, Chancellor of France for the English, to the Sire de l'Isle-Adam, Marshal of France, Captain of Paris, to two thousand men-at-arms and to the Parisian train-bands. To the last were entrusted the defence of the ramparts and the management of the artillery. They were commanded by twenty-four burgesses, called *quarteniers* because they represented the twenty-four quarters of the city. From the end of July all danger of a surprise had been guarded against.[155]

On the 10th of August, on Saint-Laurence's Eve, while the Armagnacs were encamped at La Ferté-Milon, the Saint-Martin Gate, flanked by four towers and a double drawbridge, was closed; and all men were forbidden to go to Saint-Laurent, either to the procession or to the fair, as in previous years.[156]

On the 28th of the same month, the royal army occupied Saint-Denys. Henceforth no one dared leave the city, neither for the vintage nor for the gathering of anything in the kitchen gardens, which covered the plain north of the town. Prices immediately went up.[157]

In the early days of September, the *quarteniers*, each one in his own district, had the trenches set in order and the cannons mounted on walls, gates, and towers. At the command of the aldermen, the hewers of stone for the cannon made thousands of balls.[158]

From My Lord, the Duke of Alençon, the magistrates received letters beginning thus: "To you, Provost of Paris and

Provost of the Merchants and Aldermen...." He named them by name and greeted them in eloquent language. These letters were regarded as an artifice intended to render the townsfolk suspicious of the aldermen and to incite one class of the populace against the other. The only answer sent to the Duke was a request that he would not spoil any more paper with such malicious endeavours.[159]

The chapter of Notre-Dame ordered masses to be said for the salvation of the people. On the 5th of September, three canons were authorised to make arrangements for the defence of the monastery. Those in charge of the sacristy took measures to hide the relics and the treasure of the cathedral from the Armagnac soldiers. For two hundred golden *saluts*[160] they sold the body of Saint Denys; but they kept the foot, which was of silver, the head and the crown.[161]

On Wednesday, the 7th of September, the Eve of the Virgin's Nativity, there was a procession to Sainte-Geneviève-du-Mont with the object of counteracting the evil of the times and allaying the animosity of the enemy. In it walked the canons of the Palace, bearing the True Cross.[162]

That very day the army of the Duke of Alençon and of the Maid was skirmishing beneath the walls. It retreated in the evening; and on that night the townsfolk slept in peace, for on the morrow Christians celebrated the Nativity of the Blessed Virgin.[163]

It was a great festival and a very ancient one. Its origin is described in the following manner. There was a certain holy man, who passed his life in meditation. On a day he called to mind that for many years, on the 8th of September, he had heard marvellous angelic music in the air, and he prayed to God to reveal to him the reason for this concert of instruments and of celestial voices. He was vouchsafed the answer that it was the anniversary of the birth of the glorious Virgin Mary; and he received the command to instruct the faithful in order that they on that solemn day might join their voices to the angelic chorus. The matter was reported to the Sovereign Pontiff and the other heads of the Church, who, after having prayed, fasted and consulted the witnesses and traditions of the Church, decreed that henceforth that day, the 8th of September, should be universally consecrated to the celebration of the birth of the Virgin Mary.[164]

That day were read at mass the words of the prophet Isaiah: "And there shall come forth a rod out of the stem of Jesse, and a Branch shall grow out of his roots."

The people of Paris thought that even the Armagnacs would do no work on so high a festival and would keep the third commandment.

On this Thursday, the 8th of September, about eight o'clock in the morning, the Maid, the Dukes of Alençon and of Bourbon, the Marshals of Boussac and of Rais, the Count of Vendôme, the Lords of Laval, of Albret and of Gaucourt, who with their men, to the number of ten thousand and more, had encamped in the village of La Chapelle, half-way along the road from Saint-Denys to Paris, set out on the march. At the hour of high mass, between eleven and twelve o'clock, they reached the height of Les Moulins, at the foot of which the Swine Market was held.[165] Here there was a gibbet. Fifty-six years earlier, a woman of saintly life according to the people, but according to the holy inquisitors, a heretic and *a Turlupine*, had been burned alive on that very market-place.[166]

Wherefore did the King's men appear first before the northern walls, those of Charles V, which were the strongest? It is impossible to tell. A few days earlier they had thrown a bridge across the River above Paris,[167] which looks as if they intended to attack the old fortification and get into the city from the University side. Did they mean to carry out the two attacks simultaneously? It is probable. Did they renounce the project of their own accord or against their will? We cannot tell.

Beneath the walls of Charles V they assembled a quantity of artillery, cannons, culverins, mortars; and in hand-carts they brought fagots to fill up the trenches, hurdles to bridge them over and seven hundred ladders: very elaborate material for the siege, despite their having, as we shall see, forgotten what was most necessary.[168] They came not therefore to skirmish nor to do great feats of arms. They came to attempt in broad daylight the escalading and the storming of the greatest, the most illustrious, and the most populous town of the realm; an undertaking of vast importance, proposed doubtless and decided in the royal council and with the knowledge of the King, who can have been neither indifferent nor hostile to it.[169] Charles of Valois wanted to retake Paris. It remains to be seen whether for the accomplishment of his desire he depended merely on men-at-arms and ladders.

It would seem that the Maid had not been told of the resolutions taken.[170] She was never consulted and was seldom informed of what had been decided. But she was as sure of entering the town that day as of going to Paradise when she died. For more than three years her Voices had been drumming the attack on Paris in her ears.[171] But the astonishing point is that, saint as she was, she should have consented to arm and fight on the day of the Nativity. It was contrary to her action on the 5th of May, Ascension Day, and inconsistent with what she had said on the 8th of the same month: "As ye love and honour the Sacred Sabbath do not begin the battle."[172]

True it is that afterwards, at Montepilloy, she had engaged in a skirmish on the Day of the Assumption, and thus scandalized the masters of the University. She acted according to the counsel of her Voices and her decisions depended on the vaguest murmurings in her ear. Nothing is more inconstant and more contradictory than the inspirations of such visionaries, who are but the playthings of their dreams. What is certain at least is that Jeanne now as always was convinced that she was doing right and committing no sin.[173] Arrayed on the height of Les Moulins, in front of Paris with its grey fortifications, the French had immediately before them the outermost of the trenches, dry and narrow, some sixteen or seventeen feet deep, separated by a mound from the second trench, nearly one hundred feet broad, deep and filled with water which lapped the walls of the city. Quite close, on their right, the road to Roule led up to the Saint Honoré Gate, also called the Gate of the Blind because it was near the Hospital of Les Quinze Vingts.[174] It opened beneath a castlet flanked by turrets, and for an advanced defence it had a bulwark surrounded by wooden barriers, like those of Orléans.[175]

The Parisians did not expect to be attacked on a feast day.[176] And yet the ramparts were by no means deserted, and on the walls standards could be seen waving, and especially a great white banner with a Saint Andrew's cross in silver gilt.[177]

The French arrayed themselves slightly behind the Moulin hill, which was to protect them from the stream of lead and stones beginning to be discharged from the artillery on the ramparts. There they ranged their mortars, their culverins and their cannon, ready to fire on the city walls. In this position, which commanded the widest stretch of the fortifications, was the main body of the army. Led by Messire de Saint-Vallier a knight of Dauphiné, several captains and men-at-arms approached the Saint Honoré Gate and set fire to the barriers. As the garrison of the gate had withdrawn within the fortification, and as the enemy was not seen to be coming out by any other exit, the Maréchal de Rais' company advanced with fagots, bundles and ladders right up to the ramparts. The Maid rode at the head of her company. They halted between the Saint-Denys and the Saint-Honoré Gates, but nearer the latter, and went down into the first trench, which was not difficult to cross. But on the mound they found themselves exposed to bolts and arrows which rained straight down from the walls.[178] As at Orléans, and at Les Tourelles, Jeanne had given her banner to a man of valour to hold.

When she reached the top of the mound, she cried out to the folk in Paris: "Surrender the town to the King of France."[179]

The Burgundians heard her saying also: "In Jesus' name surrender to us speedily. For if ye yield not before nightfall, we shall enter by force, whether ye will or no, and ye shall all be put to death without mercy."[180]

On the mound she remained, sounding the great dyke with her lance and marvelling to find it so full and so deep. And yet for eleven days she and her men-at-arms had been reconnoitring round the walls and seeking the most favourable point of attack. That she should not have known how to plan an attack was quite natural. But what is to be thought of the men-at-arms, who were there on the mound, taken by surprise, as baffled as she, and all aghast at finding so much water close to the Seine when the River was in flood? To be able to reconnoitre the defences of a fortress was surely the *a b c* of the trade of war. Captains and soldiers of fortune never risked advancing against a fortification without knowing first whether there were water, morass or briars, and arming themselves accordingly with siege train suitable to the occasion. When the water of the moat was deep they launched leather boats carried on horses' backs.[181] The men-at-arms of the Maréchal de Rais and my Lord of Alençon were more ignorant than the meanest adventurers. What would the doughty La Hire have thought of them? Such gross ineptitude and ignorance appeared so incredible that it was supposed that those fighting men knew the depth of the moat but concealed it from the Maid, desiring her discomfiture.[182] In such a case, while entrapping the damsel they were themselves entrapped, for there they stayed moving neither backwards nor forwards.

Certain among them idly threw fagots into the moat. Meanwhile the defenders assailed by flights of arrows, disappeared one after the other.[183] But towards four o'clock in the afternoon, the citizens arrived in crowds. The cannon of the Saint-Denys Gate thundered. Arrows and abuse flew between those above and those below. The hours passed, the sun was sinking. The Maid never ceased sounding the moat with the staff of her lance and crying out to the Parisians to surrender.

"There, wanton! There, minx!" cried a Burgundian.

And planting his cross-bow in the ground with his foot, he shot an arrow which split one of her greaves and wounded her in the thigh. Another Burgundian took aim at the Maid's standard-bearer and wounded him in the foot. The wounded man raised his visor to see whence the arrow came and straightway received another between the eyes. The Maid and the Duke of Alençon sorely regretted the loss of this man-at-arms.[184]

After she had been wounded, Jeanne cried all the more loudly that the walls must be reached and the city taken. She was placed out of reach of the arrows in the shelter of a breast-work. There she urged the men-at-arms to throw fagots into the water and make a bridge. About ten or eleven o'clock in the evening, the Sire de la Trémouille charged the combatants to retreat. The Maid would not leave the place. She was doubtless listening to her Saints and beholding celestial hosts around her. The Duke of Alençon sent for her. The aged Sire de Gaucourt[185] carried her off with the aid of a captain of Picardy, one Guichard Bournel, who did not please her on that day, and who by his treachery six months later, was to please her still less.[186] Had she not been wounded she would have resisted more strongly.[187] She yielded regretfully, saying: "In God's name! the city might have been taken."[188]

They put her on horseback; and thus she was able to follow the army. The rumour ran that she had been shot in both thighs; in sooth her wound was but slight.[189]

The French returned to La Chapelle, whence they had set out in the morning. They carried their wounded on some of the carts which they had used for the transport of fagots and ladders. In the hands of the enemy they left three hundred hand-carts, six hundred and sixty ladders, four thousand hurdles and large fagots, of which they had used but a small number.[190] Their retreat must have been somewhat hurried, seeing that, when they came to the Barn of Les Mathurins, near The Swine Market, they forsook their baggage and set fire to it. With horror it was related that, like pagans of Rome, they had cast their dead into the flames.[191] Nevertheless the Parisians dared not pursue them. In those days men-at-arms who knew their trade never retreated without laying some snare for the enemy. Consequently the King's men posted a considerable company in ambush by the roadside, to lie in wait for the light troops who should come in pursuit of the retreating army.[192] It was precisely such an ambuscade that the Parisians feared; wherefore they permitted the Armagnacs to regain their camp at La Chapelle-Saint-Denys unmolested.[193]

If we regard only the military tactics of the day, there is no doubt that the French had blundered and had lacked energy. But it was not on military tactics that the greatest reliance had been placed. Those who conducted the war, the King and his council, certainly expected to enter Paris that day. But how? As they had entered Châlons, as they had entered Reims, as they had entered all the King's good towns from Troyes to Compiègne. King Charles had shown himself determined to recover his towns by means of the townsfolk; towards Paris he acted as he had acted towards his other towns.

During the coronation march, he had entered into communication with the bishops and burgesses of the cities of Champagne; and like communications he had entered into in Paris.[194] He had dealings with the monks and notably with the Carmelites of Melun, whose Prior, Brother Pierre d'Allée, was working in his interest.[195] For some time paid agents had been watching for an opportunity of throwing the city into disorder and of bringing in the enemy in a moment of panic and confusion. During the assault they were working for him in the streets. In the afternoon, on both sides of the bridges, were heard cries of "Let every man look to his own safety! The enemy has entered! All is lost!" Such of the citizens as were listening to the sermon hastened to shut themselves in their houses. And others who were out of doors sought refuge in the churches. But the tumult was quelled. Wise men, like the clerk of the Parlement, believed that it was but a feigned attack, and that Charles of Valois looked to recover the town not so much by force of arms as by a movement of the populace.[196]

Certain monks who were acting in Paris as the King's spies, went out to him at Saint-Denys and informed him that the attempt had failed. According to them it had very nearly succeeded.[197]

The Sire de la Trémouille is said to have commanded the retreat, for fear of a massacre. Indeed, once the French had entered they were quite capable of slaughtering the townsfolk and razing the city to the ground.[198]

On the morrow, Friday the 9th, the Maid, rising with the dawn, despite her wound, asked the Duke of Alençon to have the call to arms sounded; for she was strongly determined to return to the walls of Paris, swearing not to leave them until the city should be taken.[199] Meanwhile the French captains sent a herald to Paris, charged to ask for a safe conduct for the removing of the bodies of the dead left behind in great numbers.[200]

Notwithstanding that they had suffered cruel hurt, after a retreat unmolested it is true, but none the less disastrous and involving the loss of all their siege train, several of the leaders were, like the Maid, inclined to attempt a new assault. Others would not hear of it. While they were disputing, they beheld a baron coming towards them and with him fifty nobles; it was the Sire de Montmorency, the first Christian peer of France, that is the first among the ancient vassals of the bishop of Paris. He was transferring his allegiance from the Cross of St. Andrew to the Flowers-de-luce.[201] His coming filled the King's men with courage and a desire to return to the city. The army was on its way back, when the Count of Clermont and the Duke of Bar were sent to arrest the march by order of the King, and to take the Maid back to Saint-Denys.[202]

On Saturday the 10th, at daybreak, the Duke of Alençon, with a few knights, appeared on the bank above the city, where a bridge had been thrown over the Seine some days earlier. The Maid, always eager for danger, accompanied the venturesome warriors. But the night before, the King had prudently caused the bridge to be taken down, and the little band had to retrace its steps.[203] It was not that the King had renounced the idea of taking Paris. He was thinking more than ever of the recovery of his great town; but he intended to regain it without an assault, by means of the compliance of certain burgesses.

At this same place of Saint-Denys there happened to Jeanne a misadventure, which would seem to have impressed her comrades and possibly to have lessened their faith in her good luck in war. As was customary, women of ill-fame followed the army in great numbers; each man had his own; they were called *amiètes*.[204] Jeanne could not tolerate them because they caused disorder, but more especially because their sinful lives filled her with horror. At that very time, stories like the following were circulated far and wide, and spread even into Germany.

There was a certain man in the camp, who had with him his *amiète*. She rode in armour in order not to be recognised. Now the Maid said to the nobles and captains: "There is a woman with our men." They replied that they knew of none. Whereupon the Maid assembled the army, and, approaching the woman said: "This is she."

Then addressing the wench: "Thou art of Gien and thou art big with child. Were it not so I would put thee to death. Thou hast already let one child die and thou shalt not do the same for this one."

When the Maid had thus spoken, servants took the wench and conveyed her to her own home. There they kept her under watch and ward until she was delivered of her child. And she confessed that what the Maid had said was true.

After which, the Maid again said: "There are women in the camp." Whereupon two wantons, who did not belong to the army, and had already been dismissed from it, hearing these words, rode off on horseback. But the Maid hastened after them crying: "Ye foolish women, I have forbidden you to come into my company." And she drew her sword and struck one of them on the head, so sore that she died.[205]

The tale was true; Jeanne could not suffer these wenches. Every time she met one she gave chase to her. This was precisely what she did at Gien, when she saw women of ill-fame awaiting the King's men.[206] At Château-Thierry, she espied an *amiète* riding behind a man-at-arms, and, running after her, sword in hand, she came up with her, and without striking, bade her henceforth avoid the society of men-at-arms. "If thou wilt not," she added, "I shall do thee hurt."[207]

At Saint-Denys, being accompanied by the Duke of Alençon, Jeanne pursued another of these wantons. This time she was not content with remonstrances and threats. She broke her sword over her.[208] Was it Saint Catherine's sword? So it was believed, and doubtless not without reason.[209] In those days men's minds were full of the romantic stories of Joyeuse and Durandal. It would appear that Jeanne, when she lost her sword, lost her power. A slight variation of the story was told afterwards, and it was related how the King, when he was acquainted with the matter of the broken sword, was displeased and said to the Maid: "You should have taken a stick to strike withal and should not have risked the sword you received from divine hands."[210] It was told likewise how the sword had been given to an armourer for him to join the pieces together, and that he could not, wherein lay a proof that the sword was enchanted.[211]

Before his departure, the King appointed the Count of Clermont commander of the district with several lieutenants: the Lords of Culant, Boussac, Loré, and Foucault. He constituted joint lieutenants-general the Counts of Clermont and of Vendôme, the lords Regnault de Chartres, Christophe d'Harcourt and Jean Tudert. Regnault de Chartres established himself in the town of Senlis, the lieutenant's headquarters. Having thus disposed, the King quitted Saint-Denys on the 13th of September.[212] The Maid followed him against her will notwithstanding that she had the permission of her Voices to do so.[213] She offered her armour to the image of Our Lady and to the precious body of Saint Denys.[214] This armour was white, that is to say devoid of armorial bearings.[215] She was thus following the custom of men-at-arms, who, after they had received a wound, if they did not die of it, offered their armour to Our Lady and the Saints as a token of thanksgiving. Wherefore, in those warlike days, chapels, like that of Notre-Dame de Fierbois, often presented the appearance of arsenals. To her armour the Maid added a sword which she had won before Paris.[216]

Chapter IV
The taking of Saint-Pierre-le-Moustier – Friar Richard's spiritual daughters – the siege of La Charité

HE King slept at Lagny-sur-Marne on the 14th of September, then crossed the Seine at Bray, forded the Yonne near Sens and went on through Courtenay, Châteaurenard and Montargis. On the 21st of September he reached Gien. There he disbanded the army he could no longer pay, and each man went to his own home. The Duke of Alençon withdrew into his viscounty of Beaumont-sur-Oise.[217]

Learning that the Queen was coming to meet the King, Jeanne went before her and greeted her at Selles-en-Berry.[218] She was afterwards taken to Bourges, where my Lord d'Albret, half-brother of the Sire de la Trémouille, lodged her with Messire Régnier de Bouligny. Régnier was then Receiver General. He had been one of those whose dismissal the University had requested in 1408, as being worse than useless, for they held him responsible for many of the disorders in the kingdom. He had entered the Dauphin's service, passed from the administration of the royal domain to that of taxes and attained the highest rank in the control of the finances.[219] His wife, who had accompanied the Queen to Selles, beheld the Maid and wondered. Jeanne seemed to her a creature sent by God for the relief of the King and those of France who were loyal to him. She remembered the days not so very long ago when she had seen the Dauphin and her Husband not knowing where to turn for money. Her name was Marguerite La Touroulde; she was damiselle, not dame; a comfortable *bourgeoise* and that was all.[220]

Three weeks Jeanne sojourned in the Receiver General's house. She slept there, drank there, ate there. Nearly every night, Damiselle Marguerite La Touroulde slept with her; the etiquette of those days required it. No night-gowns were worn; folk slept naked in those vast beds. It would seem that Jeanne disliked sleeping with old women.[221] Damiselle La Touroulde, although not so very old, was of matronly age;[222] she had moreover a matron's experience, and further she claimed, as we shall see directly, to know more than most matrons knew. Several times she took Jeanne to the bath and to the sweating-room.[223] That also was one of the rules of etiquette; a host was not considered to be making his guests good cheer unless he took them to the bath. In this point of courtesy princes set an example; when the King and Queen supped in the house of one of their retainers or ministers, fine baths richly ornamented were prepared for them before they came to table.[224] Mistress Marguerite doubtless did not possess what was necessary in her own house; wherefore she took Jeanne out to the bath and the sweating-room. Such are her own expressions; and they probably indicate a vapour bath[225] not a bath of hot water.

At Bourges the sweating-rooms were in the Auron quarter, in the lower town, near the river.[226] Jeanne was strictly devout, but she did not observe conventual rule; she, like chaste Suzannah therefore, might permit herself to bathe and she must have had great need to do so after having slept on straw.[227] What is more remarkable is that, after having seen Jeanne in the bath, Mistress Marguerite judged her a virgin according to all appearances.[228]

In Messire Régnier de Bouligny's house and likewise wherever she lodged, she led the life of a *béguine* but did not practise excessive austerity. She confessed frequently. Many a time she asked her hostess to come with her to matins. In the cathedral and in collegiate churches there were matins every day, between four and six, at the hour of sunset. The two women often talked together; the Receiver General's wife found Jeanne very simple and very ignorant. She was amazed to discover that the maiden knew absolutely nothing.[229]

Among other matters, Jeanne told of her visit to the old Duke of Lorraine, and how she had rebuked him for his evil life; she spoke likewise of the interrogatory to which the doctors of Poitiers had subjected her.[230] She was persuaded that these clerks had questioned her with extreme severity, and she firmly believed that she had triumphed over their ill-will. Alas! she was soon to know clerks even less accommodating.

Mistress Marguerite said to her one day: "If you are not afraid when you fight, it is because you know you will not be killed." Whereupon Jeanne answered: "I am no surer of that than are the other combatants."

Oftentimes women came to the Bouligny house, bringing paternosters and other trifling objects of devotion for the Maid to touch.

Jeanne used to say laughingly to her hostess: "Touch them yourself. Your touch will do them as much good as mine."[231]

This ready repartee must have shown Mistress Marguerite that Jeanne, ignorant as she may have been, was none the less capable of displaying a good grace and common sense in her conversation.

While in many matters this good woman found the Maid but a simple creature, in military affairs she deemed her an expert. Whether, when she judged the saintly damsel's skill in wielding arms, she was giving her own opinion or merely speaking from hearsay, as would seem probable, she at any rate declared later that Jeanne rode a horse and handled a lance as well as the best of knights and so well that the army marvelled.[232] Indeed most captains in those days could do no better.

Probably there were dice and dice-boxes in the Bouligny house, otherwise Jeanne would have had no opportunity of displaying that horror of gaming which struck her hostess. On this matter Jeanne agreed with her comrade, Friar Richard, and indeed with everyone else of good life and good doctrine.[233]

What money she had Jeanne distributed in alms. "I am come to succour the poor and needy," she used to say.[234]

When the multitude heard such words they were led to believe that this Maid of God had been raised up for something more than the glorification of the Lilies, and that she was come to dispel such ills as murder, pillage and other sins grievous to God, from which the realm was suffering. Mystic souls looked to her for the reform of the Church and the reign of Jesus Christ on earth. She was invoked as a saint, and throughout the loyal provinces were to be seen carved and painted images of her which were worshipped by the faithful. Thus, even during her lifetime, she enjoyed certain of the privileges of beatification.[235]

North of the Seine meanwhile, English and Burgundians were at their old work. The Duke of Vendôme and his company fell back on Senlis, the English descended on the town of Saint-Denys and sacked it once more. In the Abbey Church they found and carried off the Maid's armour, thus, according to the French clergy, committing undeniable sacrilege and for this reason: because they gave the monks of the Abbey nothing in exchange.

The King was then at Mehun-sur-Yèvre, quite close to Bourges, in one of the finest châteaux in the world, rising on a rock and overlooking the town. The late Duke Jean of Berry, a great builder, had erected this château with the care that he never failed to exercise in matters of art. Mehun was King Charles's favourite abode.[236]

The Duke of Alençon, eager to reconquer his duchy, was waiting for troops to accompany him into Normandy, across the marches of Brittany and Maine. He sent to the King to know if it were his good pleasure to grant him the Maid. "Many there be," said the Duke, "who would willingly come with her, while without her they will not stir from their homes." Her discomfiture before Paris had not, therefore, entirely ruined her prestige. The Sire de la Trémouille opposed her being sent to the Duke of Alençon, whom he mistrusted, and not without cause. He gave her into the care of his half-brother, the Sire d'Albret, Lieutenant of the King in his own country of Berry.[237]

The Royal Council deemed it necessary to recover La Charité, left in the hands of Perrinet Gressart at the time of the coronation campaign;[238] but it was decided first to attack Saint-Pierre-le-Moustier, which commanded the approaches to Bec-d'Allier.[239] The garrison of this little town was composed of English and Burgundians, who were constantly plundering the villages and laying waste the fields of Berry and Bourbonnais. The army for this expedition assembled at Bourges. It was commanded by my Lord d'Albret,[240] but popular report attributed the command to Jeanne. The common folk, the burgesses of the towns, especially the citizens of Orléans knew no other commander.

After two or three days' siege, the King's men stormed the town. But they were repulsed. Squire Jean d'Aulon, the Maid's steward, who some time before had been wounded in the heel and consequently walked on crutches, had retreated with the rest.[241] He went back and found Jeanne who had stayed almost alone by the side of the moat. Fearing lest harm should come to her, he leapt on to his horse, spurred towards her and cried: "What are you doing, all alone? Wherefore do you not retreat like the others?"

Jeanne doffed her sallet and replied: "I am not alone. With me are fifty thousand of my folk. I will not quit this spot till I have taken the town."

Casting his eyes around, Messire Jean d'Aulon saw the Maid surrounded by but four or five men.

More loudly he cried out to her: "Depart hence and retreat like the others."

Her only reply was a request for fagots and hurdles to fill up the moat. And straightway in a loud voice she called: "To the fagots and the hurdles all of ye, and make a bridge!"

The men-at-arms rushed to the spot, the bridge was constructed forthwith and the town taken by storm with no great difficulty. At any rate that is how the good Squire, Jean d'Aulon, told the story.[242] He was almost persuaded that the Maid's fifty thousand shadows had taken Saint-Pierre-le-Moustier.

With the little army on the Loire at that time were certain holy women who like Jeanne led a singular life and held communion with the Church Triumphant. They constituted, so to speak, a kind of flying squadron of *béguines*, which followed the men-at-arms. One of these women was called Catherine de La Rochelle; two others came from Lower Brittany.[243]

They all had miraculous visions; Jeanne saw my Lord Saint Michael in arms and Saint Catherine and Saint Margaret wearing crowns;[244] Pierronne beheld God in a long white robe and a purple cloak;[245] Catherine de La Rochelle saw a white lady, clothed in cloth of gold; and, at the moment of the consecration of the host all manner of marvels of the high mystery of Our Lord were revealed unto her.[246]

Jean Pasquerel was still with Jeanne in the capacity of chaplain.[247] He hoped to take his penitent to fight in the Crusade against the Hussites, for it was against these heretics that he felt most bitterly. But he had been entirely supplanted by the Franciscan, Friar Richard, who, after Troyes, had joined the mendicants of Jeanne's earlier days. Friar Richard dominated this little band of the illuminated. He was called their good Father. He it was who instructed them.[248] His designs for these women did not greatly differ from those of Jean Pasquerel: he intended to conduct them to those wars of the Cross, which he thought were bound to precede the impending end of the world.[249]

Meanwhile, it was his endeavour to foster a good understanding between them, which, eloquent preacher though he was, he found very difficult. Within the sisterhood there were constant suspicions and disputes. Jeanne had been on friendly terms with Catherine de la Rochelle at Montfaucon in Brie and at Jargeau; but now she began to suspect her of being a rival, and immediately she assumed an attitude of mistrust.[250] Possibly she was right. At any moment either Catherine or the Breton women might be made use of as she had been.[251] In those days a prophetess was useful in so many ways: in the edification of the people, the reformation of the Church, the leading of men-at-arms, the circulation of money, in war, in peace; no sooner did one appear than each party tried to get hold of her. It seems as if, after having employed the Maid Jeanne to deliver Orléans, the King's Councillors were now thinking of employing Dame Catherine to make peace with the Duke of Burgundy. Such a task was deemed fitting for a saint less chivalrous than Jeanne. Catherine was married and the mother of a family. In this circumstance there need be no cause for astonishment; for if the gift of prophecy be more especially reserved for virgins, the example of Judith proves that the Lord may raise up strong matrons for the serving of his people.

If we believe that, as her surname indicates, she came from La Rochelle, her origin must have inspired the Armagnacs with confidence. The inhabitants of La Rochelle, all pirates more or less, were too profitably engaged in preying upon English vessels to forsake the Dauphin's party. Moreover, he rewarded their loyalty by granting them valuable commercial privileges.[252] They had sent gifts of money to the people of Orléans; and when, in the month of May, they learned the deliverance of Duke Charles's city, they instituted a public festival to commemorate so happy an event.

The first duty of a saint in the army, it would appear, was to collect money. Jeanne was always sending letters asking the good towns for money or for munitions of war; the burgesses always promised to grant her request and sometimes they kept their promise. Catherine de la Rochelle appears to have had special revelations concerning the funds of the party; her mission, therefore, was financial, while Jeanne's was martial.

She announced that she was going to the Duke of Burgundy to conclude peace.[253] If one may judge from the little that is known of her, the inspirations of this holy dame were not very elevated, not very orderly, not very profound.

Meeting Jeanne at Montfaucon in Berry (or at Jargeau) she addressed her thus:

"There came unto me a white lady, attired in cloth of gold, who said to me: 'Go thou through the good towns and let the King give unto thee heralds and trumpets to cry: "Whosoever has gold, silver or hidden treasure, let him bring it forth instantly."'"

Dame Catherine added: "Such as have hidden treasure and do not thus, I shall know their treasure, and I shall go and find it."

She deemed it necessary to fight against the English and seemed to believe that Jeanne's mission was to drive them out of the land, since she obligingly offered her the whole of her miraculous takings.

"Wherewithal to pay your men-at-arms," she said. But the Maid answered disdainfully:

"Go back to your husband, look after your household, and feed your children."[254]

Disputes between saints are usually bitter. In her rival's missions Jeanne refused to see anything but folly and futility. Nevertheless it was not for her to deny the possibility of the white lady's visitations; for to Jeanne herself did there not descend every day as many saints, angels and archangels as were ever painted on the pages of books or the walls of monasteries? In order to make up her mind on the subject, she adopted the most effectual measures. A learned doctor may reason concerning matter and substance, the origin and the form of ideas, the dawn of impressions in the intellect, but a shepherdess will resort to a surer method; she will appeal to her own eyesight.

Jeanne asked Catherine if the white lady came every night, and learning that she did: "I will sleep with you," she said.

When night came, she went to bed with Catherine, watched till midnight, saw nothing and fell asleep, for she was young, and she had great need of sleep. In the morning, when she awoke, she asked: "Did she come?"

"She did," replied Catherine; "you were asleep, so I did not like to wake you."

"Will she not come to-morrow?"

Catherine assured her that she would come without fail.

This time Jeanne slept in the day in order that she might keep awake at night; so she lay down at night in the bed with Catherine and kept her eyes open. Often she asked: "Will she not come?"

And Catherine replied: "Yes, directly."

But Jeanne saw nothing.**[255]** She held the test to be a good one. Nevertheless she could not get the white lady attired in cloth of gold out of her head. When Saint Catherine and Saint Margaret came to her, as they delayed not to do, she spoke to them concerning this white lady and asked them what she was to think of her. The reply was such as Jeanne expected:

"This Catherine," they said, "is naught but futility and folly."**[256]**

Then was Jeanne constrained to cry: "That is just what I thought."

The strife between these two prophetesses was brief but bitter. Jeanne always maintained the opposite of what Catherine said. When the latter was going to make peace with the Duke of Burgundy, Jeanne said to her:

"Me seemeth that you will never find peace save at the lance's point."**[257]**

There was one matter at any rate wherein the White Lady proved a better prophetess than the Maid's Council, to wit, the siege of La Charité. When Jeanne wished to go and deliver that town, Catherine tried to dissuade her.

"It is too cold," she said; "I would not go."[258]

Catherine's reason was not a high one; and yet it is true Jeanne would have done better not to go to the siege of La Charité.

Taken from the Duke of Burgundy by the Dauphin in 1422, La Charité had been retaken in 1424, by Perrinet Gressart,[259] a successful captain, who had risen from the rank of mason's apprentice to that of pantler to the Duke of Burgundy and had been created Lord of Laigny by the King of England.[260] On the 30th of December, 1425, Perrinet's men arrested the Sire de La Trémouille, when he was on his way to the Duke of Burgundy, having been appointed ambassador in one of those eternal negotiations, forever in process between the King and the Duke. He was for several months kept a prisoner in the fortress which his captor commanded. He must needs pay a ransom of fourteen thousand golden crowns; and, albeit he took this sum from the royal treasury,[261] he never ceased to bear Perrinet a grudge. Wherefore it may be concluded that when he sent men-at-arms to La Charité it was in good sooth to capture the town and not with any evil design against the Maid.

The army despatched against this Burgundian captain and this great plunder of pilgrims was composed of no mean folk. Its leaders were Louis of Bourbon, Count of Montpensier, and Charles II, Sire d'Albret, La Trémouille's half-brother and Jeanne's companion in arms during the coronation campaign. The army was doubtless but scantily supplied with stores and with money.[262] That was the normal condition of armies in those days. When the King wanted to attack a stronghold of the enemy, he must needs apply to his good towns for the necessary material. The Maid, at once saint and warrior, could beg for arms with a good grace; but possibly she overrated the resources of the towns which had already given so much.

On the 7th of November, she and my Lord d'Alençon signed a letter asking the folk of Clermont in Auvergne for powder, arrows and artillery. Churchmen, magistrates, and townsfolk sent two hundredweight of saltpetre, one hundredweight of sulphur, two cases of arrows; to these they added a sword, two poniards and a battle-axe for the Maid; and they charged Messire Robert Andrieu to present this contribution to Jeanne and to my Lord d'Albret.[263]

On the 9th of November, the Maid was at Moulins in Bourbonnais.[264] What was she doing there? No one knows. There was at that time in the town an abbess very holy and very greatly venerated. Her name was Colette Boilet. She had won the highest praise and incurred the grossest insults by attempting to reform the order of Saint Clare. Colette lived in the convent of the Sisters of Saint Clare, which she had recently founded in this town. It has been thought that the Maid went to Moulins on purpose to meet her.[265] But we ought first to ascertain whether these two saints had any liking for each other. They both worked miracles and miracles which were occasionally somewhat similar;[266] but that was no reason why they should take the slightest pleasure in each other's society. One was called *La Pucelle*,[267] the other *La Petite Ancelle*.[268] But these names, both equally humble, described persons widely different in fashion of attire and in manner of life. *La Petite Ancelle* wended her way on foot, clothed in rags like a beggar-woman; *La Pucelle*, wrapped in cloth of gold, rode forth with lords on horseback. That Jeanne, surrounded by Franciscans who observed no rule, felt any veneration for the reformer of the Sisters of Saint Clare, there is no reason to believe; neither is there anything to indicate that the pacific Colette, strongly attached to the Burgundian house,[269] had any desire to hold converse with one whom the English regarded as a destroying angel.[270]

From this town of Moulins, Jeanne dictated a letter by which she informed the inhabitants of Riom that Saint-Pierre-le-

Moustier was taken, and asked them for materials of war as she had asked the folk of Clermont.[271]

Here is the letter:

Good friends and beloved, ye wit how that the town of Saint Père le Moustier hath been taken by storm; and with God's help it is our intention to cause to be evacuated the other places contrary to the King; but for this there hath been great expending of powder, arrows and other munition of war before the said town, and the lords who are in this town are but scantily provided for to go and lay siege to La Charité, whither we wend presently; I pray you as ye love the welfare and honour of the King and likewise of all others here, that ye will straightway help and send for the said siege powder, saltpetre, sulphur, arrows, strong cross-bows and other munition of war. And do this lest by failure of the said powder and other habiliments of war, the siege should be long and ye should be called in this matter negligent or unwilling. Good friends and beloved, may our Lord keep you. Written at Molins, the ninth day of November.

Jehanne.

Addressed to: My good friends and beloved, the churchmen, burgesses and townsfolk of the town of Rion.[272]

The magistrates of Riom, in letters sealed with their own seal, undertook to give Jeanne the Maid and my Lord d'Albret the sum of sixty crowns; but when the masters of the siege-artillery came to demand this sum, the magistrates would not give a farthing.[273]

The folk of Orléans, on the other hand, once more appeared both zealous and munificent; for they eagerly desired the reduction of a town commanding the Loire for seventy-five miles above their own city. They deserve to be considered the true deliverers of the kingdom; had it not been for them neither Jargeau nor Beaugency would have been taken in June. Quite in the beginning of July, when they thought the Loire campaign was to be continued, they had sent their great mortar, La Bougue, to Gien. With it they had despatched ammunition and victuals; and now, in the early days of December, at the request of the King addressed to the magistrates, they sent to La Charité all the artillery brought back from Gien; likewise eighty-nine soldiers of the municipal troops, wearing the cloak with the Duke of Orléans' colours, the white cross on the breast; with their trumpeter at their head and commanded by Captain Boiau; craftsmen of all conditions, master-masons and journeymen, carpenters, smiths; the cannoneers Fauveau, Gervaise Lefèvre and Brother Jacques, monk of the Gray friars monastery, at Orléans.[274] What became of all this artillery and of these brave folk?

On the 24th of November, the Sire d'Albret and the Maid, being hard put to it before the walls of La Charité, likewise solicited the town of Bourges. On receipt of their letter, the burgesses decided to contribute thirteen hundred golden crowns. To raise this sum they had recourse to a measure by no means unusual; it had been employed notably by the townsfolk of Orléans when, some time previously, to furnish forth Jeanne with munition of war, they had bought from a certain citizen a quantity of salt which they had put up to auction in the city barn. The townsfolk of Bourges sold by auction the annual revenue of a thirteenth part of the wine sold retail in the town. But the money thus raised never reached its destination.[275]

A right goodly knighthood was gathered beneath the walls of La Charité; besides Louis de Bourbon and the Sire d'Albret, there was the Maréchal de Broussac, Jean de Bouray, Seneschal of Toulouse, and Raymon de Montremur, a Baron of Dauphiné, who was slain there.[276] It was bitterly cold and the besiegers succeeded in nothing. At the end of a month Perrinet Gressart, who was full of craft, caused them to fall into an ambush. They raised the siege, abandoning the artillery furnished by the good towns, those fine cannon bought with the savings of thrifty citizens.[277] Their action was the less excusable because the town which had not been relieved and could not well expect to be, must have surrendered sooner or later. They pleaded that the King had sent them no victuals and no money;[278] but that was not considered an excuse and their action was deemed dishonourable. According to a knight well acquainted with points of honour in war: "One ought never to besiege a place without being sure of victuals and of pay beforehand. For to besiege a stronghold and then to withdraw is great disgrace for an army, especially when there is present with it a king or a king's lieutenant."[279]

On the 13th of December there preached to the people of Périgueux a Dominican friar, Brother Hélie Boudant, Pope Martin's Penitentiary in that town. He took as his text the great miracles worked in France by the intervention of a Maid, whom God had sent to the King. On this occasion the Mayor and the magistrates heard mass sung and presented two candles. Now for two months Brother Hélie had been under order to appear before the Parlement of Poitiers.[280] On what charge we do not know. Mendicant monks of those days were for the most part irregular in faith and in morals. The doctrine of Friar Richard himself was not altogether beyond suspicion.

At Christmas, in the year 1429, the flying squadron of *béguines* being assembled at Jargeau,[281] this good Brother said mass and administered the communion thrice to Jeanne the Maid and twice to that Pierronne of Lower Brittany, with whom our Lord conversed as friend with friend. Such an action might well be regarded, if not as a formal violation of the Church's laws, at any rate as an unjustifiable abuse of the sacrament.[282] A menacing theological tempest was then gathering and was about to break over the heads of Friar Richard's daughters in the spirit. A few days after the attack on Paris, the venerable University had had composed or rather transcribed a treatise, *De bono et maligno spiritu*, with a view probably to finding therein arguments against Friar Richard and his prophetess Jeanne, who had both appeared before the city with the Armagnacs.[283]

About the same time, a clerk of the faculty of law had published a summary reply to Chancellor Gerson's memorial concerning the Maid. "It sufficeth not," he wrote, "that one simply affirm that he is sent of God; every heretic maketh such a claim; but he must prove the truth of that mysterious mission by some miraculous work or by some special testimony in the

Bible." This Paris clerk denies that the Maid has presented any such proof, and to judge her by her acts, he believes her rather to have been sent by the Devil than by God. He reproaches her with wearing a dress forbidden to women under penalty of anathema, and he refutes the excuses for her conduct in this matter urged by Gerson. He accuses her of having excited between princes and Christian people a greater war than there had ever been before. He holds her to be an idolatress using enchantments and making false prophecies. He charges her with having induced men to slay their fellows on the two high festivals of the Holy Virgin, the Assumption and the Nativity. "Sins committed by the Enemy of Mankind, through this woman, against the Creator and his most glorious Mother. And albeit there ensued certain murders, thanks be to God they were not so many as the Enemy had intended."

"All these things do manifestly prove error and heresy," adds this devout son of the University. Whence he concludes that the Maid should be taken before the Bishop and the Inquisitor; and he ends by quoting this text from Saint Jérôme: "The unhealthy flesh must be cut off; the diseased sheep must be driven from the fold."[284]

Such was the unanimous opinion of the University of Paris concerning her in whom the French clerks beheld an Angel of the Lord. At Bruges, in November, a rumour ran and was eagerly welcomed by ecclesiastics that the University of Paris had sent an embassy to the Pope at Rome to denounce the Maid as a false prophetess and a deceiver, and likewise those who believed in her. We do not know the veritable object of this mission.[285] But there is no doubt whatever that the doctors and masters of Paris were henceforward firmly resolved that if ever they obtained possession of the damsel they would not let her go out of their hands, and certainly would not send her to be tried at Rome, where she might escape with a mere penance, and even be enlisted as one of the Pope's mercenaries.[286]

In English and Burgundian lands, not only by clerks but by folk of all conditions, she was regarded as a heretic; in those countries the few who thought well of her had to conceal their opinions carefully. After the retreat from Saint-Denys, there may have remained some in Picardy, and notably at Abbeville, who were favourable to the prophetess of the French; but such persons must not be spoken of in public.

Colin Gouye, surnamed Le Sourd, and Jehannin Daix, surnamed Le Petit, a man of Abbeville, learned this to their cost. In this town about the middle of September, Le Sourd and Le Petit were near the blacksmith's forge with divers of the burgesses and other townsfolk, among whom was a herald. They fell to talking of the Maid who was making so great a stir throughout Christendom. To certain words the herald uttered concerning her, Le Petit replied eagerly:

"Well! well! Everything that woman does and says is nought but deception."

Le Sourd spoke likewise: "That woman," he said, "is not to be trusted. Those who believe in her are mad, and there is a smell of burning about them."[287]

By that he meant that their destiny was obvious, and that they were sure to be burned at the stake as heretics.

Then he had the misfortune to add: "In this town there be many with a smell of burning about them."

Such words were for the dwellers in Abbeville a slander and a cause of suspicion. When the Mayor and the aldermen heard of this speech they ordered Le Sourd to be thrown into prison. Le Petit must have said something similar, for he too was imprisoned.[288]

By saying that divers of his fellow-citizens were suspect of heresy, Le Sourd put them in danger of being sought out by the Bishop and the Inquisitor as heretics and sorcerers of notoriously evil repute. As for the Maid, she must have been suspect indeed, for a smell of burning to be caused by the mere fact of being her partisan.

While Friar Richard and his spiritual daughters were thus threatened with a bad end should they fall into the hands of the English or Burgundians, serious troubles were agitating the sisterhood. On the subject of Catherine, Jeanne entered into an open dispute with her spiritual father. Friar Richard wanted the holy dame of La Rochelle to be set to work. Fearing lest his advice should be adopted, Jeanne wrote to her King to tell him what to do with the woman, to wit that he should send her home to her husband and children.

When she came to the King the first thing she had to say to him was: "Catherine's doings are nought but folly and futility."

Friar Richard made no attempt to hide from the Maid his profound displeasure.[289] He was thought much of at court, and it was doubtless with the consent of the Royal Council that he was endeavouring to compass the employment of Dame Catherine. The Maid had succeeded. Why should not another of the illuminated succeed?

Meanwhile the Council had by no means renounced the services Jeanne was rendering to the French cause. Even after the misfortunes of Paris and of La Charité, there were many who now as before held her power to be supernatural; and there is reason to believe that there was a party at Court intending still to employ her.[290] And even if they had wished to discard her she was now too intimately associated with the royal lilies for her rejection not to involve them too in dishonour. On the 29th of December, 1429, at Mehun-sur-Yèvre, the King gave her a charter of nobility sealed with the great seal in green wax, with a double pendant, on a strip of red and green silk.[291]

The grant of nobility was to Jeanne, her father, mother, brothers even if they were not free, and to all their posterity, male and female. It was a singular grant corresponding to the singular services rendered by a woman.

In the title she is described as Johanna d'Ay, doubtless because her father's name was given to the King's scribes by

Lorrainers who would speak with a soft drawl; but whether her name were Ay or Arc, she was seldom called by it, and was commonly spoken of as Jeanne the Maid.[292]

Chapter V
Letter to the citizens of Reims – letter to the Hussites – departure from Sully

HE folk of Orléans were grateful to the Maid for what she had done for them. Far from reproaching her with the unfortunate conclusion of the siege of La Charité, they welcomed her into their city with the same rejoicing and with as good cheer as before. On the 19th of January, 1430, they honoured her and likewise Maître Jean de Velly and Maître Jean Rabateau with a banquet, at which there was abundance of capons, partridges, hares, and even a pheasant.[293] Who that Jean de Velly was, who was feasted with her, we do not know. As for Jean Rabateau, he was none other than the King's Councillor, who had been Attorney-General at the Parlement of Poitiers since 1427.[294] He had been the Maid's host at Orléans. His wife had often seen Jeanne kneeling in her private oratory.[295] The citizens of Orléans offered wine to the Attorney-General, to Jean de Velly, and to the Maid. In good sooth, 'twas a fine feast and a ceremonious. The burgesses loved and honoured Jeanne, but they cannot have observed her very closely during the repast or they would not eight years later, when an adventuress gave herself out to be the Maid, have mistaken her for Jeanne, and offered her wine in the same manner and at the hands of the same city servant, Jacques Leprestre, as now presented it.[296]

The standard that Jeanne loved even more than her Saint Catherine's sword had been painted at Tours by one Hamish Power. He was now marrying his daughter Héliote; and when

Jeanne heard of it, she sent a letter to the magistrates of Tours, asking them to give a sum of one hundred crowns for the bride's trousseau. The nuptials were fixed for the 9th of February, 1430. The magistrates assembled twice to deliberate on Jeanne's request. They described her honourably and yet not without a certain caution as "the Maid who hath come into this realm to the King, concerning the matter of the war, announcing that she is sent by the King of Heaven against the English." In the end they refused to pay anything, because, they said, it behoved them to expend municipal funds on municipal matters and not otherwise; but they decided that for the affection and honour they bore the Maid, the churchmen, burgesses, and other townsfolk should be present in the church at the wedding, and should offer prayers for the bride and present her with bread and wine. This cost them four *livres*, ten *sous*.[297]

At a time which it is impossible to fix exactly the Maid bought a house at Orléans. To be more precise she took it on lease.[298] A lease (*bail à vente*) was an agreement by which the proprietor of a house or other property transferred the ownership to the lessee in return for an annual payment in kind or in money. The duration of such leases was usually fifty-nine years. The house that Jeanne acquired in this manner belonged to the Chapter of the Cathedral. It was in the centre of the town, in the parish of Saint-Malo, close to the Saint-Maclou Chapel, next door to the shop of an oil-seller, one Jean Feu, in the Rue des Petits-Souliers. It was in this street that, during the siege, there had fallen into the midst of five guests seated at table a stone cannon-ball weighing one hundred and sixty-four pounds, which had done no one any harm.[299] What price did the Maid give for this house? Apparently six crowns of fine gold (at sixty crowns to the mark), due half-yearly at Midsummer and Christmas, for fifty-nine years. In addition, she must according to custom have undertaken to keep the house in good condition and to pay out of her own purse the ecclesiastical dues as well as rates for wells and paving and all other taxes. Being obliged to have some one as surety, she chose as her guarantor a certain Guillot de Guyenne, of whom we know nothing further.[300]

There is no reason to believe that the Maid did not herself negotiate this agreement. Saint as she was, she knew well what it was to possess property. Such knowledge ran in her family; her father was the best business man in his village.[301] She herself was domesticated and thrifty; for she kept her old clothes, and even in the field she knew where to find them when she wanted to make presents of them to her friends. She counted up her possessions in arms and horses, valued them at twelve thousand crowns, and, apparently made a pretty accurate reckoning.[302] But what was her idea in taking this house? Did she think of living in it? Did she intend when the war was over to return to Orléans and pass a peaceful old age in a house of her own? Or was she planning for her parents to dwell there, or some Vouthon uncle, or her brothers, one of whom was in great poverty and had got a doublet out of the citizens of Orléans?[303]

On the third of March she followed King Charles to Sully.[304] The château, in which she lodged near the King, belonged to the Sire de la Trémouille, who had inherited it from his mother, Marie de Sully, the daughter of Louis I of Bourbon. It had been recaptured from the English after the deliverance of Orléans.[305] A stronghold on the Loire, on the highroad from Paris to Autun, and commanding the plain between Orléans and Briare and the ancient bridge with twenty arches, the château of Sully linked together central France and those northern provinces which Jeanne had so regretfully quitted, and whither with all her heart she longed to return to engage in fresh expeditions and fresh sieges.

During the first fortnight of March, from the townsfolk of Reims she received a message in which they confided to her fears only too well grounded.[306] On the 8th of March the Regent had granted to the Duke of Burgundy the counties of Champagne and of Brie on condition of his reconquering them.[307] Armagnacs and English vied with each other in offering the biggest and most tempting morsels to this Gargantuan Duke. Not being able to keep their promise and deliver to him Compiègne which refused to be delivered, the

French offered him in its place Pont-Sainte-Maxence.[308] But it was Compiègne that he wanted. The truces, which had been very imperfectly kept, were to have expired at Christmas, but first they had been prolonged till the 15th of March and then till Easter. In the year 1430 Easter fell on the 16th of April; and Duke Philip was only waiting for that date to put an army in the field.[309]

In a manner concise and vivacious the Maid replied to the townsfolk of Reims:

"Dear friends and beloved and mightily desired. Jehanne the Maid hath received your letters making mention that ye fear a siege. Know ye that it shall not so betide, and I may but encounter them shortly. And if I do not encounter them and they do not come to you, if you shut your gates firmly, I shall shortly be with you: and if they be there, I shall make them put on their spurs so hastily that they will not know where to take them and so quickly that it shall be very soon. Other things I will not write unto you now, save that ye be always good and loyal. I pray God to have you in his keeping. Written at Sully, the 16th day of March.

I would announce unto you other tidings at which ye would mightily rejoice; but I fear lest the letters be taken on the road, and the said tidings be seen.

Signed. Jehanne.

Addressed to my dear friends and beloved, churchmen, burgesses and other citizens of the town of Rains."[310]

There can be no doubt that the scribe wrote this letter faithfully as it was dictated by the Maid, and that he wrote her words as they fell from her lips. In her haste she now and again forgot words and sometimes whole phrases; but the sense is clear all the same. And what confidence! "You will have no siege if I encounter the enemy." How completely is this the language of chivalry! On the eve of Patay she had asked: "Have you good spurs?"[311] Here she cries: "I will make them put on their spurs." She says that soon she will be in Champagne, that she is about to start. Surely we can no longer think of her shut up in the Castle of La Trémouille as in a kind of gilded cage.[312] In conclusion, she tells her friends at Reims that she does not write unto them all that she would like for fear lest her letter should be captured on the road. She knew what it was to be cautious. Sometimes she affixed a cross to her letters to warn her followers to pay no heed to what she wrote, in the hope that the missive would be intercepted and the enemy deceived.[313]

It was from Sully that on the 23rd of March Brother Pasquerel sent the Emperor Sigismund a letter intended for the Hussites of Bohemia.[314]

The Hussites of those days were abhorred and execrated throughout Christendom. They demanded the free preaching of God's word, communion in both kinds, and the return of the Church to that evangelical life which allowed neither the wealth of priests nor the temporal power of popes. They desired the punishment of sin by the civil magistrates, a custom which could prevail only in very holy society. They were saints indeed and heretics too on every possible point. Pope Martin held the destruction of these wicked persons to be salutary, and such was the opinion of every good Catholic. But how could this armed heresy be dealt with when it routed all the forces of the Empire and the Holy See? The Hussites were too much for that worn-out ancient chivalry of Christendom, for the knighthood of France and of Germany, which was good for nothing but to be thrown on to the refuse heaps like so much old iron. And this was precisely what the towns of the realm of France did when over these knights of chivalry they placed a peasant girl.[315]

At Tachov, in 1427, the Crusaders, blessed by the Holy Father, had fled at the mere sound of the chariot wheels of the Procops.[316] Pope Martin knew not where to turn for defenders of Holy Church, one and indivisible. He had paid for the armament of five thousand English crusaders, which the Cardinal of Winchester was to lead against these accursed Bohemians; but in this force the Holy Father was cruelly disappointed; hardly had his five thousand crusaders landed in France, than the Regent of England diverted them from their route and sent them to Brie to occupy the attention of the Maid of the Armagnacs.[317]

Since her coming into France Jeanne had spoken of the crusade as a work good and meritorious. In the letter dictated before the expedition to Orléans, she summoned the English to join the French and go together to fight against the Church's foe. And later, writing to the Duke of Burgundy, she invited the son of the Duke vanquished at Nicopolis to make war against the Turks.[318] Who but the mendicants directing her can have put these crusading ideas into Jeanne's head? Immediately after the deliverance of Orléans it was said that she would lead King Charles to the conquest of the Holy Sepulchre and that she would die in the Holy Land.[319] At the same time it was rumoured that she would make war on the Hussites. In the month of July, 1429, when the coronation campaign had barely begun, it was proclaimed in Germany, on the faith of a prophetess of Rome, that by a prophetess of France the Bohemian kingdom should be recovered.[320]

Already zealous for the Crusade against the Turks, the Maid was now equally eager for the Crusade against the Hussites. Turks or Bohemians, it was all alike to her. Of one and the other her only knowledge lay in the stories full of witchcraft related to her by the mendicants of her company. Touching the Hussites, stories were told, not all true, but which Jeanne must have believed; and they cannot have pleased her. It was said that they worshipped the devil, and that they called him "the wronged one." It was told that as works of piety they committed all manner of fornication. Every Bohemian was said to be possessed by a hundred demons. They were accused of killing thousands of churchmen. Again, and this time with truth, they were charged with burning churches and monasteries. The Maid believed in the God who commanded Israel to wipe out the Philistines from the face of the earth. But recently there had arisen Cathari who held the God of the Old Testament to be none other than Lucifer or Luciabelus, author of evil, liar and murderer. The Cathari abhorred war; they refused to shed blood; they were heretics;

they had been massacred, and none remained. The Maid believed in good faith that the extirpation of the Hussites was a work pleasing to God. Men more learned than she, not like her addicted to chivalry, but of gentle life, clerks like the Chancellor Jean Gerson, believed it likewise.[321] Of these Bohemian heretics she thought what every one thought: her opinions were those of the multitude; her views were modelled on public opinion. Wherefore in all the simplicity of her heart she hated the Hussites, but she feared them not, because she feared nothing and because she believed, God helping her, that she was able to overcome all the English, all the Turks, and all the Bohemians in the world. At the first trumpet call she was ready to sally forth against them. On the 23rd of March, 1430, Brother Pasquerel sent the Emperor Sigismund a letter written in the name of the Maid and intended for the Hussites of Bohemia. This letter was indited in Latin. The following is the purport of it:

Jhesus † Maria

Long ago there reached me the tidings that ye from the true Christians that ye once were have become heretics, like unto the Saracens, that ye have abolished true religion and worship and have turned to a superstition corrupt and fatal, the which in your zeal to maintain and to spread abroad there be no shame nor cruelty ye do not dare to perpetrate. You defile the sacraments of the Church, tear to pieces the articles of her faith, overthrow her temples. The images which were made for similitudes you break and throw into the fire. Finally such Christians as embrace not your faith you massacre. What fury, what folly, what rage possesses you? That religion which God the All Powerful, which the Son, which the Holy Ghost raised up, instituted, exalted and revealed in a thousand manners, by a thousand miracles, ye persecute, ye employ all arts to overturn and to exterminate.

It is you, you who are blind and not those who have not eyes nor sight. Think ye that ye will go unpunished? Do ye not know that if God prevent not your impious violence, if he suffer you to grope on in darkness and in error, it is that he is preparing for you a greater sorrow and a greater punishment? As for me, in good sooth, were I not occupied with the English wars, I would have already come against you. But in very deed if I learn not that ye have turned from your wicked ways, I will peradventure leave the English and hasten against you, in order that I may destroy by the sword your vain and violent superstition, if I can do so in no other manner, and that I may rid you either of heresy or of life. Notwithstanding, if you prefer to return to the Catholic faith and to the light of primitive days, send unto me your ambassadors and I will tell them what ye must do. If on the other hand ye will be stiff-necked and kick against the pricks, then remember all the crimes and offences ye have perpetrated and look for to see me coming unto you with all strength divine and human to render unto you again all the evil ye have done unto others.

Given at Sully, on the 23rd of March, to the Bohemian heretics.

Signed. Pasquerel.[322]

This was the letter sent to the Emperor. How had Jeanne really expressed herself in her dialect savouring alike of the speech of Champagne and of that of l'Île de France? There can be no doubt but that her letter had been sadly embellished by the good Brother. Such Ciceronian language cannot have proceeded from the Maid. It is all very well to say that a saint of those days could do everything, could prophesy on any subject and in any tongue, so fine an epistle remains far too rhetorical to have been composed by a damsel whom even the Armagnac captains considered simple. Nevertheless, a careful examination will reveal in this missive, at any rate in the second half of it, certain of those bluntly naive passages and some of that childish assurance which are noticeable in Jeanne's genuine letters, especially in her reply to the Count of Armagnac;[323] and more than once there occurs an expression characteristic of a village sibyl. The following, for example, is quite in Jeanne's own manner: "If you will return to the bosom of the Catholic Church, send me your ambassadors; I will tell you what you have to do." And her usual threat: "Expect me with all strength human and divine."[324] As for the phrase: "If I hear not shortly of your conversion, of your return to the bosom of the Church, I will peradventure leave the English and come against you," here we may suspect the mendicant friar, less interested in the affairs of Charles VII than in those of the Church, of having ascribed to the Maid greater eagerness to set forth on the Crusade than she really felt. Good and salutary as she deemed the taking of the Cross, as far as we know her, she would never have consented to take it until she had driven the English out of the realm of France. She believed this to be her mission, and the persistence, the consistency, the strength of will she evinced in its fulfilment, are truly admirable. It is quite probable that she dictated to the good Brother some phrase like: "When I have put the English out of the kingdom, I will turn against you." This would explain and excuse Brother Pasquerel's error. It is very likely that Jeanne believed she would dispose of the English in a trice and that she already saw herself distributing good buffets and sound clouts to the renegade and infidel Bohemians. The Maid's simplicity makes itself felt through the clerk's Latin. This epistle to the Bohemians recalls, alas! that fagot placed upon the stake whereon John Huss was burning, by the pious zeal of the good wife whose saintly simplicity John Huss himself teaches us to admire.

One cannot help reflecting that Jeanne and those very men against whom she hurled menace and invective had much in common; alike they were impelled by faith, chastity, simple ignorance, pious duty, resignation to God's will, and a tendency to magnify the minor matters of devotion. Zizka[325] had established in his camp that purity of morals which the Maid was endeavouring to introduce among the Armagnacs. The peasant soldiers of Bohemia and the peasant Maid of France bearing her sword amidst mendicant monks had much in common. On the one hand and on the other, we have the religious spirit in the place of the political spirit, the fear of sin in the place of obedience to the civil law, the spiritual introduced into the temporal. Here is indeed a woeful sight and a piteous; the devout set one against the other, the innocent against the innocent, the simple against the simple, the heretic against heretics; and it is painful to think that when she is threatening with extermination the disciples of that John Huss, who had been treacherously taken and burned as a heretic, she herself is on the point of being sold to her enemies and condemned to suffer as a witch. It would have been different if this letter, at which the accomplished wits and humorists of the day looked askance, had won the approval of theologians. But they also found fault with it, an illustrious canonist, a zealous inquisitor deemed highly presumptuous this threatening of a multitude of men by a Maid.[326]

We were right in saying that she was not prepared to leave the English immediately and hasten against the Bohemians. Five days after her appeal to the Hussites she wrote to her friends at Reims and in mysterious words gave them to understand that she would come to them shortly.[327]

The partisans of Duke Philip were at that time hatching plots in the towns of Champagne, notably at Troyes and at Reims. On the 22nd of February, 1430, a canon and a chaplain were arrested and brought before the chapter for having conspired to deliver the city to the English. It was well for them that they belonged to the Church, for having been condemned to perpetual imprisonment, they obtained from the King a mitigation of their sentence, and the canon a complete remittance.[328] The aldermen and ecclesiastics of the city, fearing they would be thought badly of on the other side of the Loire, wrote to the Maid entreating her to speak well of them to the King. The following is her reply to their request:[329]

"Very good friends and beloved, may it please you to wit that I have received your letters, the which make mention how it hath been reported to the King that within the city of Reims there be many wicked persons. Therefore I give you to wit that it is indeed true that even such things have been reported to him and that he grieves much that there be folk in alliance with the Burgundians; that they would betray the town and bring the Burgundians into it. But since then the King has known the contrary by means of the assurance ye have sent him, and he is well pleased with you. And ye may believe that ye stand well in his favour; and if ye have need, he would help you with regard to the siege; and he knows well that ye have much to suffer from the hardness of those treacherous Burgundians, your adversaries: thus may God in his pleasure deliver you shortly, that is as soon as may be. So I pray and entreat you my friends dearly beloved that ye hold well the said city for the King and that ye keep good watch. Ye will soon have good tidings of me at greater length. Other things for the present I write not unto you save that the whole of Brittany is French and that the Duke is to send to the King three thousand combatants paid for two months. To God I commend you, may he keep you.

Written at Sully, the 28th of March.

Jehanne.[330]

Addressed to: My good friends and dearly beloved, the churchmen, aldermen, burgesses and inhabitants and masters of the good town of Reyms."[331]

Touching the succour to be expected from the Duke of Brittany, the Maid was labouring under a delusion. Like all other prophetesses she was ignorant of what was passing around her. Despite her failures, she believed in her good fortune; she doubted herself no more than she doubted God; and she was eager to pursue the fulfilment of her mission. "Ye shall soon have tidings of me," she said to the townsfolk of Reims. A few days after, and she left Sully to go into France and fight, on the expiration of the truces.

It has been said that she feigned an expedition of pleasure and set out without taking leave of the King, that it was a kind of innocent stratagem, an honourable flight.[332] But it was nothing of the sort.[333] The Maid gathered a company of some hundred horse, sixty-eight archers and cross-bowmen, and two trumpeters, commanded by a Lombard captain, Bartolomeo Baretta.[334] In this company were Italian men-at-arms, bearing broad shields, like some who had come to Orléans at the time of the siege; possibly they were the same.[335] She set out at the head of this company, with her brothers and her steward, the Sire Jean d'Aulon. She was in the hands of Jean d'Aulon, and Jean d'Aulon was in the hands of the Sire de la Trémouille, to whom he owed money.[336] The good squire would not have followed the Maid against the King's will.

The flying squadron of *béguines* had recently been divided by a schism. Friar Richard, who was then in high favour with Queen Marie, and who had preached the Lenten sermons of

1430[337] at Orléans, stayed behind, on the Loire, with Catherine de la Rochelle. Jeanne took with her Pierronne and the younger Breton prophetess.[338] If she went into France, it was not without the knowledge or against the will of the King and his Council. Very probably the Chancellor of the kingdom had asked La Trémouille to send her in order that he might employ her in the approaching campaign against the Burgundians, who were threatening his government of Beauvais and his city of Reims.[339] He was not very kindly disposed towards her, but already he had made use of her and he intended to do so again. Possibly his intention was to employ her in a fresh attack on Paris.

The King had not abandoned the idea of taking his great city by the peaceful methods he always preferred. Throughout Lent, between Sully and Paris, there had been a constant passing to and fro of certain Carmelite monks of Melun, disguised as artisans. These were the churchmen who, during the attack on the Porte Saint Honoré, on the Day of the Festival of Our Lady, had stirred up the popular rising which had spread from one bank of the Seine to the other. Now they were negotiating with certain influential citizens the entrance of the King's men into the rebel city. The Prior of the Melun Carmelites was directing the conspiracy.[340] There is reason to believe that Jeanne had herself seen him or one of his monks. True it is that since the 22nd or the 23rd of March it was known at Sully that the conspiracy had been discovered;[341] but perhaps the hope of success still lingered. It was to Melun that Jeanne went with her company; and it is difficult to believe that there was no connection between the conspiracy of the Carmelites and the expedition of the Maid.

Why should Charles VII's Councillors have ceased to employ her? It cannot be said that she appeared less divine to the French or less evil to the English. Her failures, either unknown, or partially known, rendered unimportant by the fame of her victories, had not dispelled the idea that within her resided invincible power. At the time when the hapless damsel with the flower of French knighthood was receiving sore treatment under the walls of La Charité at the hands of an ex-mason's apprentice, in Burgundian lands it was rumoured that she was carrying by storm a castle twelve miles from Paris.[342] She was still considered miraculous; the burgesses, the men-at-arms of her party still believed in her. And as for the *Godons*, from the Regent to the humblest swordsman of the army, they all regarded her with a terror as great as that which had possessed them at Orléans and Patay. At this time so many English soldiers and captains refused to go to France, that a special edict was issued obliging them to do so.[343] But they doubtless discovered reasons enough for not going into a country where henceforth they could hope only for hard knocks and nothing tempting; so that many declined, terrified by the enchantments of the Maid.[344]

Chapter VI
The Maid in the trenches of Melun – le seigneur de l'Ours – the child of Lagny

N Easter week, Jeanne, at the head of a band of mercenaries, is before the walls of Melun.[345] She arrives just in time to fight. The truces have expired.[346] Is it possible that the town which was subject to King Charles[347] can have refused to admit the Maid with her company when she came to it so generously? Apparently it was so. Was Jeanne able to communicate with the Carmelites of Melun? Probably. What misfortune befell her at the gates of the town? Did she suffer ill treatment at the hands of a Burgundian band? We know not. But when she was in the trenches she heard Saint Catherine and Saint Margaret saying unto her: "Thou wilt be taken before Saint John's Day."

And she entreated them: "When I am taken, let me die immediately without suffering long." And the Voices repeated that she would be taken and thus it must be.

And they added gently: "Be not troubled, be resigned. God will help thee."[348]

Saint John's Day was the 24th of June, in less than ten weeks. Many a time after that, Jeanne asked her saints at what hour she would be taken; but they did not tell her; and thus doubting she ceased to follow her own ideas and consulted the captains.[349]

On her way from Melun to Lagny-sur-Marne, in the month of May, she had to pass Corbeil. It was probably then, and in her company, that the two devout women from Lower Brittany, Pierronne and her younger sister in the spirit, were taken at Corbeil by the English.[350]

For eight months the town of Lagny had been subject to King Charles and governed by Messire Ambroise de Loré, who was energetically waging war against the English of Paris and elsewhere.[351] For the nonce Messire Ambroise de Loré was absent; but his lieutenant, Messire Jean Foucault, commanded the garrison. Shortly after Jeanne's coming to this town, tidings were brought that a company of between three and four hundred men of Picardy and of Champagne, fighting for the Duke of Burgundy, after having ranged through l'Île de France, were now on their way back to Picardy with much booty. Their captain was a valiant man-at-arms, one Franquet d'Arras.[352] The French determined to cut off their retreat. Under the command of Messire Jean Foucault, Messire Geoffroy de Saint-Bellin, Lord Hugh Kennedy, a Scotchman, and Captain Baretta, they sallied forth from the town.[353]

The Maid went with them. They encountered the Burgundians near Lagny, but failed to surprise them. Messire Franquet's archers had had time to take up their position with their backs to a hedge, in the English manner. King Charles's men barely outnumbered the enemy. A certain clerk of that time, a Frenchman, writes of the engagement. His innate ingeniousness was invincible. With candid common sense he states that this very slight numerical superiority rendered the enterprise very arduous and difficult for his party.[354] And the battle was strong indeed. The Burgundians were mightily afraid of the Maid because they believed her to be a witch and in command of armies of devils; notwithstanding, they fought right valiantly. Twice the French were repulsed; but they returned to the attack, and finally the Burgundians were all slain or taken.[355]

The conquerors returned to Lagny, loaded with booty and taking with them their prisoners, among whom was Messire Franquet d'Arras. Of noble birth and the lord of a manor, he was entitled to expect that he would be held to ransom, according to custom. Both Jean de Troissy, Bailie of Senlis,[356] and the Maid demanded him from the soldier who was his captor. It was to the Maid that he was finally delivered.[357] Did she obtain him in return for money? Probably, for soldiers were not accustomed to give up noble and profitable prisoners for nothing. Nevertheless, the Maid, when questioned on this subject, replied, that being neither mistress nor steward of France, it was not for her to give out money. We must suppose, therefore, that some one paid for her. However that may be, Captain Franquet d'Arras was given up to her, and she endeavoured to exchange him for a prisoner in the hands of the English. The man whom she thus desired to deliver was a Parisian who was called Le Seigneur de l'Ours.[358]

He was not of gentle birth and his arms were the sign of his hostelry. It was the custom in those days to give the title of Seigneur to the masters of the great Paris inns. Thus Colin, who kept the inn at the Temple Gate, was known as Seigneur du Boisseau. The hôtel de l'Ours stood in the Rue Saint-Antoine, near the Gate properly called La Porte Baudoyer, but commonly known as Porte Baudet, Baudet possessing the double advantage over Baudoyer of being shorter and more comprehensible.[359] It was an ancient and famous inn, equal in renown to the most famous, to the inn of L'Arbre Sec, in the street of that name, to the Fleur de Lis near the Pont Neuf, to the Epée in the Rue Saint-Denis, and to the Chapeau Fétu of the Rue Croix-du-Tirouer. As early as King Charles V's reign the inn was much frequented. Before huge fires the spits were turning all day long, and there were hot bread, fresh herrings, and wine of Auxerre in plenty. But since then the plunderings of men-at-arms had laid waste the countryside, and travellers no longer ventured forth for fear of being robbed and slain. Knights and pilgrims had ceased coming into the town. Only wolves came by night and devoured little children in the streets. There were no fagots in the grate, no dough in the kneading-trough. Armagnacs and Burgundians had drunk all the wine, laid waste all the vineyards, and nought was left in the cellar save a poor piquette of apples and of plums.[360]

The Seigneur de l'Ours, whom the Maid demanded, was called Jaquet Guillaume.[361] Although Jeanne, like other folk, called him Seigneur, it is not certain that he personally directed his inn, nor even that the inn was open through these years of disaster and desolation. The only ascertainable fact is that he was the proprietor of the house with the sign of the Bear (*l'Ours*). He held it by right of his wife Jeannette, and had come into possession of it in the following manner.

Fourteen years before, when King Henry with his knighthood had not yet landed in France, the host of the Bear Inn had been the King's sergeant-at-arms, one Jean Roche, a man of wealth and fair fame. He was a devoted follower of the Duke of Burgundy, and that was what ruined him. Paris was then occupied by the Armagnacs. In the year 1416, in order to turn them out of the city, Jean Roche concerted with divers burgesses. The plot was to be carried out on Easter Day, which that year fell on the 29th of April. But the Armagnacs discovered it. They threw the conspirators into prison and brought them to trial. On the first Saturday in May the Seigneur de l'Ours was carried to the market place in a tumbrel with Durand de Brie, a dyer, master of the sixty cross-bowmen of Paris, and Jean Perquin, pin-maker and brasier. All three were beheaded, and the body of the Seigneur de l'Ours was hanged at Montfaucon where it remained until the entrance of the Burgundians. Six weeks after their coming, in July, 1418, his body was taken down from gibbet and buried in consecrated ground.[362]

Now the widow of Jean Roche had a daughter by a first marriage. Her name was Jeannette; she took for her first husband a certain Bernard le Breton; for her second, Jaquet Guillaume, who was not rich. He owed money to Maître Jean Fleury, a clerk at law and the King's secretary. His wife's affairs were not more prosperous; her father's goods had been confiscated and she had been obliged to redeem a part of her maternal inheritance. In 1424, the couple were short of money, and they sold a house, concealing the fact that it was mortgaged. Being charged by the purchaser, they were thrown into prison, where they aggravated their offence by suborning two witnesses, one a priest, the other a chambermaid. Fortunately for them, they procured a pardon.[363]

The Jaquet Guillaume couple, therefore, were in a sorry plight. There remained to them, however, the inheritance of Jean Roche, the inn near the Place Baudet, at the sign of the Bear, the title of which Jaquet Guillaume bore. This second Seigneur de l'Ours was to be as strongly Armagnac as the other had been Burgundian, and was to pay the same price for his opinions.

Six years had passed since his release from prison, when, in the March of 1430, there was plotted by the Carmelites of Melun and certain burgesses of Paris that conspiracy which we mentioned on the occasion of Jeanne's departure for l'Île de France. It was not the first plot into which the Carmelites had entered; they had plotted that rising which had been on the point of breaking out on the Day of the Nativity, when the Maid was leading the attack near La Porte Saint-Honoré; but never before had so many burgesses and so many notables entered into a conspiracy. A clerk of the Treasury, Maître Jean de la Chapelle, two magistrates of the Châtelet, Maître Renaud Savin and Maître Pierre Morant, a very wealthy man, named Jean de Calais, burgesses, merchants, artisans, more than one hundred and fifty persons, held the threads of this vast web, and among them, Jaquet Guillaume, Seigneur de l'Ours.

The Carmelites of Melun directed the whole. Clad as artisans, they went from King to burgesses, from burgesses to King; they kept up the communications between those within and those without, and regulated all the details of the enterprise. One of them asked the conspirators for a written undertaking to bring the King's men into the city. Such a demand looks as if the majority of the conspirators were in the pay of the Royal Council.

In exchange for this undertaking these monks brought acts of oblivion signed by the King. For the people of Paris to be induced to receive the Prince, whom they still called Dauphin, they must needs be assured of a full and complete amnesty. For more than ten years, while the English and Burgundians had been holding the town, no one had felt altogether free from the reproach of their lawful sovereign and the men of his party. And all the more desirous were they for Charles of Valois to forget the past when they recalled the cruel vengeance taken by the Armagnacs after the suppression of the Butchers.

One of the conspirators, Jaquet Perdriel, advocated the sounding of a trumpet and the reading of the acts of oblivion on Sunday at the Porte Baudet.

"I have no doubt," he said, "but that we shall be joined by the craftsmen, who, in great numbers will flock to hear the reading."

He intended leading them to the Saint Antoine Gate and opening it to the King's men who were lying in ambush close by.

Some eighty or a hundred Scotchmen, dressed as Englishmen, wearing the Saint Andrew's cross, were then to enter the town, bringing in fish and cattle.

"They will enter boldly by the Saint-Denys Gate," said Perdriel, "and take possession of it. Whereupon the King's men will enter in force by the Porte Saint Antoine."

The plan was deemed good, except that it was considered better for the King's men to come in by the Saint-Denys Gate.

On Sunday, the 12th of March, the second Sunday in Lent, Maître Jean de la Chapelle invited the magistrate Renaud Savin to come to the tavern of *La Pomme de Pin* and meet divers other conspirators in order to arrive at an understanding touching what was best to be done. They decided that on a certain day, under pretext of going to see his vines at Chapelle-Saint-Denys, Jean de Calais should join the King's men outside the walls, make himself known to them by unfurling a white standard and bring them into the town. It was further determined that Maître Morant and a goodly company of citizens with him, should hold themselves in readiness in the taverns of the Rue Saint-Denys to support the French when they came in. In one of the taverns of this street must have been the Seigneur de l'Ours, who, dwelling near by, had undertaken to bring together divers folk of the neighbourhood.

The conspirators were acting in perfect agreement. All they now awaited was to be informed of the day chosen by the Royal Council; and they believed the attempt was to be made on the following Sunday. But on the 21st of March Brother Pierre d'Allée, Prior of the Carmelites of Melun, was taken by the English. Put to the torture, he confessed the plot and named his accomplices. On the information he gave, more than one hundred and fifty persons were arrested and tried. On the 8th of April, the Eve of Palm Sunday, seven of the most important were taken to the market-place on a tumbrel. They were: Jean de la Chapelle, clerk of the Treasury; Renaud Savin and Pierre Morant, magistrates at the Châtelet; Guillaume Perdriau; Jean le François, called Baudrin; Jean le Rigueur, baker, and Jaquet Guillaume, Seigneur de l'Ours. All seven were beheaded by the executioner, who afterwards quartered the bodies of Jean de la Chapelle and of Baudrin.

Jaquet Perdriel was merely deprived of his possessions. Jean de Calais soon procured a pardon. Jeannette, the wife of Jaquet Guillaume, was banished from the kingdom and her goods confiscated.[364]

How can the Maid have known the Seigneur de l'Ours? Possibly the Carmelites of Melun had recommended him to her, and perhaps it was on their advice that she demanded his surrender. She may have seen him in the September of 1429, at Saint-Denys or before the walls of Paris, and he may have then undertaken to work for the Dauphin and his party. Why were attempts made at Lagny to save this man alone of the one hundred and fifty Parisians arrested on the information of Brother Pierre d'Allée? Rather than Renaud Savin and Pierre Morant, magistrates at the Châtelet, rather than Jean de la Chapelle, clerk of the Treasury, why choose the meanest of the band? And how could they look to exchange a man accused of treachery for a prisoner of war? All this seems to us mysterious and inexplicable.

In the early days of May, Jeanne did not know what had become of Jaquet Guillaume. When she heard that he had been tried and put to death she was sore grieved and vexed. None the less, she looked upon Franquet as a captive held to ransom. But the Bailie of Senlis, who for some unknown reason was determined on the captain's ruin, took advantage of the Maid's vexation at Jaquet Guillaume's execution, and persuaded her to give up her prisoner.

He represented to her that this man had committed many a murder, many a theft, that he was a traitor, and that consequently he ought to be brought to trial.

"You will be neglecting to execute justice," he said, "if you set this Franquet free."

These reasons decided her, or rather she yielded to the Bailie's entreaty.

"Since the man I wished to have is dead," she said, "do with Franquet as justice shall require you."[365]

Thus she surrendered her prisoner. Was she right or wrong? Before deciding we must ask whether it were possible for her to do otherwise than she did. She was the Maid of God, the angel of the Lord of Hosts, that is clear. But the leaders of war, the captains, paid no great heed to what she said. As for the Bailie, he was the King's man, of noble birth and passing powerful.

Assisted by the judges of Lagny, he himself conducted the trial. The accused confessed that he was a murderer, a thief, and a traitor. We must believe him; and yet we cannot forbear a doubt as to whether he really was, any more than the majority of Armagnac or Burgundian men-at-arms, any more than a Damoiseau de Commercy or a Guillaume de Flavy, for example. He was condemned to death.

Jeanne consented that he should die, if he had deserved death, and seeing that he had confessed his crimes[366] he was beheaded.

When they heard of the scandalous treatment of Messire Franquet, the Burgundians were loud in their sorrow and indignation.[367] It would seem that in this matter the Bailie of Senlis and the judges of Lagny did not act according to custom. We, however, are not sufficiently acquainted with the circumstances to form an opinion. There may have been some reason, of which we are ignorant, why the King of France should have demanded this prisoner. He had a right to do so on condition that he paid the Maid the amount of the ransom. A soldier of those days, well informed in all things touching honour in war, was the author of *Le Jouvencel*. In his chivalrous romances he writes approvingly of the wise Amydas, King of Amydoine, who, learning that one of his enemies, the Sire de Morcellet, has been taken in battle and held to ransom, cries out that he is the vilest of traitors, ransoms him with good coins of the realm, and hands him over to the provost of the town and the officers of his council that they may execute justice upon him.[368] Such was the royal prerogative.

Whether it was that camp life was hardening her, or whether, like all mystics, she was subject to violent changes of mood, Jeanne showed at Lagny none of that gentleness she had displayed on the evening of Patay. The virgin who once had no other arm in battle than her standard, now wielded a sword found there, at Lagny, a Burgundian sword and a trusty. Those who regarded her as an angel of the Lord, good Brother Pasquerel, for example, might justify her by saying that the Archangel Saint Michael, the standard-bearer of celestial hosts, bore a flaming sword. And indeed Jeanne remained a saint.

While she was at Lagny, folk came and told her that a child had died at birth, unbaptised.[369] Having entered into the mother at the time of her conception, the devil held the soul of this child, who, for lack of water, had died the enemy of its Creator. The greatest anxiety was felt concerning the fate of this soul. Some thought it was in limbo, banished forever from God's sight, but the more general and better founded opinion was that it was seething in hell; for has not Saint Augustine demonstrated that souls, little as well as great, are damned because of original sin. And how could it be otherwise, seeing that Eve's fall had effaced the divine likeness in this child? He was destined to eternal death. And to think that with a few drops of water this death might have been avoided! So terrible a disaster afflicted not only the poor creature's kinsfolk, but likewise the neighbours and all good Christians in the town of Lagny. The body was carried to the Church of Saint-Pierre and placed before the image of Our Lady, which had been highly venerated ever since the plague of 1128. It was called Notre-Dame-des-Ardents because it cured burns, and when there were no burns to be cured it was called Notre-Dame-des-Aidants, or rather Des Aidances, that is, Our Lady the Helper, because she granted succour to those in dire necessity.[370]

The maidens of the town knelt before her, the little body in their midst, beseeching her to intercede with her divine Son so that this little child might have his share in the Redemption brought by our Saviour.[371] In such cases the Holy Virgin did not always deny her powerful intervention. Here it may not be inappropriate to relate a miracle she had worked thirty-seven years before.

At Paris, in 1393, a sinful creature, finding herself with child, concealed her pregnancy, and, when her time was come, was without aid delivered. Then, having stuffed linen into the throat of the girl she had brought forth, she went and threw her on to the dust-heap outside La Porte Saint-Martin-des-Champs. But a dog scented the body, and scratching away the other refuse, discovered it. A devout woman, who happened to be passing by, took this poor little lifeless creature, and, followed by more than four hundred people, bore it to the Church of Saint-Martin-des-Champs, there placed it on the altar of Our Lady, and kneeling down with the multitude of folk and the monks of the Abbey, with all her heart prayed the Holy Virgin not to suffer this innocent babe to be condemned eternally. The child stirred a little, opened her eyes, loosened the linen, which gagged her, and cried aloud. A priest baptized her on the altar of Our Lady, and gave her the name of Marie. A nurse was found, and she was fed from the breast. She lived three hours, then died and was carried to consecrated ground.[372]

In those days resurrections of unbaptised children were frequent. That saintly Abbess, Colette of Corbie, who, when Jeanne was at Lagny, dwelt at Moulins with the reformed Sisters of Saint Clare, had brought back to life two of these poor creatures: a girl, who received the name of Colette at the font and afterwards became nun, then abbess at Pont-à-Mousson; a boy, who was said to have been two days buried and whom the servant of the poor declared to be one of the elect. He died at six months, thus fulfilling the prophecy made by the saint.[373]

With this kind of miracle Jeanne was doubtless acquainted. About twenty-five miles from Domremy, in the duchy of Lorraine, near Lunéville, was the sanctuary of Notre-Dame-des-Aviots, of which she had probably heard. Notre-Dame-des-Aviots, or Our Lady of those brought back to life, was famed for restoring life to unbaptised children. By means of her intervention they lived again long enough to be made Christians.[374]

In the duchy of Luxembourg, near Montmédy, on the hill of Avioth,[375] multitudes of pilgrims worshipped an image of Our Lady brought there by angels. On this hill a church had been built for her, with slim pillars and elaborate stonework in trefoils, roses and light foliage. This statue worked all manner of miracles. At its feet were placed children born dead; they were restored to life and straightway baptized.[376]

The folk, gathered in the Church of Saint-Pierre de Lagny, around the statue of Notre-Dame-des-Aidances, hoped for a like grace. The damsels of the town prayed round the child's lifeless body. The Maid was asked to come and join them in praying to Our Lord and Our Lady. She went to the church, and knelt down with the maidens and prayed. The child was black, "as black as my coat," said Jeanne. When the Maid and the damsels had prayed, it yawned three times and its colour came back. It was baptized and straightway it died; it was buried in consecrated ground. Throughout the town this resurrection was said to be the work of the Maid. According to the tales in circulation, during the three days since its birth the child had given no sign of life;[377] but the gossips of Lagny had doubtless extended the period of its comatose condition, like those good wives who of a single egg laid by the husband of one of them, made a hundred before the day was out.

Chapter VII
Soissons and Compiègne – capture of the Maid

EAVING Lagny, the Maid presented herself before Senlis, with her own company and with the fighting men of the French nobles whom she had joined, in all some thousand horse. And for this force she demanded entrance into the town. No misfortune was more feared by burgesses than that of receiving men-at-arms, and no privilege more jealously guarded than that of keeping them outside the walls. King Charles had experienced it during the peaceful coronation campaign. The folk of Senlis made answer to the Maid that, seeing the poverty of the town in forage, corn, oats, victuals and wine, they offered her an entrance with thirty or forty of the most notable of her company and no more.[378]

It is said that from Senlis Jeanne went to the Castle of Borenglise in the parish of Elincourt, between Compiègne and Ressons; and, in ignorance as to what can have taken her there, it is supposed that she made a pilgrimage to the Church of Elincourt, which was dedicated to Saint Margaret; and it is possible that she wished to worship Saint Margaret there as she had worshipped Saint Catherine at Fierbois, in order to do honour to one of those heavenly ladies who visited her every day and every hour.[379]

In those days, in the town of Angers, was a licentiate of laws, canon of the churches of Tours and Angers and Dean of Saint-Jean d'Angers. Less than ten days before Jeanne's coming to Sainte-Marguerite d'Elincourt, on April 18, about nine o'clock in the evening, he felt a pain in the head, which lasted until four o'clock in the morning, and was so severe that he thought he must die. He prayed to Saint Catherine, for whom he professed a special devotion, and straightway was cured. In thankfulness for so great a grace, he wended on foot to the sanctuary of Saint Catherine of Fierbois; and there, on Friday, the 5th of May, in a loud voice, said a mass for the King, for "the Maid divinely worthy," and for the peace and prosperity of the realm.[380]

The Council of King Charles had made over Pont-Sainte-Maxence to the Duke of Burgundy, in lieu of Compiègne, which they were unable to deliver to him since that town absolutely refused to be delivered, and remained the King's despite the King. The Duke of Burgundy kept Pont-Sainte-Maxence which had been granted him and resolved to take Compiègne.[381]

On the 17th of April, when the truce had expired, he took the field with a goodly knighthood and a powerful army, four thousand Burgundians, Picards and Flemings, and fifteen hundred English, commanded by Jean de Luxembourg, Count of Ligny.[382]

Noble pieces of artillery did the Duke bring to that siege; notably, Remeswelle, Rouge Bombarde and Houppembière, from all three of which were fired stone balls of enormous size. Mortars, which the Duke had brought and paid ready money for to Messire Jean de Luxembourg, were brought likewise; Beaurevoir and Bourgogne, also a great "*coullard*" and a movable engine of war. The vast states of Burgundy sent their archers and cross-bowmen to Compiègne. The Duke provided himself with bows from Prussia and from Caffa in Georgia,[383] and with arrows barbed and unbarbed. He engaged sappers and miners to lay powder mines round the town and to throw Greek fire into it. In short my Lord Philip, richer than a king, the most magnificent lord in Christendom and skilled in all the arts of knighthood, was resolved to make a gallant siege.[384]

Philip, Duke of Burgundy

The town, then one of the largest and strongest in France, was defended by a garrison of between four and five hundred men,[385] commanded by Guillaume de Flavy. Scion of a noble house of that province, forever in dispute with the nobles his neighbours, and perpetually picking quarrels with the poor folk, he was as wicked and cruel as any Armagnac baron.[386] The citizens would have no other captain, and in that office they maintained him in defiance of King Charles and his chamberlains. They did wisely, for none was better able to defend the town than my Lord Guillaume, none was more set on doing his duty. When the King of France had commanded him to deliver the place he had refused point-blank; and when later the Duke promised him a good round sum and a rich inheritance in exchange for Compiègne, he made answer that the town was not his, but the King's.[387]

The Duke of Burgundy easily took Gournay-sur-Aronde, and then laid siege to Choisy-sur-Aisne, also called Choisy-au-Bac, at the junction of the Aisne and the Oise.[388]

The Gascon squire, Poton de Saintrailles and the men of his company crossed the Aisne between Soissons and Choisy, surprised the besiegers, and retired immediately, taking with them sundry prisoners.[389]

On the 13th of May, the Maid entered Compiègne, where she lodged in the Rue de l'Etoile.[390] On the morrow, the Attorneys[391] offered her four pots of wine.[392] They thereby intended to do her great honour, for they did no more for the Lord Archbishop of Reims, Chancellor of the realm, who was then in the town with the Count of Vendôme, the King's lieutenant and divers other leaders of war. These noble lords resolved to send artillery and other munitions to the Castle of Choisy, which could not hold out much longer;[393] and now, as before, the Maid was made use of.

The army marched towards Soissons in order to cross the Aisne.[394] The captain of the town was a squire of Picardy, called by the French Guichard Bournel, by the Burgundians Guichard de Thiembronne; he had served on both sides. Jeanne knew him well; he reminded her of a painful incident. He had been one of those, who finding her wounded in the trenches before Paris, had insisted on putting her on her horse against her will. On the approach of King Charles's barons and men-at-arms, Captain Guichard made the folk of Soissons believe that the whole army was coming to encamp in their town. Wherefore they resolved not to receive them. Then happened what had already befallen at Senlis: Captain Bournel received the Lord Archbishop of Reims, the Count of Vendôme and the Maid, with a small company, and the rest of the army abode that night outside the walls.[395] On the morrow, failing to obtain command of the bridge, they endeavoured to ford the river, but without success; for it was spring and the waters were high. The army had to turn back. When it was gone, Captain Bournel sold to the Duke of Burgundy the city he was charged to hold for the King of France; and he delivered it into the hand of Messire Jean de Luxembourg for four thousand golden *saluts*.[396]

At the tidings of this treacherous and dishonourable action on the part of the Captain of Soissons, Jeanne cried out that if she had him, she would cut his body into four pieces, which was no empty imagining of her wrath. As the penalty of certain crimes it was the custom for the executioner, after he had beheaded the condemned, to cut his body in four pieces, which was called quartering. So that it was as if Jeanne had said that the traitor deserved quartering. The words sounded hard to Burgundian ears; certain even believed that they heard Jeanne in her wrath taking God's name in vain. They did not hear correctly. Never had Jeanne taken the name of God or of any of his saints in vain. Far from swearing when she was angered, she used to exclaim: "God's good will!" or "Saint John!" or "By Our Lady!"[397]

Before Soissons, Jeanne and the generals separated. The latter with their men-at-arms went to Senlis and the banks of the Marne. The country between the Aisne and the Oise was no longer capable of supporting so large a number of men or such important personages. Jeanne and her company wended their way back to Compiègne.[398] Scarcely had she entered the town when she sallied forth to ravage the neighbourhood.

For example, she took part in an expedition against Pont-l'Evêque, a stronghold, some distance from Noyon, occupied by a small English garrison, commanded by Lord Montgomery.

The Burgundians, who were besieging Compiègne, made Pont-l'Evêque their base. In the middle of May, the French numbering about a thousand, commanded by Captain Poton, by Messire Jacques de Chabannes and divers others, and accompanied by the Maid, attacked the English under Lord Montgomery, and the battle was passing fierce. But the enemy, being relieved by the Burgundians of Noyon, the French must needs beat a retreat. They had slain thirty of their adversaries and had lost as many, wherefore the combat was held to have been right sanguinary.[399] There was no longer any question of crossing the Aisne and saving Choisy.

After returning to Compiègne, Jeanne, who never rested for a moment, hastened to Crépy-en-Valois, where were gathering the troops intended for the defence of Compiègne. Then, with these troops, she marched through the Forest of Guise, to the besieged town and entered it on the 23rd, at daybreak, without having encountered any Burgundians. There were none in the neighbourhood of the Forest, on the left bank of the Oise.[400]

They were all on the other side of the river. There meadowland extends for some three-quarters of a mile, while beyond rises the slope of Picardy. Because this meadow was low, damp and frequently flooded, a causeway had been built leading from the bridge to the village of Margny, which rose on the steep slope of the hill. Some two miles up the river there towered the belfry of Clairoix, at the junction of the Aronde and the Oise. On the opposite bank rose the belfry of Venette, about a mile and a quarter lower down, towards Pont-Sainte-Maxence.[401]

A little band of Burgundians commanded by a knight, Messire Baudot de Noyelles, occupied the high ground of the village of Margny. Most renowned among the men of war of the Burgundian party was Messire Jean de Luxembourg. He with his Picards was posted at Clairoix, on the banks of the Aronde, at the foot of Mount Ganelon. The five hundred English of Lord Montgomery watched the Oise at Venette. Duke Philip occupied Coudun, a good two and a half miles from the town, towards Picardy.[402] Such dispositions were in accordance with the precepts of the most experienced captains. It was their rule that when besieging a fortified town a large number of men-at-arms should never be concentrated in one spot, in one camp, as they said. In case of a sudden attack, it was thought that a large company, if it has but one base, will be surprised and routed just as easily as a lesser number, and the disaster will be grievous. Wherefore it is better to divide the besiegers into small companies and to place them not far apart, in order that they may aid one another. In this wise, when those of one body are discomfited those of another have time to put themselves in battle array for their succour. While the assailants are sore aghast at seeing fresh troops come down upon them, those who are being attacked take heart of grace. At any rate such was the opinion of Messire Jean de Bueil.[403]

That same day, the 23rd of May, towards five o'clock in the evening[404] riding a fine dapple-grey horse, Jeanne sallied forth, across the bridge, on to the causeway over the meadow. With her were her standard-bearer and her company of Lombards, Captain Baretta and his three or four hundred men, both horse and foot, who had entered Compiègne by night. She was girt with the Burgundian sword, found at Lagny, and over her armour she wore a surcoat of cloth of gold.[405] Such attire would have better beseemed a parade than a sortie; but in the simplicity of her rustic and religious soul she loved all the pompous show of chivalry.

The enterprise had been concerted between Captain Baretta, the other leaders of the party and Messire Guillaume de Flavy. The last-named, in order to protect the line of retreat for the French, had posted archers, cross-bowmen, and cannoneers at the head of the bridge, while on the river he launched a number of small covered boats, intended if need were to bring back as many men as possible.[406] Jeanne was not consulted in the matter; her advice was never asked. Without being told anything she was taken with the army as a bringer of good luck; she was exhibited to the enemy as a powerful enchantress, and they, especially if they were in mortal sin, feared lest she should cast a spell over them. Certain there were doubtless on both sides, who perceived that she did not greatly differ from other women;[407] but they were folk who believed in nothing, and that manner of person is always outside public opinion.

This time she had not the remotest idea of what was to be done. With her head full of dreams, she imagined she was setting forth for some great and noble emprise. It is said that she had promised to discomfit the Burgundians and bring back Duke Philip prisoner. But there was no question of that; Captain Baretta and those who commanded the soldiers of fortune proposed to surprise and plunder the little Burgundian outpost, which was nearest the town and most accessible. That was Margny, and there on a steep hill, which might be reached in twenty or twenty-five minutes along the causeway, was stationed Messire Baudot de Noyelles. The attempt was worth making. The taking of outposts constituted the perquisites of men-at-arms. And, albeit the enemy's positions were very wisely chosen, the assailants if they proceeded with extreme swiftness had a chance of success. The Burgundians at Margny were very few. Having but lately arrived, they had erected neither bastion nor bulwark, and their only defences were the outbuildings of the village.

It was five o'clock in the afternoon when the French set out on the march. The days being at their longest, they did not depend on the darkness for success. In those times indeed, men-at-arms were chary of venturing much in the darkness. They deemed the night treacherous, capable of serving the fool's turn as well as the wise man's, and thus ran the saw: "Night never blushes at her deed."[408]

Having climbed up to Margny, the assailants found the Burgundians scattered and unarmed. They took them by surprise; and the French set to work to strike here and there haphazard. The Maid, for her part, overthrew everything before her.

Now just at this time Sire Jean de Luxembourg and the Sire de Créquy had ridden over from their camp at Clairoix.[409]

Wearing no armour, and accompanied by eight or ten gentlemen-at-arms, they were climbing the Margny hill. They were on their way to visit Messire Baudot de Noyelles, and all unsuspecting, they were thinking to reconnoitre the defences of the town from this elevated spot, as the Earl of Salisbury had formerly done from Les Tourelles at Orléans. Having fallen into a regular skirmish, they sent to Clairoix in all haste for their arms and to summon their company, which would take a good half hour to reach the scene of battle. Meanwhile, all unarmed as they were, they joined Messire Baudot's little band, to help it to hold out against the enemy.[410] Thus to surprise my Lord of Luxembourg might be a stroke of good luck and certainly could not be bad; for in any event the Margny men would have straightway summoned their comrades of Clairoix to their aid, as they did in very deed summon the English from Venette and the Burgundians from Coudun.

Having stormed the camp and pillaged it, the assailants should in all haste have fallen back on the town with their booty; but they dallied at Margny, for what reason is not difficult to guess: that reason which so often transformed the robber into the robbed. The wearers of the white cross as well as those of the red, no matter what danger threatened them, never quitted a place as long as anything remained to be carried away.

If the mercenaries of Compiègne incurred peril by their greed, the Maid on her side by her valour and prowess ran much greater risk; never would she consent to leave a battle; she must be wounded, pierced with bolts and arrows, before she would give in.

Meanwhile, having recovered from so sudden an alarm, Messire Baudot's men armed as best they might and endeavoured to win back the village. Now they drove out the French, now they themselves were forced to retreat with great loss. The Seigneur de Créquy, among others, was sorely wounded in the face. But the hope of being reinforced gave them courage. The men of Clairoix appeared. Duke Philip himself came up with the band from Coudun. The French, outnumbered, abandoned Margny, and retreated slowly. It may be that their booty impeded their march. But suddenly espying the *Godons* from Venette advancing over the meadowland, they were seized with panic; to the cry of "*Sauve qui peut!*" they broke into one mad rush and in utter rout reached the bank of the Oise. Some threw themselves into boats, others crowded round the bulwark of the Bridge. Thus they attracted the very misfortune they feared. For the English followed so hard on the fugitives that the defenders on the ramparts dared not fire their cannon for fear of striking the French.[411]

The latter having forced the barrier of the bulwark, the English were about to enter on their heels, cross the bridge and pass into the town. The captain of Compiègne saw the danger and gave the command to close the town gate. The bridge was raised and the portcullis lowered.[412]

In the meadow, Jeanne still laboured under the heroic delusion of victory. Surrounded by a little band of kinsmen and personal retainers, she was withstanding the Burgundians, and imagining that she would overthrow everything before her.

Her comrades shouted to her: "Strive to regain the town or we are lost."

But her eyes were dazzled by the splendour of angels and archangels, and she made answer: "Hold your peace; it will be your fault if we are discomfited. Think of nought but of attacking them."

And once again she uttered those words which were forever in her mouth: "Go forward! They are ours!"[413]

Her men took her horse by the bridle and forced her to turn towards the town. It was too late; the bulwarks commanding the bridge could not be entered: the English held the head of the causeway. The Maid with her little band was penned into the corner between the side of the bulwark and the embankment of the road. Her assailants were men of Picardy, who, striking hard and driving away her protectors, succeeded in reaching her.[414]

A bowman pulled her by her cloak of cloth of gold and threw her to the ground. They all surrounded her and together cried:

"Surrender!"

Urged to give her parole, she replied: "I have plighted my word to another, and I shall keep my oath."[415]

One of those who pressed her said that he was of gentle birth. She surrendered to him.

He was an archer, by name Lyonnel, in the company of the Bastard of Wandomme. Deeming that his fortune was made, he appeared more joyful than if he had taken a king.[416]

With the Maid was taken her brother, Pierre d'Arc, Jean d'Aulon, her steward, and Jean d'Aulon's brother, Poton, surnamed the Burgundian.[417] According to the Burgundians, the French in this engagement lost four hundred fighting men, killed or drowned;[418] but according to the French most of the foot soldiers were taken up by the boats which were moored near the bank of the Oise.[419]

Had it not been for the archers, cross-bowmen and cannoneers posted at the bridge end by the Sire de Flavy, the bulwark would have been captured. The Burgundians had but twenty wounded and not one slain.[420] The Maid had not been very vigorously defended.

She was disarmed and taken to Margny.[421] At the tidings that the witch of the Armagnacs had been taken, cries and rejoicings resounded throughout the Burgundian camp. Duke Philip wished to see her. When he drew near to her, there were certain of his clergy and his knighthood who praised his piety, extolled his courage, and wondered that this mighty Duke was not afraid of the spawn of Hell.[422]

In this respect, his knighthood were as valiant as he, for many knights and squires flocked to satisfy this same curiosity. Among them was Messire Enguerrand de Monstrelet, a native of the County of Boulogne, a retainer of the House of Luxembourg, the author of the Chronicles. He heard the words the Duke addressed to the prisoner, and, albeit his calling required a good memory, he forgot them. Possibly he did not consider them chivalrous enough to be written in his book.[423]

Jeanne remained in the custody of Messire Jean de Luxembourg, to whom she belonged henceforward. The bowman, her captor, had given her up to his captain, the Bastard of Wandomme, who, in his turn, had yielded her to his Master, Messire Jean.[424]

Branches of the Luxembourg tree extended from the west to the east of Christendom, as far as Bohemia and Hungary; and it had produced six queens, an empress, four kings, and four emperors. A scion of a younger branch of this illustrious house and himself a but poorly landed cadet, Jean de Luxembourg, had with great labour won his spurs in the service of the Duke of Burgundy. When he held the Maid to ransom, he was thirty-nine years of age, covered with wounds and one-eyed.[425]

That very evening from his quarters at Coudun the Duke of Burgundy caused letters to be written to the towns of his dominions telling of the capture of the Maid. "Of this capture shall the fame spread far and wide," is written in the letter to the people of Saint-Quentin; "and there shall be bruited abroad the error and misbelief of all such as have approved and favoured the deeds of this woman."[426]

In like manner did the Duke send the tidings to the Duke of Brittany by his herald Lorraine; to the Duke of Savoy and to his good town of Ghent.[427]

The survivors of the company the Maid had taken to Compiègne abandoned the siege, and on the morrow returned to their garrisons. The Lombard Captain, Bartolomeo Baretta, Jeanne's lieutenant, remained in the town with thirty-two men-at-arms, two trumpeters, two pages, forty-eight cross bowmen, and twenty archers or targeteers.[428]

Chapter VIII
The Maid at Beaulieu – the shepherd of Gévaudan

HE tidings that Jeanne was in the hands of the Burgundians reached Paris on the morning of May the 25th.[429] On the morrow, the 26th, the University sent a summons to Duke Philip requiring him to give up his prisoner to the Vicar-General of the Grand Inquisitor of France. At the same time, the Vicar-General himself by letter required the redoubtable Duke to bring prisoner before him the young woman suspected of divers crimes savouring of heresy.[430]

> "... We beseech you in all good affection, O powerful Prince," he said, "and we entreat your noble vassals that by them and by you Jeanne be sent unto us surely and shortly, and we hope that thus ye will do as being the true protector of the faith and the defender of God's honour...."[431]

The Vicar-General of the Grand Inquisitor of France, Brother Martin Billoray,[432] Master of theology, belonged to the order of friars preachers, the members of which exercised the principal functions of the Holy office. In the days of Innocent III, when the Inquisition was exterminating Cathari and Albigenses, the sons of Dominic figured in paintings in monasteries and chapels as great white hounds spotted with black, biting at the throats of the wolves of heresy.[433] In France in the fifteenth century the Dominicans were always the dogs of the Lord; they, jointly with the bishops, drove out the heretic. The Grand Inquisitor or his Vicar was unable of his own initiative to set on foot and prosecute any judicial action; the bishops maintained their right to judge crimes committed against the Church. In matters of faith trials were conducted by two judges, the Ordinary, who might be the bishop himself or the Official, and the Inquisitor or his Vicar. Inquisitorial forms were observed.[434]

In the Maid's case it was not the Bishop only who was prompting the Holy Inquisition, but the Daughter of Kings, the Mother of Learning, the Bright and Shining Sun of France and of Christendom, the University of Paris. She arrogated to herself a peculiar jurisdiction in cases of heresy or other matters of doctrine occurring in the city or its neighbourhood; her advice was asked on every hand and regarded as authoritative over the face of the whole world, wheresoever the Cross had been set up. For a year her masters and doctors, many in number and filled with sound learning, had been clamouring for the Maid to be delivered up to the Inquisition, as being good for the welfare of the Church and conducive to the interests of the faith; for they had a deep-rooted suspicion that the damsel came not from God, but was deceived and seduced by the machinations of the Devil; that she acted not by divine power but by the aid of demons; that she was addicted to witchcraft and practised idolatry.[435]

Such knowledge as they possessed of things divine and methods of reasoning corroborated this grave suspicion. They were Burgundians and English by necessity and by inclination; they observed faithfully the Treaty of Troyes to which they had sworn; they were devoted to the Regent who showed them great consideration; they abhorred the Armagnacs, who desolated and laid waste their city, the most beautiful in the world;[436] they held that the Dauphin Charles had forfeited his rights to the Kingdom of the Lilies. Wherefore they inclined to believe that the Maid of the Armagnacs, the woman knight of the Dauphin Charles, was inspired by a company of loathsome demons. These scholars of the University were human; they believed what it was to their interest to believe; they were priests and they beheld the Devil everywhere, but especially in a woman.

Without having devoted themselves to any profound examination of the deeds and sayings of this damsel, they knew enough to cause them to demand an immediate inquiry. She called herself the emissary of God, the daughter of God; and she appeared loquacious, vain, crafty, gorgeous in her attire. She had threatened the English that if they did not quit France she would have them all slain. She commanded armies, wherefore she was a slayer of her fellow-creatures and foolhardy. She was seditious, for are not all those seditious who support the opposite party? But recently having appeared before Paris in company with Friar Richard, a heretic, and a rebel,[437] she had threatened to put the Parisians to death without mercy and committed the mortal sin of storming the city on the Anniversary of the Nativity of Our Lady. It was important to examine whether in all this she had been inspired by a good spirit or a bad.[438]

Despite his strong attachment to the interests of the Church, the Duke of Burgundy did not respond to the urgent demand of the University; and Messire Jean de Luxembourg, after having kept the Maid three or four days in his quarters before Compiègne, had her taken to the Castle of Beaulieu in Vermandois, a few leagues from the camp.[439] Like his master, he ever appeared the obedient son of Mother Church; but prudence counselled him to await the approach of English and French and to see what each of them would offer.

At Beaulieu, Jeanne was treated courteously and ceremoniously. Her steward, Messire Jean d'Aulon, waited on her in her prison; one day he said to her pitifully:

"That poor town of Compiègne, which you so dearly loved, will now be delivered into the hands of the enemies of France, whom it must needs obey."

She made answer: "No, that shall not come to pass. For not one of those places, which the King of Heaven hath conquered through me and restored to their allegiance to the fair King Charles, shall be recaptured by the enemy, so diligently will he guard them."[440]

One day she tried to escape by slipping between two planks. She had intended to shut up her guards in the tower and take to the fields, but the porter saw and stopped her. She concluded that it was not God's will that she should escape this time.[441] Notwithstanding she had far too much self-reliance to despair. Her Voices, like her enamoured of marvellous encounters and knightly adventures, told her that she must see the King of England.[442] Thus did her dreams encourage and console her in her misfortune.

Great was the mourning on the Loire when the inhabitants of the towns loyal to King Charles learnt the disaster which had befallen the Maid. The people, who venerated her as a saint, who went so far as to say that she was the greatest of all God's saints after the Blessed Virgin Mary, who erected images of her in the chapels of saints, who ordered masses to be said for her, and collects in the churches, who wore leaden medals on which she was represented as if the Church had already canonized her,[443] did not withdraw their trust, but continued to believe in her.[444] Such faithfulness scandalized the doctors and masters of the University, who reproached the hapless Maid herself with it. "Jeanne," they said, "hath so seduced the Catholic people, that many have adored her as a saint in her presence, and now in her absence they adore her still."[445]

This was indeed true of many folk and many places. The councillors of the town of Tours ordered public prayers to be offered for the deliverance of the Maid. There was a public procession in which took part the canons of the cathedral church, the clergy of the town, secular and regular, all walking barefoot.[446]

In the towns of Dauphiné prayers for the Maid were said at mass.

"*Collect.* O God, all powerful and eternal, who, in thy holy and ineffable mercy, hast commanded the Maid to restore and deliver the realm of France, and to repulse, confound and annihilate her enemies, and who hast permitted her, in the accomplishment of this holy work, ordained by thee, to fall into the hands and into the bonds of her enemies, we beseech thee, by the intercession of the Blessed Virgin Mary and of all the saints to deliver her out of their hands, without her having suffered any hurt, in order that she may finish the work whereto thou hast sent her."

"For the sake of Jesus Christ, etc."

"*Secret.* O God all powerful, Father of virtues, let thy holy benediction descend upon this sacrifice; let thy wondrous power be made manifest, that by the intercession of the Blessed Virgin Mary and of all the saints, it may deliver the Maid from the prisons of the enemy so that she may finish the work whereto thou hast sent her. Through our Lord Jesus Christ, etc."

"*Post Communion.* O God all powerful, incline thine ear and listen unto the prayers of thy people: by the virtue of the Sacrament we have just received, by the intercession of the Blessed Virgin Mary, and of all the saints, burst the bonds of the Maid, who, in the fulfilment of thy commands, hath been and is still confined in the prisons of our enemy; through thy divine compassion and thy mercy, permit her, freed from peril, to accomplish the work whereto thou hast sent her. Through our Lord Jesus Christ, etc."[447]

Learning that the Maid, whom he had once suspected of evil intentions and then recognised to be wholly good, had just fallen into the hands of the enemy of the realm, Messire Jacques Gélu, my Lord Archbishop of Embrun, despatched to King Charles a messenger bearing a letter touching the line of conduct to be adopted in such an unhappy conjuncture.[448]

Addressing the Prince, whom in childhood he had directed, Messire Jacques begins by recalling what the Maid had wrought for him by God's help and her own great courage. He beseeches him to examine his conscience and see whether he has in any wise sinned against the grace of God. For it may be that in wrath against the King the Lord hath permitted this virgin to be taken. For his own honour he urges him to strain every effort for her deliverance.

"I commend unto you," he said, "that for the recovery of this damsel and for her ransom, ye spare neither measures nor money, nor any cost, unless ye be ready to incur the ineffaceable disgrace of an ingratitude right unworthy."

Further he advises that prayers be ordered to be said everywhere for the deliverance of the Maid, so that if this disaster should have befallen through any misdoing of the King or of his people, it might please God to pardon it.[449]

Such were the words, lacking neither in strength nor in charity, of this aged prelate, who was more of a hermit than of a bishop. He remembered having been the Dauphin's Councillor in evil days and he dearly loved the King and the kingdom.

The Sire de la Trémouille and the Lord Archbishop of Reims have been suspected of desiring to get rid of the Maid and of having promoted her discomfiture. There are those who think they have discovered the treacherous methods employed to compass her defeat at Paris, at La Charité and at Compiègne.[450] But in good sooth such methods were unnecessary. At Paris there was but little chance of her being able to cross the moat, since neither she nor her companions in arms had ascertained its depth; besides, it was not the fault of the King and his Council that the Carmelites, on whom they relied, failed to open the gates. The siege of La Charité was conducted not by the Maid, but by the Sire d'Albret and divers valiant captains. In the sortie from Compiègne, it was certain that any dallying at Margny would cause the French to be cut off by the English from Venette and by the Burgundians from Clairoix and to be promptly overcome by the Burgundians from Coudun. They forgot themselves in the delights of pillage; and the inevitable result followed.

And why should the Lord Chamberlain and the Lord Archbishop have wanted to get rid of the Maid? She did not trouble them; on the contrary they found her useful and employed her. By her prophecy that she would cause the King to be anointed at Reims, she rendered an immense service to my Lord Regnault, who more than any other profited from the

Champagne expedition, more even than the King, who, while he succeeded in being crowned, failed to recover Paris and Normandy. Notwithstanding this great advantage, the Lord Archbishop felt no gratitude towards the Maid; he was a hard man and an egoist. But did he wish her harm? Had he not need of her? At Senlis he was maintaining the King's cause; and he was maintaining it well, we may be sure, since, with the towns that had returned to their liege lord, he was defending his own episcopal and ducal city, his benefices and his canonries. Did he not intend to use her against the Burgundians? We have already noted reasons for believing that towards the end of March, he had asked the Sire de la Trémouille to send her from Sully with a goodly company to wage war in l'Île-de-France. And our hypothesis is confirmed when, after they had been unhappily deprived of Jeanne's services, we find the bishop and the Chamberlain driven to replace her by someone likewise favoured with visions and claiming to be sent of God. Unable to discover a maid they had to make shift with a youth. This resolution they took a few days after Jeanne's capture and this is how it came about.

Some time before, a shepherd lad of Gévaudan, by name Guillaume, while tending his flocks at the foot of the Lozère Mountains and guarding them from wolf and lynx, had a revelation concerning the realm of France. This shepherd, like John, Our Lord's favourite disciple, was virgin. In one of the caves of the Mende Mountain, where the holy apostle Privat had prayed and fasted, his ear was struck by a heavenly voice, and thus he knew that God was sending him to the King of France. He went to Mende, just as Jeanne had gone to Vaucouleurs in order that he might be taken to the King. There he found pious folk, who, touched by his holiness and persuaded that there was power in him, provided for his equipment and for his journey, which provisions, in sooth, amounted to very little. The words he addressed to the King were much the same as those uttered by the Maid.

"Sire," he said, "I am commanded to go with your people; and without fail the English and Burgundians shall be discomfited."[451]

The King received him kindly. The clerks who had examined the Maid must have feared lest if they repulsed this shepherd lad they might be rejecting the aid of the Holy Ghost. Amos was a shepherd, and to him God granted the gift of prophecy: "I thank thee, O Father, Lord of heaven and earth, because thou hast hid these things from the wise and prudent, and hast revealed them unto babes." Matt. xi, 25.

But before this shepherd could be believed he must give a sign. The clerks of Poitiers, who in those evil days languished in dire penury, did not appear exacting in their demand for proofs; they had counselled the King to employ the Maid merely on the promise that as a token of her mission she would deliver Orléans. The Gévaudan shepherd had more than promises to allege; he showed wondrous marks on his body. Like Saint Francis he had received the stigmata; and on his hands, his feet and in his side were bleeding wounds.[452]

The mendicant monks rejoiced that their spiritual father had thus participated in the Passion of Our Lord. A like grace had been granted to the Blessed Catherine of Sienna, of the order of Saint Dominic. But if there were miraculous stigmata imprinted by Jesus Christ himself, there were also the stigmata of enchantment, which were the work of the Devil, and very important was it to distinguish between the two.[453] It could only be done by great knowledge and great piety. It would appear that Guillaume's stigmata were not the work of the devil; for it was resolved to employ him in the same manner as Jeanne, as Catherine de la Rochelle, and as the two Breton women, the spiritual daughters of Friar Richard.

When the Maid fell into the hands of the Burgundians, the Sire de la Trémouille was with the King, on the Loire, where fighting had ceased since the disastrous siege of La Charité. He sent the shepherd youth to the banks of the Oise, to the Lord Archbishop of Reims, who was there opposing the Burgundians, commanded by Duke Philip, himself. Messire Regnault had probably asked for the boy. In any case he welcomed him willingly and kept him at Beauvais, supervising and interrogating him, ready to use him at an auspicious moment. One day, either to try him or because the rumour was really in circulation, young Guillaume was told that the English had put Jeanne to death.

"Then," said he, "it will be the worse for them."[454]

By this time, after all the rivalries and jealousies which had torn asunder this company of the King's *béguines*, there remained to Friar Richard one only of his penitents, Dame Catherine of La Rochelle, who had the gift of discovering hidden treasure.[455] The young shepherd approved of the Maid as little as Dame Catherine had done.

"God suffered Jeanne to be taken," he said, "because she was puffed up with pride and because of the rich clothes she wore and because she had not done as God commanded her but according to her own will."[456]

Were these words suggested to him by the enemies of the Maid? That may be: but it is also possible that he derived them from inspiration. Saints are not always kind to one another.

Meanwhile Messire Regnault de Chartres believed himself possessed of a marvel far surpassing the marvel he had lost. He wrote a letter to the inhabitants of his town of Reims telling them that the Maid had been taken at Compiègne.

This misfortune had befallen her through her own fault, he added. "She would not take advice, but would follow her own will." In her stead God had sent a shepherd, "who says neither more nor less than Jeanne." God has strictly commanded him to discomfit the English and the Burgundians. And the Lord Archbishop neglects not to repeat the words by which the prophet of Gévaudan had represented Jeanne as proud, gorgeous in attire, rebellious of heart.[457] The Reverend Father in God, my Lord Regnault, would never have consented to employ a heretic and a sorcerer; he believed in Guillaume as he had believed in

Jeanne; he held both one and the other to have been divinely sent, in the sense that all which is not of the devil is of God. It was sufficient for him that no evil had been found in the child, and he intended to essay him, hoping that Guillaume would do what Jeanne had done. Whether the Archbishop thus acted rightly or wrongly the issue was to decide, but he might have exalted the shepherd without denying the Saint who was so near her martyrdom. Doubtless he deemed it necessary to distinguish between the fortune of the kingdom and the fortune of Jeanne. And he had the courage to do it.

Chapter IX
The Maid at Beaurevoir – Catherine de la Rochelle at Paris – execution of La Pierronne

THE Maid had been taken captive in the diocese of Beauvais.[458] At that time the Bishop Count of Beauvais was Pierre Cauchon of Reims, a great and pompous clerk of the University of Paris, which had elected him rector in 1403. Messire Pierre Cauchon was not a moderate man; with great ardour he had thrown himself into the Cabochien riots.[459] In 1414, the Duke of Burgundy had sent him on an embassy to the Council of Constance to defend the doctrines of Jean Petit;[460] then he had appointed him Master of Requests in 1418, and finally raised him to the episcopal see of Beauvais.[461] Standing equally high in the favour of the English, Messire Pierre was Councillor of King Henry VI, Almoner of France and Chancellor to the Queen of England. Since 1423, his usual residence had been at Rouen. By their submission to King Charles the people of Beauvais had deprived him of his episcopal revenue.[462] And, as the English said and believed that the army of the King of France was at that time commanded by Friar Richard and the Maid, Messire Pierre Cauchon, the impoverished Bishop of Beauvais, had a personal grievance against Jeanne. It would have been better for his own reputation that he should have abstained from avenging the Church's honour on a damsel who was possibly an idolatress, a soothsayer and the invoker of devils, but who had certainly incurred his personal ill-will. He was in the Regent's pay;[463] and the Regent was filled with bitter hatred of the Maid.[464] Again for his reputation's sake, my Lord Bishop of Beauvais should have reflected that in prosecuting Jeanne for a matter of faith he was serving his master's wrath and furthering the temporal interests of the great of this world. On these things he did not reflect; on the contrary, this case at once temporal and spiritual, as ambiguous as his own position, excited his worst passions. He flung himself into it with all the thoughtlessness of the violent. A maiden to be denounced, a heretic and an Armagnac to boot, what a feast for the prelate, the Councillor of King Henry! After having concerted with the doctors and masters of the University of Paris, on the 14th of July, he presented himself before the camp of Compiègne and demanded the Maid as subject to his jurisdiction.[465]

He supported his demand by letters from the *Alma Mater* to the Duke of Burgundy and the Lord Jean de Luxembourg.

The University made known to the most illustrious Prince, the Duke of Burgundy, that once before it had claimed this woman, called the Maid, and had received no reply.

"We greatly fear," continued the doctors and masters, "that by the false and seductive power of the Hellish Enemy and by the malice and subtlety of wicked persons, your enemies and adversaries who, it is said, are making every effort to deliver this woman by crooked means, will in some manner remove her out of your power.

"Wherefore, the University hopes that so great a dishonour may be spared to the most Christian name of the house of France, and again it supplicates your Highness, the Duke of Burgundy, to deliver over this woman either to the Inquisitor of the evil of heresy or to my Lord Bishop of Beauvais within whose spiritual jurisdiction she was captured."

Here follows the letter which the doctors and masters of the University entrusted to the Lord Bishop of Beauvais for the Lord Jean de Luxembourg:

Most noble, honoured and powerful lord, to your high nobility we very affectionately commend us. Your noble wisdom doth well know and recognise that all good Catholic knights should employ their strength and their power first in God's service and then for the common weal. Above all, the first oath of the order of knighthood is to defend and keep the honour of God, the Catholic Faith and holy Church. This sacred oath was present to your mind when you employed your noble power and your person in the taking of the woman who calleth herself the Maid, by whom the glory of God hath been infinitely offended, the Faith deeply wounded and the Church greatly dishonoured: for through her there have arisen in this kingdom, idolatries, errors, false doctrines and other evils and misfortunes without end. And in truth all loyal Christians must give unto you hearty thanks for having rendered so great service to our holy Faith and to all the kingdom. As for us, we thank God with all our hearts, and you we thank for your noble prowess as affectionately as we may. But such a capture alone would be but a small thing were it not followed by a worthy issue whereby this woman may answer for the offences she hath committed against our merciful Creator, his faith and his holy Church, as well as for her other evil deeds which are said to be without number. The mischief would be greater than ever, the people would be wrapped in yet grosser error than before and his Divine Majesty too insufferably offended, if matters continued in their present state, or if it befell that this woman were delivered or retaken, as we are told, is wished, plotted and endeavoured by divers of our enemies, by all secret ways and by what is even worse by bribe or by ransom. But it is our hope that God will not permit so great an evil to betide his people, and that your great and high wisdom will not suffer it so to befall but will provide against it as becometh your nobility.

For if without the retribution that behoveth she were to be delivered, irreparable would be the dishonour which should fall on your great nobility and on all those who have dealt in this matter. But your good and noble wisdom will know how to devise means whereby such scandal shall cease as soon as may be, whereof there is great need. And because all delay in this matter is very perilous and very injurious to this kingdom, very kindly and with a cordial affection do we beseech your powerful and honoured nobility to grant that for the glory of God, for the maintenance of the Holy Catholic Faith, for the good and honour of the kingdom, this woman be delivered up to justice and given over here to the Inquisitor of the Faith, who hath demanded her and doth now demand her urgently, in order that he may examine the grievous charges under which she labours, so that God may be satisfied and the folk duly edified in good and holy doctrine. Or, an it please you better, hand over this woman to the reverend Father in God, our highly honoured Lord Bishop of Beauvais, who it is said hath likewise claimed her, because she was taken within his jurisdiction. This prelate and this inquisitor are judges of this woman in matters of faith; and every Christian of whatsoever estate owes them obedience in this case under heavy penalty of the law. By so doing you will attain to the love and grace of the most High and you will be the means of exalting the holy Faith, and likewise will you glorify your own high and noble name and also that of the most high and most powerful Prince, our redoubtable Lord and yours, my Lord of Burgundy. Every man shall be required to pray God for the prosperity of your most noble worship, whom may it please God our Saviour in his grace, to guide and keep in all his affairs and finally to grant eternal joy.

Given at Paris, the 14th day of July, 1430.[466]

At the same time that he bore these letters, the Reverend Father in God, the Bishop of Beauvais was charged to offer money.[467] To us it seems strange indeed that just at the very time when, by the mouth of the University, he was representing to the Lord of Luxembourg that he could not sell his prisoner without committing a crime, the Bishop should himself offer to purchase her. According to these ecclesiastics, Jean would incur terrible penalties in this world and in the next, if in conformity with the laws and customs of war he surrendered a prisoner held to ransom in return for money, and he would win praise and blessing if he treacherously sold his captive to those who wished to put her to death. But at least we might expect that this Lord Bishop who had come to buy this woman for the Church, would purchase her with the Church's money. Not at all! The purchase money is furnished by the English. In the end therefore she is delivered not to the Church but to the English. And it is a priest, acting in the interests of God and of his Church, by virtue of his episcopal jurisdiction, who concludes the bargain. He offers ten thousand golden francs, a sum in return for which, he says, according to the custom prevailing in France, the King has the right to claim any prisoner even were he of the blood royal.[468]

There can be no doubt whatever that the high and solemn ecclesiastic, Pierre Cauchon, suspected Jeanne of witchcraft. Wishing to bring her to trial, he exercised his ecclesiastical functions. But he knew her to be the enemy of the English as well as of himself; there is no doubt on that point. So when he wished to bring her to trial he acted as the Councillor of King Henry. Was it a witch or the enemy of the English he was buying with his ten thousand gold francs? And if it were merely a witch and an idolatress that the Holy Inquisitor, that the University, that the Ordinary demanded for the glory of God, and at the price of gold, wherefore so much ado, wherefore so great an expenditure of money? Would it not be better in this matter to act in concert with the ecclesiastics of King Charles's party? The Armagnacs were neither infidels nor heretics; they were neither Turks nor Hussites; they were Catholics; they acknowledged the Pope of Rome to be the true head of Christendom. The Dauphin Charles and his clergy had not been excommunicated. Neither those who regarded the Treaty of Troyes as invalid nor those who had sworn to it had been pronounced anathema by the Pope. This was not a question of faith. In the provinces ruled over by King Charles the Holy Inquisition prosecuted heresy in a curious manner and the secular arm saw to it that the sentences pronounced by the Church did not remain a dead letter. The Armagnacs burned witches just as much as the French and the Burgundians. For the present doubtless they did not believe the Maid to be possessed by devils; most of them on the contrary were inclined to regard her as a saint. But might they not be undeceived? Would it not be good Christian charity to present them with fine canonical arguments? If the Maid's case were really a case for the ecclesiastical court why not join with Churchmen of both parties and take her before the Pope and the Council? And just at that time a Council for the reformation of the Church and the establishment of peace in the kingdom was sitting in the town of Bâle; the University was sending its delegates, who would there meet the ecclesiastics of King Charles, also Gallicans and firmly attached to the privileges of the Church of France.[469] Why not have this Armagnac prophetess tried by the assembled Fathers? But for the sake of Henry of Lancaster and the glory of Old England matters had to take another turn. The Regent's Councillors were already accusing Jeanne of witchcraft when she summoned them in the name of the King of Heaven to depart out of France. During the siege of Orléans, they wanted to burn her heralds and said that if they had her they would burn her also at the stake. Such in good sooth was their firm intent and their unvarying intimation. This does not look as if they would be likely to hand her over to the Church as soon as she was taken. In their own kingdom they burned as many witches and wizards as possible; but they had never suffered the Holy Inquisition to be established in their land, and they were ill acquainted with that form of justice. Informed that Jeanne was in the hands of the Sire de Luxembourg, the Great Council of England were unanimously in favour of her being purchased at any price. Divers lords recommended that as soon as they obtained possession of the Maid she should be sewn in a sack and cast into the river. But one of them (it is said to have been the Earl of Warwick) represented to them that she ought first to be tried, convicted of heresy and witchcraft by an ecclesiastical tribunal, and then solemnly degraded in order that her King might be degraded with her.[470] What a disgrace for Charles of Valois, calling himself King of France, if the University of Paris, if the French ecclesiastical dignitaries, bishops, abbots, canons, if in short the Church Universal were to declare that a witch had sat in his Council and that a witch led his host, that one possessed had conducted him to his impious, sacrilegious and void anointing! Thus would the trial of the Maid be the trial of Charles VII, the condemnation of the Maid the condemnation of Charles VII. The idea seemed good to them and was adopted.

The Lord Bishop of Beauvais was eager to put it into execution. He, a priest and Councillor of State, was consumed with a desire, under the semblance of trying an unfortunate heretic, to sit in judgment on the descendant of Clovis, of Saint Charlemagne and of Saint Louis.

Early in August, the Sire de Luxembourg had the Maid taken from Beaulieu, which was not safe enough, to Beaurevoir, near Cambrai.[471] There dwelt Dame Jeanne de Luxembourg and Dame Jeanne de Béthune. Jeanne de Luxembourg was the aunt of Lord Jean, whom she loved dearly. Among the great of this world she had lived as a saint, and she had never married. Formerly lady-in-waiting to Queen Ysabeau, King Charles VII's godmother, one of the most important events of her life had been to solicit from Pope Martin the canonisation of her Brother, the Cardinal of Luxembourg, who had died at Avignon in his ninetieth year. She was known as the Demoiselle de Luxembourg. She was sixty-seven years of age, infirm and near her end.[472]

Jeanne de Béthune, widow of Lord Robert de Bar, slain at the Battle of Azincourt, had married Lord Jean in 1418. She was reputed pitiful, because, in 1424, she had obtained from her husband the pardon of a nobleman of Picardy, who had been brought prisoner to Beaurevoir and was in great danger of being beheaded and quartered.[473]

These two ladies treated Jeanne kindly. They offered her woman's clothes or cloth with which to make them; and they urged her to abandon a dress which appeared to them unseemly. Jeanne refused, alleging that she had not received permission from Our Lord and that it was not yet time; later she admitted that had she been able to quit man's attire, she would have done so at the request of these two dames rather than for any other dame of France, the Queen excepted.[474]

A noble of the Burgundian party, one Aimond de Macy, often came to see her and was pleased to converse with her. To him she seemed modest in word and in deed. Still Sire Aimond, who was but thirty, had found her personally attractive.[475] If certain witnesses of her own party are to be believed, Jeanne, although beautiful, did not inspire men with desire.

This singular grace however applied to the Armagnacs only; it was not extended to the Burgundians, and Seigneur Aimond did not experience it, for one day he tried to thrust his hand into her bosom. She resisted and repulsed him with all her strength. Lord Aimond concluded as more than one would have done in his place that this was a damsel of rare virtue. He took warning.[476]

Confined in the castle keep, Jeanne's mind was for ever running on her return to her friends at Compiègne; her one idea was to escape. Somehow there reached her evil tidings from France. She got the idea that all the inhabitants of Compiègne over seven years of age were to be massacred, "to perish by fire and sword," she said; and indeed such a fate was bound to overtake them if the town were taken.

Confiding her distress and her unconquerable desire to Saint Catherine, she asked: "How can God abandon to destruction those good folk of Compiègne who have been so loyal to their Lord?"[477]

And in her dream, surrounded by saints, like the donors in church pictures, kneeling and in rapture, she wrestled with her heavenly counsellors for the poor folk of Compiègne.

What she had heard of their fate caused her infinite distress; she herself would rather die than continue to live after such a destruction of worthy people. For this reason she was strongly tempted to leap from the top of the keep. And because she knew all that could be said against it, she heard her Voices putting her in mind of those arguments.

Nearly every day Saint Catherine said to her: "Do not leap, God will help both you and those of Compiègne."

And Jeanne replied to her: "Since God will help those of Compiègne, I want to be there."

And once again Saint Catherine told her the marvellous story of the shepherdess and the King: "To all things must you be resigned. And you will not be delivered until you have seen the King of the English."

To which Jeanne made answer: "But in good sooth I do not desire to see him. I would rather die than fall into the hands of the English."[478]

One day she heard a rumour that the English had come to fetch her. The arrival of the Lord Bishop of Beauvais who came to offer the blood money at Beaurevoir may have given rise to the report.[479] Straightway Jeanne became frantic and beside herself. She ceased to listen to her Voices, who forbade her the fatal leap. The keep was at least seventy feet high; she commended her soul to God and leapt.

Having fallen to the ground, she heard cries: "She is dead."

The guards hurried to the spot. Finding her still alive, in their amazement they could only ask: "Did you leap?"

She felt sorely shaken; but Saint Catherine spoke to her and said: "Be of good courage. You will recover." At the same time the Saint gave her good tidings of her friends. "You will recover and the people of Compiègne will receive succour." And she added that this succour would come before Saint Martin's Day in the winter.[480]

Henceforth Jeanne believed that it was her saints who had helped her and guarded her from death. She knew well that she had been wrong in attempting such a leap, despite her Voices.

Saint Catherine said to her: "You must confess and ask God to forgive you for having leapt."

Jeanne did confess and ask pardon of Our Lord. And after her confession Saint Catherine made known unto her that God had forgiven her. For three or four days she remained without eating or drinking; then she took some food and was whole.[481]

Another story was told of the leap from Beaurevoir; it was related that she had tried to escape through a window letting herself down by a sheet or something that broke; but we must believe the Maid: she says she leapt; if she had been attached to a cord, she would not have committed sin and would not have confessed. This leap was known and the rumour spread abroad that she had escaped and joined her own party.[482]

Meanwhile the Lenten sermons at Orléans had been delivered by that good preacher, Friar Richard, who was ill content with Jeanne, and whom Jeanne disliked and had quitted. The townsfolk as a token of regard presented him with the image of Jesus sculptured in copper by a certain Philippe, a metal-worker of the city. And the bookseller, Jean Moreau, bound him a book of hours at the town's expense.[483]

He brought back Queen Marie to Jargeau and succeeded in obtaining her favour. Jeanne was spared the bitterness of learning that while she was languishing in prison her friends at Orléans, her fair Dauphin and his Queen Marie, were making good cheer for the monk who had turned from her to prefer a dame Catherine whom she considered worthless.[484] Only lately the idea of employing Dame Catherine had filled Jeanne with alarm; she wrote to her King about it, and as soon as she saw him besought him not to employ her. However the King set no store by what she had said; he agreed to Friar Richard's favourite being allowed to set forth on her mission to obtain money from the good towns and to negotiate peace with the Duke of Burgundy. But perhaps this saintly dame was not possessed of all the wisdom necessary for the performance of man's work and King's service. For immediately she became a cause of embarrassment to her friends.

Being in the town of Tours, she fell to saying: "In this town there be carpenters who work, but not at houses, and if ye have not a care, this town is in the way to a bad end and there be those in the town that know it."[485]

This was a denunciation in the form of a parable. Dame Catherine was thereby accusing the churchmen and burgesses of

Tours of working against Charles of Valois, their lord. The woman must have been held to have influence with the King, his kinsmen and his Council; for the inhabitants of Tours took fright and sent an Augustinian monk, Brother Jean Bourget, to King Charles, to the Queen of Sicily, to the Bishop of Séez, and to the Lord of Trèves, to inquire whether the words of this holy woman had been believed by them. The Queen of Sicily and the Councillors of King Charles gave the monk letters wherein they announced to the townsfolk of Tours that they had never heard of such things, and King Charles declared that he had every confidence in the churchmen, the burgesses and the other citizens of his town of Tours.[486]

Dame Catherine had in like manner slandered the inhabitants of Angers.[487]

Whether, following the example of the Blessed Colette of Corbie, this devout person wished to pass from one party to the other, or whether she had chanced to be taken captive by Burgundian men-at-arms, she was brought before the Official at Paris. In their interrogation of her the ecclesiastics appear to have been concerned less about her than about the Maid Jeanne, whose prosecution was then being instituted.

On the subject of the Maid, Catherine said: "Jeanne has two counsellors, whom she calls Counsellors of the Spring."[488]

Such was the confused recollection of the conversations she had had at Jargeau and at Montfaucon. The term Council was the one Jeanne usually employed when speaking of her Voices; but Dame Catherine was confusing Jeanne's heavenly visitants with what the Maid had told her of the Gooseberry Spring at Domremy.

If Jeanne felt unkindly towards Catherine, Catherine did not feel kindly towards Jeanne. She did not assert Jeanne's mission to be nought; but she let it be clearly understood that the hapless damsel, then a prisoner in the hands of the Burgundians, was addicted to invoking evil spirits.

"If Jeanne be not well guarded," Catherine told the Official, "she will escape from prison with the aid of the devil."[489]

Whether Jeanne was or was not aided by the devil was a matter to be decided between herself and the doctors of the church. But it is certain that her one thought was to burst her bonds, and that she was ceaselessly imagining means of escape. Catherine de la Rochelle knew her well and wished her ill.

Catherine was released. Her ecclesiastical judges would not have treated her so leniently had she spoken well of the Maid. The La Rochelle Dame returned to King Charles.[490]

The two religious women who had followed Jeanne on her departure from Sully and had been taken at Corbeil, Pierronne of Lower Brittany and her companion, had been confined in ecclesiastical prisons at Paris since the spring. They openly said that God had sent them to succour the Maid Jeanne. Friar Richard had been their spiritual father and they had been in the Maid's company. Wherefore they were strongly suspected of having offended against God and his Holy Religion. The Grand Inquisitor of France, Brother Jean Graverent, Prior of the Jacobins at Paris, prosecuted them according to the forms usual in that country. He proceeded in concurrence with the Ordinary, represented by the official.

Pierronne maintained and believed it to be true that Jeanne was good, and that what she did was well done and according to God's will. She admitted that on the Christmas night of that year, at Jargeau, Friar Richard had twice given her the body of Jesus Christ and had given it three times to Jeanne.[491] Besides, the fact had been well proved by information gathered from eye-witnesses. The judges, who were authorities on this subject, held that the monk should not thus have lavished the bread of angels on such women. However, since frequent communion was not formally forbidden by canon law, Pierronne could not be censured for having received it. The informers, who were then giving evidence against Jeanne, did not remember the three communions at Jargeau.[492]

Heavier charges weighed upon the two Breton women. They were labouring under the accusation of witchcraft and sorcery.

Pierronne stated and took her oath that God often appeared to her in human form and spoke to her as friend to friend, and that the last time she had seen him he was clothed in a purple cloak and a long white robe.[493]

The illustrious masters who were trying her, represented to her that to speak thus of such apparitions was to blaspheme. And these women were convicted of being possessed by evil spirits, who caused them to err in word and in deed.

On Sunday, the 3rd of September, 1430, they were taken to the Parvis Notre Dame to hear a sermon. Platforms had been erected as usual, and Sunday had been chosen as the day in order that folk might benefit from this edifying spectacle. A famous doctor addressed a charitable exhortation to both women. One of them, the youngest, as she listened to him and looked at the stake that had been erected, was filled with repentance. She confessed that she had been seduced by an angel of the devil and duly renounced her error.

Pierronne, on the contrary, refused to retract. She obstinately persisted in the belief that she saw God often, clothed as she had said. The Church could do nothing for her. Given over to the secular arm, she was straightway conducted to the stake which had been prepared for her, and burned alive by the executioner.[494]

Thus did the Grand Inquisitor of France and the Bishop of Paris cruelly cause to perish by an ignominious death one of those women who had followed Friar Richard, one of the saints of the Dauphin Charles. But the most famous of these women and the most abounding in works was in their hands. The death of La Pierronne was an earnest of the fate reserved for the Maid.

Chapter X
Beaurevoir – Arras – Rouen – the trial for lapse

N the month of September, 1430, two inhabitants of Tournai, the chief alderman, Bietremieu Carlier, and the chief Councillor, Henri Romain, were returning from the banks of the Loire, whither their town had despatched them on a mission to the King of France. They stopped at Beaurevoir. Albeit this place lay upon their direct route and afforded them a halt between two stages of their journey, one cannot help supposing some connection to have existed between their mission to Charles of Valois and their arrival in the domain of the Sire de Luxembourg. The existence of such a connection seems all the more probable when we remember the attachment of their fellow-citizens to the Fleurs-de-Lis, and when we know the relations already existing between the Maid and these emissaries.[495]

It has been said that the district of the provost of Tournai was loyal to the King of France, who had granted it freedom and privileges. Message after message it sent him; it organised public processions in his honour, and it was ready to grant him anything, so long as he demanded neither men nor money. The alderman, Carlier, and the Councillor, Romain, had both previously gone to Reims as representatives of their town to witness the anointing and the coronation of King Charles. There they had doubtless seen the Maid in her glory and had held her to be a very great saint. In those days, their town, attentively watching the progress of the royal army, was in regular correspondence with the warlike *béguine*, and with her confessor, Friar Richard, or more probably Friar Pasquerel. To-day they wended to the castle, wherein she was imprisoned in the hands of her cruel enemies. We know not what it was they came to say to the Sire de Luxembourg, nor even whether he received them. He cannot have refused to hear them if he thought they came to make secret offers on the part of King Charles for the ransom of the Maid, who had fought in his battles. We know not, either, whether they were able to see the prisoner. The idea that they did enter her presence is quite tenable; for in those days it was generally easy to approach captives, and passers by when they visited them were given every facility for the performance of one of the seven works of mercy.

One thing, however, is certain; that when they left Beaurevoir, they carried with them a letter which Jeanne had given them, charging them to deliver it to the magistrates of their town. In this letter she asked the folk of Tournai, for the sake of her Lord the King and in view of the good services she had rendered him, to send unto her twenty or thirty crowns, that she might employ them for her necessities.[496]

It was the custom in those days thus to permit prisoners to beg their bread.

It is said that the Demoiselle de Luxembourg, who had just made her will, and had but a few days longer to live,[497] entreated her noble nephew not to give the Maid up to the English.[498] But what power had this good dame against the Norman gold of the King of England and against the anathemas of Holy Church? For if my Lord Jean had refused to give up this damsel suspected of enchantments, of idolatries, of invoking devils and committing other crimes against religion, he would have been excommunicated. The venerable University of Paris had not neglected to make him aware that a refusal would expose him to heavy legal penalties.[499]

The Sire de Luxembourg, meanwhile, was ill at ease; he feared that in his castle of Beaurevoir, a prisoner worth ten thousand golden livres was not sufficiently secure in case of a descent on the part of the French or of the English or of the Burgundians, or of any of those folk, who, caring nought for Burgundy or England or France, might wish to carry her off, cast her into a pit, and hold her to ransom, according to the custom of brigands in those days.[500]

Towards the end of September, he asked his lord, the Duke of Burgundy, who ruled over fine towns and strong cities, if he would undertake the safe custody of the Maid. My Lord Philip consented and, by his command, Jeanne was taken to Arras. This town was encircled by high walls; it had two castles, one of which, La Cour-le-Comte, was in the centre of the town. It was probably in the cells of Cour-le-Comte that Jeanne was confined, under the watch and ward of my Lord David de Brimeu, Lord of Ligny, Knight of the Golden Fleece, Governor of Arras.

At that time it was rare for prisoners to be kept in isolation.[501] At Arras, Jeanne received visitors; and among others, a Scotsman, who showed her her portrait, in which she was represented kneeling on one knee and presenting a letter to her King.[502] This letter might be supposed to have been from the Sire de Baudricourt, or from any other clerk or captain by whom the painter may have thought Jeanne to have been sent to the Dauphin; it might have been a letter announcing to the King the deliverance of Orléans or the victory of Patay.

This was the only portrait of herself Jeanne ever saw and, for her own part, she never had any painted; but during the brief duration of her power, the inhabitants of the French towns placed images of her, carved and painted, in the chapels of the saints, and wore leaden medals on which she was represented; thus in her case following a custom established in honour of the saints canonised by the Church.[503]

Many Burgundian lords, and among them a knight, one Jean de Pressy, Controller of the Finances of Burgundy, offered her woman's dress, as the Luxembourg dame had done, for her own good and in order to avoid scandal; but for nothing in the world would Jeanne have cast off the garb which she had assumed according to divine command.

She also received in her prison at Arras a clerk of Tournai, one Jean Naviel, charged by the magistrates of his town to deliver to her the sum of twenty-two golden crowns. This ecclesiastic enjoyed the confidence of his fellow citizens, who employed him in the town's most urgent affairs. In the May of this year, 1430, he had been sent to Messire Regnault de Chartres, Chancellor of King Charles. He had been taken by the Burgundians at the same time as Jeanne and held to ransom; but out of that predicament he soon escaped and at no great cost.

He acquitted himself well of his mission[504] to the Maid, and, it would seem, received nothing for his trouble, doubtless because he wanted the reward of this work of mercy to be placed to his account in heaven.[505]

Neither the capture of the Maid nor the retreat of the men-at-arms she had brought, put an end to the siege of Compiègne. Guillaume de Flavy and his two brothers, Charles and Louis, and Captain Baretta with his Italians, and the five hundred of the garrison[506] displayed skill, vigour, and untiring energy. The Burgundians conducted the siege in the same manner as the English had conducted that of Orléans; mines, trenches, bulwarks, cannonades and bastions, those gigantic and absurd erections good for nothing but for burning. The suburbs of the town Guillaume de Flavy had demolished because they were in the way of his firing; boats he had sunk in order to bar the river. To the mortars and huge *couillards* of the Burgundians he replied with his artillery, and notably with those little copper culverins which did such good service.[507] If the gay cannoneer of Orléans and Jargeau, Maître Jean de Montesclère, were absent, there was a shoemaker of Valenciennes, an artilleryman, named Noirouffle, tall, dark, terrible to see, and terrible to hear.[508] The townsfolk of Compiègne, like those of Orléans, made unsuccessful sallies. One day Louis de Flavy, the governor's brother, was killed by a Burgundian bullet. But none the less on that day Guillaume did as he was wont to do and made the minstrels play to keep his men-at-arms in good cheer.[509]

Henry VI
(from a portrait in the "Election Chamber" at Eton, reproduced by permission of the Provost)

In the month of June the bulwark, defending the bridge over the Oise, like les Tourelles at Orléans which defended the bridge over the Loire, was captured by the enemy without bringing about the reduction of the town. In like manner, the capture of Les Tourelles had not occasioned the fall of the town of Duke Charles.[510]

As for the bastions, they were just as little good on the Oise as they had been on the Loire; everything passed by them. The Burgundians were unable to invest Compiègne because its circumference was too great.[511] They were short of money; and their men-at-arms, for lack of food and of pay, deserted with that perfect assurance which in those days characterised alike mercenaries of the red cross and of the white.[512] To complete his misfortunes, Duke Philip was obliged to take away some of the troops engaged in the siege and send them against the inhabitants of Liège who had revolted.[513] On the 24th of October, a relieving army, commanded by the Count of Vendôme and the Marshal de Boussac, approached Compiègne. The English and the Burgundians having turned to encounter them, the garrison and all the inhabitants of the town, even the women, fell upon the rear of the besiegers and routed them.[514] The relieving army entered Compiègne. The flaring of the bastions was a fine sight. The Duke of Burgundy lost all his artillery.[515] The Sire de Luxembourg, who had come to Beaurevoir, where he had received the Count Bishop of Beauvais, now appeared before Compiègne just in time to bear his share in the disaster.[516] The same causes which had constrained the English to depart, as they put it, from Orléans, now obliged the Burgundians to leave Compiègne. But in those days the most ordinary events must needs have a supernatural cause assigned to them, wherefore the deliverance of the town was attributed to the vow of the Count of Vendôme, who, in the cathedral of Senlis, had promised an annual mass to Notre-Dame-de-la-Pierre if the place were not taken.[517]

The Lord Treasurer of Normandy raised aids to the amount of eighty thousand *livres tournois*, ten thousand of which were to be devoted to the purchase of Jeanne. The Count Bishop of Beauvais, who was taking this matter to heart, urged the Sire de Luxembourg to come to terms, mingled threats with coaxings, and caused the Norman gold to glitter before his eyes. He seemed to fear, and his fear was shared by the masters and doctors of the University, that King Charles would likewise make an offer, that he would promise more than King Henry's ten thousand golden francs and that in the end, by dint of costly gifts, the Armagnacs would succeed in winning back their fairy-godmother.[518] The rumour ran that King Charles, hearing that the English were about to gain possession of Jeanne for a sum of money, sent an ambassador to warn the Duke of Burgundy not on any account to consent to such an agreement, adding that if he did, the Burgundians in the hands of the King of France would be made to pay for the fate of the Maid.[519] Doubtless the rumour was false; albeit the fears of the Lord Bishop and the masters of the Paris University were not entirely groundless; and it is certain that from the banks of the Loire the negotiations were being attentively followed with a view to intervention at a favourable moment.

Besides, some sudden descent of the French was always to be feared. Captain La Hire was ravaging Normandy, the knight Barbazan, la Champagne, and Marshal de Boussac, the country between the Seine, the Marne and the Somme.[520]

At length, about the middle of November, the Sire de Luxembourg consented to the bargain; Jeanne was delivered up to the English. It was decided to take her to Rouen, through Ponthieu, along the sea-shore, through the north of Normandy, where there would be less risk of falling in with the scouts of the various parties.

From Arras she was taken to the Château of Drugy, where the monks of Saint-Riquier were said to have visited her in prison.[521] She was afterwards taken to Crotoy, where the castle walls were washed by the ocean waves. The Duke of Alençon, whom she called her fair Duke, had been imprisoned there after the Battle of Verneuil.[522] At the time of her arrival,

Maître Nicolas Gueuville, Chancellor of the Cathedral church of Notre Dame d'Amiens, was a prisoner in that castle in the hands of the English. He heard her confess and administered the Communion to her.[523] And there on that vast Bay of the Somme, grey and monotonous, with its low sky traversed by sea-birds in their long flight, Jeanne beheld coming down to her the visitant of earlier days, the Archangel Saint Michael; and she was comforted. It was said that the damsels and burgesses of Abbeville went to see her in the castle where she was imprisoned.[524] At the time of the coronation, these burgesses had thought of turning French; and they would have done so if King Charles had come to their town; he did not come; and perhaps it was through Christian charity that the folk of Abbeville visited Jeanne; but those among them who thought well of her did not say so, for fear they too should be suspected of heresy.[525]

The doctors and masters of the University pursued her with a bitterness hardly credible. In November, after they had been informed of the conclusion of the bargain between Jean de Luxembourg and the English, they wrote through their rector to the Lord Bishop of Beauvais reproaching him for his delay in the matter of this woman and exhorting him to be more diligent.

"For you it is no slight matter, holding as you do so high an office in God's Church," ran this letter, "that the scandals committed against the Christian religion be stamped out, especially when such scandals arise within your actual jurisdiction."[526]

Filled with faith and zeal for the avenging of God's honour, these clerks were, as they said, always ready to burn witches. They feared the devil; but, perchance, though they may not have admitted it even to themselves, they feared him twenty times more when he was Armagnac.

Jeanne was taken out of Crotoy at high tide and conveyed by boat to Saint-Valery, then to Dieppe, as is supposed, and certainly in the end to Rouen.[527]

She was conducted to the old castle, built in the time of Philippe-Auguste on the slope of the Bouvreuil hill.[528] King Henry VI, who had come to France for his coronation, had been there since the end of August. He was a sad, serious child, harshly treated by the Earl of Warwick, who was governor of the castle.[529] The castle was strongly fortified;[530] it had seven towers, including the keep. Jeanne was placed in a tower looking on to the open country.[531] Her room was on the middle storey, between the dungeon and the state apartment. Eight steps led up to it.[532] It extended over the whole of that floor, which was forty-three feet across, including the walls.[533] A stone staircase approached it at an angle. There was but a dim light, for some of the window slits had been filled in.[534] From a locksmith of Rouen, one Étienne Castille, the English had ordered an iron cage, in which it was said to be impossible to stand upright. If the reports of the ecclesiastical registrars are to be believed, Jeanne was placed in it and chained by the neck, feet, and hands,[535] and left there till the opening of the trial. At Jean Salvart's, at *l'Écu de France*, in front of the Official's courtyard,[536] a mason's apprentice saw the cage weighed. But no one ever found Jeanne in it. If this treatment were inflicted on Jeanne, it was not invented for her; when Captain La Hire, in the February of this same year, 1430, took Château Gaillard, near Rouen, he found the good knight Barbazan in an iron cage, from which he would not come out, alleging that he was a prisoner on parole.[537] Jeanne, on the contrary, had been careful to promise nothing, or rather she had promised to escape as soon as she could.[538] Therefore the English, who believed that she had magical powers, mistrusted her greatly.[539] As she was being prosecuted by the Church, she ought to have been detained in an ecclesiastical prison,[540] but the *Godons* were resolved to keep her in their custody. One among them said she was dear to them because they had paid dearly for her. On her feet they put shackles and round her waist a chain padlocked to a beam five or six feet long. At night this chain was carried over the foot of her bed and attached to the principal beam.[541] In like manner, John Huss, in 1415, when he was delivered up to the Bishop of

Constance and transferred to the fortress of Gottlieben, was chained night and day until he was taken to the stake.

Five English men-at-arms,[542] common soldiers (*houspilleurs*), guarded the prisoner;[543] they were not the flower of chivalry. They mocked her and she rebuked them, a circumstance they must have found consolatory. At night two of them stayed behind the door; three remained with her, and constantly troubled her by saying first that she would die, then that she would be delivered. No one could speak to her without their consent.[544]

Nevertheless folk entered the prison as if it were a fair (*comme au moulin*); people of all ranks came to see Jeanne as they pleased. Thus Maître Laurent Guesdon, Lieutenant of the Bailie of Rouen, came,[545] and Maître Pierre Manuel, Advocate of the King of England, who was accompanied by Maître Pierre Daron, magistrate of the city of Rouen. They found her with her feet in shackles, guarded by soldiers.[546]

Maître Pierre Manuel felt called upon to tell her that for certain she would never have come there if she had not been brought. Sensible persons were always surprised when they saw witches and soothsayers falling into a trap like any ordinary Christian. The King's Advocate must have been a sensible person, since his surprise appeared in the questions he put to Jeanne.

"Did you know you were to be taken?" he asked her.

"I thought it likely," she replied.

"Then why," asked Maître Pierre again, "if you thought it likely, did you not take better care on the day you were captured?"

"I knew neither the day nor the hour when I should be taken, nor when it should happen."[547]

A young fellow, one Pierre Cusquel, who worked for Jean Salvart, also called Jeanson, the master-mason of the castle, through the influence of his employer, was permitted to enter the tower. He also found Jeanne bound with a long chain attached to a beam, and with her feet in shackles. Much later, he claimed to have warned her to be careful of what she said, because her life was involved in it. It is true that she talked volubly to her guards and that all she said was reported to her judges. And it may have happened that the young Pierre, whose master was on the English side, wished to advise her and even did so. There is a suspicion, however, that like so many others he was merely boasting.[548]

The Sire Jean de Luxembourg came to Rouen. He went to the Maid's tower accompanied by his brother, the Lord Bishop of Thérouanne, Chancellor of England; and also by Humphrey, Earl of Stafford, Constable of France for King Henry; and the Earl of Warwick, Governor of the Castle of Rouen. At this interview there was also present the young Seigneur de Macy, who held Jeanne to be of very modest bearing, since she had repulsed his attempted familiarity.

"Jeanne," said the Sire de Luxembourg, "I have come to ransom you if you will promise never again to bear arms against us."

These words do not accord with our knowledge of the negotiation for the purchase of the Maid. They seem to indicate that even then the contract was not complete, or at any rate that the vendor thought he could break it if he chose. But the most remarkable point about the Sire de Luxembourg's speech is the condition on which he says he will ransom the Maid. He asks her to promise never again to fight against England and Burgundy. From these words it would seem to have been his intention to sell her to the King of France or to his representative.[549]

There is no evidence, however, of this speech having made any impression on the English. Jeanne set no store by it.

"In God's name, you do but jest," she replied; "for I know well that it lieth neither within your will nor within your power."

It is related that when he persisted in his statement, she replied:

"I know that these English will put me to death, believing that afterwards they will conquer France."

Since she certainly did not believe it, it seems highly improbable that she should have said that the English would have put her to death. Throughout the trial she was expecting, on the faith of her Voices, to be delivered. She knew not how or when that deliverance would come to pass, but she was as certain of it as of the presence of Our Lord in the Holy Sacrament. She may have said to the Sire de Luxembourg: "I know that the English want to put me to death." Then she repeated courageously what she had already said a thousand times:

"But were there one hundred thousand *Godons* more than at present, they would not conquer the kingdom."

On hearing these words, the Earl of Stafford unsheathed his sword and the Earl of Warwick had to restrain his hand.[550] That the English Constable of France should have raised his sword against a woman in chains would be incredible, did we not know that about this time this Earl of Stafford, hearing some one speak well of Jeanne, straightway wished to transfix him.[551]

In order that the Bishop and Vidame of Beauvais might exercise jurisdiction at Rouen it was necessary that a concession of territory should be granted him. The archiepiscopal see of Rouen was vacant.[552] For this concession, therefore, the Bishop of Beauvais applied to the chapter, with whom he had had misunderstandings.[553] The canons of Rouen lacked neither firmness nor independence; more of them were honest than dishonest; some were highly educated, well-lettered and even kind-hearted. None of them nourished any ill will toward the English. The Regent Bedford himself was a canon of Rouen, as Charles VII was a canon of Puy.[554] On the 20th of October, in that same year 1430, the Regent, donning surplice and amice, had distributed the dole of bread and wine for the chapter.[555] The canons of Rouen were not prejudiced in favour of the Maid of the Armagnacs; they agreed to the demand of the Bishop of Beauvais and granted him the formal concession of territory.[556]

On the 3rd of January, 1431, by royal decree, King Henry ordered the Maid to be given up to the Bishop and Count of Beauvais, reserving to himself the right to bring her before him, if she should be acquitted by the ecclesiastical tribunal.[557]

Nevertheless she was not placed in the Church prison, in one of those dungeons near the Booksellers' Porch, where in the shadow of the gigantic cathedral there rotted unhappy wretches who had erred in matters of faith.[558] There she would have endured sufferings far more terrible than even the horrors of her military tower. The wrong the Great Council of England inflicted on Jeanne by not handing her over to the ecclesiastical powers of Rouen was far less than the indignity they thereby inflicted on her judges.

With the way thus opened before him, the Bishop of Beauvais proceeded with all the violence one might expect from a Cabochien, albeit that violence was qualified by worldly arts and canonical knowledge.[559] As promoter in the case, that is, as the magistrate who was to conduct the prosecution, he selected one Jean d'Estivet, called Bénédicité, canon of Bayeux and of Beauvais, Promoter-General of the diocese of Beauvais. Jean d'Estivet was a friend of the Lord Bishop, and had been driven out of the diocese by the French at the same time. He was suspected of hostility to the Maid.[560] The Lord Bishop appointed Jean de la Fontaine, master of arts, licentiate of canon law, to be "councillor commissary" of the trial.[561] One of the clerks of the ecclesiastical court of Rouen, Guillaume Manchon, priest, he appointed first registrar.

In the course of instructing this official as to what would be expected of him, the Lord Bishop said to Messire Guillaume:

"You must do the King good service. It is our intention to institute an elaborate prosecution (*un beau procès*) against this Jeanne."[562]

As to the King's service, the Lord Bishop did not mean that it should be rendered at the expense of justice; he was a man of some priestly pride and was not likely to reveal his own evil designs. If he spoke thus, it was because in France, for a century at least, the jurisdiction of the Inquisition had been regarded as the jurisdiction of the King.[563] And as for the expression "an elaborate prosecution" (*un beau procès*), that meant a trial in which legal forms were observed and irregularities avoided, for it was a case in which were interested the doctors and masters of the realm of France and indeed the whole of Christendom. Messire Guillaume Manchon, well skilled in legal procedure, was not likely to err in a matter of legal language. An elaborate trial was a strictly regular trial. It was said, for example, that "N – – and N – – had by elaborate judicial procedure found such an one to be guilty."[564]

Charged by the Bishop to choose another registrar to assist him, Guillaume Manchon selected as his colleague Guillaume Colles, surnamed Boisguillaume, who like him was a notary of the Church.[565]

Jean Massieu, priest, ecclesiastical dean of Rouen, was appointed usher of the court.[566]

In that kind of trial, which was very common in those days, there were strictly only two judges, the Ordinary and the Inquisitor. But it was the custom for the Bishop to summon as councillors and assessors persons learned in both canon and civil law. The number and the rank of those councillors varied according to the case. And it is clear that the obstinate upholder of a very pestilent heresy must needs be more particularly and more ceremoniously tried than an old wife, who had sold herself to some insignificant demon, and whose spells could harm nothing more important than cabbages. For the common wizard, for the multitude of those females, or *mulierculæ*, as they were described by one inquisitor who boasted of having burnt many, the judges were content with three or four ecclesiastical advocates and as many canons.[567] When it was a question of a very notable personage who had set a highly pernicious example, of a king's advocate, for instance like Master Jean Segueut, who that very year, in Normandy, had spoken against the temporal power of the Church, a large assembly of doctors and prelates, English and French, were convoked, and the doctors and masters of the University of Paris were consulted in writing.[568] Now it was fitting that the Maid of the Armagnacs should be yet more elaborately and more solemnly tried, with a yet greater concourse of doctors and of prelates; and thus it was ordained by the Lord Bishop of Beauvais. As councillors and assessors he summoned the canons of Rouen in as great a number as possible. Among those who answered his summons we may mention Raoul Roussel, treasurer of the chapter; Gilles Deschamps, who had been chaplain to the late King, Charles VI, in 1415; Pierre Maurice, doctor in theology, rector of the University of Paris in 1428; Jean Alespée, one of the sixteen who during the siege of 1418 had gone robed in black and with cheerful countenance to place at the feet of King Henry V the life and honour of the city; Pasquier de Vaux, apostolic notary at the Council of Constance, President of the Norman *Chambre des Comptes*; Nicolas de Vendères, whose candidature for the vacant see of Rouen was being advocated by a powerful party; and, lastly, Nicolas Loiseleur. For the same purpose, the Lord Bishop summoned the abbots of the great Norman abbeys, Mont Saint-Michel-au-Péril-de-la-Mer, Fécamp, Jumièges, Préaux, Mortemer, Saint-Georges de Boscherville, la Trinité-du-mont-Sainte-Catherine, Saint-Ouen, Bec, Cormeilles, the priors of Saint-Lô, of Rouen, of Sigy, of Longueville, and the abbot of Saint Corneille of Compiègne. He summoned twelve ecclesiastical advocates; likewise famous doctors and masters of the University of Paris, Jean Beaupère, rector in 1412; Thomas Fiefvé, rector in 1427; Guillaume Erart, Nicolas Midi,[569] and that young doctor, abounding in knowledge and in modesty, the brightest star in the Christian firmament of the day, Thomas de Courcelles.[570] The Lord Bishop is bent upon turning the tribunal, which is to try Jeanne, into a veritable synod; it is indeed a provincial council, before which she is cited. Moreover, in effect, it is not only Jeanne the Maid, but Charles of Valois, calling himself King of France, and lawful successor of Charles VI who is to be brought to justice. Wherefore are assembled so many croziered and mitred abbots, so many renowned doctors and masters.

Nevertheless, there were other bright and shining lights of the Church, whom the Bishop of Beauvais neglected to summon. He consulted the two bishops of Coutances and Lisieux; he did not consult the senior bishop of Normandy, the Bishop of Avranches, Messire Jean de Saint-Avit, whom the chapter of the cathedral had charged with the duty of ordination throughout the diocese during the vacancy of the see of Rouen. But Messire Jean de Saint-Avit was considered and rightly considered to favour King Charles.[571] On the other hand those English doctors and masters, residing at Rouen, who had been consulted in Segueut's trial, were not consulted in that of Jeanne.[572] The doctors and masters of the University of Paris, the abbots of Normandy, the chapter of Rouen, held firmly to the Treaty of Troyes; they were as prejudiced as the English clerks against the Maid and the Dauphin Charles, and they were less suspected; it was all to the good.[573]

On Tuesday, the 9th of January, my Lord of Beauvais summoned eight councillors to his house: the abbots of Fécamp and of Jumièges, the prior of Longueville, the canons Roussel, Venderès, Barbier, Coppequesne and Loiseleur.

"Before entering upon the prosecution of this woman," he said to them, "we have judged it good, maturely and fully to confer with men learned and skilled in law, human and divine, of whom, thank God, there be great number in this city of Rouen."

The opinion of the doctors and masters was that information should be collected concerning the deeds and sayings publicly imputed to this woman.

The Lord Bishop informed them that already certain information had been obtained by his command, and that he had decided to order more to be collected, which would be ultimately presented to the Council.[574]

It is certain that a tabellion[575] of Andelot in Champagne, Nicolas Bailly, requisitioned by Messire Jean de Torcenay,

Bailie of Chaumont for King Henry, went to Domremy, and with Gérard Petit, provost of Andelot, and divers mendicant monks, made inquiry touching Jeanne's life and reputation. The interrogators heard twelve or fifteen witnesses and among others Jean Hannequin[576] of Greux and Jean Bégot, with whom they lodged.[577] We know from Nicolas Bailly himself that they gathered not a single fact derogatory to Jeanne. And if we may believe Jean Moreau, a citizen of Rouen, Maître Nicolas, having brought my Lord of Beauvais the result of his researches, was treated as a wicked man and a traitor; and obtained no reward for his expenditure or his labour.[578] This is possible, but it seems strange. It can in no wise be true, however, that neither at Vaucouleurs nor at Domremy, nor in the neighbouring villages was anything discovered against Jeanne. Quite on the contrary, numbers of accusations were collected against the inhabitants in general, who were addicted to evil practices, and in particular against Jeanne, who held intercourse with fairies,[579] carried a mandrake in her bosom, and disobeyed her father and mother.[580]

Abundant information was forthcoming, not only from Lorraine and from Paris, but from the districts loyal to King Charles, from Lagny, Beauvais, Reims, and even from so far as Touraine and Berry;[581] which was information enough to burn ten heretics and twenty witches. Devilries were discovered which filled the priests with horror: the finding of a lost cup and gloves, the exposure of an immoral priest, the sword of Saint Catherine, the restoration of a child to life. There was also a report of a rash letter concerning the Pope and there were many other indications of witchcraft, heresy, and religious error.[582] Such information was not to be included among the documents of the trial.[583] It was the custom of the Holy Inquisition to keep secret the evidence and even the names of the witnesses.[584] In this case the Bishop of Beauvais might have pleaded as an excuse for so doing the safety of the deponents, who might have suffered had he published information gathered in provinces subject to the Dauphin Charles. Even if their names were concealed, they would be identified by their evidence. For the purposes of the trial, Jeanne's own conversation in prison was the best source of information: she spoke much and without any of the reserve which prudence might have dictated.

A painter, whose name is unknown, came to see her in her tower. He asked her aloud and before her guards what arms she bore, as if he wished to represent her with her escutcheon. In those days portraits were very seldom painted from life, except of persons of very high rank, and they were generally represented kneeling and with clasped hands in an attitude of prayer. Though in Flanders and in Burgundy there may have been a few portraits bearing no signs of devotion, they were very rare. A portrait naturally suggested a person praying to God, to the Holy Virgin, or to some saint. Wherefore the idea of painting the Maid's picture doubtless must have met with the stern disapproval of her ecclesiastical judges. All the more so because they must have feared that the painter would represent this excommunicated woman in the guise of a saint, canonised by the Church, as the Armagnacs were wont to do.

A careful consideration of this incident inclines us to think that this man was no painter but a spy. Jeanne told him of the arms which the King had granted to her brothers: an azure shield bearing a sword between two golden *fleurs de lis*. And our suspicion is confirmed when at the trial she is reproached with pomp and vanity for having caused her arms to be painted.[585]

Sundry clerks introduced into her prison gave her to believe that they were men-at-arms of the party of Charles of Valois.[586] In order to deceive her, the Promoter himself, Maître Jean d'Estivet, disguised himself as a poor prisoner.[587] One of the canons of Rouen, who was summoned to the trial, by name Maître Nicolas Loiseleur, would seem to have been especially inventive of devices for the discovery of Jeanne's heresies. A native of Chartres, he was not only a master of arts, but was greatly renowned for astuteness. In 1427 and 1428 he carried through difficult negotiations, which detained him long months in Paris. In 1430 he was one of those deputed by the chapter to go to the Cardinal of Winchester in order to obtain an audience of King Henry and commend to him the church of Rouen. Maître Nicolas Loiseleur was therefore a *persona grata* with the Great Council.[588]

Having concerted with the Bishop of Beauvais and the Earl of Warwick, he entered Jeanne's prison, wearing a short jacket like a layman. The guards had been instructed to withdraw; and Maître Nicolas, left alone with his prisoner, confided to her that he, like herself, was a native of the Lorraine Marches, a shoemaker by trade, one who held to the French party and had been taken prisoner by the English. From King Charles he brought her tidings which were the fruit of his own imagination. No one was dearer to Jeanne than her King. Thus having won her confidence, the pseudo-shoemaker asked her sundry questions concerning the angels and saints who visited her. She answered him confidingly, speaking as friend to friend, as countryman to countryman. He gave her counsel, advising her not to believe all these churchmen and not to do all that they asked her; "For," he said, "if thou believest in them thou shalt be destroyed."

Many a time, we are told, did Maître Nicolas Loiseleur act the part of the Lorraine shoemaker. Afterwards he dictated to the registrars all that Jeanne had said, providing thus a valuable source of information of which a memorandum was made to be used during the examination. It would even appear that during certain of these visits the registrars were stationed at a peep-hole in an adjoining room.[589] If we may believe the rumours current in the town, Maître Nicolas also disguised himself as Saint Catherine, and by this means brought Jeanne to say all that he wanted.

He may not have been proud of such deceptions, but at any rate he made no secret of them.[590] Many famous masters approved him; others censured him.[591]

The angel of the schools, Thomas de Courcelles, when Nicolas told him of his disguises, counselled him to abandon them.

Afterwards the registrars pretended that it had been extremely repugnant to them thus to overhear in hiding a conversation so craftily contrived. The golden age of inquisitorial justice must have been well over when so strict a doctor as Maître Thomas was willing thus to criticise the most solemn forms of that justice. Inquisitorial proceedings must indeed have fallen into decay when two notaries of the Church dream of eluding its most common prescriptions. The clerks who disguised themselves as soldiers, the Promoter who took on the semblance of a poor prisoner, were exercising the most regular functions of the judicial system instituted by Innocent III.

In acting the shoemaker and Saint Catherine, if he were seeking the salvation and not the destruction of the sinner, if, contrary to public report, far from inciting her to rebellion, he was reducing her to obedience, if, in short, he were but deceiving her for her own temporal and spiritual good, Maître Nicolas Loiseleur was proceeding in conformity with established rules. In the *Tractatus de Hæresi* it is written: "Let no man approach the heretic, save from time to time two persons of faith and tact, who may warn him with precaution and as having compassion upon him, to eschew death by confessing his errors, and who may promise him that by so doing he shall escape death by fire; for the fear of death, and the hope of life may peradventure soften a heart which could be touched in no other wise."[592]

The duty of registrars was laid down in the following manner:

"Matters shall be ordained thus, that certain persons shall be stationed in a suitable place so as to surprise the confidences of heretics and to overhear their words."[593]

As for the Bishop of Beauvais, who had ordained and permitted such procedure, he found his justification and approbation in the words of the Apostle Saint Paul to the Corinthians: "I did not burden you: nevertheless, being crafty, I caught you with guile." "*Ego vos non gravavi; sed cum essem astutus, dolo vos cepi*" (II Corinthians xii, 16).[594]

Meanwhile, when Jeanne saw the Promoter, Jean d'Estivet, in his churchman's habit she did not recognise him. And Maître Nicolas Loiseleur also often came to her in monkish dress. In this guise he inspired her with great confidence; she confessed to him devoutly and had no other confessor.[595] She saw him sometimes as a shoemaker and sometimes as a canon and never perceived that he was the same person. Wherefore we must indeed believe her to have been incredibly simple in certain respects; and these great theologians must have realised that it was not difficult to deceive her.

It was well known to all men versed in science, divine and human, that the Enemy never entered into dealings with a maid without depriving her of her virginity.[596] At Poitiers the French clerks had thought of it, and when Queen Yolande assured them that Jeanne was a virgin, they ceased to fear that she was sent by the devil.[597] The Lord Bishop of Beauvais in a different hope awaited a similar examination. The Duchess of Bedford herself went to the prison. She was assisted by Lady Anna Bavon and another matron. It has been said that the Regent was hidden meanwhile in an adjoining room and looking through a hole in the wall.[598] This is by no means certain, but it is not impossible; he was at Rouen a fortnight after Jeanne had been brought there.[599] Whether the charge were groundless or well founded he was seriously reproached for this curiosity. If there were many who in his place would have been equally curious, every one must judge for himself; but we must bear in mind that my Lord of Bedford believed Jeanne a witch, and that it was not the custom in those days to treat witches with the respect due to ladies. We must remember also that this was a matter in which Old England was greatly concerned, and the Regent loved his country with all his heart and all his strength.

Upon the examination of the Duchess of Bedford as upon that of the Queen of Sicily Jeanne appeared a virgin. The matrons knew various signs of virginity; but for us a more certain sign is Jeanne's own word. When she was asked wherefore she called herself the Maid, whether she were one in reality, she replied: "I may tell you that such I am."[600] The judges, as far as we know, set no store by this favourable result of the examination. Did they believe with the wise King Solomon that in such matters all inquiry is vain, and did they reject the matrons' verdict by virtue of the saying: *Virginitatis probatio non minus difficilis quam custodia*? No, they knew well that she was indeed a virgin. They allowed it to be understood when they did not assert the contrary.[601] And since they persisted in believing her a witch, it must have been because they imagined her to have given herself to devils who had left her as they found her. The morals of devils abounded in such inconsistencies, which were the despair of the most learned doctors; every day new inconsistencies were being discovered.

On Saturday, the 13th of January, the Lord Abbot of Fécamp, the doctors and masters, Nicolas de Venderès, Guillaume Haiton, Nicolas Coppequesne, Jean de la Fontaine, and Nicolas Loiseleur, met in the house of the Lord Bishop. There was read to them the information concerning the Maid gathered in Lorraine and elsewhere. And it was decided that according to this information a certain number of articles should be drawn up in due form; which was done.[602]

On Tuesday, the 23rd of January, the doctors and masters above named considered the terms of these articles, and, finding them sufficient, they decided that they might be used for the examination. Then they resolved that the Bishop of Beauvais should order a preliminary inquiry as to the deeds and sayings of Jeanne.[603]

On Tuesday, the 13th of February, Jean d'Estivet, called Bénédicité, Promoter, Jean de la Fontaine, Commissioner, Boisguillaume and Manchon, Registrars, and Jean Massieu, Usher, took the oath faithfully to discharge their various offices. Then straightway Maître Jean de la Fontaine, assisted by two registrars, proceeded to the preliminary inquiry.[604]

On Monday, the 19th of February, at eight o'clock in the morning, the doctors and masters assembled, to the number of eleven, in the house of the Bishop of Beauvais; there they heard the reading of the articles and the preliminary information. Whereupon they gave it as their opinion, and, in conformity with this opinion, the Bishop decided that there was matter sufficient to justify the woman called the Maid being cited and charged touching a question of faith.[605]

But now a fresh difficulty arose. In such a trial it was necessary for the accused to appear at once before the Ordinary and before the Inquisitor. The two judges were equally necessary for the validity of the trial. Now the Grand Inquisitor for the realm of France, Brother Jean Graverent, was then at Saint-Lô, prosecuting on a religious charge a citizen of the town, one Jean Le Couvreur.[606] In the absence of Brother Jean Graverent, the Bishop of Beauvais had invited the Vice-Inquisitor for the diocese of Rouen to proceed against Jeanne conjointly with himself. Meanwhile the Vice-Inquisitor seemed not to understand; he made no response; and the Bishop was left in embarrassment with his lawsuit on his hands.

This Vice-Inquisitor was Brother Jean Lemaistre, Prior of the Dominicans of Rouen, bachelor of theology, a monk right prudent and scrupulous.[607] At length in answer to a summons from the Usher, at four o'clock on the 19th of February, 1413, he appeared in the house of the Bishop of Beauvais. He declared himself ready to intervene provided that he had the right to do so, which he doubted. As the reason for his uncertainty he alleged that he was the Inquisitor of Rouen; now the Bishop of Beauvais was exercising his jurisdiction as bishop of the diocese of Beauvais, but on borrowed territory; wherefore was it not rather for the Inquisitor of Beauvais not for the Inquisitor of Rouen, to sit on the judgment seat side by side with the Bishop?[608] He declared that he would ask the Grand Inquisitor of France for an authorisation which should hold good for the diocese of Beauvais. Meanwhile he consented to act in order to satisfy his own conscience and to prevent the proceedings from lapsing, which, in the opinion of all, must have ensued had the trial been instituted without the concurrence of the Holy Inquisition.[609] All preliminary difficulties were now removed.

The Maid was cited to appear on Wednesday, the 21st of February,[610] 1431.

On that day, at eight o'clock in the morning, the Bishop of Beauvais, the Vicar of the Inquisitor, and forty-one Councillors and Assessors assembled in the castle chapel. Fifteen of them were doctors in theology, five doctors in civil and canon law, six bachelors in theology, eleven bachelors in canon law, four licentiates in civil law. The Bishop sat as judge. At his side were the Councillors and Assessors, clothed either in the fine camlet of canons or in the coarse cloth of mendicants, expressive, the one of sacerdotal solemnity, the other of evangelical meekness. Some glared fiercely, others cast down their eyes. Brother Jean Lemaistre, Vice-Inquisitor of the faith, was among them, silent, in the black and white livery of poverty and obedience.[611]

Before bringing in the accused, the usher informed the Bishop that Jeanne, to whom the citation had been delivered, had replied that she would be willing to appear, but she demanded that an equal number of ecclesiastics of the French party should be added to those of the English party. She requested also the permission to hear mass.[612] The Bishop refused both demands;[613] and Jeanne was brought in, dressed as a man, with her feet in shackles. She was made to sit down at the table of the registrars.

And now from the very outset these theologians and this damsel regarded each other with mutual horror and hatred. Contrary to the custom of her sex, a custom which even loose women did not dare to infringe, she displayed her hair, which was brown and cut short over the ears. It was possibly the first time that some of those young monks seated behind their elders had ever seen a woman's hair. She wore hose like a youth. To them her dress appeared immodest and abominable.[614] She exasperated and irritated them. Had the Bishop of Beauvais insisted on her appearing in hood and gown their anger against her would have been less violent. This man's attire brought before their minds the works performed by the Maid in the camp of the Dauphin Charles, calling himself king. By the stroke of a magic wand she had deprived the English men-at-arms of all their strength, and thereby she had inflicted sore hurt on the majority of the churchmen who were to judge her. Some among them were thinking of the benefices of which she had despoiled them; others, doctors and masters of the University, recalled how she had been about to lay Paris waste with fire and sword;[615] others again, canons and abbots, could not forgive her perchance for having struck fear into their hearts even in remote Normandy. Was it possible for them to pardon the havoc she had thus wrought in a great part of the Church of France, when they knew she had done it by sorcery, by divination and by invoking devils? "A man must be very ignorant if he will deny the reality of magic," said Sprenger. As they were very learned, they saw magicians and wizards where others would never have suspected them; they held that to doubt the power of demons over men and things was not only heretical and impious, but tending to subvert the whole natural and social order. These doctors, seated in the castle chapel, had burned each one of them ten, twenty, fifty witches, all of whom had confessed their crimes. Would it not have been madness after that to doubt the existence of witches?

To us it seems curious that beings capable of causing hail-storms and casting spells over men and animals should allow themselves to be taken, judged, tortured, and burned without making any defence; but it was constantly occurring; every ecclesiastical judge must have observed it. Very learned men were able to account for it: they explained that wizards and witches lost their power as soon as they fell into the hands of churchmen. This explanation was deemed sufficient. The hapless Maid had lost her power like the others; they feared her no longer.

At least Jeanne hated them as bitterly as they hated her. It was natural for unlettered saints, for the fair inspired, frank of mind, capricious, and enthusiastic to feel an antipathy towards doctors all inflated with knowledge and stiffened with scholasticism. Such an antipathy Jeanne had recently felt towards clerks, even when as at Poitiers they had been on the French side, and had not wished her evil and had not greatly troubled her. Wherefore we may easily imagine how intense was the repulsion with which the clerks of Rouen now inspired her. She knew that they sought to compass her death. But she feared them not; confidently she awaited from her saints and angels the fulfilment of their promise, their coming for her deliverance. She knew not when nor how her deliverance should come; but that come it would she never once doubted. To doubt it would indeed have been to doubt Saint Michael, Saint Catherine, and even Our Lord; it would have been to believe evil of her Voices. They had told her to fear nothing, and of nothing was she afeard.[616] Fearless simplicity; whence came her confidence in her Voices if not from her own heart?

The Bishop required her to swear, according to the prescribed form with both hands on the holy Gospels, that she would reply truly to all that should be asked her.

She could not. Her Voices forbade her telling any one of the revelations they had so abundantly vouchsafed to her.

She answered: "I do not know on what you wish to question me. You might ask me things that I would not tell you."

And when the Bishop insisted on her swearing to tell the whole truth:

"Touching my father and mother and what I did after my coming into France I will willingly swear," she said; "but touching God's revelations to me, those I have neither told nor communicated to any man, save to Charles my King. And nought of them will I reveal, were I to lose my head for it."

Then, either because she wished to gain time or because she counted on receiving some new directions from her *Council*, she added that in a week she would know whether she might so reveal those things.

At length she took the oath, according to the prescribed form, on her knees, with both hands on the missal.[617] Then she answered concerning her name, her country, her parents, her baptism, her godfathers and godmothers. She said that to the best of her knowledge she was about nineteen years of age.[618]

Questioned concerning her education, she replied: "From my mother I learnt my Paternoster, my Ave Maria and my Credo."

But, asked to repeat her Paternoster, she refused, for, she said, she would only say it in confession. This was because she wanted the Bishop to hear her confess.[619]

The assembly was profoundly agitated; all spoke at once. Jeanne with her soft voice had scandalised the doctors.

The Bishop forbade her to leave her prison, under pain of being convicted of the crime of heresy.

She refused to submit to this prohibition. "If I did escape," she said, "none could reproach me with having broken faith, for I never gave my word to any one."

Afterwards she complained of her chains.

The Bishop told her they were on account of her attempt to escape.

She agreed: "It is true that I wanted to escape, and I still want to, just like every other prisoner."[620]

Such a confession was very bold, if she had rightly understood the judge when he said that by flight from prison she would incur the punishment of a heretic. To escape from an ecclesiastical prison was to commit a crime against the Church, but it was folly as well as crime; for the prisons of the Church are penitentiaries, and the prisoner who refuses salutary penance is as foolish as he is guilty; for he is like a sick man who refuses to be cured. But Jeanne was not, strictly speaking, in an ecclesiastical prison; she was in the castle of Rouen, a prisoner of war in the hands of the English. Could it be said that if she escaped she would incur excommunication and the spiritual and temporal penalties inflicted on the enemies of religion? There lay the difficulty. The Lord Bishop removed it forthwith by an elaborate legal fiction. Three English men-at-arms, John Grey, John Berwoist, and William Talbot, were appointed by the King to be Jeanne's custodians. The Bishop, acting as an ecclesiastical judge, himself delivered to them their charge, and made them swear on the holy Gospels to bind the damsel and confine her.[621] In this wise the Maid became the prisoner of our holy Mother, the Church; and she could not burst her bonds without falling into heresy. The second sitting was appointed for the next day, the 22nd of February.[622]

Chapter XI
The trial for lapse (*continued*)

HEN a record of the proceedings came to be written down after the first sitting, a dispute arose between the ecclesiastical notaries and the two or three royal registrars who had likewise taken down the replies of the accused. As might be expected, the two records differed in several places. It was decided that on the contested points Jeanne should be further examined.[623] The notaries of the Church complained also that they experienced great difficulty in seizing Jeanne's words on account of the constant interruptions of the bystanders.

In a trial by the Inquisition there was no place fixed for the examination any more than for the other acts of the procedure. The judges might examine the accused in a chapel, in a chapter-house, or even in a prison or a torture-chamber. According to Messire Guillaume Manchon it was in order to escape from the tumult of the first sitting,[624] and because there was no longer any reason for proceeding with such solemn ceremony as at the opening of the trial, that the judge and his councillors met in the Robing Room, a little chamber at one end of the castle hall;[625] and two English guards were stationed at the door. According to the rules of inquisitorial procedure, the assessors were not bound to be present at all the deliberations.[626] This time forty-two were present, twenty-six of the original ones and six newly appointed. Among these high clerics was Brother Jean Lemaistre, Vice Inquisitor of the Faith, a humble preaching friar. No longer as in the days of Saint Dominic was the Vice Inquisitor the hunting hound of the Lord, now he was but the dog of the Bishop, a poor monk, who dared neither to do nor to abstain from doing. Such was the result of the assertion of Gallican independence against papal supremacy. Dumb and timid, Brother Jean Lemaistre was the last and the least of all the brethren in that assembly, but he was ever looking for the day when he should be sovereign judge and without appeal.[627]

Jeanne was brought in by the Usher, Messire Jean Massieu. Again she endeavoured to avoid taking the oath to tell everything; but she had to swear on the Gospel.[628]

She was examined by Maître Jean Beaupère, doctor in theology. In his University of Paris he was regarded as a scholar of light and leading; it had twice appointed him rector. It had charged him with the functions of chancellor in the absence of Gerson, and, in 1419, had sent him with Messire Pierre Cauchon to the town of Troyes, to give aid and counsel to King Charles VI. Three years later it had despatched him to the Queen of England and the Duke of Gloucester to enlist their support in its endeavour to obtain the confirmation of its privileges. King Henry VI had just appointed him canon of Rouen.[629]

Maître Jean's first question to Jeanne was what was her age when she left her father's house. She was unable to say, although on the previous day she had stated her present age to be about nineteen.[630]

Interrogated as to the occupations of her childhood, she replied that she was busy with household duties and seldom went into the fields with the cattle.

"For spinning and sewing," she said, "I am as good as any woman in Rouen."[631]

Thus even in things domestic she displayed her ardour and her chivalrous zeal; at the spinning-wheel and with the needle she challenged all the women in a town, without knowing one of them.

Questioned as to her confessions and her communions, she answered that she confessed to her parish priest or to another priest when the former was not able to hear her. But she refused to say whether she had received the communion on other feast-days than Easter.[632]

In order to take her unawares, Maître Jean Beaupère proceeded without method, passing abruptly from one subject to another. Suddenly he spoke of her Voices. She gave him the following reply:

"Being thirteen years of age, I heard the Voice of God, bidding me lead a good life. And the first time I was sore afeard. And the Voice came almost at the hour of noon, in summer, in my father's garden...."

She heard the Voice on the right towards the church. Rarely did she hear it without seeing a light. This light was in the direction whence the Voice came.[633]

When Jeanne said that her Voice spoke to her from the right, a doctor more learned and more kindly disposed than Maître Jean would have interpreted this circumstance favourably; for do we not read in Ezekiel that the angels were upon the right hand of the dwelling; do we not find in the last chapter of Saint Mark, that the women beheld the Angel seated on the right, and finally does not Saint Luke expressly state that the Angel appeared unto Zacharias on the right of the altar burning with incense; whereupon the Venerable Bede observes: "he appeared on the right as a sign that he was the bringer of divine mercy."[634] But such things never occurred to the examiner. Thinking to embarrass Jeanne, he asked how she came to see the light if it appeared at her side.[635] Jeanne made no reply, and as if distraught, she said:

"If I were in a wood I should easily hear the Voices coming towards me.... It seems to me to be a Voice right worthy. I believe that this Voice was sent to me by God. After having heard it three times I knew it to be the voice of an angel."

"What instruction did this Voice give you for the salvation of your soul?"

"It taught me to live well, to go to church, and it told me to fare forth into France."[636]

Then Jeanne related how, by the command of her Voice, she had gone to Vaucouleurs, to Sire Robert de Baudricourt, whom she had recognised without ever having seen him before, how the Duke of Lorraine had summoned her to cure him, and how she had come into France.[637]

Thereafter she was brought to say that she knew well that God loved the Duke of Orléans and that concerning him she had had more revelations than concerning any man living, save the King; that she had been obliged to change her woman's dress for man's attire and that her *Council* had advised her well.[638]

The letter to the English was read before her. She admitted having dictated it in those terms, with the exception of three passages. She had not said *body for body* nor *chieftain of war*; and she had said *surrender to the King* in the place *of surrender to the Maid.* That the judges had not tampered with the text of the letter we may assure ourselves by comparing it with other texts, which did not pass through their hands, and which contain the expressions challenged by Jeanne.[639]

In the beginning of her career, she believed that Our Lord, the true King of France, had ordained her to deliver the government of the realm to Charles of Valois, as His deputy. The words in which she gave utterance to this idea are reported by too many persons strangers one to another for us to doubt her having spoken them. "The King shall hold the kingdom as a fief (*en commande*); the King of France is the lieutenant of the King of Heaven." These are her own words and she did actually say to the Dauphin: "Make a gift of your realm to the King of Heaven."[640] But we are bound to admit that at Rouen not one of these mystic ideas persists, indeed there they seem altogether beyond her. In all her replies to her examiners, she seems incapable of any abstract reasoning whatsoever and of any speculation however simple, so that it is hard to understand how she should ever have conceived the idea of the temporal rule of Jesus Christ over the Land of the Lilies. There is nothing in her speech or in her thoughts to suggest such meditations, wherefore we are led to believe that this politico-theology had been taught her in her tender, teachable years by ecclesiastics desiring to remove the woes of Church and kingdom, but that she had failed to seize its spirit or grasp its inner meaning. Now, in the midst of a hard life lived with men-at-arms, whose simple souls accorded better with her own than the more cultivated minds of the early directors of her meditations, she had forgotten even the phraseology in which those suggested meditations were expressed. Interrogated concerning her coming to Chinon, she replied:

"Without let or hindrance I went to my King. When I reached the town of Sainte-Catherine de Fierbois, I sent first to the town of Château-Chinon, where my King was. I arrived there about the hour of noon and lodged in an inn, and, after dinner, I went to my King who was in his castle."

If we may believe the registrars, they never ceased wondering at her memory. They were amazed that she should recollect exactly what she had said a week before.[641] Nevertheless her memory was sometimes curiously uncertain, and we have reason for thinking with the Bastard that she waited two days at the inn before being received by the King.[642]

With regard to this audience in the castle of Chinon, she told her judges she had recognised the King as she had recognised the Sire de Baudricourt, by revelation.[643]

The interrogator asked her: "When the Voice revealed your King to you, was there any light?"[644]

This question bore upon matters which were of great moment to her judges; for they suspected the Maid of having committed a sacrilegious fraud, or rather witchcraft, with the complicity of the King of France. Indeed, they had learnt from their informers that Jeanne boasted of having given the King a sign in the form of a precious crown.[645] The following is the actual truth of the matter:

The legend of Saint Catherine relates that on a day she received from the hand of an angel a resplendent crown and placed it on the head of the Empress of the Romans. This crown was the symbol of eternal blessedness.[646] Jeanne, who had been brought up on this legend, said that the same thing had happened to her. In France she had told sundry marvellous stories of crowns, and in one of these stories she imagined herself to be in the great hall of the castle at Chinon, in the midst of the barons, receiving a crown from the hand of an angel to give it to her King.[647] This was true in a spiritual sense, for she had taken Charles to his anointing and to his coronation. Jeanne was not quick to grasp the distinction between two kinds of truth. She may, nevertheless, have doubted the material reality of this vision. She may even have held it to be true in a spiritual sense only. In any case, she had of her own accord promised Saint Catherine and Saint Margaret not to speak of it to her judges.[648]

"Saw you any angel above the King?"

She refused to reply.[649]

This time nothing more was said of the crown. Maître Jean Beaupère asked Jeanne if she often heard the Voice.

"Not a day passes without my hearing it. And it is my stay in great need."[650]

She never spoke of her Voices without describing them as her refuge and relief, her consolation and her joy. Now all theologians agreed in believing that good spirits when they depart leave the soul filled with joy, with peace, and with comfort, and as proof they cited the angel's words to Zacharias and Mary: "Be not afraid."[651] This reason, however, was not strong enough to persuade clerks of the English party that Voices hostile to the English were of God.

And the Maid added: "Never have I required of them any other final reward than the salvation of my soul."[652]

The examination ended with a capital charge: the attack on Paris on a feast day. It was in this connection possibly that Brother Jacques of Touraine, a friar of the Franciscan order, who from time to time put a question, asked Jeanne whether she had ever been in a place where Englishmen were being slain.

"In God's name, was I ever in such a place?" Jeanne responded vehemently. "How glibly you speak. Why did they not depart from France and go into their own country?"

A nobleman of England, who was in the chamber, on hearing these words, said to his neighbours: "By my troth she is a good woman. Why is she not English?"[653]

The third public sitting was appointed for two days thence, Saturday, the 24th of February.[654]

It was Lent. Jeanne observed the fast very strictly.[655]

On Friday, the 23rd, in the morning, she was awakened by her Voices themselves. She arose from her bed and remained seated, her hands clasped, giving thanks. Then she asked what she should reply to her judges, beseeching the Voices thereupon to take counsel of Our Lord. First the Voices uttered words she could not understand. That happened sometimes, in difficult circumstances especially. Then they said:[656] "Reply boldly, God will aid thee."

That day she heard them a second time at the hour of vespers and a third time when the bells were ringing the *Ave Maria* in the evening. In the night of Friday and Saturday they came and revealed to her many secrets for the weal of the King of France. Thereupon she received great consolation.[657] Very probably they repeated the assurance that she would be delivered from the hands of her enemies, and that on the other hand her judges stood in great danger.

She depended absolutely on her Voices for direction. When she was in difficulty as to what to say to her judges, she prayed to Our Lord; she addressed him devoutly, saying: "Good God, for the sake of thy holy Passion, I beseech thee if thou lovest me to reveal unto me what I should reply to these churchmen. Touching my dress I know well how I was commanded to put it on; but as to leaving it I know nothing. In this may it please thee to teach me."

Then straightway the Voices came.[658]

At the third sitting, held in the Robing Chamber, there were present sixty-two assessors, of whom twenty were new.[659]

Jeanne showed a greater repugnance than before to swearing on the holy Gospels to reply to all that should be asked her. In charity the Bishop warned her that this obstinate refusal caused her to be suspected, and he required her to swear, under pain of being convicted upon all the charges.[660] Such was indeed the rule in a trial by the Inquisition. In 1310 a *béguine*, one La Porète, refused to take the oath as required by the Holy Inquisitor of the Faith, Brother Guillaume of Paris. She was excommunicated forthwith, and without being further examined, after lengthy proceedings, she was handed over to the Provost of Paris, who caused her to be burned alive. Her piety at the stake drew tears from all the bystanders.[661]

Still the Bishop failed to force an unconditional oath from the Maid; she swore to tell the truth on all she knew concerning the trial, reserving to herself the right to be silent on everything which in her opinion did not concern it. She spoke freely of the Voices she had heard the previous day, but not of the revelations touching the King. When, however, Maître Jean Beaupère appeared desirous to know them, she asked for a fortnight's delay before replying, sure that before then she would be delivered; and straightway she fell to boasting of the secrets her Voices had confided to her for the King's weal.

"I would wish him to know them at this moment," she said; "even if as the result I were to drink no wine from now till Easter."[662]

"Drink no wine from now till Easter!" Did she thus casually use an expression common in that land of the rose-tinted wine (*vin gris*), a drop or two of which with a slice of bread sufficed the Domremy women for a meal?[663] Or had she caught this manner of speech with the habit of dealing hard clouts and good blows from the men-at-arms of her company? Alas! what hypocras was she to drink during the five weeks before Easter! She was merely making use of a current phrase, as was frequently her custom, and attributing no precise meaning to it, unless it were that wine vaguely suggested to her mind the idea of cordiality and the hope that after her deliverance she would see the Lords of France filling a cup in her honour.

Maître Jean Beaupère asked her whether she saw anything when she heard her Voices.

She replied: "I cannot tell you everything. I am not permitted. The Voice is good and worthy.... To this question I am not bound to reply."

And she asked them to give her in writing the points concerning which she had not given an immediate reply.[664]

What use did she intend to make of this writing? She did not know how to read; she had no counsel. Did she want to show the document to some false friend, like Loiseleur, who was deceiving her? Or was it her intent to present it to her saints?

Maître Beaupère asked whether her Voice had a face and eyes.

She refused to answer and quoted a saying frequently on the lips of children: "One is often hanged for having spoken the truth."[665]

Maître Beaupère asked: "Do you know whether you stand in God's grace?"

This was an extremely insidious question; it placed Jeanne in the dilemma of having to avow herself sinful or of appearing unpardonably bold. One of the assessors, Maître Jean Lefèvre of the Order of the Hermit Friars, observed that she was not bound to reply. There was murmuring throughout the chamber.

But Jeanne said: "If I be not, then may God bring me into it; if I be, then may God keep me in it."[666]

The assessors were astonished at so ready an answer. And yet no improvement ensued in their disposition towards her. They admitted that touching her King she spoke well, but for the rest she was too subtle, and with a subtlety peculiar to women.[667]

Thereafter, Maître Jean Beaupère examined Jeanne concerning her childhood in her village. He essayed to show that she had been cruel, had displayed a homicidal tendency from her earliest years, and had been addicted to those idolatrous practices which had given the folk of Domremy a bad name.[668]

Then he touched on a point of prime importance in elucidating the obscure origin of Jeanne's mission:

"Were you not regarded as the one who was sent from the Oak Wood?"

In this direction he might have succeeded in obtaining important revelations. False prophecies had indeed established Jeanne's reputation in France; but these clerks were incapable of discriminating amongst all these pseudo-Bedes and pseudo-Merlins.[669]

Jeanne replied: "When I came to the King, certain asked me whether there were in my country a wood called the Oak Wood; because of prophecies saying that from the neighbourhood of this wood should come a damsel who would work wonders. But to such things I paid no heed."

This statement we must needs believe; but if she denied credence to the prophecy of Merlin touching the Virgin of the Oak Wood, she paid good heed to the prophecy foretelling the appearance of a Deliverer in the person of a Maid coming from the Lorraine Marches, since she repeated that prophecy to the two Leroyers and to her Uncle Lassois, with an emphasis which filled them with astonishment. Now we must admit that the two prophecies are as alike as two peas.[670]

Passing abruptly from Merlin the Magician, Maître Jean Beaupère asked: "Jeanne, will you have a woman's dress?"

She answered: "Give me one; and I will accept it and depart. Otherwise I will not have it. I will be content with this one, since God is pleased for me to wear it."

On this reply, which contained two errors tending to heresy, the Lord Bishop adjourned the court.[671]

The morrow, the 25th of February, was the first Sunday in Lent. On that day or another, but probably on that day, my Lord Bishop sent Jeanne a shad. Having partaken of this fish she had fever and was seized with vomiting.[672] Two masters of arts of the Paris University, both doctors of medicine, Jean Tiphaine and Guillaume Delachambre, assessors in the trial, were summoned by the Earl of Warwick, who said to them:

"According to what has been told me, Jeanne is sick. I have summoned you to devise measures for her recovery. The King would not for the world have her die a natural death. She is dear to him, for he has bought her dearly; his intent is that she die not, save by the hand of justice, and that she should be burned. Do all that may be necessary, therefore, visit her attentively, and endeavour to restore her."[673]

Conducted to Jeanne by Maître Jean d'Estivet, the doctors inquired of her the cause of her suffering.

She answered that she had eaten a carp sent her by the Lord Bishop of Beauvais, and that she believed it to be the cause of her sickness.

Did Jeanne suspect the Bishop of designing to poison her? That is what Maître Jean d'Estivet thought, for he flew into a violent rage:

"Whore!" he cried, "it is thine own doing; thou hast eaten herrings and other things which have made thee ill."

"I have not," she answered.

They exchanged insults, and Jeanne's sickness thereupon grew worse.[674]

The doctors examined her and found that she had fever. Wherefore they decided to bleed her.

They informed the Earl of Warwick, who became anxious:

"A bleeding!" he cried; "take heed! She is artful and might kill herself."

Nevertheless Jeanne was bled and recovered.[675]

On Monday, the 26th, there was no examination.[676] On the opening of the fourth sitting, Tuesday, the 27th, Maître Jean Beaupère asked her how she had been, which inquiry touched her but little. She replied drily:

"You can see for yourself. I am as well as it is possible for me to be."[677]

This sitting was held in the Robing Chamber in the presence of fifty-four assessors.[678] Five of them had not been present before, and among them was Maître Nicolas Loiseleur, canon of Rouen, whose share in the proceedings had been to act the Lorraine shoemaker and Saint Catherine of Alexandria.[679]

Maître Jean Beaupère, as on the previous Saturday, was curious to know whether Jeanne had heard her Voices. She heard them every day.[680]

He asked her: "Is it an angel's voice that speaketh unto you, or the voice of a woman saint or of a man saint? Or is it God speaking without an interpreter?"

Said Jeanne: "This voice is the voice of Saint Catherine and of Saint Margaret; and on their heads are beautiful crowns, right rich and right precious. I am permitted to tell you so by Messire. If you doubt it send to Poitiers, where I was examined."[681]

She was right in appealing to the clerks of France. The Armagnac doctors had no less authority in matters of faith than the English and Burgundian doctors. Were they not all to meet at the Council?

The examiner asked: "How know ye that they are these two saints? Know ye them one from another?"

Said Jeanne: "Well do I know who they are; and I do know one from the other."

"How?"

"By the greeting they give me."[682]

Let not Jeanne be hastily taxed with error or untruth. Did not the Angel salute Gideon (Judges vi), and Raphaël salute Tobias (Tobit xii)?[683]

Thereafter Jeanne gave another reason: "I know them because they call themselves by name."[684]

When she was asked whether her saints were both clothed alike, whether they were of the same age, whether they spoke at once, whether one of them appeared before the other, she refused to reply, saying she had not permission to do so.[685]

Maître Jean Beaupère inquired which of the apparitions came to her the first when she was about thirteen.

Jeanne said: "It was Saint Michael. I beheld him with my eyes. And he was not alone, but with him were angels from heaven. It was by Messire's command alone that I came into France."

"Did you actually behold Saint Michael and these angels in the body?"

"I saw them with the eyes of my head as plainly as I see you; and when they went away I wept and should have liked them to take me with them."

"In what semblance was Saint Michael?"[686]

She was not permitted to say.

She was asked whether she had received permission from God to go into France and whether God had commanded her to put on man's dress.

By keeping silence on this point she became liable to be suspected of heresy, and however she replied she laid herself open to serious charges, – she either took upon herself homicide and abomination, or she attributed it to God, which manifestly was to blaspheme.

Concerning her coming into France, she said: "I would rather have been dragged by the hair of my head than have come into France without permission from Messire." Concerning her dress she added: "Dress is but a little thing, less than nothing. It was not according to the counsel of any man of this world that I put on man's clothing. I neither wore this attire nor did anything save by the command of Messire and his angels."[687]

Maître Jean Beaupère asked: "When you behold this Voice coming towards you, is there any light?"

Then she replied with a jest, as at Poitiers: "Every light cometh not to you, my fair lord."[688]

After all it was virtually against the King of France that these doctors of Rouen were proceeding with craft and with cunning.

Maître Jean Beaupère threw out the question: "How did your King come to have faith in your sayings?"

"Because they were proved good to him by signs and also because of his clerks."

"What revelations were made unto your King?"

"That you will not hear from me this year."

As he listened to the damsel's words, must not my Lord of Beauvais, who was in the counsels of King Henry, have reflected on that verse in the Book of Tobias (xii, 7): "It is good to keep close the secret of a king"?

Thereafter Jeanne was called upon to reply at length concerning the sword of Saint Catherine. The clerks suspected her of having found it by the art of divination, and by invoking the aid of demons, and of having cast a spell over it. All that she was able to say did not remove their suspicions.[689]

Then they passed on to the sword she had captured from a Burgundian.

"I wore it at Compiègne," she said, "because it was good for dealing sound clouts and good buffets."[690] The buffet was a flat blow, the clout was a side stroke. Some moments later, on the subject of her banner, she said that, in order to avoid killing any one, she bore it herself when they charged the enemy. And she added: "I have never slain any one."[691]

The doctors found that her replies varied.[692] Of course they varied. But if like her every hour of the day and night the doctors had been seeing the heavens descending, if all their thoughts, all their instincts, good and bad, all their desires barely formulated, had been undergoing instant transformation into divine commands, their replies would likewise have varied, and they would have doubtless been in such a state of illusion that in their words and in their actions they would have displayed less good sense, less gentleness and less courage.

The examinations were long; they lasted between three and four hours.[693] Before closing this one, Maître Jean Beaupère wished to know whether Jeanne had been wounded at Orléans. This was an interesting point. It was generally admitted that witches lost their power when they shed blood. Finally, the doctors quibbled over the capitulation of Jargeau, and the court adjourned.[694]

A famous Norman clerk, Maître Jean Lohier, having come to Rouen, the Count Bishop of Beauvais commanded that he should be informed concerning the trial. On the first Saturday in Lent, the 24th of February, the Bishop summoned him to his house near Saint-Nicolas-le-Painteur, and invited him to give his opinion of the proceedings. The views of Maître Jean Lohier greatly disturbed the Bishop. Off he rushed to the doctors and masters, Jean Beaupère, Jacques de Touraine, Nicolas Midi, Pierre Maurice, Thomas de Courcelles, Nicolas Loiseleur, and said to them:

"Here's Lohier, who holds fine views concerning our trial! He wants to object to everything, and says that our proceedings are invalid. If we were to take his advice we should begin everything over again, and all we have done would be worthless! It is easy to see what he is aiming at. By Saint John, we will do nothing of the kind; we will go on with our trial now it is begun."

The next day, in the Church of Notre Dame, Guillaume Manchon met Maître Jean Lohier and asked him:

"Have you seen anything of the records of the trial?"

"I have," replied Maître Jean. "This trial is void. It is impossible to support it on many grounds: firstly, it is not in regular form."[695]

By that he meant that proceedings should not have been taken against Jeanne without preliminary inquiries concerning the probability of her guilt; either he did not know of the inquiries instituted by my Lord of Beauvais, or he deemed them insufficient.[696]

"Secondly," continued Maître Jean Lohier, "the judges and assessors when they are trying this case are shut up in the castle, where they are not free to utter their opinions frankly. Thirdly, the trial involves divers persons who are not called, notably it touches the reputation of the King of France, to whose party Jeanne belonged, yet neither he nor his representative is cited. Fourthly, neither documents nor definite written charges have been produced, wherefore this woman, this simple girl, is left to reply without guidance to so many masters, to such great doctors and on such grave matters, especially those concerning her revelations. For all these reasons the trial appears to me to be invalid." Then he added: "You see how they proceed. They will catch her if they can in her words. They take advantage of the statements in which she says, 'I know for certain,' concerning her apparitions. But if she were to say, 'It seems to me,' instead of 'I know for certain,' it is my opinion that no man could convict her. I perceive that the dominant sentiment which actuates them is one of hatred. Their intention is to bring her to her death. Wherefore I shall stay here no longer. I cannot witness it. What I say gives offence."[697]

That same day Maître Jean left Rouen.[698]

A somewhat similar incident occurred with regard to Maître Nicolas de Houppeville, a famous cleric. In conference with certain churchmen, he expressed the opinion that to appoint as Jeanne's judges members of the party hostile to her was not a correct method of procedure; and he added that Jeanne had already been examined by the clerks of Poitiers and by the Archbishop of Reims, the metropolitan of this very Bishop of Beauvais. Hearing of this expression of opinion, my Lord of Beauvais flew into a violent rage, and summoned Maître Nicolas to appear before him. The latter replied that the Official of Rouen was his superior, and that the Bishop of Beauvais was not his judge. If it be true, as is related, that Maître Nicolas was thereafter cast into the King's prison, it was doubtless for a reason more strictly judicial than that of having offended the Lord Bishop of Beauvais. It is more probable, however, that this famous cleric did not wish to act as assessor, and that he left Rouen in order to avoid being summoned to take part in the trial.[699]

Certain ecclesiastics, among others Maître Jean Pigache, Maître Pierre Minier, and Maître Richard de Grouchet, discovered long afterwards that being threatened they had given their opinions under the influence of fear. "We were present at that trial," they said, "but throughout the proceedings we were always contemplating flight."[700] As a matter of fact, no violence was done to any man's opinions, and such as refused to attend the trial were in no way molested. Threats! But why should there be any? Was it difficult to convict a witch in those days? Jeanne was no witch. But, then, neither were the others. Still, between

Jeanne and the other alleged witches there was this difference, that Jeanne had cast her spells in favour of the Armagnacs, and to convict her was to render a service to the English, who were the masters. This was a point to be taken into consideration; but there was something else which ought also to be borne in mind by thoughtful folk: such a conviction would at the same time offend the French, who were in a fair way to become the masters once more in the place of the English. These matters were very perplexing to the doctors; but the second consideration had less weight with them than the first; they had no idea that the French were so near reconquering Normandy.

The fifth session of the court took place in the usual chamber on the 1st of March, in the presence of fifty-eight assessors, of whom nine had not sat previously.[701]

The first question the examiner put Jeanne was:

"What say you of our Lord the Pope, and whom think you to be the true pope?"

She adroitly made answer by asking another question: "Are there two?"[702]

No, there were not two; Clement VIII's abdication had put an end to the schism; the great rift in the Church had been closed for thirteen years and all Christian nations recognized the Pope of Rome; even France who had become resigned to the disappearance of her Avignon popes. There was something, however, which neither the accused nor her judges knew; on that 1st of March, 1431, far from there being two popes, there was not even one; the Holy See had fallen vacant by the death of Martin V on the 20th of February, and the vacancy was only to be filled on the 3rd of March, by the election of Eugenius IV.[703]

The examiner in questioning Jeanne concerning the Holy See was not without a motive. That motive became obvious when he asked her whether she had not received a letter from the Count of Armagnac. She admitted having received the letter and having replied to it.

Copies of these two letters were included in the evidence to be used at the trial. They were read to Jeanne.

It appeared that the Count of Armagnac had asked the Maid by letter which of the three popes was the true one, and that Jeanne had replied to him, likewise by letter, that for the moment she had not time to answer, but that she would do so at her leisure when she should come to Paris.

Having heard these two letters read, Jeanne declared that the one attributed to her was only partially hers. And since she always dictated and could never read what had been taken down, it is conceivable that hasty words, uttered with her foot in the stirrup, may not have been accurately transcribed; but in a series of involved and contradictory replies she was unable to demonstrate how that which she had dictated differed from the written text;[704] and in itself the letter appears much more likely to have proceeded from an ignorant visionary than from a clerk who would have some knowledge, however little, of church affairs.

It contains certain words and turns of expression which are to be found in Jeanne's other letters. There can hardly be any doubt that this letter is by her; she had forgotten it. There is nothing surprising in that; her memory, as we have seen, was curiously liable to fail her.[705]

On this document the judges based the most serious of charges; they regarded it as furnishing proof of a most blamable temerity. What arrogance on the part of this woman, so it seemed to them, to claim to have been told by God himself that which the Church alone is entitled to teach! And to undertake by means of an inner illumination to point out the true pope, was that not to commit grave sin against the Bride of Christ, and with sacrilegious hand to rend the seamless robe of our Lord?

For once Jeanne saw clearly how her judges were endeavouring to entrap her, wherefore she twice declared her belief in the Sovereign Pontiff of Rome.[706] How bitterly she would have smiled had she known that the lights of the

University of Paris, these famous doctors who held it mortal sin to believe in the wrong pope, themselves believed in his Holiness about as much as they disbelieved in him; that at that very time certain of their number, Maître Thomas de Courcelles, so great a doctor, Maître Jean Beaupère, the examiner, Maître Nicolas Loiseleur, who acted the part of Saint Catherine, were hastening to despatch her, in order that they might bestride their mules and amble away to Bâle, there in the Synagogue of Satan to hurl thunderbolts against the Holy Apostolic See, and diabolically to decree the subjection of the Pope to the Council, the confiscation of his annates, dearer to him than the apple of his eye, and finally his own deposition.[707] Now would have been the time for her to have cried, with the voice of a simple soul, to the priests so keen to avenge upon her the Church's honour: "I am more of a Catholic than you!" And the words in her mouth would have been even more appropriate than on the lips of the Limousin clerk of old. Yet we must not reproach these clerics for having been good Gallicans at Bâle, but rather for having been cruel and hypocritical at Rouen.

In her prison the Maid prophesied before her guard, John Grey. Informed of these prophecies, the judges wished to hear them from Jeanne's own mouth.

"Before seven years have passed," she said to them, "the English shall lose a greater wager than any they lost at Orléans. They shall lose everything in France. They shall suffer greater loss than ever they have suffered in France, and that shall come to pass because God shall vouchsafe unto the French great victory."

"How do you know this?"

"I know it by revelation made unto me and that this shall befall within seven years. And greatly should I sorrow were it further delayed. I know it by revelation as surely as I know that you are before my eyes at this moment."

"When shall this come to pass?"

"I know neither the day nor the hour."

"But the year?"

"That ye shall not know for the present. But I should wish it to be before Saint John's Day."

"Did you not say that it should come to pass before Saint Martin in the winter?"

"I said that before Saint Martin in the winter many things should befall and it might be that the English would be discomfited."

Whereupon the examiner asked Jeanne whether when Saint Michael came to her he was accompanied by Saint Gabriel.

Jeanne replied: "I do not remember."[708]

She did not remember whether, in the multitude of angels who visited her, was the Angel Gabriel who had saluted Our Lady and announced unto her the salvation of mankind. So many angels and archangels had she seen that this one had not particularly impressed her.

After an answer of such perfect simplicity how could these priests proceed to question her on her visions? Were they not sufficiently edified? But no! These innocent answers whetted the examiner's zeal. With intense ardour and copious amplification, passing from angels to saints, he multiplied petty and insidious questions. Did you see the hair on their heads? Had they rings in their ears? Was there anything between their crowns and their hair? Was their hair long and hanging? Had they arms? How did they speak? What kind of voices had they?[709]

This last question touched on an important theological point. Demons, whose voices are as rasping as a cart wheel or a winepress screw, cannot imitate the sweet tones of saints.[710]

Jeanne replied that the Voice was beautiful, sweet, and soft, and spoke in French.

Whereupon she was asked craftily wherefore Saint Margaret did not speak English.

She replied: "How should she speak English, since she is not on the side of the English?"[711]

Two hundred years before, a poet of Champagne had said that the French language, which Our Lord created beautiful and graceful, was the language of Paradise.

She was afterwards asked concerning her rings. This was a hard matter; in those days there were many magic rings or rings bearing amulets. They were fashioned by magicians under the influence of planets; and, by means of wonder-working herbs and stones, these rings had spells cast upon them and received miraculous virtues. Constellation rings worked miracles. Jeanne, alas! had possessed but two poor rings, one of brass, inscribed with the names Jésus and Marie, which she received from her father and mother, the other her brother had given her. The Bishop kept the latter; the other had been taken from her by the Burgundians.[712]

An attempt was made to incriminate her in a pact made with the Devil near the Fairy Tree. She was not to be caught thus, but retorted by prophesying her deliverance and the destruction of her enemies. "Those who wish to banish me from this world may very likely leave it before me.... I know that my King will win the realm of France."

She was asked what she had done with her mandrake. She said she had never had one.[713]

Then the examiner appeared to be seized with curiosity concerning Saint Michael. "Was he clothed?"

She replied: "Doubt ye that Messire lacks wherewithal to clothe himself?"

"Had he hair?"

"Wherefore should he have cut it off?"

"Did he hold scales?"

"I don't know."[714]

Their object was to ascertain whether she saw Saint Michael as he was represented in the churches, with scales for weighing souls.[715]

When she said that at the sight of the Archangel it seemed to her she was not in a state of mortal sin, the examiner fell to arguing on the subject of her conscience. She replied like a true Christian.[716] Then he returned to the miracle of the sign, which had not been referred to since the first sitting, to the mystery of Chinon, to that wondrous crown, which Jeanne, following Saint Catherine of Alexandria, believed she had received from the hand of an angel. But she had promised Saint Catherine and Saint Margaret to say nothing about it.

"When you showed the King the sign was there any one with him?"

"I think there was no other person, albeit there were many folk not far off."

"Did you see a crown on the King's head when you gave him this sign?"

"I cannot say without committing perjury."

"Had your King a crown at Reims?"

"My King, methinketh, took with pleasure the crown he found at Reims. But afterwards a very rich crown was brought him. He did not wait for it, because he wished to hurry on the ceremony according to the request of the inhabitants of Reims who desired to rid their town of the burden of men-at-arms. If he had waited he would have had a crown a thousand times more rich."

"Have you seen that richer crown?"

"I cannot tell you without committing perjury. If I have not seen it I have heard tell how rich and how magnificent it is."[717]

Jeanne suffered intensely from being deprived of the sacraments. One day when Messire Jean Massieu, performing the office of ecclesiastical usher, was taking her before her judges, she asked him whether there were not on the way some church or chapel in which was the body of Our Lord Jesus Christ.[718]

Messire Jean Massieu, dean of Rouen, was a cleric of manners dissolute; his inveterate lewdness had involved him in difficulties with the Chapter and with the Official.[719] He may have been neither as brave nor as frank as he wished to make out, but he was not hard or pitiless.

He told his prisoner that there was a chapel on the way. And he pointed out to her the chapel of the castle.

Then she besought him urgently to take her into the chapel in order that she might worship Messire and pray.

Readily did Messire Jean Massieu consent; and he permitted her to kneel before the sanctuary. Devoutly bending, Jeanne offered her prayer.

The Lord Bishop, being informed of this incident, was highly displeased. He instructed the Usher that in the future such devotions must not be tolerated.

And the Promoter, Maître Jean d'Estivet, on his part, addressed many a reprimand to Messire Jean Massieu.

"Rascal," he said, "what possesses thee to allow an excommunicated whore to approach a church without permission? If ever thou doest the like again I will imprison thee in that tower, where for a month thou wilt see neither sun nor moon."

Messire Jean Massieu heeded not this threat. And the Promoter, perceiving this, himself took up his post at the chapel door when Jeanne went that way. Thus he prevented the hapless damsel from engaging in her devotions.[720]

The sixth sitting was held in the same court as before, in the presence of forty-one assessors, of whom six or seven were new, and among them was Maître Guillaume Erart, doctor in theology.[721]

In the beginning, the examiner asked Jeanne whether she had seen Saint Michael and the saints, and whether she had seen anything but their faces. He insisted: "You must say what you know."

"Rather than say all that I know, I would have my head cut off."[722]

They puzzled her with questions touching the nature of angelic bodies. She was simple; with her own eyes she had seen Saint Michael; she said so and could not say otherwise.

The examiner, now as always, informed of the words she had let fall in prison, asked her whether she had heard her Voices.

"Yes, in good sooth. They told me that I should be delivered. But I know neither the day nor the hour. And they told me to have good courage, and to be of good cheer."[723]

Of all this the judges believed nothing, because demonologists teach that witches lose their power when an officer of Holy Church lays hands upon them.

The examiner recurred to her man's dress. Then he endeavoured to find out whether she had cast spells over the banners of her companions in arms.

He sought out by what secret power she led the soldiers.

This power she was willing to reveal: "I said to them: 'Go on boldly against the English;' and at the same time I went myself."[724]

In this examination, which was the most diffuse and the most captious of all, the following curious question was put to the accused: "When you were before Jargeau, what was it you were wearing behind your helmet? Was there not something round?"[725]

At the siege of Jargeau she had been struck on the head by a huge stone which had not hurt her; and this her own party deemed miraculous.[726] Did the judges of Rouen imagine that she wore a golden halo, like the saints, and that this halo had protected her?

Later she was examined on a more ordinary subject, concerning a picture in the house of her host at Orléans, representing three women: Justice, Peace, Union.

Jeanne knew nothing about it;[727] she was no connoisseur in tapestry and in paintings, like the Duke of Bar and the Duke of Orléans; neither were her judges, not on this occasion at any rate. And if they were concerned about a picture in the house of Maître Boucher, it was not so much on account of the painting as of the doctrine. These three women that the wealthy Maître Boucher kept in his house were doubtless nude. The painters of those days depicted on small panels allegories and bathing scenes, and they painted nude women. Full foreheads, round heads, golden hair, short figures of small build but with embonpoint, their nudity minutely represented and but thinly veiled; many such were produced in Flanders and in Italy. The illustrious masters, to whom those pictures appeared corrupt and indecent, doubtless wished to reproach Jeanne with having looked at them in the house of the treasurer of the Duke of Orléans. It is not difficult to divine what were the doctors' suspicions when they are found asking Jeanne whether Saint Michael wore clothes, in what manner she greeted her saints, and how she gave them her rings to touch.[728]

They also wanted to make her admit that she had caused herself to be honoured as a saint. She disconcerted them by the following reply: "The poor folk came to me readily, because I did them no hurt, but aided them to the best of my power."[729]

Then the examination ranged over many and various subjects: Friar Richard; the children Jeanne had held over the baptismal fonts; the good wives of the town of Reims who touched rings with her; the butterflies caught in a standard at Château Thierry.[730]

In this town, certain of the Maid's followers were said to have caught butterflies in her standard. Now doctors in theology knew for a certainty that necromancers sacrificed butterflies to the devil. A century before, at Pamiers, the tribunal of the Holy Inquisition had condemned the Carmelite Pierre Recordi, who was accused of having celebrated such a sacrifice. He had killed a butterfly and the devil had revealed his presence by a breath of wind.[731] Jeanne's judges may have wished to involve her in similar fashion, or their design may have been quite different. In war a butterfly in the cap was a sign either of unconditional surrender or of the possession of a safe conduct.[732] Were the judges accusing her or her followers of having feigned to surrender in order treacherously to attack the enemy? They were quite capable of making such a charge. However that may be, the examiner passed on to inquire concerning a lost glove found by Jeanne in the town of Reims.[733] It was important to know whether it had been discovered by magic art. Then the magistrate returned to several of the capital charges of the trial: communion received in man's dress; the hackney of the Bishop of Senlis, which Jeanne had taken, thus committing a kind of sacrilege; the discoloured child she had brought back to life at Lagny; Catherine de La Rochelle, who had recently borne witness against her before the Official at Paris; the siege of La Charité which she had been obliged to raise; the leap which she had made in her despair from the keep of Beaurevoir, and, finally, certain blasphemy she was falsely accused of having uttered at Soissons concerning Captain Bournel.[734]

Then the Lord Bishop declared the examination concluded. He added, however, that should it appear expedient to interrogate Jeanne more fully, certain doctors and masters would be appointed for that purpose.[735]

Accordingly, on Saturday, March the 10th, Maître Jean de la Fontaine, the Bishop's commissioner, went to the prison. He was accompanied by Nicolas Midi, Gérard Feuillet, Jean Fécard, and Jean Massieu.[736] The first point touched upon at this inquiry was the sortie from Compiègne. The priests took great pains to prove to Jeanne that her Voices must be bad or that she must have failed to understand them since her obedience to them had brought about her destruction. Jacques Gélu[737] and Jean Gerson had foreseen this dilemma and had met it in anticipation with elaborate theological arguments.[738] She was examined concerning the paintings on her standard, and she replied:

"Saint Catherine and Saint Margaret bade me take the standard and bear it boldly, and have painted upon it the King of Heaven. And this, much against my will, I told to my King. Touching its meaning I know nought else."[739]

They tried to make her out avaricious, proud, and ostentatious because she possessed a shield and arms, a stable, chargers, demi-chargers, and hackneys, and because she had money with which to pay her household, some ten to twelve thousand livres.[740] But the point on which they questioned her most closely was the sign which had already been twice discussed in the public examinations. On this subject the doctors displayed an insatiable curiosity. For the sign was the exact reverse of the coronation at Reims; it was an anointing, not with divine unction but with magic charm, the crowning of the King of France by a witch. Maître Jean de la Fontaine had this advantage over Jeanne, he knew what she was going to say and what she wished to conceal. "What is the sign that was given to your King?"

"It is beautiful and honourable and very credible; it is the best and the richest in the world...."

"Does it still last?"

"It is well to know that it lasts and will last for a thousand years. My sign is in the King's treasury."

"Is it of gold or silver, or of precious stones, or is it a crown?"

"Nothing more will I tell unto you and no man can devise anything so rich as is this sign. Nevertheless, the sign that you need is that God should deliver me out of your hands and no surer sign can he send you...."

"When the sign came to your King what reverence did you make to it?"

"I thanked Our Lord for having delivered me from the troubles caused me by the clerks of our party, who were arguing against me. And I knelt down several times. An angel from God and from none other gave the sign to my King. And many times did I give thanks to Our Lord. The clerks ceased to attack me when they had seen the said sign."[741]

"Did the churchmen of your party behold the sign?"

"When my King and such as were with him had seen the sign and also the angel who gave it, I asked my King whether he were pleased, and he replied that he was. Then I departed and went into a little chapel near by. I have since heard that after my departure more than three hundred persons saw the sign. For love of me and in order that I should be questioned no further, God was pleased to permit this sign to be seen by all those of my party who did see it."

"Did your King and you make any reverence to the angel when he brought the sign?"

"Yes, for my part, I did. I knelt and took off my hood."[742]

Chapter XII
The trial for lapse (*continued*)

N Monday, the 12th of March, Brother Jean Lemaistre received from Brother Jean Graverent, Inquisitor of France, an order to proceed against and to pronounce the final sentence on a certain woman, named Jeanne, commonly called the Maid.[743] On that same day, in the morning, Maître Jean de la Fontaine, in presence of the Bishop, for the second time examined Jeanne in her prison.[744]

He first returned to the sign. "Did not the angel who brought the sign speak?"

"Yes, he told my King that he must set me to work in order that the country might soon be relieved."

"Was the angel, who brought the sign, the angel who first appeared unto you or another?"

"It was always the same and never did he fail me."

"But inasmuch as you have been taken hath not the angel failed you with regard to the good things of this life?"

"Since it is Our Lord's good pleasure, I believe it was best for me to be taken."

"In the good things of grace hath not your angel failed you?"

"How can he have failed me when he comforteth me every day?"[745]

Maître Jean de la Fontaine then put her a subtle question and one as nearly approaching humour as was permissible in an ecclesiastical trial.

"Did Saint Denys ever appear to you?"[746]

Saint Denys, patron of the most Christian kings, Saint Denys, the war cry of France, had allowed the English to take his abbey, that rich church, to which queens came to receive their crowns, and wherein kings had their burying. He had turned English and Burgundian, and it was not likely he would come to hold converse with the Maid of the Armagnacs.

To the question: "Were you addressing God himself when you promised to remain a virgin?" she replied:

"It sufficed to give the promise to the messengers of God, to wit, Saint Catherine and Saint Margaret."[747]

They had sought to entrap her, for a vow must be made directly to God. However, it might be argued, that it is lawful to promise a good thing to an angel or to a man; and that this good thing, thus promised, may form the substance of a vow. One vows to God what one has promised to the saints. Pierre of Tarentaise (iv, dist: xxviii, a. 1) teaches that all vows should be made to God: either to himself directly or through the mediation of his saints.[748]

According to a statement made during the inquiry, Jeanne had given a promise of marriage to a young peasant. Now the examiner endeavoured to prove that she had been at liberty to break her vow of virginity made in an irregular form; but Jeanne maintained that she had not promised marriage, and she added:

"The first time I heard my Voices, I vowed to remain a virgin as long as it should please God."

But this time it was Saint Michael and not the saints who had appeared to her.[749] She herself found it difficult to unravel the tangled web of her dreams and her ecstasies. And from these vague visions of a child the doctors were laboriously essaying to elaborate a capital charge.

Then a very grave and serious question was asked her by the examiner: "Did you speak to your priest or to any other churchman of those visions which you say were vouchsafed to you?"

"No, I spoke of them only to Robert de Baudricourt and to my King."[750]

The vavasour of Champagne, a man of mature years and sound sense, when in the days of King John, he, like the Maid, had heard a Voice in the fields bidding him go to his King, went straightway and told his priest. The latter commanded him to fast for three days, to do penance, and then to return to the field where the Voice had spoken to him.

The vavasour obeyed. Again the Voice was heard repeating the command it had previously given. The peasant again told his priest, who said to him: "My brother, thou and I will abstain and fast for three days, and I will pray for thee to Our Lord Jesus Christ." This they did, and on the fourth day the good man returned to the field. After the Voice had spoken for the third time, the priest enjoined his parishioner to go forthwith and fulfil his mission, since such was the will of God.[751]

There is no doubt that, according to all appearances, this vavasour had acted with greater wisdom than La Romée's daughter. By concealing her visions from the priest the latter had slighted the authority of the Church Militant. Still there might be urged in her defence the words of the Apostle Paul, that where the spirit of God is there is liberty.[752] If ye be led of the Spirit ye are not under the law.[753] Was she a heretic or was she a saint? Therein lay the whole trial.

Then came this remarkable question: "Have you received letters from Saint Michael or from your Voices?"

She replied: "I have not permission to tell you; but in a week I will willingly say all I know."[754]

Such was her manner of speaking when there was something she wanted to conceal but not to deny. The question must have been embarrassing therefore. Moreover, these interrogatories were based on a good store of facts either true or false; and in the questions addressed to the Maid we may generally discern a certain anticipation of her replies. What were those letters from Saint Michael and her other saints, the existence of which she did not deny, but which were never produced by her judges? Did certain of her party send them in the hope that she would carry out their intentions, while under the impression that she was obeying divine commands?

Without insisting further for the present, the examiner passed on to another grievance:

"Have not your Voices called you daughter of God, daughter of the Church, great-hearted damsel?"

"Before the siege of Orléans and since, every day when they speak to me, many times have they called me *Jeanne the Maid, daughter of God.*"[755]

The examination was suspended and resumed in the afternoon.

Maître Jean de la Fontaine questioned Jeanne concerning a dream of her father, of which the judges had been informed in the preliminary inquiry.[756]

Sad it is to reflect that when Jeanne was accused of the sin of having broken God's commandment, "Thou shalt honour thy father and thy mother," neither her mother nor any of her kin asked to be heard as witnesses. And yet there were churchmen in her family;[757] but a trial on a question of faith struck terror into all hearts.

Again her man's dress was reverted to, and not for the last time.[758] We marvel at the profound meditations into which the Maid's doublet and hose plunged these clerics. They contemplated them with gloomy terror and in the light of the precepts of Deuteronomy.

Thereafter they questioned her touching the Duke of Orléans. Their object was to show from her own replies that her Voices had deceived her when they promised the prisoner's deliverance. Here they easily succeeded. Then she pleaded that she had not had sufficient time.

"Had I continued for three years without let or hindrance I should have delivered him."

In her revelations there had been mentioned a term shorter than three years and longer than one.[759]

Questioned again touching the sign vouchsafed to her King, she replied that she would take counsel with Saint Catherine.

On the morrow, Tuesday, the 13th of March, the Bishop and the Vice-Inquisitor went to her prison. For the first time the Vice-Inquisitor opened his mouth:[760] "Have you promised and sworn to Saint Catherine that you will not tell this sign?"

He spoke of the sign given to the King. Jeanne replied:

"I have sworn and I have promised that I will not myself reveal this sign, because I was too urgently pressed to tell it. I vow that never again will I speak of it to living man."[761]

Then she continued forthwith: "The sign was that the Angel assured my King, when bringing him the crown, that he should have the whole realm of France, with God's help and my labours, and that he should set me to work. That is to say, he should grant me men-at-arms. Otherwise he would not be so soon crowned and anointed."

"In what manner did the Angel bring the crown? Did he place it on your King's head?"

"It was given to an archbishop, to the Archbishop of Reims, meseemeth in the King's presence. The said Archbishop received it and gave it to the King; and I myself was present; and it is put in the King's treasury."

"To what place was the crown brought?"

"To the King's chamber in the castle of Chinon."

"On what day and at what hour?"

"The day I know not, the hour was full day. No further recollection have I of the hour or of the month. But meseemeth it was the month of April or March; it will be two years this month or next April. It was after Easter."[762]

"On the first day that you saw the sign did your King see it?"

"Yes. He had it the same day."

"Of what was the crown made?"

"It is well to know that it was of fine gold, and so rich that I cannot count its riches; and the crown meant that he would hold the realm of France."

"Were there jewels in it?"

"I have told you that I do not know."

"Did you touch it or kiss it?"

"No."

"Did the Angel who bore it come from above, or did he come from the earth?"

"He came from above. I understand that he came by Our Lord's command, and he came in by the door of the chamber."

"Did the Angel come along the ground, walking from the door of the room?"

"When he was come before the King he did him reverence, bowing low before him and uttering the words concerning the sign which I have already repeated; and thereupon the Angel recalled to the King's mind the great patience he had had in the midst of the long tribulation that had befallen him; and as he came towards the King the Angel walked and touched the ground."

"How far was it from the door to the King?"

"Methinketh it was a full lance's length;[763] and as he had come so he returned. When the Angel came, I accompanied him and went with him up the steps into the King's chamber; and the Angel went in first. And I said to the King: 'Sire, behold your sign; take it.'"[764]

In a spiritual sense we may say that this fable is true. This crown, which "flowers sweetly and will flower sweetly if it be well guarded,"[765] is the crown of victory. When the Maid beholds the Angel who brought it, it is her own image that appears before her. Had not a theologian of her own party said that she might be called an angel? Not that she had the nature of an angel, but she did the work of one.[766]

She began to describe the angels who had come with her to the King:

"So far as I saw, certain among them were very like, the others different. Some had wings. Some wore crowns, others did not. And they were with Saint Catherine and Saint Margaret, and they accompanied the Angel of whom I have spoken and the other angels also into the chamber of the King."[767]

And thus for a long time, as she was pressed by her interrogator, she continued to tell these marvellous stories one after another.

When she was asked for the second time whether the Angel had written her letters, she denied it.[768] But now it was the Angel who bore the crown and not Saint Michael who was in question. And despite her having said they were one and the same, she may have distinguished between them. Therefore we shall never know whether she did receive letters from Saint Michael the Archangel, or from Saint Catherine and from Saint Margaret.

Thereafter the examiner inquired touching a cup lost at Reims and found by Jeanne as well as the gloves.[769] Saints sometimes condescended to find things that had been lost, as is proved by the example of Saint Antony of Padua. It was always with the help of God. Necromancers imitated their powers by invoking the aid of demons and by profaning sacred things.

She was also questioned concerning the priest who had a concubine. Here again she was reproached with being possessed of a magic gift of clairvoyance. It was by magic she had known that this priest had a concubine. Many other such things were reported of her. For example, it was said that at the sight of a certain loose woman she knew that this woman had killed her child.[770]

Then recurred the same old questions: "When you went to the attack on Paris did you receive a revelation from your Voices? Was it revealed to you that you should go against La Charité? Was it a revelation that caused you to go to Pont-l'Evêque?"

She denied that she had then received any revelation from her Voices.

The last question was: "Did you not say before Paris, 'Surrender the town in the name of Jesus'?"

She answered that she had not spoken those words, but had said, "Surrender the town to the King of France."[771]

The Parisians who were engaged in repelling the attack had heard her saying, "Surrender to us speedily in the name of Jesus." These words are consistent with all we know of Jeanne in the early years of her career. She believed it to be the will of Messire that the towns of the realm should surrender to her, whom he had sent to reconquer them. We have noticed already that at the time of her trial Jeanne had completely lost touch with her early illuminations and that she spoke in quite another language.

On the morrow, Wednesday, the 14th of March, there were two more examinations in the prison. The morning interrogatory turned on the leap from Beaurevoir. She confessed to having leapt without permission from her Voices, preferring to die rather than to fall into the hands of the English.[772]

She was accused of blasphemy against God; but that was false.[773]

The Bishop intervened: "You have said that we, the Lord Bishop, run great danger by bringing you to trial. Of what danger were you speaking? In what peril do we stand, we, your judges, and others?"

"I said to my Lord of Beauvais: 'You declare that you are my judge, I know not if you be. But take heed that ye judge not wrongly, for thus would ye run great danger; and I warn you, so that if Our Lord chastise you for it, I have done my duty by warning you.'"

"What is this peril or this danger?"

"Saint Catherine has told me that I shall have succour. I know not whether it will be my deliverance from prison, or whether, during the trial, some tumult shall arise whereby I shall be delivered. I think it will be either one or the other. My Voices most often tell me I shall be delivered by a great victory. And afterwards they say to me: 'Be thou resigned, grieve not at thy martyrdom; thou shalt come in the end to the kingdom of Paradise.' This do my Voices say unto me simply and absolutely. I mean to say without fail. And I call my martyrdom the trouble and anguish I suffer in prison. I know not whether still greater sufferings are before me, but I wait on the Lord."[774]

It would seem that thus her Voices promised the Maid at once a spiritual and a material deliverance, but the two could hardly occur together. This reply, expressive alike of fear and of illusion, was one to call forth pity from the hardest; and yet her judges regarded it merely as a means whereby they might entrap her. Feigning to understand that from her revelations she derived a heretical confidence in her eternal salvation, the examiner put to her an old question in a new form. She had already given it a saintly answer. He inquired whether her Voices had told her that she would finally come to the kingdom of Paradise if she continued in the assurance that she would be saved and not condemned in Hell. To this she replied with that perfect faith with which her Voices inspired her: "I believe what my Voices have told me touching my salvation as strongly as if I were already in Paradise."

Such a reply was heretical. The examiner, albeit he was not accustomed to discuss the Maid's replies, could not forbear remarking that this one was of great importance.[775]

Accordingly in the afternoon of that same day, she was shown a consequence of her error; to wit, that if she received from her Voices the assurance of eternal salvation she needed not to confess.[776]

On this occasion Jeanne was questioned touching the affair of Franquet d'Arras. The Bailie of Senlis had done wrong in asking the Maid for her prisoner,[777] the Lord Franquet,[778] in order to put him to death, and Jeanne's judges now incriminated her.

The examiner pointed out the mortal sins with which the accused might be charged: first, having attacked Paris on a feast-day; second, having stolen the hackney of the Lord Bishop of Senlis; third, having leapt from Beaurevoir; fourth, having worn man's dress; fifth, having consented to the death of a prisoner of war. Touching all these matters, Jeanne did not believe that she had committed mortal sin; but with regard to the leap from Beaurevoir she acknowledged that she was wrong, and that she had asked God to forgive her.[779]

It was sufficiently established that the accused had fallen into religious error. The tribunal of the Inquisition, out of its abounding mercy, desired the salvation of the sinner. Wherefore on the morning of the very next day, Thursday, the 15th of March, my Lord of Beauvais exhorted Jeanne to submit to the Church, and essayed to make her understand that she ought to obey the Church Militant, for the Church Militant was one thing and the Church Triumphant another. Jeanne listened to him dubiously.[780] On that day she was again questioned touching her flight from the château of Beaulieu and her intention to leave the tower without the permission of my Lord of Beauvais. As to the latter she was firmly resolute.

"Were I to see the door open, I would go, and it would be with the permission of Our Lord. I firmly believe that if I were to see the door open and if my guards and the other English were beyond power of resistance, I should regard it as my permission and as succour sent unto me by Our Lord. But without permission I would not go, save that I might essay to go, in order to know whether it were Our Lord's will. The proverb says: 'Help thyself and God will help thee.'[781] This I say so that, if I were to go, it should not be said I went without permission."[782]

Then they reverted to the question of her wearing man's dress.

"Which would you prefer, to wear a woman's dress and hear mass, or to continue in man's dress and not to hear mass?"

"Promise me that I shall hear mass if I am in woman's dress, and then I will answer you."

"I promise you that you shall hear mass when you are in woman's dress."

"And what do you say if I have promised and sworn to our King not to put off these clothes? Nevertheless, I say unto you: 'Have me a robe made, long enough to touch the ground, but without a train. I will go to mass in it; then, when I come back, I will return to my present clothes.'"

"You must wear woman's dress altogether and without conditions."

"Send me a dress like that worn by your burgess's daughters, to wit, a long *houppelande*; and I will take it and even a woman's hood to go and hear mass. But with all my heart I entreat you to leave me these clothes I am now wearing, and let me hear mass without changing anything."[783]

Her aversion to putting off man's dress is not to be explained solely by the fact that this dress preserved her best against the violence of the men-at-arms; it is possible that no such objection existed. She was averse to wearing woman's dress because she had not received permission from her Voices; and we may easily divine why not. Was she not a chieftain of war? How humiliating for such an one to wear petticoats like a townsman's wife! And above all things just now, when at any moment the French might come and deliver her by some great feat of arms. Ought they not to find their Maid in man's attire, ready to put on her armour and fight with them?

Thereafter the examiner asked her whether she would submit to the Church, whether she made a reverence to her Voices, whether she believed the saints, whether she offered them lighted candles, whether she obeyed them, whether in war she had ever done anything without their permission or contrary to their command.[784]

Then they came to the question which they held to be the most difficult of all:

"If the devil were to take upon himself the form of an angel, how would you know whether he were a good angel or a bad?"

She replied with a simplicity which appeared presumptuous: "I should easily discern whether it were Saint Michael or an imitation of him."[785]

Two days later, on Saturday, the 17th of March, Jeanne was examined in her prison both morning and evening.[786]

Hitherto she had been very loath to describe the countenance and the dress of the angel and the saints who had visited her in the village. Maître Jean de la Fontaine endeavoured to obtain some light on this subject.

"In what form and semblance did Saint Michael come to you? Was he tall and how was he clothed?"

"He came in the form of a true *prud'homme*."[787]

Jeanne was not one to believe she saw the Archangel in a long doctor's robe or wearing a cope of gold. Moreover it was not thus that he figured in the churches. There he was represented in painting and in sculpture, clothed in glittering armour, with a golden crown on his helmet.[788] In such guise did he appear to her "in the form of a right true *prud'homme*," to take a word from the *Chanson de Roland*, where a great sword thrust is called the thrust of a *prud'homme*. He came to her in the garb of a great knight, like Arthur and Charlemagne, wearing full armour.

Once again the examiner put to Jeanne that question on which her life or death depended:

"Will you submit all your deeds and sayings, good or bad, to the judgment of our mother, Holy Church?"

"As for the Church, I love her and would maintain her with all my power, for religion's sake," the Maid replied; "and I am not one to be kept from church and from hearing mass. But as for the good works which I have wrought, and touching my coming, for them I must give an account to the King of Heaven, who has sent me to Charles, son of Charles, King of France. And you will see that the French will shortly accomplish a great work, to which God will appoint them, in which they will shake nearly all France. I say it in order that when it shall come to pass, it may be remembered that I have said it."[789]

But she was unable to name the time when this great work should be accomplished; and Maître Jean de la Fontaine returned to the point on which Jeanne's fate depended.

"Will you submit to the judgment of the Church?"

"I appeal to Our Lord, who hath sent me, to Our Lady and to all the blessed saints in Paradise. To my mind Our Lord and his Church are one, and no distinction should be made. Wherefore do you essay to make out that they are not one?"

In justice to Maître Jean de la Fontaine we are bound to admit the lucidity of his reply. "There is the Church Triumphant, in which are God, his saints, the angels and the souls that are saved," he said. "There is also the Church Militant, which is our Holy Father, the Pope, the Vicar of God on earth; the cardinals, the prelates of the Church and the clergy, with all good Christians and Catholics; and this Church in its assembly cannot err, for it is moved by the Holy Ghost. Will you appeal to the Church Militant?"

"I am come to the King of France from God, from the Virgin Mary and all the blessed saints in Paradise and from the Church Victorious above and by their command. To this Church I submit all the good deeds I have done and shall do. As to replying whether I will submit to the Church Militant, for the present, I will make no further answer."[790]

Again she was offered a woman's dress in which to hear mass; she refused it.

"As for a woman's dress, I will not take it yet, not until it be Our Lord's will. And if it should come to pass that I be taken to judgment and there divested of my clothes, I beg my lords of the Church the favour of a woman's smock and covering for my head. I would rather die than deny what Our Lord hath caused me to do. I believe firmly that Our Lord will not let it come to pass that I should be cast so low, and that soon I shall have help from God, and that by a miracle."

Thereafter the following questions were put to her: "Do you not believe to-day that fairies are evil spirits?"

"I do not know."

"Do you know whether Saint Catherine and Saint Margaret hate the English?"

"They love what Our Lord loves and hate what God hates."

"Does God hate the English?"

"Touching the love or hatred of God for the English and what he will do for their souls I know nothing. But I do know that they will all be driven out of France, save those who die there, and that God will send victory to the French and defeat to the English."

"Was God on the side of the English when they prospered in France?"

"I know not whether God hated the French. But I believe that he permitted them to be beaten for their sins, if they were in sin."[791]

Jeanne was asked certain questions touching the banner on which she had caused angels to be painted.

She replied that she had had angels painted as she had seen them represented in churches.[792]

At this point the examination was adjourned. The last interrogation in the prison[793] took place after dinner. She had now endured fifteen in twenty-five days, but her courage never flagged. This last time the subjects were more than usually diverse and confused. First, the examiner essayed to discover by what charms and evil practices good fortune and victory had attended the standard painted with angelic figures. Then he wanted to know wherefore the clerks put on Jeanne's letters the sacred names of Jésus and Marie.[794]

Then came the following subtle question: "Do you believe that if you were married your Voices would come to you?"

It was well known that she dearly cherished her virginity. Certain of her words might be interpreted to mean that she considered this virginity to be the cause of her good fortune; wherefore her examiners were curious to know whether if she were adroitly approached she might not be brought to cast scorn on the married state and to condemn intercourse between husbands and wives. Such a condemnation would have been a grievous error, savouring of the heresy of the Cathari.[795]

She replied: "I know not and I appeal to Our Lord."[796] Then there followed another question much more dangerous for one who like Jeanne loved her King with all her heart.

"Do you think and firmly believe that your King did right to kill or cause to be killed my Lord of Burgundy?"

"It was sore pity for the realm of France."[797]

Then did the examiner put to her this grave question: "Do you hold yourself bound to answer the whole truth to the Pope, God's Vicar, on all that may be asked you touching religion and your conscience?"

"I demand to be taken before him. Then will I make unto him such answer as behoveth."[798]

These words involved an appeal to the Pope, and such an appeal was lawful. "In doubtful matters touching on religion," said St. Thomas, "there ought always to be an appeal to the Pope or to the General Council." If Jeanne's appeal were not in regular judicial form, it was not her fault. She was ignorant of legal matters and neither guide nor counsel had been granted to her. To the best of her knowledge, and according to wont and justice, she appealed to the common father of the faithful.

The doctors and masters were silent. And thus was closed against the accused the one way of deliverance remaining to her. She was now hopelessly lost. It is not surprising that Jeanne's judges, who were partisans of England, ignored her right of appeal; but it is surprising that the doctors and masters of the French party, the clerks of the provinces loyal to King Charles, did not all and with one voice sign an appeal and demand that the Maid, who had been judged worthy by her examiners at Poitiers, should be taken before the Pope and the Council.

Instead of replying to Jeanne's request, the examiners inquired further concerning those much discussed magic rings and apparitions of demons.[799]

"Did you ever kiss and embrace the Saints, Catherine and Margaret?"

"I embraced them both."

"Were they of a sweet savour?"

"It is well to know. Yea, their savour was sweet."

"When embracing them did you feel heat or anything else?"

"I could not have embraced them without feeling and touching them."

"What part did you kiss, face or feet?"

"It is more fitting to kiss their feet than their faces."

"Did you not give them chaplets of flowers?"

"I have often done them honour by crowning with flowers their images in churches. But to those who appeared to me never have I given flowers as far as I can remember."

"Know you aught of those who consort with fairies?"

"I have never done so nor have I known anything about them. Yet I have heard of them and that they were seen on Thursdays; but I do not believe it, and to me it seems sorcery."[800]

Then came a question touching her standard, deemed enchanted by her judges. It elicited one of those epigrammatic replies she loved.

"Wherefore was your standard rather than those of the other captains carried into the church of Reims?"

"It had been in the contest, wherefore should it not share the prize?"[801]

Now that the inquiries and examinations were concluded, it was announced that the preliminary trial was at an end. The so-called trial in ordinary opened on the Tuesday after Palm

Sunday, the 27th of March, in a room near the great hall of the castle.[802]

Before ordering the deed of accusation to be read, my Lord of Beauvais offered Jeanne the aid of an advocate.[803] If this offer had been postponed till then, it was doubtless because in his opinion Jeanne had not previously needed such aid. It is well known that a heretic's advocate, if he would himself escape falling into heresy, must strictly limit his methods of defence. During the preliminary inquiry he must confine himself to discovering the names of the witnesses for the prosecution and to making them known to the accused. If the heretic pleaded guilty then it was useless to grant him an advocate.[804] Now my Lord maintained that the accusation was founded not on the evidence of witnesses but on the avowals of the accused. And this was doubtless his reason for not offering Jeanne an advocate before the opening of the trial in ordinary, which bore upon matters of doctrine.

The Lord Bishop thus addressed the Maid: "Jeanne," said he, "all persons here present are churchmen of consummate knowledge, whose will and intention it is to proceed against you in all piety and kindness, seeking neither vengeance nor corporal chastisement, but your instruction and your return into the way of truth and salvation. As you are neither learned nor sufficiently instructed in letters or in the difficult matters which are to be discussed, to take counsel of yourself, touching what you should do or reply, we offer you to choose as your advocate one or more of those present, as you will. If you will not choose, then one shall be appointed for you by us, in order that he may advise you touching what you may do or say...."[805]

Considering what the method of procedure was, this was a gracious offer. And even though my Lord of Beauvais obliged the accused to choose from among the counsellors and assessors, whom he had himself summoned to the trial, he did more than he was bound to do. The choice of a counsel did not belong to the accused; it belonged to the judge, whose duty it was to appoint an honest, upright person. Moreover, it was permissible for an ecclesiastical judge to refuse to the end to grant the accused any counsel whatsoever. Nicolas Eymeric, in his *Directorium*, decides that the Bishop and the Inquisitor, acting conjointly, may constitute authority sufficient for the interpretation of the law and may proceed informally, *de plano*, dispensing with the ceremony of appointing counsel and all the paraphernalia of a trial.[806]

We may notice that my Lord of Beauvais offered the accused an advocate on the ground of her ignorance of things divine and human, but without taking her youthfulness into account. In other courts of law proceedings against a minor – that is, a person under twenty-five – who was not assisted by an advocate, were legally void.[807] If this rule had been binding in Inquisitorial procedure the Bishop, by his offer of legal aid, would have avoided any breach of this rule; and as the choice of an advocate lay with him, he might well have done so without running any risk. "Our justice is not like theirs," Bernard Gui rightly said, when he was comparing inquisitorial procedure with that of the other ecclesiastical courts which conformed to the Roman law.

Jeanne did not accept the judge's offer: "First," she said, "touching what you admonish me for my good and in matters of religion, I thank you and the company here assembled. As for the advocate you offer me, I also thank you, but it is not my intent to depart from the counsel of Our Lord. As for the oath you wish me to take, I am ready to swear to speak the truth in all that concerns your suit."[808]

Thereupon Maître Thomas de Courcelles began to read in French the indictment which the Promoter had drawn up in seventy articles.[809] This text set forth in order the deeds with which Jeanne had already been reproached and which were groundlessly held to have been confessed by her and duly proved. There were no less than seventy distinct charges of horrible crimes committed against religion and Holy Mother Church. Questioned on each article, Jeanne with heroic candour repeated her previous replies. The tedious reading of this long accusation was continued and completed on the 28th of March, the Wednesday after Palm Sunday.[810] As was her wont, she asked for delay in order to reply on certain points. On Easter Eve, the 31st of March, the time granted having expired, my Lord of Beauvais went to the prison, and, in the presence of the doctors and masters of the University, demanded the promised replies. They nearly all touched on the one accusation which included all the rest, the heresy in which all heresies were comprehended, – the refusal to obey the Church Militant. Jeanne finally declared her resolve to appeal to Our Lord rather than to any man; this was to set at naught the authority of the Pope and the Council.[811]

The doctors and masters of the University of Paris advised that an epitome should be made of the Promoter's voluminous indictment, its chief points selected, and the seventy charges considerably reduced.[812] Maître Nicolas Midi, doctor in theology, performed this task and submitted it when done to the judges and assessors.[813] One of them proposed emendations. Brother Jacques of Touraine, a friar of the Franciscan order, who was charged to draw up the document in its final stage, admitted most of the corrections requested.[814] In this wise the incriminating propositions,[815] which the judges claimed, but claimed falsely, to have derived from the replies of the accused, were resolved into twelve articles.[816]

These twelve articles were not communicated to Jeanne. On Thursday, the 12th of April, twenty-one masters and doctors met in the chapel of the Bishop's Palace, and, after having examined the articles, engaged in a conference, the result of which was unfavourable to the accused.[817]

According to them, the apparitions and revelations of which she boasted came not from God. They were human inventions, or the work of an evil spirit. She had not received signs sufficient to warrant her believing in them. In the case of this woman these doctors and masters discovered lies; a lack of verisimilitude; faith lightly given; superstitious divinings; deeds scandalous and irreligious; sayings rash, presumptuous, full of boasting; blasphemies against God and his saints. They found her to have lacked piety in her behaviour towards father and mother; to have come short in love towards her neighbour; to have been addicted to idolatry, or at any rate to the invention of lying tales and to schismatic conversation destructive of the unity, the authority and the power of the Church; and, finally, to have been skilled in the black art and to have strongly inclined to heresy.[818]

Had she not been sustained and comforted by her heavenly Voices, the Voices of her own heart, Jeanne would never have endured to the end of this terrible trial. Not only was she being tortured at once by the princes of the Church and the rascals of the army, but her sufferings of body and mind were such as could never have been borne by any ordinary human being. Yet she suffered them without her constancy, her faith, her divine hope, one might almost say her cheerfulness, ever being diminished. Finally she gave way; her physical strength, but not her courage, was exhausted; she fell a victim to an illness which was expected to be fatal. She seemed near her end, or rather, alas! near her release.[819]

On Wednesday, the 18th of April, my Lord of Beauvais and the Vice-Inquisitor of the Faith went to her with divers doctors and masters to exhort her in all charity; she was still very seriously sick.[820] My Lord of Beauvais represented to her that when on certain difficult matters she had been examined before persons of great wisdom, many things she had said had been noted as contrary to religion. Wherefore, considering that she was but an unlettered woman, he offered to provide her with men learned and upright who would instruct her. He requested the doctors present to give her salutary counsel, and he invited her herself, if any other such persons were known to her, to indicate them, promising to summon them without fail.

"The Church," he added, "never closes her heart against those who will return to her."

Jeanne answered that she thanked him for what he had said for her salvation, and she added: "Meseemeth, that seeing the sickness in which I lie, I am in great danger of death. If it be thus, then may God do with me according to his good pleasure. I demand that ye permit me to confess, that ye also give me the body of my Saviour and bury me in holy ground."

My Lord of Beauvais represented to her that if she would receive the sacraments she must submit to the Church.

"If my body die in prison," she replied, "I depend on you to have it put in holy ground; if you do not, then I appeal to Our Lord."[821]

Then she vehemently maintained the truth of the revelations she had received from God, Saint Michael, Saint Catherine, and Saint Margaret.

And when she was asked yet again whether she would submit herself and her acts to Holy Mother Church, she replied: "Whatever happens to me, I will never do or say aught save what I have already said at the trial."[822]

The doctors and masters one after the other exhorted her to submit to Holy Mother Church. They quoted numerous passages from Holy Writ. They promised her the body of Our Lord if she would obey; but she remained resolute.

"Touching this submission," she said, "I will reply naught save what I have said already. I love God, I serve him, I am a good Christian, and I wish with all my power to aid and support Holy Church."[823]

In times of great need recourse was had to processions. "Do you not wish," she was asked, "that a fine and famous procession be ordained to restore you to a good estate if you be not therein?"

She replied, "I desire the Church and all Catholics to pray for me."[824]

Among the doctors consulted there were many who recommended that she should be again instructed and charitably admonished. On Wednesday, the 2nd of May, sixty-three reverend doctors and masters met in the Robing Room of the castle.[825] She was brought in, and Maître Jean de Castillon, doctor in theology, Archdeacon of Évreux,[826] read a document in French, in which the deeds and sayings with which Jeanne was reproached were summed up in six articles. Then many doctors and masters addressed to her in turn admonitions and charitable counsels. They exhorted her to submit to the Church Militant Universal, to the Holy Father the Pope and to the General Council. They warned her that if the Church abandoned her, her soul would stand in great peril of the penalty of eternal fire, whilst her body might be burned in an earthly fire, and that by the sentence of other judges.

Jeanne replied as before.[827] On the morrow, Thursday, the 3rd of May, the day of the Invention of the Holy Cross, the Archangel Gabriel appeared to her. She was not sure whether she had seen him before. But this time she had no doubt. Her Voices told her that it was he, and she was greatly comforted.

That same day she asked her Voices whether she should submit to the Church and obey the exhortation of the clerics.

Her Voices replied: "If thou desirest help from Our Lord, then submit to him all thy doings."

Jeanne wanted to know from her Voices whether she would be burned.

Her Voices told her to wait upon the Lord and he would help her.[828] This mystic aid strengthened Jeanne's heart.

Among heretics and those possessed, such obstinacy as hers was not unparalleled. Ecclesiastical judges were well acquainted with the stiff-neckedness of women who had been deceived by the Devil. In order to force them to tell the truth, when admonitions and exhortations failed, recourse was had to torture. And even such a measure did not always succeed. Many of these wicked females (*mulierculæ*) endured the cruellest suffering with a constancy passing the ordinary strength of human nature. The doctors would not believe such constancy to be natural; they attributed it to the machinations of the Evil One.

The devil was capable of protecting his servants even when they had fallen into the hands of judges of the Church; he granted them strength to bear the torture in silence. This strength was called the gift of taciturnity.[829]

On Wednesday, the 9th of May, Jeanne was taken to the great tower of the castle, into the torture-chamber. There my Lord of Beauvais, in the presence of the Vice Inquisitor and nine doctors and masters, read her the articles, to which she had hitherto refused to reply; and he threatened her that if she did not confess the whole truth she would be put to the torture.[830]

The instruments were prepared; the two executioners, Mauger Leparmentier, a married clerk, and his companion, were in readiness close by her, awaiting the Bishop's orders.

Six days before Jeanne had received great comfort from her Voices. Now she replied resolutely: "Verily, if you were to tear my limbs asunder and drive my soul out of my body, naught else would I tell you, and if I did say anything unto you, I would always maintain afterwards that you had dragged it from me by force."[831]

My Lord of Beauvais decided to defer the torture, fearing that it would do no good to so hardened a subject.[832] On the following Saturday, he deliberated in his house, with the Vice-Inquisitor and thirteen doctors and masters; opinion was divided. Maître Raoul Roussel advised that Jeanne should not be tortured lest ground for complaint should be given against a trial so carefully conducted. It would seem that he anticipated the Devil's granting Jeanne the gift of taciturnity, whereby in diabolical silence she would be able to brave the tortures of the Holy Inquisition. On the other hand Maître Aubert Morel, licentiate in canon law, counsellor to the Official of Rouen, Canon of the Cathedral, and Maître Thomas de Courcelles, deemed it expedient to apply torture. Maître Nicolas Loiseleur, master of arts, Canon of Rouen, whose share in the proceedings had been to act Saint Catherine and the Lorraine shoemaker, had no very decided opinion on the subject, still it seemed to him by no means unprofitable that Jeanne for her soul's welfare should be tortured. The majority of doctors and masters agreed that for the present there was no need to subject her to this trial. Some gave no reasons, others alleged that it behoved them yet once again to warn her charitably. Maître Guillaume Erard, doctor in theology, held that sufficient material for the pronouncing of a sentence existed already.[833] Thus among those, who spared Jeanne the torture, were to be found the least merciful; for the spirit of ecclesiastical tribunals was such that to refuse to torture an accused was in certain cases to refuse him mercy.

To the trial of Marguerite la Porète, the judges summoned no experts.[834] Touching the charges held as proven, they submitted a written report to the University of Paris. The University gave its opinion on everything but the truth of the charges. This reservation was merely formal, and the decision of the University had the force of a sentence. In Jeanne's trial this precedent was cited. On the 21st of April, Maître Jean Beaupère, Maître Jacques de Touraine and Maître Nicolas Midi left Rouen, and, at the risk of being attacked on the road by men-at-arms, journeyed to Paris in order to present the twelve articles to their colleagues of the University.

On the 28th of April, the University, meeting in its general assembly at Saint-Bernard, charged the Holy Faculty of Theology and the Venerable Faculty of Decrees with the examination of the twelve articles.[835]

On the 14th of May, the deliberations of the two Faculties were submitted to all the Faculties in solemn assembly, who ratified them and made them their own. The University then sent them to King Henry, beseeching his Royal Majesty to execute justice promptly, in order that the people, so greatly scandalised by this woman, be brought back to good doctrine and holy faith.[836] It is worthy of notice that in a trial, in which the Pope, represented by the Vice-Inquisitor, was one judge, and the King, represented by the Bishop, another, the Eldest Daughter of Kings[837] should have communicated directly with the King of France, the guardian of her privileges.

According to the Sacred Faculty of Theology, Jeanne's apparitions were fictitious, lying, deceptive, inspired by devils. The sign given to the King was a presumptuous and pernicious lie, derogatory to the dignity of angels. Jeanne's belief in the visitations of Saint Michael, Saint Catherine and Saint Margaret was an error rash and injurious because Jeanne placed it on the same plane as the truths of religion. Jeanne's predictions were but superstitions, idle divinations and vain boasting. Her statement that she wore man's dress by the command of God was blasphemy, a violation of divine law and ecclesiastical sanction, a contemning of the sacraments and tainted with idolatry. In the letters she had dictated, Jeanne appeared treacherous, perfidious, cruel, sanguinary, seditious, blasphemous and in favour of tyranny. In setting out for France she had broken the commandment to honour father and mother, she had given an occasion for scandal, she had committed blasphemy and had fallen from the faith. In the leap from Beaurevoir, she had displayed a pusillanimity bordering on despair and homicide; and, moreover, it had caused her to utter rash statements touching the remission of her sin and erroneous pronouncements concerning free will. By proclaiming her confidence in her salvation, she uttered presumptuous and pernicious lies; by saying that Saint Catherine and Saint Margaret did not speak English, she blasphemed these saints and violated the precept: "Thou shalt love thy neighbour." The honours she rendered these saints were nought but idolatry and the worship of devils. Her refusal to submit her doings to the Church tended to schism, to the denial of the unity and authority of the Church and to apostasy.[838]

The doctors of the Faculty of Theology were very learned. They knew who the three evil spirits were whom Jeanne in her delusion took for Saint Michael, Saint Catherine, and Saint Margaret. They were Belial, Satan, and Behemoth. Belial, worshipped by the people of Sidon, was sometimes represented as an angel of great beauty; he is the demon of disobedience. Satan is the Lord of Hell; and Behemoth is a dull, heavy creature, who feeds on hay like an ox.[839]

The venerable Faculty of Decrees decided that this schismatic, this erring woman, this apostate, this liar, this soothsayer, be charitably exhorted and duly warned by competent judges, and that if notwithstanding she persisted in refusing to abjure her error, she must be given up to the secular arm to receive due chastisement.[840] Such were the deliberations and decisions which the Venerable University of Paris submitted to the examination and to the verdict of the Holy Apostolic See and of the sacrosanct General Council.

Meanwhile, where were the clerks of France? Had they nothing to say in this matter? Had they no decision to submit to the Pope and to the Council? Why did they not urge their opinions in opposition to those of the Faculties of Paris? Why did they keep silence? Jeanne demanded the record of the Poitiers trial. Wherefore did those Poitiers doctors, who had recommended the King to employ the Maid lest, by rejecting her, he should refuse the gift of the Holy Spirit, fail to send the record to Rouen?[841] Before the Maid espoused their waning cause, these Poitiers doctors, these magistrates, these University professors banished from Paris, advocates and counsellors of an exiled Parlement, had not a robe to their backs nor shoes for their children. Now, thanks to the Maid, they were every day regaining new hope and vigour. And yet they left her, who had so nobly served their King, to be treated as a heretic and a reprobate. Where were Brother Pasquerel, Friar Richard, and all those churchmen who but lately surrounded her in France and who looked to go with her to the Crusade against the Bohemians and the Turks? Why did they not demand a safe-conduct and come and give evidence at the trial? Or at least why did they not send their evidence? Why did not the Archbishop of Embrun, who but recently gave such noble counsels to the King, send some written statement in favour of the Maid to the judges at Rouen? My Lord of Reims, Chancellor of the Kingdom, had said that she was proud but not heretical. Wherefore now, acting contrary to his own interests and honour, did he refrain from testifying in favour of her through whom he had recovered his episcopal city? Wherefore did he not assert his right and do his duty as metropolitan and censure and suspend his suffragan, the Bishop of Beauvais, who was guilty of prevarication in the administration of justice? Why did not the illustrious clerics, whom King Charles had appointed deputies at the Council of Bâle, undertake to bring the cause of the Maid before the Council? And finally, why did not the priests, the ecclesiastics of the realm, with one voice demand an appeal to the Holy Father?

They all with one accord, as if struck dumb with astonishment, remained passive and silent. Can they have feared that too searching a light would be cast on Jeanne's cause by that illustrious University, that Sun of the Church, which was consulted on religious matters by all Christian states? Can they have suspected that this woman, who in France had been considered a saint, might after all have been inspired by the devil? But if what they had once believed they still held to be true, if they believed that the Maid had come from God to lead their King to his glorious coronation, then what are we to think of those clerks, those ecclesiastics who denied the Daughter of God, on the eve of her passion?

Chapter XIII
The abjuration – the first sentence

N Saturday, the 19th of May, the doctors and masters, to the number of fifty, assembled in the archiepiscopal chapel of Rouen. There they unanimously declared their agreement with the decision of the University of Paris; and my Lord of Beauvais ordained that a new charitable admonition be addressed to Jeanne.[842] Accordingly, on Wednesday the 23rd, the Bishop, the Vice-Inquisitor, and the Promoter went to a room in the castle, near Jeanne's cell. They were accompanied by seven doctors and masters, by the Lord Bishop of Noyon and by the Lord Bishop of Thérouanne.[843] The latter, brother to Messire Jean de Luxembourg who had sold the Maid, was held one of the most notable personages of the Great Council of England; he was Chancellor of France for King Henry, as Messire Regnault de Chartres was for King Charles.[844]

The accused was brought in, and Maître Pierre Maurice, doctor in theology, read to her the twelve articles as they had been abridged and commented upon, in conformity with the deliberations of the University; the whole was drawn up as a discourse addressed to Jeanne directly:[845]

Article I

First, Jeanne, thou saidst that at about the age of thirteen, thou didst receive revelations and behold apparitions of angels and of the Saints, Catherine and Margaret, that thou didst behold them frequently with thy bodily eyes, that they spoke unto thee and do still oftentimes speak unto thee, and that they have said unto thee many things that thou hast fully declared in thy trial.

The clerks of the University of Paris and others have considered the manner of these revelations and apparitions, their object, the substance of the things revealed, the person to whom they were revealed; all points touching them have they considered. And now they pronounce these revelations and apparitions to be either lying fictions, deceptive and dangerous, or superstitions, proceeding from spirits evil and devilish.

Article II

Item, thou hast said that thy King received a sign, by which he knew that thou wast sent of God: to wit that Saint Michael, accompanied by a multitude of angels, certain of whom had wings, others crowns, and with whom were Saint Catherine and Saint Margaret, came to thee in the town of Château-Chinon; and that they all entered with thee and went up the staircase of the castle, into the chamber of thy King, before whom the angel who wore the crown made obeisance. And once didst thou say that this crown which thou callest a sign, was delivered to the Archbishop of Reims who gave it to thy King, in the presence of a multitude of princes and lords whom thou didst call by name.

Now concerning this sign, the aforesaid clerks declare it to lack verisimilitude, to be a presumptuous lie, deceptive, pernicious, a thing counterfeited and attacking the dignity of angels.

Article III

Item, thou hast said that thou knewest the angels and the saints by the good counsel, the comfort and the instruction they gave thee, because they told thee their names and because the saints saluted thee. Thou didst believe also that it was Saint Michael who appeared unto thee; and that the deeds and sayings of this angel and these saints are good thou didst believe as firmly as thou believest in Christ.

Now the clerks declare such signs to be insufficient for the recognition of the said saints and angels. The clerks maintain that thou hast lightly believed and rashly affirmed, and further that when thou sayst thou dost believe as firmly etc., thou dost err from the faith.

Article IV

Item, thou hast said thou art assured of certain things which are to come, that thou hast known hidden things, that thou hast also recognized men whom thou hadst never seen before, and this by the Voices of Saint Catherine and Saint Margaret.

Thereupon the clerks declare that in these sayings are superstition, divination, presumptuous assertion and vain boasting.

Article V

Item, thou hast said that by God's command and according to his will, thou hast worn and dost still wear man's apparel. Because thou hast God's commandment to wear this dress thou hast donned a short tunic, jerkin, and hose with many points. Thou dost even wear thy hair cut short above the ears, without keeping about thee anything to denote the feminine sex, save what nature hath given thee. And oftentimes hast thou in this garb received the Sacrament of the Eucharist. And albeit thou hast been many times admonished to leave it, thou wouldest not, saying that thou wouldst liefer die than quit this apparel, unless it were by God's command; and that if thou wert still in this dress and with those of thine own party it would be for the great weal of France. Thou sayest also that for nothing wouldst thou take an oath not to wear this dress and bear these arms; and for all this that thou doest thou dost plead divine command.

In such matters the clerks declare that thou blasphemest against God, despising him and his Sacraments, that thou dost transgress divine law, Holy Scripture and the canons of the Church, that thou thinkest evil and dost err from the faith, that thou art full of vain boasting, that thou art addicted to idolatry and worship of thyself and thy clothes, according to the customs of the heathen.

Article VI

Item, thou hast often said, that in thy letters thou hast put these names, *Jhesus Maria*, and the sign of the cross, to warn those to whom thou didst write not to do what was indicated in the letter. In other letters thou hast boasted that thou wouldst slay all those who did not obey thee, and that by thy blows thou wouldst prove who had God on his side. Also hast thou oftentimes said that all thy deeds were by revelation and according to divine command.

Touching such affirmations the clerks declare thee to be a traitor, perfidious, cruel, desiring human bloodshed, seditious, an instigator of tyranny, a blasphemer of God's commandments and revelations.

Article VII

Item, thou sayest that according to revelations vouchsafed unto thee at the age of seventeen, thou didst leave thy parents' house against their will, driving them almost mad. Thou didst go to Robert de Baudricourt, who, at thy request, gave thee man's apparel and a sword, also men-at-arms to take thee to thy King. And being come to the King, thou didst say unto him that his enemies should be driven away, thou didst promise to bring him into a great kingdom, to make him victorious over his foes, and that for this God had sent thee. These things thou sayest thou didst accomplish in obedience to God and according to revelation.

In such things the clerks declare thee to have been irreverent to thy father and mother, thus disobeying God's command; to have given occasion for scandal, to have blasphemed, to have erred from the faith and to have made a rash and presumptuous promise.

Article VIII

Item, thou hast said, that voluntarily thou didst leap from the Tower of Beaurevoir, preferring rather to die than to be delivered into the hands of the English and to live after the destruction of Compiègne. And albeit Saint Catherine and Saint Margaret forbade thee to leap, thou couldst not restrain thyself. And despite the great sin thou hast committed in offending these saints, thou didst know by thy Voices, that after thy confession, thy sin was forgiven thee.

This deed the clerks declare thee to have committed through cowardice turning to despair and probably to suicide. In this matter likewise thou didst utter a rash and presumptuous statement in asserting that thy sin is forgiven, and thou dost err from the faith touching the doctrine of free will.

Article IX

Item, thou hast said that Saint Catherine and Saint Margaret promised to lead thee to Paradise provided thou didst remain a virgin; and that thou hadst vowed and promised them to cherish thy virginity, and of that thou art as well assured as if already thou hadst entered into the glory of the Blessed. Thou believest that thou hast not committed mortal sin. And it seemeth to thee that if thou wert in mortal sin the saints would not visit thee daily as they do.

Such an assertion the clerks pronounce to be a pernicious lie, presumptuous and rash, that therein lieth a contradiction of what thou hadst previously said, and that finally thy beliefs do err from the true Christian faith.

Article X

Item, thou hast declared it to be within thy knowledge that God loveth certain living persons better than thee, and that this thou hast learnt by revelation from Saint Catherine and Saint Margaret: also that those saints speak French, not English, since they are not on the side of the English. And when thou knewest that thy Voices were for thy King, you didst fall to disliking the Burgundians.

Such matters the clerks pronounce to be a rash and presumptuous assertion, a superstitious divination, a blasphemy uttered against Saint Catherine and Saint Margaret, and a transgression of the commandment to love our neighbours.

Article XI

Item, thou hast said that to those whom thou callest Saint Michael, Saint Catherine and Saint Margaret, thou didst do reverence, bending the knee, taking off thy cap, kissing the ground on which they trod, vowing to them thy virginity: that in the instruction of these saints, whom thou didst invoke and kiss and embrace, thou didst believe as soon as they appeared unto thee, and without seeking counsel from thy priest or from any other ecclesiastic. And, notwithstanding, thou believest that these Voices came from God as firmly as thou believest in the Christian religion and the Passion of Our Lord Jesus Christ. Moreover thou hast said that did any evil spirit appear to thee in the form of Saint Michael thou wouldest know such a spirit and distinguish him from the saint. And again hast thou said, that of thine own accord, thou hast sworn not to reveal the sign thou gavest to thy King. And finally thou didst add: "Save at God's command."

Now touching these matters, the clerks affirm that supposing thou hast had the revelations and beheld the apparitions of which thou boastest and in such a manner as thou dost say, then art thou an idolatress, an invoker of demons, an apostate from the faith, a maker of rash statements, a swearer of an unlawful oath.

Article XII

Item, thou hast said that if the Church wished thee to disobey the orders thou sayest God gave thee, nothing would induce thee to do it; that thou knowest that all the deeds of which thou hast been accused in thy trial were wrought according to the command of God and that it was impossible for thee to do otherwise. Touching these deeds, thou dost refuse to submit to the judgment of the Church on earth or of any living man, and will submit therein to God alone. And moreover thou didst declare this reply itself not to be made of thine own accord but by God's command; despite the article of faith: *Unam sanctam Ecclesiam catholicam*, having been many times declared unto thee, and notwithstanding that it behoveth all Christians to submit their deeds and sayings to the Church militant especially concerning revelations and such like matters.

Wherefore the clerks declare thee to be schismatic, disbelieving in the unity and authority of the Church, apostate and obstinately erring from the faith.[846]

Having completed the reading of the articles, Maître Pierre Maurice, on the invitation of the Bishop, proceeded to exhort Jeanne. He had been rector of the University of Paris in 1428.[847] He was esteemed an orator. He it was who, on the 5th of June, had discoursed in the name of the chapter, before King Henry VI on the occasion of his entering Rouen. He would seem to have been distinguished by some knowledge of and taste for ancient letters, and to have been possessed of precious manuscripts, amongst which were the comedies of Terence and the *Æneid* of Virgil.[848]

In terms of calculated simplicity did this illustrious doctor call upon Jeanne to reflect on the effects of her words and sayings, and tenderly did he exhort her to submit to the Church. After the wormwood he offered her the honey; he spoke to her in words kind and familiar. With remarkable adroitness he entered into the feelings and inclinations of the maiden's heart. Seeing her filled with knightly enthusiasm and loyalty to King Charles, whose coronation was her doing, he drew his comparisons from chivalry, thereby essaying to prove to her that she ought rather to believe in the Church Militant than in her Voices and apparitions.

"If your King," he said to her, "had appointed you to defend a fortress, forbidding you to let any one enter it, would you not refuse to admit whomsoever claiming to come from him did not present letters and some other token. Likewise, when Our Lord Jesus Christ, on his ascension into heaven, committed to the Blessed Apostle Peter and to his successors the government of his Church, he forbade them to receive such as claimed to come in his name but brought no credentials."

And, to bring home to her how grievous a sin it was to disobey the Church, he recalled the time when she waged war, and put the case of a knight who should disobey his king:

"When you were in your King's dominion," he said to her, "if a knight or some other owing fealty to him had arisen, saying, 'I will not obey the King; I will not submit either to him or to his officers,' would you not have said, 'He is a man to be censured'? What say you then of yourself, you who, engendered in Christ's religion, having become by baptism the daughter of the Church and the bride of Christ, dost now refuse obedience to the officers of Christ, that is, to the prelates of the Church?"[849]

Thus did Maître Pierre Maurice endeavour to make Jeanne understand him. He did not succeed. Against the courage of this child all the reasons and all the eloquence of the world would have availed nothing. When Maître Pierre had finished speaking, Jeanne, being asked whether she did not hold herself bound to submit her deeds and sayings to the Church, replied:

"What I have always held and said in the trial that will I maintain.... If I were condemned and saw the fagots lighted, and the executioner ready to stir the fire, and I in the fire, I would say and maintain till I died nought other than what I said during the trial."

At these words the Bishop declared the discussion at an end, and deferred the pronouncing of the sentence till the morrow.[850]

The next day, the Thursday after Whitsuntide and the 24th day of May, early in the morning, Maître Jean Beaupère visited Jeanne in her prison and warned her that she would be shortly taken to the scaffold to hear a sermon.

"If you are a good Christian," he said, "you will agree to submit all your deeds and sayings to Holy Mother Church, and especially to the ecclesiastical judges."

Maître Jean Beaupère thought he heard her reply, "So I will."[851]

If such were her answer, then it must have been because, worn out by a flight of agony, her physical courage quailed at the thought of death by burning.

Just when he was leaving her, as she stood near a door, Maître Nicolas Loiseleur gave her the same advice, and in order to induce her to follow it, he made her a false promise:

"Jeanne, believe me," he said. "You have your deliverance in your own hands. Wear the apparel of your sex, and do what shall be required of you. Otherwise you stand in danger of death. If you do as I tell you, good will come to you and no harm. You will be delivered into the hands of the Church."[852]

She was taken in a cart and with an armed guard to that part of the town called Bourg-l'Abbé, lying beneath the castle walls. And but a short distance away the cart was stopped, in the cemetery of Saint-Ouen, also called *les aitres*[853] *Saint-Ouen.* Here a highly popular fair was held every year on the feast day of the patron saint of the Abbey.[854] Here it was that Jeanne was to hear the sermon, as so many other unhappy creatures had done before her. Places like this, to which the folk could flock in crowds, were generally chosen for these edifying spectacles. On the border of this vast charnel-house for a hundred years there had towered a parish church, and on the south there rose the nave of the abbey. Against the magnificent edifice of the church two scaffolds had been erected,[855] one large, the other smaller. They were west of the porch which was called *portail des Marmousets*, because of the multitudes of tiny figures carved upon it.[856]

On the great scaffold the two judges, the Lord Bishop and the Vice-Inquisitor, took their places. They were assisted by the most reverend Cardinal of Winchester, the Lord Bishops of Thérouanne, of Noyon, and of Norwich, the Lord Abbots of Fécamp, of Jumièges, of Bec, of Corneilles, of Mont-Saint-Michel-au-Péril-de-la-Mer, of Mortemart, of Préaux, and of Saint-Ouen of Rouen, where the assembly was held, the Priors of Longueville and of Saint-Lô, also many doctors and bachelors in theology, doctors and licentiates in canon and civil law.[857] Likewise were there many high personages of the English party. The other scaffold was a kind of pulpit. To it ascended the doctor who, according to the use and custom of the Holy Inquisition was to preach the sermon against Jeanne. He was Maître Guillaume Erard, doctor in theology, canon of the churches of Langres and of Beauvais.[858] At this time he was very eager to go to Flanders, where he was urgently needed; and he confided to his young servitor, Brother Jean de Lenisoles, that the preaching of this sermon caused him great inconvenience. "I want to be in Flanders," he said. "This affair is very annoying for me."[859]

From one point of view, however, he must have been pleased to perform this duty, since it afforded him the opportunity of attacking the King of France, Charles VII, and of thereby showing his devotion to the English cause, to which he was strongly attached.

Jeanne, dressed as a man, was brought up and placed at his side, before all the people.[860]

Maître Guillaume Erard began his sermon in the following manner:

"I take as my text the words of God in the Gospel of Saint John, chapter xv: 'The branch cannot bear fruit of itself, except it abide in the vine.'[861] Thus it behoveth all Catholics to remain abiding in Holy Mother Church, the true vine, which the hand of Our Lord Jesus Christ hath planted. Now this Jeanne, whom you see before you, falling from error into error, and from crime into crime, hath become separate from the unity of Holy Mother Church and in a thousand manners hath scandalised Christian people."

Then he reproached her with having failed, with having sinned against royal Majesty and against God and the Catholic Faith; and all these things must she henceforth eschew under pain of death by burning.

He declaimed vehemently against the pride of this woman. He said that never had there appeared in France a monster so great as that which was manifest in Jeanne; that she was a witch, a heretic, a schismatic, and that the King, who protected her, risked the same reproach from the moment that he became willing to recover his throne with the help of such a heretic.[862]

Towards the middle of his sermon, he cried out with a loud voice:

"Ah! right terribly hast thou been deceived, noble house of France, once the most Christian of houses! Charles, who calls himself thy head and assumes the title of King hath, like a heretic and schismatic, received the words of an infamous woman, abounding in evil works and in all dishonour. And not he alone, but all the clergy in his lordship and dominion, by whom this woman, so she sayeth, hath been examined and not rejected. Full sore is the pity of it."[863]

Two or three times did Maître Guillaume repeat these words concerning King Charles. Then pointing at Jeanne with his finger he said:

"It is to you, Jeanne, that I speak; and I say unto you that your King is a heretic and a schismatic."

At these words Jeanne was deeply wounded in her love for the Lilies of France and for King Charles. She was moved with great feeling, and she heard her Voices saying unto her:

"Reply boldly to the preacher who is preaching to you."[864]

Then obeying them heartily, she interrupted Maître Jean:

"By my troth, Messire," she said to him, "saving your reverence, I dare say unto you and swear at the risk of my life, that he is the noblest Christian of all Christians, that none loveth better religion and the Church, and that he is not at all what you say."[865]

Maître Guillaume ordered the Usher, Jean Massieu, to silence her.[866] Then he went on with his sermon, and concluded with these words: "Jeanne, behold my Lords the Judges, who oftentimes have summoned you and required you to submit all your acts and sayings to Mother Church. In these acts and sayings were many things which, so it seemed to these clerics, were good neither to say nor to maintain."[867]

"I will answer you," said Jeanne. Touching the article of submission to the Church, she recalled how she had asked for all the deeds she had wrought and the words she had uttered to be reported to Rome, to Our Holy Father the Pope, to whom, after God, she appealed. Then she added: "And as for the sayings I have uttered and the deeds I have done, they have all been by God's command."[868]

She declared that she had not understood that the record of her trial was being sent to Rome to be judged by the Pope.

"I will not have it thus," she said. "I know not what you will insert in the record of these proceedings. I demand to be taken to the Pope and questioned by him."[869]

They urged her to incriminate her King. But they wasted their breath.

"For my deeds and sayings I hold no man responsible, neither my King nor another."[870]

"Will you abjure all your deeds and sayings? Will you abjure such of your deeds and sayings as have been condemned by the clerks?"

"I appeal to God and to Our Holy Father, the Pope."

"But that is not sufficient. We cannot go so far to seek the Pope. Each Ordinary is judge in his own diocese. Wherefore it is needful for you to appeal to Our Holy Mother Church, and to hold as true all that clerks and folks well learned in the matter say and determine touching your actions and your sayings."[871]

Admonished with yet a third admonition, Jeanne refused to recant.[872] With confidence she awaited the deliverance promised by her Voices, certain that of a sudden there would come men-at-arms from France and that in one great tumult of fighting-men and angels she would be liberated. That was why she had insisted on retaining man's attire.

Two sentences had been prepared: one for the case in which the accused should abjure her error, the other for the case in which she should persevere. By the first there was removed from Jeanne the ban of excommunication. By the second, the tribunal, declaring that it could do nothing more for her, abandoned her to the secular arm. The Lord Bishop had them both with him.[873]

He took the second and began to read: "In the name of the Lord, Amen. All the pastors of the Church who have it in their hearts faithfully to tend their flocks...."[874]

Meanwhile, as he read, the clerks who were round Jeanne urged her to recant, while there was yet time. Maître Nicolas Loiseleur exhorted her to do as he had recommended, and to put on woman's dress.[875]

Maître Guillaume Erard was saying: "Do as you are advised and you will be delivered from prison."[876]

Then straightway came the Voices unto her and said: "Jeanne, passing sore is our pity for you! You must recant what you have said, or we abandon you to secular justice.... Jeanne, do as you are advised. Jeanne, will you bring death upon yourself!"[877]

The sentence was long and the Lord Bishop read slowly:

"We judges, having Christ before our eyes and also the honour of the true faith, in order that our judgment may proceed from the Lord himself, do say and decree that thou hast been a liar, an inventor of revelations and apparitions said to be divine; a deceiver, pernicious, presumptuous, light of faith, rash, superstitious, a soothsayer, a blasphemer against God and his saints. We declare thee to be a contemner of God even in his sacraments, a prevaricator of divine law, of sacred doctrine and of ecclesiastical sanction, seditious, cruel, apostate, schismatic, having committed a thousand errors against religion, and by all these tokens rashly guilty towards God and Holy Church.[878]"

Time was passing. Already the Lord Bishop had uttered the greater part of the sentence.[879] The executioner was there, ready to take off the condemned in his cart.[880]

Then suddenly, with hands clasped, Jeanne cried that she was willing to obey the Church.[881]

The judge paused in the reading of the sentence.

An uproar arose in the crowd, consisting largely of English men-at-arms and officers of King Henry. Ignorant of the customs of the Inquisition, which had not been introduced into their country, these *Godons* could not understand what was going on; all they knew was that the witch was saved. Now they held Jeanne's death to be necessary for the welfare of England; wherefore the unaccountable actions of these doctors and the Lord Bishop threw them into a fury. In their Island witches were not treated thus; no mercy was shown them, and they were burned speedily. Angry murmurs arose; stones were thrown at the registrars of the trial.[882] Maître Pierre Maurice, who was doing his best to strengthen Jeanne in the resolution she had taken, was threatened and the *coués* very nearly made short work with him.[883] Neither did Maître Jean Beaupère and the delegates from the University of Paris escape their share of the insults. They were accused of favouring Jeanne's errors.[884] Who better than they knew the injustice of these reproaches?

Certain of the high personages sitting on the platform at the side of the judge complained to the Lord Bishop that he had not gone on to the end of the sentence but had admitted Jeanne to repentance.

He was even reproached with insults, for one was heard to cry: "You shall pay for this."

He threatened to suspend the trial.

"I have been insulted," he said. "I will proceed no further until honourable amends have been done me."[885]

In the tumult, Maître Guillaume Erard unfolded a double sheet of paper, and read Jeanne the form of abjuration, written down according to the opinion of the masters. It was no longer than the Lord's Prayer and consisted of six or seven lines of writing. It was in French and began with these words: "I, Jeanne...." The Maid submitted therein to the sentence, the judgment, and the commandment of the Church; she acknowledged having committed the crime of high treason and having deceived the people. She undertook never again to bear arms or to wear man's dress or her hair cut round her ears.[886]

When Maître Guillaume had read the document, Jeanne declared she did not understand it, and wished to be advised thereupon.[887] She was heard to ask counsel of Saint Michael.[888] She still believed firmly in her Voices, albeit they had not aided her in her dire necessity, neither had spared her the shame of denying them. For, simple as she was, at the bottom of her heart she knew well what the clerks were asking of her; she realised that they would not let her go until she had pronounced a great recantation. All that she said was merely in order to gain time and because she was afraid of death; yet she could not bring herself to lie.

Without losing a moment Maître Guillaume said to Messire Jean Massieu, the Usher: "Advise her touching this abjuration."

And he passed him the document.[889]

Messire Jean Massieu at first made excuse, but afterwards he complied and warned Jeanne of the danger she was running by her refusal to recant.

"You must know," he said, "that if you oppose any of these articles you will be burned. I counsel you to appeal to the Church Universal as to whether you should abjure these articles or not."

Maître Guillaume Erard asked Jean Massieu: "Well, what are you saying to her?"

Jean Massieu replied: "I make known unto Jeanne the text of the deed of abjuration and I urge her to sign it. But she declares that she knoweth not whether she will."

At this juncture, Jeanne, who was still being pressed to sign, said aloud: "I wish the Church to deliberate on the articles. I appeal to the Church Universal as to whether I should abjure them. Let the document be read by the Church and the clerks into whose hands I am to be delivered. If it be their counsel that I ought to sign it and do what I am told, then willingly will I do it."[890]

Maître Guillaume Erard replied: "Do it now, or you will be burned this very day."

And he forbade Jean Massieu to confer with her any longer.

Whereupon Jeanne said that she would liefer sign than be burned.[891]

Then straightway Messire Jean Massieu gave her a second reading of the deed of abjuration. And she repeated the words after the Usher. As she spoke her countenance seemed to express a kind of sneer. It may have been that her features were contracted by the violent emotions which swayed her and that the horrors and tortures of an ecclesiastical trial may have overclouded her reason, subject at all times to strange vagaries, and that after such bitter suffering there may have come upon her the actual paroxysm of madness. On the other hand it may have been that with sound sense and calm mind she was mocking at the clerks of Rouen; she was quite capable of it, for she had mocked at the clerks of Poitiers. At any rate she had a jesting air, and the bystanders noticed that she pronounced the words of her abjuration with a smile.[892] And her gaiety, whether real or apparent, roused the wrath of those burgesses, priests, artisans, and men-at-arms who desired her death.

"'Tis all a mockery. Jeanne doth but jest,"[893] they cried.

Among the most irate was Master Lawrence Calot, Secretary to the King of England. He was seen to be in a violent rage and to approach first the judge and then the accused. A noble of Picardy who was present, the very same who had essayed familiarities with Jeanne in the Castle of Beaurevoir, thought he saw this Englishman forcing Jeanne to sign a paper.[894] He was mistaken. In every crowd there are those who see things that never happen. The Bishop would not have permitted such a thing; he was devoted to the Regent, but on a question of form he would never have given way. Meanwhile, under this storm of insults, amidst the throwing of stones and the clashing of swords, these illustrious masters, these worthy doctors grew pale. The Prior of Longueville was awaiting an opportunity to make an apology to the Cardinal of Winchester.[895]

On the platform a chaplain of the Cardinal violently accused the Lord Bishop. "You do wrong to accept such an abjuration. 'Tis a mere mockery," he said.

"You lie," retorted my Lord Pierre. "I, the judge of a religious suit, ought to seek the salvation of this woman rather than her death."

The Cardinal silenced his chaplain.[896]

It is said that the Earl of Warwick came up to the judges and complained of what they had done, adding: "The King is not well served, since Jeanne escapes."

And it is stated that one of them replied: "Have no fear, my Lord. She will not escape us long."[897]

It is hardly credible that any one should have actually said so, but doubtless there were many at that time who thought it.

With what scorn must the Bishop of Beauvais have regarded those dull minds, incapable of understanding the service he was rendering to Old England by forcing this damsel to acknowledge that all she had declared and maintained in honour of her King was but lying and illusion.

With a pen that Massieu gave her Jeanne made a cross at the bottom of the deed.[898]

In the midst of howls and oaths from the English, my Lord of Beauvais read the more merciful of the sentences. It relieved Jeanne from excommunication and reconciled her to Holy Mother Church.[899] Further the sentence ran:

"... Because thou hast rashly sinned against God and Holy Church, we, thy judges, that thou mayest do salutary penance, out of our Grace and moderation, do condemn thee finally and definitely to perpetual prison, with the bread of sorrow and the water of affliction, so that there thou mayest weep over thy offences and commit no other that may be an occasion of weeping."[900]

This penalty, like all other penalties, save death and mutilation, lay within the power of ecclesiastical judges. They inflicted it so frequently that in the early days of the Holy Inquisition, the Fathers of the Council of Narbonne said that stones and mortar would become as scarce as money.[901] It was a penalty doubtless, but one which in character and significance differed from the penalties inflicted by secular courts; it was a penance. According to the mercy of ecclesiastical law, prison was a place suitable for repentance, where, in one perpetual penance, the condemned might eat the bread of sorrow and drink the waters of affliction.

How foolish was he, who by refusing to enter that prison or by escaping from it, should reject the salutary healing of his soul! By so doing he was fleeing from the gentle tribunal of penance, and the Church in sadness cut him off from the communion of the faithful. By inflicting this penalty, which a good Catholic must needs regard rather as a favour than a punishment, my Lord the Bishop and my Lord the Holy Vicar of the Inquisition were conforming to the custom, whereby our Holy Mother Church became reconciled to heretics. But had they power to execute their sentence? The prison to which they condemned Jeanne, the expiatory prison, the salutary confinement, must be in a dungeon of the Church. Could they send her there?

Jeanne, turning towards them, said: "Now, you Churchmen, take me to your prison. Let me be no longer in the hands of the English."[902]

Many of those clerics had promised it to her.[903] They had deceived her. They knew it was not possible; for it had been stipulated that the King of England's men should resume possession of Jeanne after the trial.[904]

The Lord Bishop gave the order: "Take her back to the place whence you brought her."[905]

He, a judge of the Church, committed the crime of surrendering the Church's daughter reconciled and penitent, to laymen. Among them she could not mourn over her sins; and they, hating her body and caring nought for her soul, were to tempt her and cause her to fall back into error.

While Jeanne was being taken back in the cart to her tower in the fields, the soldiers insulted her and their captains did not rebuke them.[906]

Thereafter, the Vice-Inquisitor and with him divers doctors and masters, went to her prison and charitably exhorted her. She promised to wear woman's apparel, and to let her head be shaved.[907]

The Duchess of Bedford, knowing that she was a virgin, saw to it that she was treated with respect.[908] As the ladies of Luxembourg had done formerly, she essayed to persuade her to wear the clothing of her sex. By a certain tailor, one Jeannotin Simon, she had had made for Jeanne a gown which she had hitherto refused to wear. Jeannotin brought the garment to the prisoner, who this time did not refuse it. In putting it on, Jeannotin touched her bosom, which she resented. She boxed his ears;[909] but she consented to wear the gown provided by the Duchess.

Chapter XIV
The trial for relapse – second sentence – death of the Maid

N the following Sunday, which was Trinity Sunday, there arose a rumour that Jeanne had resumed man's apparel. The report spread rapidly from the castle down the narrow streets where lived the clerks in the shadow of the cathedral. Straightway notaries and assessors hastened to the tower which looked on the fields.

In the outer court of the castle they found some hundred men-at-arms, who welcomed them with threats and curses.[910] These fellows did not yet understand that the judges had conducted the trial so as to bring honour to old England and dishonour to the French. They did not realise what it meant when the Maid of the Armagnacs, who hitherto had obstinately persisted in her utterances, was at length brought to confess her impostures. They did not see how great was the advantage to their country when it was published abroad throughout the world that Charles of Valois had been conducted to his coronation by a heretic. But no, the only idea these brutes were capable of grasping was the burning of the girl prisoner who had struck terror into their hearts. The doctors and masters they treated as traitors, false counsellors and Armagnacs.[911]

In the castle yard is Maître André Marguerie, bachelor in decrees, archdeacon of Petit-Caux, King's Counsellor,[912] who is inquiring what has happened. He had displayed great assiduity in the trial. The Maid he held to be a crafty damsel.[913] Now again he desired to give an expert's judgment touching what had just occurred.

"That Jeanne is to be seen dressed as a man is not everything," he said. "We must know what motives induced her to resume masculine attire."

Maître André Marguerie was an eloquent orator, one of the shining lights of the Council of Constance. But, when a man-at-arms raised his axe against him and called out "Traitor! Armagnac!" Maître Marguerie asked no further questions, but speedily departed, and went to bed very sick.[914]

The next day, Monday the 25th, there came to the castle the Vice-Inquisitor, accompanied by divers doctors and masters. The Registrar, Messire Guillaume Manchon, was summoned. He was such a coward that he dared not come save under the escort of one of the Earl of Warwick's men-at-arms.[915] They found Jeanne wearing man's apparel, jerkin and short tunic, with a hood covering her shaved head. Her face was in tears and disfigured by terrible suffering.[916]

She was asked when and why she had assumed this attire.

She replied: "'Tis but now that I have donned man's dress and put off woman's."

"Wherefore did you put it on and who made you?"

"I put it on of my own will and without constraint. I had liefer wear man's dress than woman's."

"You promised and swore not to wear man's dress."

"I never meant to take an oath not to wear it."

"Wherefore did you return to it?"

"Because it is more seemly to take it and wear man's dress, being amongst men, than to wear woman's dress.... I returned to it because the promise made me was not kept, to wit, that I should go to mass and should receive my Saviour and be loosed from my bonds."

"Did you not abjure, and promise not to return to this dress?"

"I had liefer die than be in bonds. But if I be allowed to go to mass and taken out of my bonds and put in a prison of grace, and given a woman to be with me, I will be good and do as the Church shall command."

"Have you heard your Voices since Thursday?"

"Yes."

"What did they say unto you?"

"They told me that through Saint Catherine and Saint Margaret God gave me to wit his sore pity for the treachery, to which I consented in abjuring and recanting to save my life, and that in saving my life I was losing my soul. Before Thursday my Voices had told me what I should do and what I did do on that day. On the scaffold my Voices told me to reply boldly to the preacher. He is a false preacher.... Many things did he say that I have never done. If I were to say that God has not sent me I should be damned. It is true that God has sent me. My Voices have since told me that by confessing I committed a great wickedness which I ought never to have done. All that I said I uttered through fear of the fire."[917]

Thus spake Jeanne in sore sorrow. And now what becomes of those monkish tales of attempted violence related long afterwards by a registrar and two churchmen?[918] And how can Messire Massieu make us believe that Jeanne, unable to find her petticoats, put on her hose in order not to appear before her guards unclothed?[919] The truth is very different. It is Jeanne herself who confesses bravely and simply. She repented of her abjuration, as of the greatest sin she had ever committed. She could not forgive herself for having lied through fear of death. Her Voices, who, before the sermon at Saint-Ouen had foretold that she would deny them, now came to her and spoke of "the sore pity of her treachery." Could they say otherwise since they were the voices of her own heart? And could Jeanne fail to listen to them since she had always listened to them whenever they had counselled her to sacrifice and self-abnegation?

It was out of obedience to her heavenly *Council* that Jeanne had returned to man's apparel, because she would not purchase her life at the price of denying the Angel and the Saints, and because with her whole heart and soul she rebelled against her recantation.

Still the English were seriously to blame for having left her man's clothes. It would have been more humane to have taken them from her, since if she wore them she must needs die. They had been put in a bag.[920] Her guards may even be suspected of having tempted her by placing under her very eyes those garments which recalled to her days of happiness. They had taken away all her few possessions, even her poor brass ring, everything save that suit which meant death to her.

To blame also were her ecclesiastical judges who should not have sentenced her to imprisonment if they foresaw that they could not place her in an ecclesiastical prison, nor have commanded her a penance which they knew they were unable to enforce. Likewise to blame were the Bishop of Beauvais and the Vice-Inquisitor; because after having, for the good of her sinful soul, prescribed the bread of bitterness and the water of affliction, they gave her not this bread and this water, but delivered her in disgrace into the hands of her cruel enemies.

When she uttered the words, "God by Saint Catherine and Saint Margaret hath given me to wit the sore pity of the treason to which I consented," Jeanne consummated the sacrifice of her life.[921]

The Bishop and the Inquisitor had now to proceed in conformity with the law. The interrogatory however lasted a few moments longer.

"Do you believe that your Voices are Saint Margaret and Saint Catherine?"

"Yes, and they come from God."

"Tell us the truth touching the crown."

"To the best of my knowledge I told you the truth of everything at the trial."

"On the scaffold, at the time of your abjuration, you did acknowledge before us your judges and before many others, and in the presence of the people, that you had falsely boasted your Voices to be those of Saint Catherine and Saint Margaret."

"I did not mean thus to do or to say. I did not deny, neither did I intend to deny, my apparitions and to say that they were not Saint Margaret and Saint Catherine. All that I have said was through fear of the fire, and I recanted nothing that was not contrary to the truth. I had liefer do my penance once and for all, to wit by dying, than endure further anguish in prison. Whatsoever abjuration I have been forced to make, I never did anything against God and religion. I did not understand what was in the deed of abjuration, wherefore I did not mean to abjure anything unless it were Our Lord's will. If the judges wish I will resume my woman's dress. But nothing else will I do."[922]

Coming out of the prison, my Lord of Beauvais met the Earl of Warwick accompanied by many persons. He said to him: "Farewell. *Faites bonne chère.*" It is said that he added, laughing: "It is done! We have caught her."[923] The words are his, doubtless, but we are not certain that he laughed.

On the morrow, Tuesday the 29th, he assembled the tribunal in the chapel of the Archbishop's house. The forty-two assessors present were informed of what had happened on the previous day and invited to state their opinions, the nature of which might easily be anticipated.[924] Every heretic who retracted his confession was held a perjurer, not only impenitent but relapsed. And the relapsed were given up to the secular arm.[925]

Maître Nicholas de Venderès, canon, archdeacon, was the first to state his opinion.

"Jeanne is and must be held a heretic. She must be delivered to the secular authority."[926]

The Lord Abbot of Fécamp expressed his opinion in the following terms: "Jeanne has relapsed. Nevertheless it is well that the terms of her abjuration once read to her, be read a second time and explained, and that at the same time she be reminded of God's word. This done, it is for us, her judges, to declare her a heretic and to abandon her to the secular authority, entreating it to deal leniently with her."[927]

This plea for leniency was a mere matter of form. If the Provost of Rouen had taken it into consideration he also would have been excommunicated, with a further possibility of temporal punishment.[928] And yet there were certain counsellors who even wished to dispense with this empty show of pity, urging that there was no need for such a supplication.

Maître Guillaume Erard and sundry other assessors, among whom were Maîtres Marguerie, Loiseleur, Pierre Maurice, and Brother Martin Ladvenu, were of the opinion of my Lord Abbot of Fécamp.[929]

Maître Thomas de Courcelles advised the woman being again charitably admonished touching the salvation of her soul.

Such likewise was the opinion of Brother Isambart de la Pierre.[930]

The Lord Bishop, having listened to these opinions, concluded that Jeanne must be proceeded against as one having relapsed. Accordingly he summoned her to appear on the morrow, the 30th of May, in the old Market Square.[931]

On the morning of that Wednesday, the 30th of May, by the command of my Lord of Beauvais, the two young friars preachers, bachelors in theology, Brother Martin Ladvenu and Brother Isambart de la Pierre, went to Jeanne in her prison. Brother Martin told her that she was to die that day.

At the approach of this cruel death, amidst the silence of her Voices, she understood at length that she would not be delivered. Cruelly awakened from her dream, she felt heaven and earth failing her, and fell into a deep despair.

"Alas!" she cried, "shall so terrible a fate betide me as that my body ever pure and intact shall to-day be burned and reduced to ashes? Ah me! Ah me! Liefer would I be seven times beheaded than thus be burned. Alas! had I been in the prison of the Church, to which I submitted, and guarded by ecclesiastics and not by my foes and adversaries, so woeful a misfortune as this would not have befallen me. Oh! I appeal to God, the great judge, against this violence and these sore wrongs with which I am afflicted."[932]

While she was lamenting, the doctors and masters, Nicolas de Venderès, Pierre Maurice and Nicolas Loiseleur, entered the prison; they came by order of my Lord of Beauvais.[933] On the previous day thirty-nine counsellors out of forty-two, declaring that Jeanne had relapsed, had added that they deemed it well she should be reminded of the terms of her abjuration.[934] Wherefore, according to the counsel of these clerics, the Lord Bishop had sent certain learned doctors to the relapsed heretic and had resolved to come to her himself.

She must needs submit to one last examination.

"Do you believe that your Voices and apparitions come from good or from evil spirits?"

"I know not; but I appeal to my Mother the Church."[935]

Maître Pierre Maurice, a reader of Terence and Virgil, was filled with pity for this hapless Maid.[936] On the previous day he had declared her to have relapsed because his knowledge of theology forced him to it; and now he was concerned for the salvation of this soul in peril, which could not be saved except by recognising the falseness of its Voices.

"Are they indeed real?" he asked her.

She replied, "Whether they be good or bad, they appeared to me."

She affirmed that with her eyes she had seen, with her ears heard, the Voices and apparitions which had been spoken of at the trial.

She heard them most frequently, she said, at the hour of compline and of matins, when the bells were ringing.[937]

Maître Pierre Maurice, being the Pope's secretary, was debarred from openly professing the Pyrrhonic philosophy. He inclined, however, to a rational interpretation of natural phenomena, if we may judge from his remarking to Jeanne that the ringing of bells often sounded like voices.

Without describing the exact form of her apparitions, Jeanne said they came to her in a great multitude and were very tiny. She believed in them no longer, being fully persuaded that they had deceived her.

Maître Pierre Maurice asked about the Angel who had brought the crown.

She replied that there had never been a crown save that promised by her to her King, and that the Angel was herself.[938]

At that moment the Lord Bishop of Beauvais and the Vice-Inquisitor entered the prison, accompanied by Maître Thomas de Courcelles and Maître Jacques Lecamus.[939]

At the sight of the Judge who had brought her to such a pass she cried, "Bishop, I die through you."

He replied by piously admonishing her. "Ah! Jeanne, bear all in patience. You die because you have not kept your promise and have returned to evil-doing.[940] Now, Jeanne," he asked her, "you have always said that your Voices promised you deliverance; you behold how they have deceived you, wherefore tell us the truth."

She replied, "Verily, I see that they have deceived me."[941]

The Bishop and the Vice-Inquisitor withdrew. They had triumphed over a poor girl of twenty.

"If after their condemnation heretics repent, and if the signs of their repentance are manifest, the sacraments of confession and the Eucharist may not be denied them, provided they demand them with humility."[942] Thus ran the sacred decretals. But no recantation, no assurance of conformity, could save the relapsed heretic. He was permitted confession, absolution, and communion; which means that at the bar of the Sacrament the sincerity of his repentance and conversion was believed in. But at the same time it was declared judicially that his repentance was not believed in and that consequently he must die.[943]

Brother Martin Ladvenu heard Jeanne's confession. Then he sent Messire Massieu, the Usher, to my Lord of Beauvais, to inform him that she asked to be given the body of Jesus Christ.

The Bishop assembled certain doctors to confer on this subject; and after they had deliberated, he replied to the Usher: "Tell Brother Martin to give her the communion and all that she shall ask."[944]

Messire Massieu returned to the castle to bear this reply to Brother Martin. For a second time Brother Martin heard Jeanne in confession and gave her absolution.[945]

A cleric, one Pierre, brought the body of Our Lord in an unceremonious fashion, on a paten covered with the cloth used to put over the chalice, without lights or procession, without surplice or stole.[946]

This did not please Brother Martin, who sent to fetch a stole and candles.

Then, taking the consecrated host in his fingers and presenting it to Jeanne, he said: "Do you believe this to be the body of Christ?"

"Yes, and it alone is able to deliver me."

And she entreated that it should be given to her.

"Do you still believe in your Voices?" asked the officiating priest.

"I believe in God alone, and will place no trust in the Voices who have thus deceived me."[947]

And shedding many tears she received the body of Our Lord very devoutly. Then to God, to the Virgin Mary and to the saints she offered prayers beautiful and reverent and gave such signs of repentance that those present were moved to tears.[948]

Contrite and sorrowful she said to Maître Pierre Maurice:[949] "Maître Pierre, where shall I be this evening?"

"Do you not trust in the Lord?" asked the canon.

"Yea, God helping me, I shall be in Paradise."[950]

Maître Nicolas Loiseleur exhorted her to correct the error she had caused to grow up among the people.

"To this end you must openly declare that you have been deceived and have deceived the folk and that you humbly ask pardon."

Then, fearing lest she might forget when the time came for her to be publicly judged, she asked Brother Martin to put her in mind of this matter and of others touching her salvation.[951]

Maître Loiseleur went away giving signs of violent grief. Walking through the streets like a madman, he was howled at by the *Godons*.[952]

It was about nine o'clock in the morning when Brother Martin and Messire Massieu took Jeanne out of the prison, wherein she had been in bonds one hundred and seventy-eight days. She was placed in a cart, and, escorted by eighty men-at-arms, was driven along the narrow streets to the Old Market Square, close to the River.[953] This square was bordered on the east by a wooden market-house, the butcher's market, on the west by the cemetery of Saint-Sauveur, on the edge of which, towards the square, stood the church of Saint-Sauveur.[954] In this place three scaffolds had been raised, one against the northern gable of the market-house; and in its erection several tiles of the roof had been broken.[955] On this scaffold Jeanne was to be stationed, there to listen to the sermon. Another and a larger scaffold had been erected adjoining the cemetery. There the judges and the prelates were to sit.[956] The pronouncing of sentence in a religious trial was an act of ecclesiastical jurisdiction. For the place of its pronouncement the Inquisitor and the Ordinary preferred consecrated territory, holy ground. True it is that a bull of Pope Lucius forbade such sentences to be given in churches and cemeteries; but the judges eluded this rule by recommending the secular arm to modify its sentence. The third scaffold, opposite the second, was of plaster, and stood in the middle of the square, on the spot whereon executions usually took place. On it was piled the wood for the burning. On the stake which surmounted it was a scroll bearing the words:

"Jehanne, who hath caused herself to be called the Maid, a liar, pernicious, deceiver of the people, soothsayer, superstitious, a blasphemer against God, presumptuous, miscreant, boaster, idolatress, cruel, dissolute, an invoker of devils, apostate, schismatic, and heretic."[957]

The square was guarded by one hundred and sixty men-at-arms. A crowd of curious folk pressed behind the guards, the windows were filled and the roofs covered with onlookers. Jeanne was brought on to the scaffold which had its back to the market-house gable. She wore a long gown and hood.[958] Maître Nicolas Midi, doctor in theology, came up on to the same platform and began to preach to her.[959] As the text of his sermon he took the words of the Apostle in the first Epistle to the Corinthians:[960] "And whether one member suffer, all the members suffer with it." Jeanne patiently listened to the sermon.[961]

Then my Lord of Beauvais, in his own name and that of the Vice-Inquisitor, pronounced the sentence.

He declared Jeanne to be a relapsed heretic.

"We declare that thou, Jeanne, art a corrupt member, and in order that thou mayest not infect the other members, we are resolved to sever thee from the unity of the Church, to tear thee from its body, and to deliver thee to the secular power. And we reject thee, we tear thee out, we abandon thee, beseeching this same secular power, that touching death and the mutilation of the limbs, it may be pleased to moderate its sentence...."[962]

By this formula, the ecclesiastical judge withdrew from any share in the violent death of a fellow creature: *Ecclesia abhorret a sanguine*.[963] But every one knew how much such an entreaty was worth; and all were aware that if the impossible had happened and the magistrate had granted it, he would have been subject to the same penalties as the heretic. Things had now come to such a pass that had the city of Rouen belonged to King Charles, he himself could not have saved the Maid from the stake.

When the sentence was announced Jeanne breathed heart-rending sighs. Weeping bitterly, she fell on her knees, commended her soul to God, to Our Lady, to the blessed saints of Paradise, many of whom she mentioned by name. Very humbly did she ask for mercy from all manner of folk, of whatsoever rank or condition, of her own party and of the enemy's, entreating them to forgive the wrong she had done them and to pray for her. She asked pardon of her judges, of the English, of King Henry, of the English princes of the realm. Addressing all the priests there present she besought each one to say a mass for the salvation of her soul.[964]

Thus for one half hour did she continue with sighs and tears to give expression to the sentiments of humiliation and contrition with which the clerics had inspired her.[965]

And even now she did not neglect to defend the honour of the fair Dauphin, whom she had so greatly loved.

She was heard to say: "It was never my King who induced me to do anything I have done, either good or evil."[966]

Many of the bystanders wept. A few English laughed. Certain of the captains, who could make nothing of the edifying ceremonial of ecclesiastical justice, grew impatient. Seeing Messire Massieu in the pulpit and hearing him exhort Jeanne to make a good end, they cried:

"What now, priest! Art thou going to keep us here to dinner?"[967]

At Rouen, when a heretic was given up to the secular arm, it was customary to take him to the town hall, where the town council made known unto him his sentence.[968] In Jeanne's case these forms were not observed. The Bailie, Messire le Bouteiller, who was present, waved his hand and said: "Take her, take her."[969] Straightway, two of the King's sergeants dragged her to the base of the scaffold and placed her in a cart which was waiting. On her head was set a great fool's cap made of paper, on which were written the words: "*Hérétique, relapse, apostate, idolâtre*"; and she was handed over to the executioner.[970]

A bystander heard her saying: "Ah! Rouen, sorely do I fear that thou mayest have to suffer for my death."[971]

She evidently still regarded herself as the messenger from Heaven, the angel of the realm of France. Possibly the illusion, so cruelly reft from her, returned at last to enfold her in its beneficent veil. At any rate, she appears to have been crushed; all that remained to her was an infinite horror of death and a childlike piety.

The ecclesiastical judges had barely time to descend and flee from a spectacle which they could not have witnessed without violating the laws of clerical procedure. They were all weeping: the Lord Bishop of Thérouanne, Chancellor of England, had his eyes full of tears. The Cardinal of Winchester, who was said never to enter a church save to pray for the death of an enemy,[972] had pity on this damsel so woeful and so contrite. Brother Pierre Maurice, the canon who was a reader of the Æneid, could not keep back his tears. All the priests who had delivered her to the executioner were edified to see her make so holy an end. That is what Maître Jean Alespée meant when he sighed: "I would that my soul were where I believe the soul of that woman to be."[973] To himself and the hapless sufferer he applied the following lines from the *Dies iræ*:

Qui Mariam absolvisti,
Mihi quoque spem dedisti.[974]

But none the less he must have believed that by her heresies and her obstinacy she had brought death on herself.

The two young friars preachers and the Usher Massieu accompanied Jeanne to the stake.

She asked for a cross. An Englishman made a tiny one out of two pieces of wood, and gave it to her. She took it devoutly and put it in her bosom, on her breast. Then she besought Brother Isambart to go to the neighbouring church to fetch a cross, to bring it to her and hold it before her, so that as long as she lived, the cross on which God was crucified should be ever in her sight.

Massieu asked a priest of Saint-Sauveur for one, and it was brought. Jeanne weeping kissed it long and tenderly, and her hands held it while they were free.[975]

As she was being bound to the stake she invoked the aid of Saint Michael; and now at length no examiner was present to ask her whether it were really he she saw in her father's garden. She prayed also to Saint Catherine.[976]

When she saw a light put to the stake, she cried loudly, "Jesus!" This name she repeated six times.[977] She was also heard asking for holy water.[978]

It was usual for the executioner, in order to cut short the sufferings of the victim, to stifle him in dense smoke before the flames had had time to ascend; but the Rouen executioner was too terrified of the prodigies worked by the Maid to do thus; and besides he would have found it difficult to reach her, because the Bailie had had the plaster scaffold made unusually high.

Wherefore the executioner himself, hardened man that he was, judged her death to have been a terribly cruel one.[979]

Once again Jeanne uttered the name of Jesus; then she bowed her head and gave up her spirit.[980]

As soon as she was dead the Bailie commanded the executioner to scatter the flames in order to see that the prophetess of the Armagnacs had not escaped with the aid of the devil or in some other manner.[981] Then, after the poor blackened body had been shown to the people, the executioner, in order to reduce it to ashes, threw on to the fire coal, oil and sulphur.

In such an execution the combustion of the corpse was rarely complete.[982] Among the ashes, when the fire was extinguished, the heart and entrails were found intact. For fear lest Jeanne's remains should be taken and used for witchcraft or other evil practices,[983] the Bailie had them thrown into the Seine.[984]

Chapter XV
After the death of the Maid – the end of the Shepherd – la Dame des Armoises

IN the evening, after the burning, the executioner, as was his wont, went whining and begging to the monastery of the preaching friars. The creature complained that he had found it very difficult to make an end of Jeanne. According to a legend invented afterwards, he told the monks that he feared damnation for having burned a saint.[985] Had he actually spoken thus in the house of the Vice-Inquisitor he would have been straightway cast into the lowest dungeon, there to await a trial for heresy, which would have probably resulted in his being sentenced to suffer the death he had inflicted on her whom he had called a saint. And what could have led him to suppose that the woman condemned by good Father Lemaistre and my Lord of Beauvais was not a bad woman? The truth is that in the presence of these friars he arrogated to himself merit for having executed a witch and taken pains therein, wherefore he came to ask for his pot of wine. One of the monks, who happened to be a friar preacher, Brother Pierre Bosquier, forgot himself so far as to say that it was wrong to have condemned the Maid. These words, albeit they were heard by only a few persons, were carried to the Inquisitor General. When he was summoned to answer for them, Brother Pierre Bosquier declared very humbly that his words were altogether wrong and tainted with heresy, and that indeed he had only uttered them when he was full of wine. On his knees and with clasped hands he entreated Holy Mother Church, his judges and the most redoubtable lords to pardon him. Having regard to his repentance and in consideration of his cloth and of his having spoken in a state of intoxication, my Lord of Beauvais and the Vice-Inquisitor showed indulgence to Brother Pierre Bosquier. By a sentence pronounced on the 8th of August, 1431, they condemned him to be imprisoned in the house of the friars preachers and fed on bread and water until Easter.[986]

On the 12th of June the judges and counsellors, who had sat in judgment on Jeanne, received letters of indemnity from the Great Council. What was the object of these letters? Was it in case the holders of them should be proceeded against by the French? But in that event the letters would have done them more harm than good.[987]

The Lord Chancellor of England sent to the Emperor, to the Kings and to the princes of Christendom, letters in Latin; to the prelates, dukes, counts, lords, and all the towns of France, letters in French.[988] Herein he made known unto them that King Henry and his Counsellors had had sore pity on the Maid, and that if they had caused her death it was through their zeal for the faith and their solicitude Christian folk.[989]

In like tenor did the University of Paris write to the Holy Father, the Emperor and the College of Cardinals.[990]

On the 4th of July, the day of Saint-Martin-le-Bouillant, Master Jean Graverent, Prior of the Jacobins, Inquisitor of the Faith, preached at Saint-Martin-des-Champs. In his sermon he related the deeds of Jeanne, and told how for her errors and shortcomings she had been delivered to the secular judges and burned alive.

Then he added: "There were four, three of whom have been taken, to wit, this Maid, Pierronne, and her companion. One, Catherine de la Rochelle, still remaineth with the Armagnacs. Friar Richard, the Franciscan, who attracted so great a multitude of folk when he preached in Paris at the Innocents and elsewhere, directed these women; he was their spiritual father."[991]

With Pierronne burned in Paris, her companion eating the bread of bitterness and drinking the water of affliction in the prison of the Church, and Jeanne burned at Rouen, the royal company of *béguines* was now almost entirely annihilated. There only remained to the King the holy dame of La Rochelle, who had escaped from the hands of the Paris Official; but her indiscreet talk had rendered her troublesome.[992] While his penitents were being discredited, good Friar Richard himself had fallen on evil days. The Vicars in the diocese of Poitiers and the Inquisitor of the Faith had forbidden him to preach. The great orator, who had converted so many Christian folk, could no longer thunder against gaming-tables and dice, against women's finery, and mandrakes arrayed in magnificent attire. No longer could he declare the coming of Antichrist nor prepare souls for the terrible trials which were to herald the imminent end of the world. He was ordered to lie under arrest in the Franciscan monastery at Poitiers. And doubtless it was with no great docility that he submitted to the sentence of his superiors; for on Friday, the 23rd of March, 1431, we find the Ordinary and the Inquisitor, asking aid in the execution of the sentence from the Parliament of Poitiers, which did not refuse it. Why did Holy Church exercise such severity towards a preacher endowed with so wondrous a power of moving sinful souls? We may at any rate suspect the reason. For some time the English and Burgundian clergy had been accusing him of apostasy and magic. Now, owing to the unity of the Church in general and to that of the Gallican Church in particular, owing also to the authority of that bright sun of Christendom, the University of Paris, when a clerk was suspected of error and heresy by the doctors of the English and Burgundian party he came to be looked at askance by the clergy who were loyal to King Charles. Especially was this so when in a matter touching the Catholic faith, the University had pronounced against him and in favour of the English. It is quite likely that the clerks of Poitiers had been prejudiced against Friar Richard by Pierronne's conviction and even by the Maid's trial. The good brother, who persisted in preaching the end of the world, was strongly suspected of dealing in the black art. Wherefore, realising the fate which was threatening him, he fled, and was never heard of again.[993]

None the less, however, did the counsellors of King Charles continue to employ the devout in the army. At the time of the disappearance of Friar Richard and his penitents, they were making use of a young shepherd whom my Lord the Archbishop, Duke of Reims and Chancellor of the kingdom, had proclaimed to be Jeanne's miraculous successor. And it was in the following circumstance that the shepherd was permitted to display his power.

The war continued. Twenty days after Jeanne's death the English in great force marched to recapture the town of Louviers. They had delayed till then, not, as some have stated, because they despaired of succeeding in anything as long as the Maid lived, but because they needed time to collect money and engines for the siege.[994] In the July and August of this same year, at Senlis and at Beauvais, my Lord of Reims, Chancellor of France and the Maréchal de Boussac, were upholding the French cause. And we may be sure that my Lord of Reims was upholding it with no little vigour since at the same time he was defending the benefices which were so dear to him.[995] A Maid had reconquered them, now he intended a lad to hold them. With this object he employed the little shepherd, Guillaume, from the Lozère Mountains, who, like Saint Francis of Assisi and Saint Catherine of Sienna, had received stigmata. A party of French surprised the Regent at Mantes and were on the point of taking him prisoner. The alarm was given to the army besieging Louviers; and two or three companies of men-at-arms were despatched. They hastened to Mantes, where they learnt that the Regent had succeeded in reaching Paris. Thereupon, having been reinforced by troops from Gournay and certain other English garrisons, being some two thousand strong and commanded by the Earls of Warwick, Arundel, Salisbury, and Suffolk, and by Lord Talbot and Sir Thomas Kiriel, the English made bold to march upon Beauvais. The French, informed of their approach, left the town at daybreak, and marched out to meet them in the direction of Savignies. King Charles's men, numbering between eight hundred and one thousand combatants, were commanded by the Maréchal de Boussac, the Captains La Hire, Poton, and others.[996]

The shepherd Guillaume, whom they believed to be sent of God, was at their head, riding side-saddle and displaying the miraculous wounds in his hands, his feet, and his left side.[997]

When they were about two and a half miles from the town, just when they least expected it, a shower of arrows came down upon them. The English, informed by their scouts of the French approach, had lain in wait for them in a hollow of the road. Now they attacked them closely both in the van and in the rear. Each side fought valiantly. A considerable number were slain, which was not the case in most of the battles of those days, when few but the fugitives were killed. But the French, feeling themselves surrounded, were seized with panic, and thus brought about their own destruction. Most of them, with the Maréchal de Boussac and Captain La Hire, fled to the town of Beauvais. Captain Poton and the shepherd, Guillaume, remained in the hands of the English, who returned to Rouen in triumph.[998]

Poton made sure of being ransomed in the usual manner. But the little shepherd could not hope for such a fate; he was suspected of heresy and magic; he had deceived Christian folk and accepted from them idolatrous veneration. The signs of our Saviour's passion that he bore upon him helped him not a whit; on the contrary the wounds, by the French held to have been divinely imprinted, to the English seemed the marks of the devil.

Guillaume, like the Maid, had been taken in the diocese of Beauvais. The Lord Bishop of this town, Messire Pierre Cauchon, who had claimed the right to try Jeanne, made a similar claim for Guillaume; and the shepherd was granted what the Maid had been refused, he was cast into an ecclesiastical prison.[999] He would seem to have been less difficult to guard than Jeanne and also less important. But the English had recently learnt what was involved in a trial by the Inquisition; they now knew how lengthy and how punctilious it was. Moreover, they did not see how it would profit them if this shepherd were convicted of heresy. If the French had set their hope of success in war[1000] in Guillaume as they had done in Jeanne, then that hope was but short-lived. To put the Armagnacs to shame by proving that their shepherd lad came from the devil, that game was not worth the candle. The youth was taken to Rouen and thence to Paris.[1001]

He had been a prisoner for four months when King Henry VI, who was nine years old, came to Paris to be crowned in the church of Notre Dame with the two crowns of France and England. With high pomp and great rejoicing he made his entrance into the city on Sunday, the 16th of December. Along the route of the procession, in the Rue du Ponceau-Saint-Denys, had been constructed a fountain adorned with three sirens; and from their midst rose a tall lily stalk, from the buds and blossoms of which flowed streams of wine and milk. Folk flocked to drink of the fountain; and around its basin men disguised as savages entertained them with games and sham fights.

From the Porte Saint-Denys to the Hôtel Saint-Paul in the Marais, the child King rode beneath a great azure canopy, embroidered with flowers-de-luce in gold, borne first by the four aldermen hooded and clothed in purple, then by the corporations, drapers, grocers, money-changers, goldsmiths and hosiers. Before him went twenty-five heralds and twenty-five trumpeters; followed by nine handsome men and nine beautiful ladies, wearing magnificent armour and bearing great shields, representing the nine *preux* and the nine *preuses*, also by a number of knights and squires. In this brilliant procession appeared the little shepherd Guillaume; he no longer stretched out his arms to show the wounds of the passion, for he was strongly bound.[1002]

After the ceremony he was conducted back to prison, whence he was taken later to be sewn in a sack and thrown into the Seine.[1003] Even the French admitted that Guillaume was but a simpleton and that his mission was not of God.[1004]

In 1433, the Constable, with the assistance of the Queen of Sicily, caused the capture and planned the assassination of La Trémouille. It was the custom of the nobles of that day to appoint counsellors for King Charles and afterwards to kill them. However, the sword which was to have caused the death of La Trémouille, owing to his corpulence, failed to inflict a mortal wound. His life was saved, but his influence was dead. King Charles tolerated the Constable as he had tolerated the Sire de la Trémouille.[1005]

The latter left behind him the reputation of having been grasping and indifferent to the welfare of the kingdom. Perhaps his greatest fault was that he governed in a time of war and pillage, when friends and foes alike were devouring the realm. He was charged with the destruction of the Maid, of whom he was said to have been jealous. This accusation proceeds from the House of Alençon, with whom the Lord Chamberlain was not popular.[1006] On the contrary, it must be admitted, that after the Lord Chancellor, La Trémouille was the boldest in employing the Maid, and if later she did thwart his plans there is nothing to prove that it was his intention to have her destroyed by the English. She destroyed herself and was consumed by her own zeal.

Rightly or wrongly, the Lord Chamberlain was held to be a bad man; and, although his successor in the King's favour, the Duc de Richemont, was avaricious, hard, violent, incredibly stupid, surly, malicious, always beaten and always discontented, the exchange appeared to be no loss. The Constable came in a fortunate hour, when the Duke of Burgundy was making peace with the King of France.

In the words of a Carthusian friar, the English who had entered the kingdom by the hole made in Duke John's head on the Bridge of Montereau, only retained their hold on the kingdom by the hand of Duke Philip. They were but few in number, and if the giant were to withdraw his hand a breath of wind would suffice to blow them away. The Regent died of sorrow and wrath, beholding the fulfilment of the horoscope of

King Henry VI: "Exeter shall lose what Monmouth hath won."[1007]

On the 13th of April, 1436, the Count of Richemont entered Paris. The nursing mother of Burgundian clerks and *Cabochien* doctors, the University herself, had helped to mediate peace.[1008]

Now, one month after Paris had returned to her allegiance to King Charles, there appeared in Lorraine a certain damsel. She was about twenty-five years old. Hitherto she had been called Claude; but she now made herself known to divers lords of the town of Metz as being Jeanne the Maid.[1009]

At this time, Jeanne's father and eldest brother were dead.[1010] Isabelle Romée was alive. Her two youngest sons were in the service of the King of France, who had raised them to the rank of nobility and given them the name of Du Lys. Jean, the eldest, called Petit-Jean,[1011] had been appointed Bailie of Vermandois, then Captain of Chartres. About this year, 1436, he was provost and captain of Vaucouleurs.[1012]

The youngest, Pierre, or Pierrelot, who had fallen into the hands of the Burgundians before Compiègne at the same time as Jeanne, had just been liberated from the prison of the Bastard of Vergy.[1013]

Both brothers believed that their sister had been burned at Rouen. But when they were told that she was living and wished to see them, they appointed a meeting at La-Grange-aux-Ormes, a village in the meadows of the Sablon, between the Seille and the Moselle, about two and a half miles south of Metz. They reached this place on the 20th of May. There they saw her and recognised her immediately to be their sister; and she recognised them to be her brothers.[1014]

She was accompanied by certain lords of Metz, among whom was a man right noble, Messire Nicole Lowe, who was chamberlain to Charles VII.[1015] By divers tokens these nobles recognised her to be the Maid Jeanne who had taken King Charles to be crowned at Reims. These tokens were certain signs on the skin.[1016] Now there was a prophecy concerning Jeanne which stated her to have a little red mark beneath the ear.[1017] But this prophecy was invented after the events to which it referred. Consequently we may believe the Maid to have been thus marked. Was this the token by which the nobles of Metz recognised her?

We do not know by what means she claimed to have escaped death; but there is reason to think[1018] that she attributed her deliverance to her holiness. Did she say that an angel had saved her from the fire? It might be read in books how in the ancient amphitheatres lions licked the bare feet of virgins, how boiling oil was as soothing as balm to the bodies of holy martyrs; and how according to many of the old stories nothing short of the sword could take the life of God's maidens. These ancient histories rested on a sure foundation. But if such tales had been related of the fifteenth century they might have appeared less credible. And this damsel does not seem to have employed them to adorn her adventure. She was probably content to say that another woman had been burned in her place.

According to a confession she made afterwards, she came from Rome, where, accoutred in harness of war, she had fought valiantly in the service of Pope Eugenius. She may even have told the Lorrainers of the feats of prowess she had there accomplished.

Now Jeanne had prophesied (at least so it was believed) that she would die in battle against the infidel and that her mantle would fall upon a maid of Rome. But such a saying, if it were known to these nobles of Metz, would be more likely to denounce this so-called Jeanne as an imposture than witness to the truth of her mission.[1019] However this might be, they believed what this woman told them.

Perhaps, like many a noble of the republic,[1020] they were more inclined to King Charles than to the Duke of Burgundy. And we may be sure that, chivalrous knights as they were, they esteemed chivalry wherever they found it; wherefore, because of her valour they admired the Maid; and they made her good cheer.

Messire Nicole Lowe gave her a charger and a pair of hose. The charger was worth thirty francs – a sum well-nigh royal – for of the two horses which at Soissons and at Senlis the King gave the Maid Jeanne, one was worth thirty-eight livres ten sous, and the other thirty-seven livres ten sous.[1021] Not more than sixteen francs had been paid for the horse with which she had been provided at Vaucouleurs.[1022]

Nicole Grognot, governor of the town,[1023] offered a sword to the sister of the Du Lys brothers; Aubert Boullay presented her with a hood.[1024]

She rode her horse with the same skill which seven years earlier, if we may believe some rather mythical stories, had filled with wonder the old Duke of Lorraine.[1025] And she spoke certain words to Messire Nicole Lowe which confirmed him in his belief that she was indeed that same Maid Jeanne who had fared forth into France. She had the ready tongue of a prophetess, and spoke in symbols and parables, revealing nought of her intent.

Her power would not come to her before Saint John the Baptist's Day, she said. Now this was the very time which the Maid, after the Battle of Patay, in 1429, had fixed for the extermination of the English in France.[1026]

This prophecy had not been fulfilled and consequently had not been mentioned again. Jeanne, if she ever uttered it, and it is quite possible that she did, must have been the first to forget it. Moreover, Saint John's Day was a term commonly cited in leases, fairs, contracts, hirings, etc., and it is quite conceivable that the calendar of a prophetess may have been the same as that of a labourer.

The day after their arrival at La Grange-aux-Ormes, Monday, the 21st of May, the Du Lys brothers took her, whom they held to be their sister, to that town of Vaucouleurs[1027] whither Isabelle Romée's daughter had gone to see Sire Robert de Baudricourt. In this town, in the year 1436, there were still living many persons of different conditions, such as the Leroyer couple and the Seigneur Aubert d'Ourches,[1028] who had seen Jeanne in February, 1429.

After a week at Vaucouleurs she went to Marville, a small town between Corny and Pont-á-Mousson. There she spent Whitsuntide and abode for three weeks in the house of one Jean Quenat.[1029] On her departure she was visited by sundry inhabitants of Metz, who gave her jewels, recognising her to be the Maid of France.[1030] Jeanne, it will be remembered, had been seen by divers knights of Metz at the time of King Charles's coronation at Reims. At Marville, Geoffroy Desch, following the example of Nicole Lowe, presented the so-called Jeanne with a horse. Geoffroy Desch belonged to one of the most influential families of the Republic of Metz. He was related to Jean Desch, municipal secretary in 1429.[1031]

From Marville, she went on a pilgrimage to Notre Dame de Liance, called Lienche by the Picards and known later as Notre Dame de Liesse. At Liance was worshipped a black image of the Virgin, which, according to tradition, had been brought by the crusaders from the Holy Land. The chapel containing this image was situated between Laon and Reims. It was said, by the priests who officiated there, to be one of the halting places on the route of the coronation procession, where the kings and their retinues were accustomed to stop on their return from Reims; but this is very likely not to be true. Whether it were such a halting place or no, there is no doubt that the folk of Metz displayed a particular devotion to Our Lady of Liance; and it seemed fitting that Jeanne, who had escaped from an English prison, should go and give thanks for her marvellous deliverance to the Black Virgin of Picardy.[1032]

Thence she went on her way to Arlon, to Elisabeth of Gorlitz, Duchess of Luxembourg, an aunt by marriage of the Duke of Burgundy.[1033] She was an old woman, who had been twice a widow. By extortion and oppression she had made herself detested by her vassals. By this princess Jeanne was well received. There was nothing strange in that. Persons living holy lives and working miracles were much sought after by princes and nobles who desired to discover secrets or to obtain the fulfilment of some wish. And the Duchess of Luxembourg might well believe this damsel to be the Maid Jeanne herself, since the brothers Du Lys, the nobles of Metz and the folk of Vaucouleurs were of that opinion.

For the generality of men, Jeanne's life and death were surrounded by marvels and mysteries. Many had from the first doubted her having perished by the hand of the executioner. Certain were curiously reticent on this point; they said: "the English had her publicly burnt at Rouen, or some other woman like her."[1034] Others confessed that they did not know what had become of her.[1035]

Thus, when throughout Germany and France the rumour spread that the Maid was alive and had been seen near Metz, the tidings were variously received. Some believed them, others did not. An ardent dispute, which arose between two citizens of Arles, gives some idea of the emotion aroused by such tidings. One maintained that the Maid was still alive; the other asserted that she was dead; each one wagered that what he said was true. This was no light wager, for it was made and registered in the presence of a notary, on the 27th of June, 1436, only five weeks after the interview at La Grange-aux-Ormes.[1036]

Meanwhile, in the beginning of August, the Maid's eldest brother, Jean du Lys, called Petit-Jean, had gone to Orléans to announce that his sister was alive. As a reward for these good tidings, he received for himself and his followers ten pints of wine, twelve hens, two goslings, and two leverets.[1037]

The birds had been purchased by two magistrates; the name of one, Pierre Baratin, is to be found in the account books of the fortress, in 1429,[1038] at the time of the expedition to Jargeau; the other was an old man of sixty-six, a burgess passing rich, Aignan de Saint-Mesmin.[1039]

Messengers were passing to and fro between the town of Duke Charles and the town of the Duchess of Luxembourg. On the 9th of August a letter from Arlon reached Orléans. About the middle of the month a pursuivant arrived at Arlon. He was called Cœur-de-Lis, in honour of the heraldic symbol of the city of Orléans, which was a lily-bud, a kind of trefoil. The magistrates of Orléans had sent him to Jeanne with a letter, the contents of which are unknown. Jeanne gave him a letter for the King, in which she probably requested an audience. He took it straight to Loches, where King Charles was negotiating the betrothal of his daughter Yolande to Prince Amedée of Savoie.[1040]

After forty-one days' journey the pursuivant returned to the magistrates, who had despatched him on the 2nd of September. The messenger complained of a great thirst, wherefore the magistrates, according to their wont, had him served in the chamber of the town-hall with bread, wine, pears, and green walnuts. This repast cost the town two *sous* four *deniers* of Paris, while the pursuivant's travelling expenses amounted to six *livres* which were paid in the following month. The town varlet who provided the walnuts was that same Jacquet Leprestre who had served during the siege. Another letter from the Maid had been received by the magistrates on the 25th of August.[1041]

Jean du Lys proceeded just as if his miracle-working sister had in very deed been restored to him. He went to the King, to whom he announced the wonderful tidings. Charles cannot have entirely disbelieved them since he ordered Jean du Lys to be given a gratuity of one hundred francs. Whereupon Jean promptly demanded these hundred francs from the King's treasurer, who gave him twenty. The coffers of the victorious King were not full even then.

Having returned to Orléans, Jean appeared before the town-council. He gave the magistrates to wit that he had only eight francs, a sum by no means sufficient to enable him and four retainers to return to Lorraine. The magistrates gave him twelve francs.[1042]

Every year until then the anniversary of the Maid had been celebrated in the church of Saint-Sanxon[1043] on the eve of Corpus Christi and on the previous day. In 1435, eight ecclesiastics of the four mendicant orders sang a mass for the repose of Jeanne's soul. In this year, 1436, the magistrates had four candles burnt, weighing together nine and a half pounds, and pendent therefrom the Maid's escutcheon, a silver shield bearing the crown of France. But when they heard the Maid was alive they cancelled the arrangements for a funeral service in her memory.[1044]

While these things were occurring in France, Jeanne was still with the Duchess of Luxembourg. There she met the young Count Ulrich of Wurtemberg, who refused to leave her. He had a handsome cuirasse made for her and took her to Cologne. She still called herself the Maid of France sent by God.[1045]

Since the 24th of June, Saint John the Baptist's Day, her power had returned to her. Count Ulrich, recognising her supernatural gifts, entreated her to employ them on behalf of himself and his friends. Being very contentious, he had become seriously involved in the schism which was then rending asunder the diocese of Trèves. Two prelates were contending for the see; one, Udalric of Manderscheit, appointed by the chapter, the other Raban of Helmstat, Bishop of Speyer, appointed by the Pope.[1046] Udalric took the field with a small force and twice besieged and bombarded the town of which he called himself the true shepherd. These proceedings brought the greater part of the diocese on to his side.[1047] But although aged and infirm, Raban too had weapons; they were spiritual but powerful: he pronounced an interdict against all such as should espouse the cause of his rival.

Count Ulrich of Wurtemberg, who was among the most zealous of Udalric's supporters, questioned the Maid of God concerning him.[1048] Similar cases had been submitted to the first Jeanne when she was in France. She had been asked, for example, which of the three popes, Benedict, Martin, or Clement, was the true father of the faithful, and without immediately pronouncing on the subject she had promised to designate the Pope to whom obedience was due, after she had reached Paris and rested there.[1049] The second Jeanne replied with even more assurance; she declared that she knew who was the true archbishop and boasted that she would enthrone him.

According to her, it was Udalric of Manderscheit, he whom the Chapter had appointed. But when Udalric was summoned before the Council of Bâle, he was declared an usurper; and the fathers did what it was by no means their unvarying rule to do, – they confirmed the nomination of the Pope.

Unfortunately the Maid's intervention in this dispute attracted the attention of the Inquisitor General of the city of Cologne, Heinrich Kalt Eysen, an illustrious professor of theology. He inquired into the rumours which were being circulated in the city touching the young prince's protégée; and he learnt that she wore unseemly apparel, danced with men, ate and drank more than she ought, and practised magic. He was informed notably that in a certain assembly the Maid tore a table-cloth and straightway restored it to its original condition, and that having broken a glass against the wall she with marvellous skill put all its pieces together again. Such deeds caused Kalt Eysen to suspect her strongly of heresy and witchcraft. He summoned her before his tribunal; she refused to appear. This disobedience displeased the Inquisitor General, and he sent to fetch the defaulter. But the young Count of Wurtemberg hid his Maid in his house, and afterwards contrived to get her secretly out of the town. Thus she escaped the fate of her whom she was willing only partially to imitate. As he could do nothing else, the Inquisitor excommunicated her.[1050] She took refuge at Arlon with her protectress, the Duchess of Luxembourg. There she met Robert des Armoises, Lord of Tichemont. She may have seen him before, in the spring, at Marville, where he usually resided. This nobleman was probably the son of Lord Richard, Governor of the Duchy of Bar in 1416. Nothing is known of him, save that he surrendered this territory to the foreigner without the Duke of Bar's consent, and then beheld it confiscated and granted to the Lord of Apremont on condition that he should conquer it.

It was not extraordinary that Lord Robert should be at Arlon, seeing that his château of Tichemont was near this town. He was poor, albeit of noble birth.[1051]

The so-called Maid married him,[1052] apparently with the approval of the Duchess of Luxembourg. According to the opinion of the Holy Inquisitor of Cologne, this marriage was contracted merely to protect the woman against the interdict and to save her from the sword of the Church.[1053]

Soon after her marriage she went to live at Metz in her husband's house, opposite the church of Sainte-Ségolène, over the Sainte-Barbe Gate. Henceforth she was Jeanne du Lys, the Maid of France, the Lady of Tichemont. By these names she is described in a contract dated the 7th of November, 1436, by which Robert des Armoises and his wife, authorised by him, sell to Collard de Failly, squire, dwelling at Marville, and to Poinsette, his wife, one quarter of the lordship of Haraucourt. At the request of their dear friends, Messire Robert and Dame Jeanne, Jean de Thoneletil, Lord of Villette, and Saubelet de Dun, Provost of Marville, as well as the vendors, put their seals to the contract to testify to its validity.[1054]

In her dwelling, opposite the Sainte-Ségolène Church, la Dame des Armoises gave birth to two children.[1055] Somewhere in Languedoc[1056] there was an honest squire who, when he heard of these births, seriously doubted whether Jeanne the Maid and la Dame des Armoises could be one and the same person. This was Jean d'Aulon, who had once been Jeanne's steward. From information he had received from women who knew, he did not believe her to be the kind of woman likely to have children.[1057]

According to Brother Jean Nider, doctor in theology of the University of Vienne, this fruitful union turned out badly. A priest, and, as he says, a priest who might more appropriately be called a pander, seduced this witch with words of love and carried her off. But Brother Jean Nider adds that the priest secretly took la Dame des Armoises to Metz and there lived with her as his concubine.[1058] Now it is proved that her own home was in that very town; hence we may conclude that this friar preacher does not know what he is talking about.[1059]

The fact of the matter is that she did not remain longer than two years in the shadow of Sainte-Ségolène.

Although she had married, it was by no means her intention to forswear prophesying and chivalry. During her trial Jeanne had been asked by the examiner: "Jeanne, was it not revealed to you that if you lost your virginity your good fortune would cease and your Voices desert you?" She denied that such things had been revealed to her. And when he insisted, asking her whether she believed that if she were married her Voices would still come to her, she answered like a good Christian: "I know not, and I appeal to God."[1060] Jeanne des Armoises likewise held that good fortune had not forsaken her on account of her marriage. Moreover, in those days of prophecy there were both widows and married women who, like Judith of Bethulia, acted by divine inspiration. Such had been Dame Catherine de la Rochelle, although perhaps after all she had not done anything so very great.[1061]

In the summer of 1439, la Dame des Armoises went to Orléans. The magistrates offered her wine and meat as a token of gladness and devotion. On the first of August they gave her a dinner and presented her with two hundred and ten livres of Paris as an acknowledgment of the service she had rendered to the town during the siege. These are the very terms in which this expenditure is entered in the account books of that city.[1062]

If the folk of Orléans did actually take her for the real Maid, Jeanne, then it must have been more on account of the evidence of the Du Lys brothers, than on that of their own eyes. For, when one comes to think of it, they had seen her but very seldom. During that week in May, she had only appeared before them armed and on horseback. Afterwards in June, 1429, and

January, 1430, she had merely passed through the town. True it was she had been offered wine and the magistrates had sat at table with her;[1063] but that was nine years ago. And the lapse of nine years works many a change in a woman's face. They had seen her last as a young girl, now they found her a woman and the mother of two children. Moreover they were guided by the opinion of her kinsfolk. Their attitude provokes some astonishment, however, when one thinks of the conversation at the banquet, and of the awkward and inconsistent remarks the dame must have uttered. If they were not then undeceived, these burgesses must have been passing simple and strongly prejudiced in favour of their guest.

And who can say that they were not? Who can say that, after having given credence to the tidings brought by Jean du Lys, the townsfolk did not begin to discover the imposture? That the belief in the survival of Jeanne was by no means general in the city, during the visit of la Dame des Armoises, is proved by the entries in the municipal accounts of sums expended on the funeral services, which we have already mentioned. Supposing we abstract the years 1437 and 1438, the anniversary service had at any rate been held in 1439, two days before Corpus-Christi, and only about three months before the banquet on the 1st of August.[1064] Thus these grateful burgesses of Orléans were at one and the same time entertaining their benefactress at banquets and saying masses in memory of her death.

La Dame des Armoises only spent a fortnight with them. She left the city towards the end of July. Her departure would seem to have been hasty and sudden. She was invited to a supper, at which she was to have been presented with eight pints of wine, but when the wine was served she had gone, and the banquet had to be held without her.[1065] Jean Quillier and Thévanon of Bourges were present. This Thévanon may have been that Thévenin Villedart, with whom Jeanne's brothers dwelt during the siege.[1066] In Jean Quillier we recognise the young draper who, in June, 1429, had furnished fine Brussels cloth of purple, wherewith to make a gown for the Maid.[1067]

La Dame des Armoises had gone to Tours, where she gave herself out to be the true Jeanne. She gave the Bailie of Touraine a letter for the King; and the Bailie undertook to see that it was delivered to the Prince, who was then at Orléans, having arrived there but shortly after Jeanne's departure. The Bailie of Touraine in 1439 was none other than that Guillaume Bellier who ten years before as lieutenant of Chinon had received the Maid into his house and committed her to the care of his devout wife.[1068]

To the messenger, who bore this letter, Guillaume Bellier also gave a note for the King written by himself, and "touching the deeds of la Dame des Armoises."[1069] We know nothing of its purport.[1070]

Shortly afterwards the Dame went off into Poitou. There she placed herself at the service of Seigneur Gille de Rais, Marshal of France.[1071] He it was who in his early youth had conducted the Maid to Orléans, had been with her throughout the coronation campaign, had fought at her side before the walls of Paris. During Jeanne's captivity he had occupied Louviers and pushed on boldly to Rouen. Now throughout the length and breadth of his vast domains he was kidnapping children, mingling magic with debauchery, and offering to demons the blood and the limbs of his countless victims. His monstrous doings spread terror round his castles of Tiffauges and Machecoul, and already the hand of the Church was upon him.

According to the Holy Inquisitor of Cologne, la Dame des Armoises practised magic; but it was not as an invoker of demons that the Maréchal de Rais employed her; he placed her in authority over the men-at-arms,[1072] in somewhat the same position as Jeanne had occupied at Lagny and Compiègne. Did she do great prowess? We do not know. At any rate she did not hold her office long; and after her it was bestowed on a Gascon squire, one Jean de Siquemville.[1073] In the spring of 1440 she was near Paris.[1074]

For nearly two years and a half the great town had been loyal to King Charles. He had entered the city, but had failed to restore it to prosperity. Deserted houses were everywhere falling into ruins; wolves penetrated into the suburbs and devoured little children.[1075] The townsfolk, who had so recently been Burgundian, could not all forget how the Maid in company with Friar Richard and the Armagnacs had attacked the city on the day of the Nativity of Our Lady. There were many, doubtless, who bore her ill will and believed she had been burned for her sins; but her name no longer excited universal reprobation as in 1429. Certain even among her former enemies regarded her as a martyr to the cause of her liege lord.[1076] Even in Rouen such an opinion was not unknown, and it was much more likely to be held in the city of Paris which had lately turned French. At the rumour that Jeanne was not dead, that she had been recognised by the people of Orléans and was coming to Paris, the lower orders in the city grew excited and disturbances were threatening.

Under Charles of Valois in 1440, the spirit of the University was just the same as it had been under Henry of Lancaster in 1431. It honoured and respected the King of France, the guardian of its privileges and the defender of the liberties of the Gallican Church. The illustrious masters felt no remorse at having demanded and obtained the chastisement of the rebel and heretic, Jeanne the Maid. Whosoever persists in error is a heretic; whosoever essays and fails to overthrow the powers that be is a rebel. It was God's will that in 1440 Charles of Valois should possess the city of Paris; it had not been God's will in 1429; wherefore the Maid had striven against God. With equal bitterness would the University, in 1440, have proceeded against a Maid of the English.

The magistrates who had returned to their Paris homes from their long dreary exile at Poitiers sat in the Parlement side by side with the converted Burgundians.[1077] In the days of adversity these faithful servants of King Charles had set the Maid to work, but now in 1440 it was none of their business to maintain publicly the truth of her mission and the purity of her faith. Burned by the English, that was all very well. But a trial conducted by a bishop and a vice-inquisitor with the concurrence of the University is not an English trial; it is a trial at once essentially Gallican and essentially Catholic. Jeanne's name was forever branded throughout Christendom. That ecclesiastical sentence could be reversed by the Pope alone. But the Pope had no intention of doing this. He was too much afraid of displeasing the King of Catholic England; and moreover were he once to admit that an inquisitor of the faith had pronounced a wrong sentence he would undermine all human authority. The French clerks submit and are silent. In the assemblies of the clergy no one dares to utter Jeanne's name.

Fortunately for them neither the doctors and masters of the University nor the sometime members of the Parlement of Poitiers share the popular delusion touching la Dame des Armoises. They have no doubt that the Maid was burned at Rouen. And they fear lest this woman, who gives herself out to be the deliverer of Orléans, may arouse a tumult by her entrance into the city. Wherefore the Parlement and the University send out men-at-arms to meet her. She is arrested and brought to the Palais.[1078]

She was examined, tried and sentenced to be publicly exhibited. In the Palais de Justice, leading up from the court called the Cour-de-Mai, there was a marble slab on which malefactors were exhibited. La Dame des Armoises was put up there and shown to the people whom she had deceived. The usual sermon was preached at her and she was forced to confess publicly.[1079]

She declared that she was not the Maid, that she was married to a knight and had two sons. She told how one day, in her mother's presence, she heard a woman speak slightingly of her; whereupon she proceeded to attack the slanderer, and, when her mother restrained her, she turned her blows against her parent. Had she not been in a passion she would never have struck her mother. Notwithstanding this provocation, here was a special case and one reserved for the papal jurisdiction. Whosoever had raised his hand against his father or his mother, as likewise against a priest or a clerk, must go and ask forgiveness of the Holy Father, to whom alone belonged the power of convicting or acquitting the sinner. This was what she had done. "I went to Rome," she said, "attired in man's apparel. I engaged as a soldier in the war of the Holy Father Eugenius, and in this war I twice committed homicide."

When had she journeyed to Rome? Probably before the exile of Pope Eugenius to Florence, about the year 1433, when the condottieri of the Duke of Milan were advancing to the gates of the Eternal City.[1080]

We do not find either the University, or the Ordinary, or the Grand Inquisitor demanding the trial of this woman, who was suspected of witchcraft and of homicide, and who was attired in unseemly garments. She was not prosecuted as a heretic, doubtless because she was not obstinate, and obstinacy alone constitutes heresy.

Henceforth she attracted no further attention. It is believed, but on no very trustworthy evidence, that she ended by returning to Metz, to her husband, le Chevalier des Armoises, and that she lived quietly and respectably to a good old age, dwelling in the house over the door of which were her armorial bearings, or rather those of Jeanne the Maid, the sword, the crown and the Lilies.[1081]

The success of this fraud had endured four years. After all it is not so very surprising. In every age people have been loath to believe in the final end of existences which have touched their imagination; they will not admit that great personalities can be struck down by death like ordinary folk; such an end to a noble career is repugnant to them. Impostors, like la Dame des Armoises, never fail to find some who will believe in them. And the Dame appeared at a time which was singularly favourable to such a delusion; intellects had been dulled by long suffering; communication between one district and another was rendered impossible or difficult, and what was happening in one place was unknown quite near at hand; in the minds of men there reigned dimness, ignorance, confusion.

But even then folk would not have been imposed upon so long by this pseudo-Jeanne had it not been for the support given her by the Du Lys brothers. Were they her dupes or her accomplices? Dull-witted as they may have been, it seems hardly credible that the adventuress could have imposed upon them. Admitting that she very closely resembled La Romée's daughter, the woman from La Grange-aux-Ormes cannot possibly for any length of time have deceived two men who knew Jeanne intimately, having been brought up with her and come with her into France.

If they were not imposed upon, then how can we account for their conduct? They had lost much when they lost their sister. When he arrived at La Grange-aux-Ormes, Pierre du Lys had just quitted a Burgundian prison; his ransom had been paid with his wife's dowry, and he was then absolutely destitute.[1082] Jean, Bailie of Vermandois, afterwards Governor of Chartres and about 1436 Bailie of Vaucouleurs, was hardly more prosperous.[1083] Such circumstances explained much. And yet it is unlikely that they of themselves alone and unsupported would have played a game so difficult, so risky, and so dangerous. From the little we know of their lives we should conclude that they were both too simple, too naïf, too placid, to carry on such an intrigue.

We are tempted to believe that they were urged on by some higher and greater power. Who knows? Perhaps by certain indiscreet persons in the service of the King of France. The condemnation and death of Jeanne was a serious attack upon the prestige of Charles VII. May he not have had in his household or among his counsellors certain subjects who were rashly jealous enough to invent this appearance, in order to spread abroad the belief that Jeanne the Maid had not died the death of a witch, but that by virtue of her innocence and her holiness she had escaped the flames? If this were so, then we may regard the imposture of the pseudo-Jeanne, invented at a time when it seemed impossible ever to obtain a papal revision of the trial of 1431, as an attempt, surreptitious and fraudulent and speedily abandoned, to bring about her rehabilitation.

Such a hypothesis would explain why the Du Lys brothers were not punished or even disgraced, when they had put themselves in the wrong, had deceived King and people and committed the crime of high treason. Jean continued provost of Vaucouleurs for many a long year, and then, when relieved of his office, received a sum of money in lieu of it. Pierre, as well as his mother, La Romée, was living at Orléans. In 1443 he received from Duke Charles, who had returned to France three years before, the grant of an island in the Loire, l'Île-aux-Bœufs,[1084] which was fair grazing land. Nevertheless, he remained poor, and was constantly receiving help from the Duke and the townsfolk of Orléans.[1085]

Chapter XVI
After the death of the Maid (*continued*) – the Rouen judges at the council of Bâle and the pragmatic sanction – the rehabilitation trial – the Maid of Sarmaize – the Maid of Le Mans

ROM year to year the Council of Bâle drew out its deliberations in a series of sessions well nigh as lengthy as the tail of the dragon in the Apocalypse. Its manner of reforming at once the Church, its members, and its head struck terror into the hearts of the sovereign Pontiff and the Sacred College. Sorrowfully did Æneus Sylvius exclaim, "There is assembled at Bâle, not the Church of God indeed, but the synagogue of Satan."[1086] But though uttered by a Roman cardinal, even such an expression can hardly be termed violent when applied to the synod which established free elections to bishoprics, suppressed the right of bestowing the pallium, of exacting annates and payments to the papal chancery, and which was endeavouring to restore the papacy to evangelical poverty. The King of France and the Emperor, on the other hand, looked favourably on the Council when it essayed to bridle the ambition and greed of the Bishop of Rome.

Now among the Fathers who displayed the greatest zeal in the reformation of the Church were the masters and doctors of the University of Paris, those who had sat in judgment on Jeanne the Maid, and notably Maître Nicolas Loiseleur and Maître

Thomas de Courcelles. Charles VII convoked an assembly of the clergy of the realm in order to examine the canons of Bâle. The assembly met in the Sainte-Chapelle at Bourges, on the 1st of May, 1438. Master Thomas de Courcelles, appointed delegate by the Council, there conferred with the Lord Bishop of Castres. Now in 1438 the Bishop of Castres was that elegant humanist, that zealous counsellor of the crown, who, in style truly Ciceronian, complained in his letters that so closely was he bound to his glebe, the court, that no time remained to him to visit his spouse.[1087] He was none other than that Gérard Machet, the King's confessor, who had, in 1429, along with the clerks at Poitiers, pleaded the authority of prophecy in favour of the Maid, in whom he found nought but sincerity and goodness.[1088] Maître Thomas de Courcelles at Rouen had urged the Maid's being tortured and delivered to the secular arm.[1089] At the Bourges assembly the two churchmen agreed touching the supremacy of General Councils, the freedom of episcopal elections, the suppression of annates and the rights of the Gallican Church. At that moment it was not likely that either one or the other remembered the poor Maid. From the deliberations of this assembly, in which Maître Thomas played an important part, there issued the solemn edict promulgated by the King on the 7th of July, 1438; the Pragmatic Sanction. By this edict the canons of Bâle became the constitution of the Church of France.[1090]

The Emperor also agreed to the reforms of Bâle. So audacious did the Fathers become that they summoned Pope Eugenius to appear before their tribunal. When he refused to obey their summons, they deposed him, declaring him to be disobedient, obstinate, rebellious, a breaker of rules, a perturber of ecclesiastical unity, a perjurer, a schismatic, a hardened heretic, a squanderer of the treasures of the Church, scandalous, simoniacal, pernicious and damnable.[1091] Such was the condemnation of the Holy Fathers pronounced among other doctors by Maître Jean Beaupère, Maître Thomas de Courcelles and Maître Nicolas Loiseleur, who had all three so sternly reproached Jeanne with having refused to submit to the

Pope.[1092] Maître Nicolas had been extremely energetic throughout the Maid's trial, playing alternately the parts of the Lorraine prisoner and Saint Catherine; when she was led to the stake he had run after her like a madman.[1093] This same Maître Nicolas now displayed great activity in the Council wherein he attained to some eminence. He upheld the view that the General Council canonically convoked, was superior to the Pope and in a position to depose him. And albeit this canon was a mere master of arts, he made such an impression on the Fathers at Bâle that in 1439, they despatched him to act as juris-consult at the Diet of Mainz. Meanwhile his attitude was strongly displeasing to the chapter which had sent him as deputy to the Council. The canons of Rouen sided with the Sovereign Pontiff and against the Fathers, on this point joining issue with the University of Paris. They disowned their delegate and sent to recall him on the 28th of July, 1438.[1094]

Maître Thomas de Courcelles, one of those who had declared the Pope disobedient, obstinate, rebellious and the rest, was nominated one of the commissioners to preside over the election of a new pope, and, like Loiseleur, a delegate to the Diet of Mainz. But, unlike Loiseleur, he was not disowned by those who had appointed him, for he was the deputy of the University of Paris who recognised the Pope of the Council, Felix, to be the true Father of the Faithful.[1095] In the assembly of the French clergy held at Bourges in the August of 1440, Maître Thomas spoke in the name of the Fathers of Bâle. He discoursed for two hours to the complete satisfaction of the King.[1096] Charles VII, while remaining loyal to Pope Eugenius, maintained the Pragmatic Sanction. Maître Thomas de Courcelles was henceforth one of the pillars of the French Church.

Meanwhile the English government had declared for the Pope and against the Council.[1097] My Lord Pierre Cauchon, who had become Bishop of Lisieux, was Henry VI's ambassador at the Council. And at Bâle a somewhat unpleasant experience befell him. By reason of his translation to the see of Lisieux he owed Rome annates to the amount of 400 golden florins. In

Germany he was informed by the Pope's Treasurer that by his failure to pay this sum, despite the long delays granted to him, he had incurred excommunication, and that being excommunicate, by presuming to celebrate divine service he had committed irregularity.[1098] Such accusations must have caused him considerable annoyance. But after all, such occurrences were frequent and of no great consequence. On churchmen these thunderbolts fell but lightly, doing them no great hurt.

From 1444, the realm of France, disembarrassed alike of adversaries and of defenders, was free to labour, to work at various trades, to engage in commerce and to grow rich. In the intervals between wars and during truces, King Charles's government, by the interchange of natural products and of merchandise, also, we may add, by the abolition of tolls and dues on the Rivers Seine, Oise, and Loire, effected the actual conquest of Normandy. Thus, when the time for nominal conquest came, the French had only to take possession of the province. So easy had this become, that in the rapid campaign of 1449,[1099] even the Constable was not beaten, neither was the Duke of Alençon. In his royal and peaceful manner Charles VII resumed possession of his town of Rouen, just as twenty years before he had taken Troyes and Reims, as the result of an understanding with the townsfolk and in return for an amnesty and the grant of rights and privileges to the burghers. He entered the city on Monday, the 10th of November, 1449.

The French government felt itself strong enough even to attempt the reconquest of that essentially English province, Aquitaine. In 1451, my Lord the Bastard, now Count of Dunois, took possession of the fortress of Blaye. Bordeaux and Bayonne surrendered in the same year. In the following manner did the Lord Bishop of Le Mans celebrate these conquests, worthy of the majesty of the most Christian King.

"Maine, Normandy, Aquitaine, these goodly provinces have returned to their allegiance to the King. Almost without the shedding of French blood hath this been accomplished. It hath not been necessary to overthrow the ramparts of many strongly walled towns, or to demolish their fortifications or for the inhabitants to suffer either pillage or murder."[1100]

Indeed Normandy and Maine were quite content at being French once more. The town of Bordeaux was alone in regretting the English, whose departure spelt its ruin. It revolted in 1452; and then after considerable difficulty was reconquered once and for all.

King Charles, henceforth rich and victorious, now desired to efface the stain inflicted on his reputation by the sentence of 1431. He wanted to prove to the whole world that it was no witch who had conducted him to his coronation. He was now eager to appeal against the condemnation of the Maid. But this condemnation had been pronounced by the church, and the Pope alone could order it to be cancelled. The King hoped to bring the Pope to do this, although he knew it would not be easy. In the March of 1450, he proceeded to a preliminary inquiry;[1101] and matters remained in that position until the arrival in France of Cardinal d'Estouteville, the legate of the Holy See. Pope Nicolas had sent him to negotiate with the King of France a peace with England and a crusade against the Turks. Cardinal d'Estouteville, who belonged to a Norman family, was just the man to discover the weak points in Jeanne's trial. In order to curry favour with Charles, he, as legate, set on foot a new inquiry at Rouen, with the assistance of Jean Bréhal, of the order of preaching friars, the Inquisitor of the Faith in the kingdom of France. But the Pope did not approve of the legate's intervention;[1102] and for three years the revision was not proceeded with. Nicolas V would not allow it to be thought that the sacred tribunal of the most holy Inquisition was fallible and had even once pronounced an unjust sentence. And there existed at Rome a stronger reason for not interfering with the trial of 1431: the French demanded revision; the English were opposed to it; and the Pope did not wish to annoy the English, for they were then just as good and even better Catholics than the French.[1103]

In order to relieve the Pope from embarrassment and set him at his ease, the government of Charles VII invented an expedient: the King was not to appear in the suit; his place was to be taken by the family of the Maid. Jeanne's mother, Isabelle Romée de Vouthon, who lived in retirement at Orléans,[1104] and her two sons, Pierre and Jean du Lys, demanded the revision.[1105] By this legal artifice the case was converted from a political into a private suit. At this juncture Nicolas V died, on the 24th of March, 1455. His successor, Calixtus III, a Borgia, an old man of seventy-eight, by a rescript dated the 11th of June, 1455, authorised the institution of proceedings. To this end he appointed Jean Jouvenel des Ursins, Archbishop of Reims, Guillaume Chartier, Bishop of Paris, and Richard Olivier, Bishop of Coutances, who were to act conjointly with the Grand Inquisitor of France.[1106]

From the first it was agreed that certain of those concerned in the original trial were not now to be involved, "for they had been deceived." Notably it was admitted that the Daughter of Kings, the Mother of Learning, the University of Paris, had been led into error by a fraudulent indictment consisting of twelve articles. It was agreed that the whole responsibility should be thrown on to the Bishop of Beauvais and the Promoter, Guillaume d'Estivet, who were both deceased. The precaution was necessary. Had it not been taken, certain doctors very influential with the King and very dear to the Church of France would have been greatly embarrassed.

On the 7th of November, 1455, Isabelle Romée and her two sons, followed by a long procession of innumerable ecclesiastics, laymen, and worthy women, approached the church of Notre Dame in Paris to demand justice from the prelates and papal commissioners.[1107]

Informers and accusers in the trial of the late Jeanne were summoned to appear at Rouen on the 12th of December. Not one came.[1108] The heirs of the late Messire Pierre Cauchon declined all liability for the deeds of their deceased kinsman, and touching the civil responsibility, they pleaded the amnesty granted by the King on the reconquest of Normandy.[1109] As had been expected, the proceedings went forward without any obstacle or even any discussion.

Inquiries were instituted at Domremy, at Orléans, at Paris, at Rouen.[1110] The friends of Jeannette's childhood, Hauviette, Mengette, either married or grown old; Jeannette, the wife of Thévenin; Jeannette, the widow of Estellin; Jean Morel of Greux; Gérardin of Épinal, the Burgundian, and his wife Isabellette, who had been godmother to Jacques d'Arc's daughter; Perrin, the bell-ringer; Jeanne's uncle Lassois; the Leroyer couple and a score of peasants from Domremy all appeared. Bertrand de Poulengy, then sixty-three and gentleman of the horse to the King of France, was heard; likewise Jean de Novelompont, called Jean de Metz, who had been raised to noble rank and was now living at Vaucouleurs, where he held some military office. Gentlemen and ecclesiastics of Lorraine and Champagne were examined.[1111] Burgesses of Orléans were also called, and notably Jean Luillier, the draper, who in June, 1429, had furnished fine Brussels cloth of purple for Jeanne's gown and ten years later had been present at the banquet given by the magistrates of Orléans in honour of the Maid who, as it was believed, had escaped burning.[1112] Jean Luillier was the most intelligent of the witnesses; as for the others, of whom there were about two dozen townsmen and townswomen, of between fifty and sixty years of age, they did little but repeat his evidence.[1113] He spoke well; but the fear of the English dazzled him and he saw many more of them than there had ever been.

Touching the examination at Poitiers there were called an advocate, a squire, a man of business, François Garivel, who was fifteen at the time of Jeanne's interrogation.[1114] The only cleric summoned was Brother Seguin of Limousin.[1115] The clerics of Poitiers were first as disinclined to risk themselves in this matter as were those of Rouen; a burnt child dreads the fire. La Hire and Poton of Saintrailles were dead. The survivors of Orléans and of Patay were called; the Bastard Jean, now Count of Dunois and Longueville, who gave his evidence like a clerk;[1116] the old

Sire de Gaucourt, who in his eighty-fifth year made some effort of memory, and for the rest gave the same evidence as the Count of Dunois;[1117] the Duke of Alençon, on the point of making an alliance with the English and of procuring a powder with which to dry up the King,[1118] but who was none the less talkative and vain-glorious;[1119] Jeanne's steward, Messire Jean d'Aulon, who had become a knight, a King's Counsellor and Seneschal of Beaucaire,[1120] and the little page Louis de Coutes, now a noble of forty-two.[1121] Brother Pasquerel too was called; even in his old-age he remained superficial and credulous.[1122] And there was heard also the widow of Maître René de Bouligny, Demoiselle Marguerite la Toroulde, who delicately and with a good grace related what she remembered.[1123]

Care was taken not to summon the Lord Archbishop of Rouen, Messire Raoul Roussel, as a witness of the actual incidents of the trial, albeit he had sat in judgment on the Maid, side by side with my Lord of Beauvais. As for the Vice Inquisitor of Religion, Brother Jean Lemaistre, he might have been dead, so completely was he ignored. Nevertheless, certain of the assessors were called: Jean Beaupère, canon of Paris, of Besançon and of Rouen; Jean de Mailly, Lord Bishop of Noyon; Jean Lefèvre, Bishop of Démétriade; divers canons of Rouen, sundry ecclesiastics who appeared some unctuous, others stern and frowning;[1124] and, finally, the most illustrious Thomas de Courcelles, who, after having been the most laborious and assiduous collaborator of the Bishop of Beauvais, recalled nothing when he came before the commissioners for the revision.[1125]

Among those who had been most zealous to procure Jeanne's condemnation were those who were now most eagerly labouring for her rehabilitation. The registrars of the Lord Bishop of Beauvais, the Boisguillaumes, the Manchons, the Taquels, all those ink-pots of the Church who had been used for her death sentence, worked wonders when that sentence had to be annulled; all the zeal they had displayed in the institution of the trial they now displayed in its revision; they were prepared to discover in it every possible flaw.[1126]

The Bastard of Orleans
(from an old engraving)

And in what a poor and paltry tone did these benign fabricators of legal artifices denounce the cruel iniquity which they had themselves perpetrated in due form! Among them was the Usher, Jean Massieu, a dissolute priest,[1127] of scandalous morals, but a kindly fellow for all that, albeit somewhat crafty and the inventor of a thousand ridiculous stories against Cauchon, as if the old Bishop were not black enough already.[1128] The revision commissioners produced a couple of sorry monks, Friar Martin Ladvenu and Friar Isambart de la Pierre, from the monastery of the preaching friars at Rouen. They wept in a heart-rending manner as they told of the pious end of that poor Maid, whom they had declared a heretic, then a relapsed heretic, and had finally burned alive. There was not one of the clerks charged with the examination of Jeanne but was touched to the heart at the memory of so saintly a damsel.[1129]

Huge piles of memoranda drawn up by doctors of high repute, canonists, theologians and jurists, both French and foreign, were furnished for the trial. Their chief object was to establish by scholastic reasoning that Jeanne had submitted her deeds and sayings to the judgment of the Church and of the Holy Father. These doctors proved that the judges of 1431 had been very subtle and Jeanne very simple. Doubtless, it was the best way to make out that she had submitted to the Church; but they over-reached themselves and made her too simple. According to them she was absolutely ignorant, almost an idiot, understanding nothing, imagining that the clerics who examined her in themselves alone constituted the Church Militant. This had been the impression of the doctors on the French side in 1429. *La Pucelle*, "*une puce*," said the Lord Archbishop of Embrun.[1130]

But there was another reason for making her appear as weak and imbecile as possible. Such a representation exalted the power of God, who through her had restored the King of France to his inheritance.

Declarations confirming this view of the Maid were obtained by the commissioners from most of the witnesses. She was simple, she was very simple, she was absolutely simple, they repeated one after the other. And they all in the same words added: "Yes, she was simple, save in deeds of war, wherein she was well skilled."[1131] Then the captains said how clever she was in placing cannon, albeit they knew well to the contrary. But how could she have failed to be well versed in deeds of war, since God himself led her against the English? And in this possession of the art of war by an unskilled girl lay the miracle.

The Grand Inquisitor of France, Jean Bréhal, in his reminiscence enumerates the reasons for believing that Jeanne came from God. One of the proofs which seems to have struck him most forcibly is that her coming is foretold in the prophecies of Merlin, the Magician.[1132]

Believing that he could prove from one of Jeanne's answers that her first apparitions were in her thirteenth year, Brother Jean Bréhal argues that the fact is all the more credible seeing that this number 13, composed of 3, which indicates the Blessed Trinity, and of 10, which expresses the perfect observation of the Decalogue, is marvellously favourable to divine visitations.[1133]

On the 16th of June, 1455, the sentence of 1431 was declared unjust, unfounded, iniquitous. It was nullified and pronounced invalid.

Thus was honour restored to the messenger of the coronation, thus was her memory reconciled with the Church. But that abundant source whence on the appearance of this child there had flowed so many pious legends and heroic fables was henceforth dried up. The rehabilitation trial added little to the popular legend. It rendered it possible to connect with Jeanne's death the usual incidents narrated of the martyrdom of virgins, such as the dove taking flight from the stake, the name of Jesus written in letters of flame, the heart intact in the ashes.[1134] The miserable deaths of the wicked judges were insisted upon. True it is that Jean d'Estivet, the Promoter, was found dead in a dove-cot,[1135] that Nicolas Midi was attacked by leprosy, that Pierre Cauchon died when he was being shaved.[1136] But, among those who aided and accompanied the Maid, more than one came to a bad end. Sire Robert de Baudricourt, who had sent Jeanne to the King, died in prison, excommunicated for having laid waste the lands of the chapter of Toul.[1137] The Maréchal de Rais was sentenced to death.[1138] The Duke of Alençon, convicted of high treason, was pardoned only to fall under a new condemnation and to die in captivity.[1139]

Two years after Charles VII had ordered the preliminary inquiry into the trial of 1431, a woman, following the example of la Dame des Armoises, passed herself off as the Maid Jeanne.

At this time there lived in the little town of Sarmaize, between the Marne and the Meuse, two cousins german of the Maid, Poiresson and Périnet, both sons of the late Jean de Vouthon, Isabelle Romée's brother, who in his lifetime had been a thatcher by trade. Now, on a day in 1452, it befell that the curé of Notre Dame de Sarmaize, Simon Fauchard, being in the market-house of the town, there came to him a woman dressed as a youth who asked him to play at tennis with her.

He consented, and when they had begun their game the woman said to him, "Say boldly that you have played tennis with the Maid." And at these words Simon Fauchard was right joyful.

The woman afterwards went to the house of Périnet, the carpenter, and said, "I am the Maid; I come to visit my Cousin Henri."

Périnet, Poiresson, and Henri de Vouthon made her good cheer and kept her in their house, where she ate and drank as she pleased.[1140]

Then, when she had had enough, she went away.

Whence came she? No one knows. Whither did she go? She may probably be recognised in an adventuress, who not long afterwards, with her hair cut short and a hood on her head, wearing doublet and hose, wandered through Anjou, calling herself Jeanne the Maid. While the doctors and masters, engaged in the revision of the trial, were gathering evidence of Jeanne's life and death from all parts of the kingdom, this false Jeanne was finding credence with many folk. But she became involved in difficulties with a certain Dame of Saumoussay,[1141] and was cast into the prison of Saumur, where she lay for three months. At the end of this time, having been banished from the dominions of the good King René, she married one Jean Douillet; and, by a document dated the 3rd day of February, 1456, she received permission to return to Saumur, on condition of living there respectably and ceasing to wear man's apparel.[1142]

About this time there came to Laval in the diocese of Le Mans, a damsel between eighteen and twenty-two, who was a native of a neighbouring place called Chassé-les-Usson. Her father's name was Jean Féron and she was commonly called Jeanne la Férone.

She was inspired from heaven, and the names Jesus and Mary were for ever on her lips; yet the devil cruelly tormented her. The Dame de Laval, mother of the Lords André and Guy, being now very aged, marvelled at the piety and the sufferings of the holy damsel; and she sent her to Le Mans, to the Bishop.

Since 1449, the see of Le Mans had been held by Messire Martin Berruyer of Touraine. In his youth he had been professor of philosophy and rhetoric at the University of Paris. Later he had devoted himself to theology and had become one of the directors of the College of Navarre. Although he was infirm with age, his learning was such that he was consulted by the commissioners for the rehabilitation trial,[1143] whereupon he drew up a memorandum touching the Maid. Herein he believes her to have been verily sent of God because she was abject and very poor and appeared well nigh imbecile in everything that did not concern her mission. Messire Martin argues that it was by reason of the King's virtues that God had vouchsafed to him the help of the Maid.[1144] Such an idea found favour with the theologians of the French party.

The Lord Bishop, Martin Berruyer, heard Jeanne la Férone in confession, renewed her baptism, confirmed her in the faith and gave her the name of Marie, in gratitude for the abounding grace which the most Holy Virgin, Mother of God, had granted to his servant.

This maid was subject to the violent attacks of evil spirits. Many a time did my Lord of Mans behold her covered with bleeding wounds, struggling in the grasp of the enemy, and on several occasions he delivered her by means of exorcisms. Greatly was he edified by this holy damsel, who made known unto him marvellous secrets, who abounded in pious revelations and noble Christian utterances. Wherefore in praise of La Férone he wrote many letters[1145] to princes and communities of the realm.

The Queen of France, who was then very old and whose husband had long ago deserted her, heard tell of the Maid of Le Mans, and wrote to Messire Martin Berruyer, requesting him to make the damsel known unto her.

Thus there befel, what we have seen happening over and over again in this history, that when a devout person, leading a contemplative life uttered prophecies, those in places of authority grew curious concerning her and desired to submit her to the judgment of the Church that they might know whether the goodness that appeared in her were true or false. Certain officers of the King visited La Férone at Le Mans.

As revelations touching the realm of France had been vouchsafed to her, she spoke to them the following words:

"Commend me very humbly to the King and bid him recognise the grace which God granteth unto him, and lighten the burdens of his people."

In the December of 1460, she was summoned before the Royal Council, which was then sitting at Tours, while the King, who was sick of an ulcer in the leg, was residing in the Château of Les Montils.[1146] The Maid of Le Mans was examined in like manner as the Maid Jeanne had been, but the result was unfavourable; she was found wanting in everything. Brought before the ecclesiastical court she was convicted of imposture. It appeared that she was no maid, but was living in concubinage with a cleric, that certain persons in the service of my Lord of Le Mans instructed her in what she was to say, and that such was the origin of the revelations she made to the Reverend Father in God, Messire Martin Berruyer, under the seal of the confession. Convicted of being a hypocrite, an idolatress, an invoker of demons, a witch, a magician, lascivious, dissolute, an enchantress, a mine of falsehood, she was condemned to have a fool's cap put on her head and to be preached at in public, in the towns of Le Mans, Tours and Laval. On the 2nd of May, 1461, she was exhibited to the folk at Tours, wearing a paper cap and over her head a scroll on which her deeds were set forth in lines of Latin and of French. Maître Guillaume de Châteaufort, Grand Master of the Royal College of Navarre, preached to her. Then she was cast into close confinement in a prison, there to weep over her sins for the space of seven years, eating the bread of sorrow and drinking the water of affliction;[1147] at the end of which time she rented a house of ill fame.[1148]

On Wednesday, the 22nd of July, 1461, covered with ulcers internal and external, believing himself poisoned and perhaps not without reason, Charles VII died, in the fifty-ninth year of his age, in his Château of Mehun-sur-Yèvre.[1149]

On Thursday, the 6th of August, his body was borne to the Church of Saint-Denys in France and placed in a chapel hung with velvet; the nave was draped with black satin, the vault was covered with blue cloth embroidered with flowers-de-luce.[1150] During the ceremony, which took place on the following day, a funeral oration was delivered on Charles VII. The preacher was no less a personage than the most highly renowned professor at the University of Paris, the doctor, who according to the Princes of the Roman Church was ever aimable and modest, he who had been the stoutest defender of the liberties of the Gallican Church, the ecclesiastic who, having declined a Cardinal's hat, bore to the threshold of an illustrious old age none other title than that of Dean of the Canons of Notre Dame de Paris, Maître Thomas de Courcelles.[1151] Thus it befell that the assessor of Rouen, who had been the most bitterly bent on procuring Jeanne's cruel condemnation, celebrated the memory of the victorious King whom the Maid had conducted to his solemn coronation.

Appendices

Appendix I
Letter from Doctor G. Dumas

Y DEAR MASTER, – You ask for my medical opinion in the case of Jeanne d'Arc. Had I been able to examine it at my leisure with the Doctors Tiphaine and Delachambre, who were summoned before the tribunal at Rouen, I might have found it difficult to come to any definite conclusion. And even more difficult do I find it now, when my diagnosis must necessarily be retrospective and based upon examinations conducted by persons who never dreamed of attempting to discover the existence of any nervous disease. However since they ascribed what we now call disease to the influence of the devil, their questions are not without significance for us. Therefore with many reservations I will endeavour to answer your question.

Of Jeanne's inherited constitution we know nothing; and of her personal antecedents we are almost entirely ignorant. Our only information concerning such matters comes from Jean d'Aulon, who, on the evidence of several women, states[1152] that she was never fully developed, a condition which frequently occurs in neurotic subjects.

We should, however, be unable to arrive at any conclusion concerning Jeanne's nervous constitution had not her judges, and in particular Maître Jean Beaupère, in the numerous examinations to which they subjected her, elicited certain significant details on the subject of her hallucinations.

Maître Beaupère begins by inquiring very judiciously whether Jeanne had fasted the day before she first heard her voices. Whence we infer that the interdependence of inanition and hallucinations was recognised by this illustrious professor of theology. Before condemning Jeanne as a witch he wanted to make sure that she was not merely suffering from weakness. Some time later we find Saint Theresa suspecting that the visions said to have been seen by a certain nun were merely the result of long fasting. Saint Theresa insisted on the nun's partaking of food, and the visions ceased.

Jeanne replies that she had only fasted since the morning, and Maître Beaupère proceeds to ask:

Q. "In what direction did you hear the voice?"

A. "I heard it on the right, towards the church."

Q. "Was the voice accompanied by any light?"

A. "I seldom heard it without there being a light. This light appeared in the direction whence the voice came."[1153]

We might wonder whether by the expression "*à droite*" (*a latere dextro*) Jeanne meant her own right side or the position of the church in relation to her; and in the latter case, the information would have no clinical significance; but the context leaves no doubt as to the veritable meaning of her words.

"How can you," urges Jean Beaupère, "see this light which you say appears to you, if it is on your right?"

If it had been merely a question of the situation of the church and not of Jeanne's own right side, she would only have had to turn her face to see the light in front of her, and Jean Beaupère's objection would have been pointless.

Consequently at about the age of thirteen, at the period of puberty, which for her never came, Jeanne would appear to have been subject on her right side to unilateral hallucinations of sight and hearing. Now Charcot[1154] considered unilateral hallucinations of sight to be common in cases of hysteria.[1155] He even thought that in hysterical subjects they are allied to a hemianæsthesia situated on the same side of the body, and which in Jeanne would be on the right side. Jeanne's trial might have proved the existence of this hemianæsthesia, an extremely significant symptom in the diagnosis of hysteria, if the judges had applied torture or merely had examined the skin of the subject in order to discover anæsthesia patches which were called marks of the devil.[1156] But from the merely oral examination which took place we can only draw inferences concerning Jeanne's general physical condition. In case excessive importance should be attached to such inferences I should add that in the diagnosis of hysteria contemporary neurologists pay less attention than did Charcot to unilateral hallucinations of sight.

The other characteristics of Jeanne's hallucinations revealed by her examinations during the trial are no less interesting than these, although they do not lead to any more certain conclusions.

Those visions and voices, which the subject refers to an external source and which are so characteristic of hysterical hallucinations, proceed suddenly from the subconscious self. Jeanne's conscious self was so far from being prepared for her voices that she declares she was very much afraid when she first heard them: "I was thirteen when I heard a voice coming from God telling me to lead a good life. And the first time I was very much afraid. This voice came to me about noon; it was in the summer, in my father's garden."[1157]

And then straightway the voice becomes imperative. It demands an obedience which is not refused: "It said to me: 'Go forth into France,' and I could no longer stay where I was."[1158]

Her visions all occur in the same manner. They appeal to the senses in exactly the same way and are received by the Maid with equal credulity.

Finally, these hallucinations of hearing and of sight are soon associated with similar hallucinations of smell and touch, which serve to confirm Jeanne's belief in their reality.

Q. "Which part of Saint Catherine did you touch?"

A. "You will hear nothing more."

Q. "Did you kiss or embrace Saint Catherine or Saint Margaret?"

A. "I embraced them both."

Q. "In embracing them did you feel heat or anything?"

A. "I could not embrace them without feeling and touching them."[1159]

Because they thus appeal to the senses and seem to possess a certain material reality, hysterical hallucinations make a profound and ineffaceable impression on those who experience them. The subjects speak of them as being actual and very striking facts. When they become accusers, as so many women do who claim to have been the victims of imaginary assaults, they support their assertions in the most energetic fashion.

Not only does Jeanne see, hear, smell and touch her saints, she joins the procession of angels they bring in their train. With them she performs actual deeds, as if there were perfect unity between her life and her hallucinations.

"I was in my lodging, in the house of a good woman, near the *château* of Chinon, when the angel came. And then he and I went together to the King."

Q. "Was this angel alone?"

A. "This angel was with a goodly company of other angels.[1160] They were with him, but not every one saw them.... Some were very much alike; others were not, or at any rate not as I saw them. Some had wings. Certain even wore crowns, and in their company were Saint Catherine and Saint Margaret. With the angel aforesaid and with the other angels they went right into the King's chamber."

Q. "Tell us how the angel left you."

A. "He left me in a little chapel, and at his departure I was very sorrowful, and I even wept. Willingly would I have gone away with him; I mean my soul would have gone."[1161]

In all these hallucinations there is the same objective clearness, the same subjective certitude as in toxic hallucinations; and this clearness, this certitude, may in Jeanne's case suggest hysteria.

But if in certain respects Jeanne resembles hysterical subjects, in others she differs from them. She seems early to have acquired an independence of her visions and an authority over them.

Without ever doubting their reality, she resists them and sometimes disobeys them, when, for example, in defiance of Saint Catherine, she leaps from her prison of Beaurevoir: "Well nigh every day Saint Catherine told me not to leap and that God would come to my aid, and also would succour those of Compiègne. And I said to Saint Catherine: 'Since God is to help those of Compiègne, I want to be with them.'"[1162]

On another occasion she assumes such authority over her visions that she can make the two saints come at her bidding when they do not come of themselves.

Q. "Do you call these saints, or do they come without being called?"

A. "They often come without being called, and sometimes when they did not come I asked God to send them speedily."[1163]

All this is not in the accepted manner of the hysterical, who are usually somewhat passive with regard to their nervous fits and hallucinations. But Jeanne's dominance over her visions is a characteristic I have noted in many of the higher mystics and in those who have attained notoriety. This kind of subject, after having at first passively submitted to his hysteria, afterwards uses it rather than submits to it, and finally by means of it attains in his ecstasy to that divine union after which he strives.

If Jeanne were hysterical, such a characteristic would help us to determine the part played by the neurotic side of her nature in the development of her character and in her life.

If there were any hysterical strain in her nature, then it was by means of this hysterical strain that the most secret sentiments of her heart took shape in the form of visions and celestial voices. Her hysteria became the open door by which the divine – or what Jeanne deemed the divine – entered into her life. It strengthened her faith and consecrated her mission; but in her intellect and in her will Jeanne remains healthy and normal. Nervous pathology can therefore cast but a feeble light on Jeanne's nature. It can reveal only one part of that spirit which your book resuscitates in its entirety. With the expression of my respectful admiration, believe me, my dear master,

Doctor G. Dumas.

Appendix II
The farrier of Salon

OWARDS the end of the seventeenth century, there lived at Salon-en-Crau, near Aix, a farrier, one François Michel. He came of a respectable family. He himself had served in the cavalry regiment of the Chevalier de Grignan. He was held to be a sensible man, honest and devout. He was close on forty when, in February, 1697, he had a vision.

Returning to his home one evening, he beheld a spectre, holding a torch in its hand. This spectre said to him:

"Fear nothing. Go to Paris and speak to the King. If thou dost not obey this command thou shalt die. When thou shalt approach to within a league of Versailles, I will not fail to make known unto thee what things thou shalt say to his Majesty. Go to the Governor of thy province, who will order all that is necessary for thy journey."

The figure which thus addressed him was in the form of a woman. She wore a royal crown and a mantle embroidered with flowers-de-luce of gold, like the late Queen, Marie-Thérèse, who had died a holy death full fourteen years before.

The poor farrier was greatly afraid. He fell down at the foot of a tree, knowing not whether he dreamed or was awake. Then he went back to his house, and told no man of what he had seen.

Two days afterwards he passed the same spot. There again he beheld the same spectre, who repeated the same orders and the same threats. The farrier could no longer doubt the reality of what he saw; but as yet he could not make up his mind what to do.

A third apparition, more imperious and more importunate than the first, reduced him to obedience. He went to Aix, to the Governor of the province; he saw him and told him how he had been given a mission to speak to the King. The Governor at first paid no great heed to him. But the visionary's patient persistence could not fail to impress him. Moreover, since the King was personally concerned in the matter, it ought not to be entirely neglected. These considerations led the Governor to inquire from the magistrates of Salon touching the farrier's family and manner of life. The result of these inquiries was very favourable. Accordingly the Governor deemed it fitting to proceed forthwith to action. In those days no one was quite sure whether advice, very useful to the most Christian of Kings, might not be sent by some member of the Church Triumphant through the medium of a common artisan. Still less were they sure that some plot in which the welfare of the State was concerned might not be hatched under colour of an apparition. In both contingencies, the second of which was quite probable, it would be advisable to send François Michel to Versailles. And this was the decision arrived at by the Governor.

For the transport of François Michel he adopted measures at once sure and inexpensive. He confided him to an officer who was taking recruits in that direction. After having received the communion in the church of the Franciscans, who were edified by his pious bearing, the farrier set out on February 25 with his Majesty's young soldiers, with whom he travelled as far as La Ferté-sous-Jouarre. On his arrival at Versailles, he asked to see the King or at least one of his Ministers of State. He was directed to M. de Barbezieux, who, when he was still very young, had succeeded his father, M. de Louvois, and in that position had displayed some talent. But the good farrier declined to tell him anything, because he was not a Minister of State.

And it was true that Barbezieux, although a Minister, was not a Minister of State. But that a farrier from Provence should be capable of drawing such a distinction occasioned considerable surprise.

M. de Barbezieux doubtless did not evince such scorn for this compatriot of Nostradamus as would have been shown in his place by a man of broader mind. For he, like his father, was addicted to the practice of astrology, and he was always inquiring concerning his horoscope of a certain Franciscan friar who had predicted the hour of his death.

We do not know whether he gave the King a favourable report of the farrier, or whether the latter was admitted to the presence of M. de Pomponne, who was then at the head of the administration of Provence. But we do know that Louis XIV consented to see the man. He had him brought up the steps leading to the marble courtyard, and then granted him a lengthy audience in his private apartments.

On the morrow, as the King was coming down his private staircase on his way out hunting, he met Marshal de Duras, who was Captain of the King's bodyguard for the day. With his usual freedom of speech the Marshal spoke to the King of the farrier, using a common saying:

"Either the man is mad, or the King is not noble."

At these words the King, contrary to his usual habit, paused and turned to the Marshal de Duras:

"Then I am not noble," he said, "for I talked to him for a long time, and he spoke very sensibly; I assure you he is far from being mad."

The last words he uttered with so solemn a gravity that those who were present were astonished.

Persons who claim to be inspired are expected to show some sign of their mission. In a second interview, François Michel showed the King a sign in fulfilment of a promise he had given. He reminded him of an extraordinary circumstance which the son of Anne of Austria believed known to himself alone. Louis XIV himself admitted it, but for the rest preserved a profound silence touching this interview.

Saint Simon, always eager to collect every court rumour, believed it was a question of some phantom, which more than twenty years before had appeared to Louis XIV in the Forest of Saint-Germain.

For the third and last time the King received the farrier of Salon.

The courtiers displayed so much curiosity in this visionary that he had to be shut up in the monastery of Des Rècollets. There the little Princess of Savoy, who was shortly to marry the Duke of Burgundy, came to see him with several lords and ladies of the court.

He appeared slow to speak, good, simple, and humble. The King ordered him to be furnished with a fine horse, clothes, and money; then he sent him back to Provence.

Public opinion was divided on the subject of the apparition which had appeared to the farrier and the mission he had received from it. Most people believed that he had seen the spirit of Marie-Thérèse; but some said it was Nostradamus.[1164]

It was only at Salon, where he slept in the church of the Franciscans, that this astrologer was absolutely believed in. His "Centuries," which appeared at Paris and at Lyon in no less than ten editions in the course of one century, entertained the credulous throughout the kingdom. In 1693, there had just been published a book of the prophecies of Nostradamus showing how they had been fulfilled in history from the reign of Henry II down to that of Louis the Great.

It came to be believed that in the following mysterious quatrain the farrier's coming had been prophesied:

"Le penultiesme du surnom du Prophète,
Prendra Diane pour son iour et repos:

Loing vaguera par frénétique teste,
En délivrant un grand peuple d'impos."[1165]

An attempt was made to apply these obscure lines to the poor prophet of Salon. In the first line he is said to figure as one of the twelve minor prophets, Micah, which name is closely allied to Michel. In the second line Diane was said to be the mother of the farrier, who was certainly called by that name. But if the line means anything at all, it is more likely to refer to the day of the moon, Monday. It was carefully pointed out that in the third line *frénétique* means not *mad* but *inspired.* The fourth and only intelligible line would suggest that the spectre bade Michel ask the King to lessen the taxes and dues which then weighed so heavily on the good folk of town and country:

En délivrant un grand peuple d'impos. This was enough to make the farrier popular and to cause those unhappy sufferers to centre in this poor windbag their hopes for a better future. His portrait was engraved in copper-plate, and below it was written the quatrain of Nostradamus. M. d'Argenson,[1166] who was at the head of the police department, had these portraits seized. They were suppressed, so says the *Gazette d'Amsterdam*, on account of the last line of the quatrain written beneath the portrait, the line which runs: *En délivrant un grand peuple d'impos*. Such an expression was hardly likely to please the court.

No one ever knew exactly what was the mission the farrier received from his spectre. Subtle folk suspected one of Madame de Maintenon's intrigues. She had a friend at Marseille, a Madame Arnoul, who was as ugly as sin, it was said, and yet who managed to make men fall in love with her. They thought that this Madame Arnoul had shown Marie-Thérèse to the good man of Salon in order to induce the King to live honourably with widow Scarron. But in 1697 widow Scarron had been married to Louis for twelve years at least; and one cannot see why ghostly aid should have been necessary to attach the old King to her.

On his return to his native town, François Michel shoed horses as before.

He died at Lançon, near Salon, on December 10, 1726.[1167]

Appendix III
Martin de Gallardon

GNACE THOMAS MARTIN was by calling a husbandman. A native of Gallardon in Eure-et-Loir, he dwelt there with his wife and four children in the beginning of the nineteenth century. Those who knew him tell us that he was of average height, with brown straight hair, a calm glance, a thin countenance and an air of quiet and assurance. A pencil portrait, which his son, M. le Docteur Martin, has kindly sent me, gives a more exact idea of the visionary. The portrait, which is in profile, presents a forehead curiously high and straight, a long narrow head, round eyes, broad nostrils, a compressed mouth, a protruding chin, hollow cheeks and an air of austerity. He is dressed as a *bourgeois*, with a collar and white cravat.

According to the evidence of his brother, a man both physically and mentally sound, his was the gentlest of natures; he never sought to attract attention; in his regular piety there was nothing ecstatic. Both the mayor and the priest of Gallardon confirmed this description. They agreed in representing him to have been a good simple creature, with an intellect well-balanced although not very active.

In 1816 he was thirty-three. On January 15 in this year he was alone in his field, over which he was spreading manure, when in his ear he heard a voice which had not been preceded by footsteps. Then he turned his head in the direction of the voice and saw a figure which alarmed him. In comparison with human size it was but slight; its countenance, which was very thin, dazzled by its unnatural whiteness. It was wearing a high hat and a frock-coat of a light colour, with laced shoes.

It said in a kindly tone: "You must go to the King; you must warn him that his person is in danger, that wicked people are seeking to overthrow his Government."

It added further recommendations to Louis XVIII touching the necessity of having an efficient police, of keeping holy the Sabbath, of ordering public prayers and of suppressing the disorders of the Carnival. If such measures be neglected, it said, "France will fall into yet greater misfortunes." All this was doubtless nothing more or less than what M. La Perruque, Priest of Gallardon, had a hundred times repeated from the pulpit on Sunday.

Martin replied:

"Since you know so much about it, why don't you perform your errand yourself? Why do you appeal to a poor man like me who knows not how to express himself?"

Then the unknown replied to Martin:

"It is not I who will go, but you; do as I command you."

As soon as he had uttered these words, his feet rose from the ground, his body bent, and with this double movement he vanished.

From this time onwards, Martin was haunted by the mysterious being. One day, having gone down into his cellar, he found him there. On another occasion, during vespers, he saw him in church, near the holy water stoup, in a devout attitude. When the service was over, the unknown accompanied Martin on his way home and again commanded him to go and see the King. The farmer told his relatives who were with him, but neither of them had seen or heard anything.

Tormented by these apparitions, Martin communicated them to his priest, M. La Perruque. He, being certain of the good faith of his parishioner and deeming that the case ought to be submitted to the diocesan authority, sent the visionary to the Bishop of Versailles. The Bishop was then M. Louis Charrier de la Roche, a priest who in the days of the Revolution had taken the oath to the Republic. He resolved to subject Martin to a thorough examination; and from the first he told him to ask the unknown what was his name, and who it was who sent him.

But when the messenger in the light-coloured frock-coat appeared again, he declared that his name must remain unknown.

"I come," he added, "from him who has sent me, and he who has sent me is above me."

He may have wished to conceal his name; but at least he did not conceal his views; the vexation he displayed on the escape of La Valette[1168] proved that in politics he was an ultra Royalist of the most violent type.

Meanwhile the Comte de Bréteuil, Prefect of Eure-et-Loir, had been told of the visionary at the same time as the Bishop. He also questioned Martin. He expected to find him a nervous, agitated person; but when he found him tranquil, speaking simply, but with logical sequence and precision, he was very astonished.

Like M. l'Abbé La Perruque he deemed the matter sufficiently important to bring before the higher authorities. Accordingly he sent Martin, under the escort of a lieutenant of *gendarmerie*, to the Ministre de la Police Générale.

Having reached Paris on March 8, Martin lodged with the *gendarme* at the Hôtel de Calais, in the Rue Montmartre. They occupied a double-bedded room. One morning, when Martin was in bed, he beheld an apparition and told Lieutenant André, who could see nothing, although it was broad daylight. Indeed, Martin's visitations became so frequent that they ceased to cause him either surprise or concern. It was only to the abrupt disappearance of the unknown that he could never grow accustomed. The voice continued to give the same command.

One day it told him that if it were not obeyed France would not know peace until 1840.

In 1816 the Ministre de la Police Générale was the Comte Decazes who was afterwards created a duke. He was in the King's confidence. But he knew that the extreme Royalists were hatching plots against his royal master. Decazes wished to see the good man from Gallardon, suspecting doubtless, that he was but a tool in the hands of the Extremists. Martin was brought to the Minister, who questioned him and at once perceived that the poor creature was in no way dangerous. He spoke to him as he would to a madman, endeavouring to regard the subject of his mania as if it were real, and so he said:

"Don't be agitated; the man who has been troubling you is arrested; you will have nothing more to fear from him."

But these words did not produce the desired effect. Three or four hours after this interview, Martin again beheld the unknown, who, after speaking to him in his usual manner, said: "When you were told that I had been arrested, you were told a lie; he who said so has no power over me."

On Sunday, March 10, the unknown returned; and on that day he disclosed the matter concerning which the Bishop of Versailles had inquired, and which he had said at first he would never reveal.

"I am," he declared, "the Archangel Raphaël, an angel of great renown in the presence of God, and I have received power to afflict France with all manner of suffering."

Three days later, Martin was shut up in Charenton on the certificate of Doctor Pinel, who stated him to be suffering from intermittent mania with alienation of mind.

He was treated in the kindest manner and was even permitted to enjoy some appearance of liberty. Pinel himself originated the humane treatment of the insane. Martin in the asylum was not forsaken by the blessed Raphaël. On Friday, the

15th, as the peasant was tying his shoe laces, the Archangel in his frock-coat of a light colour, spoke to him these words:

"Have faith in God. If France persists in her incredulity, the misfortunes I have predicted will happen. Moreover, if they doubt the truth of your visions, they have but to cause you to be examined by doctors in theology."

These words Martin repeated to M. Legros; Director of the Royal Institution of Charenton, and asked him what a doctor in theology was. He did not know the meaning of the term. In the same manner, when he was at Gallardon he had asked the priest, M. La Perruque, the meaning of certain expressions the voice had used. For example, he did not understand the wild frenzy of France [*le délvie de la France*] nor the evils to which she would fall a victim [*elle serait en proie*]. But there is nothing that need puzzle us in such ignorance, if it really existed. Martin may well have remembered the words he did not understand and which he afterwards attributed to his Archangel still without understanding them.

The visions recurred at brief intervals. On Sunday, March 31, the Archangel appeared to him in the garden, took his hand, which he pressed affectionately, opened his coat and displayed a bosom of so dazzling a whiteness that Martin could not bear to gaze on it. Then he took off his hat.

"Behold my forehead," he said, "and give heed that it beareth not the mark of the beast whereby the fallen angels were sealed."

Louis XVIII expressed a desire to see Martin and to question him. The King, like his favourite Minister, believed the visionary to be a tool in the hands of the extreme party.

On Tuesday, April 2, Martin was taken to the Tuileries and brought into the King's closet, where was also M. Decazes. As soon as the King saw the farmer, he said to him: "Martin, I salute you."

Then he signed to his Minister to withdraw. Thereupon Martin, according to his own telling, repeated to the King all that the Archangel had revealed to him, and disclosed to Louis XVIII sundry secret matters concerning the years he had spent in exile; finally he made known to him certain plots which had been formed against his person. Then the King, profoundly agitated and in tears, raised his hands and his eyes to heaven and said to Martin:

"Martin, these are things which must never be known save to you and to me."

The visionary promised him absolute secrecy.

Such was the interview of April 2, according to the account given of it by Martin, who then, under the influence of M. La Perruque's sermons, was an infatuated Royalist. It would be interesting to know more of this priest whose inspiration is obvious throughout the whole story. Louis XVIII agreed with M. Decazes that the man was quite harmless; and he was sent back to his plough.

Later, the agents of one of those false dauphins so numerous under the Restoration, got hold of Martin and made use of him in their own interest. After Louis XVIII's death, under the influence of these adventurers, the poor man, reconstituting the story of his interview with the late King, introduced into it other revelations he claimed to have received and completely changed the whole character of the incident. In this second version the passionate Royalist of 1816 was transformed into an accusing prophet, who came to the King's own palace to denounce him as a usurper and a regicide, forbidding him in God's name to be crowned at Reims.

Such ramblings I cannot relate at length. They are to be found fully detailed in the book of M. Paul Marin. The author of this work would have done well to indicate that these follies were suggested to the unhappy man by the partisans of Naundorf, who was passing himself off as the Duke of Normandy, who had escaped from the Temple.

Thomas Ignace Martin died at Chartres in 1834. It is alleged, but it has never been proved, that he was poisoned.[1169]

Appendix IV
Iconographical note

HERE is no authentic picture of Jeanne. From her we know that at Arras she saw in the hands of a Scotsman a picture in which she was represented on her knees presenting a letter to her King. From her we know also that she never caused to be made either image or painting of herself, and that she was not aware of the existence of any such image or painting. The portrait painted by the Scotsman, which was doubtless very small, is unfortunately lost and no copy of it is known.[1170] The slight pen-and-ink figure, drawn on a register of May 10, 1429, by a clerk of the Parlement of Paris, who had never seen the Maid, must be regarded as the mere scribbling of a scribe who was incapable of even designing a good initial letter.[1171] I shall not attempt to reconstruct the iconography of the Maid.[1172] The bronze equestrian statue in the Cluny Museum produces a grotesque effect that one is tempted to believe deliberate, if one may ascribe such an intention to an old sculptor. It dates from the reign of Charles VIII. It is a Saint George or a Saint Maurice, which, at a time doubtless quite recent, was taken to represent the Maid. Between the legs of the miserable jade, on which the figure is mounted, was engraved the inscription: *La pucelle dorlians*, a description which would not have been employed in the fifteenth century.[1173] About 1875, the Cluny Museum exhibited another statuette, slightly larger, in painted wood, which was also believed to be fifteenth century, and to represent Jeanne d'Arc. It was relegated to the store-room, when it turned out to be a bad seventeenth-century

Saint Maurice from a church at Montargis.[1174] Any saint in armour is frequently described as a Jeanne d'Arc. This is what happened to a small fifteenth-century head wearing a helmet, found buried in the ground at Orléans, broken off from a statue and still bearing traces of painting: a work in good style and with a charming expression.[1175] I have not patience to relate how many initial letters of antiphonaries and sixteenth-, seventeenth- and even eighteenth-century miniatures have been touched up or repainted and passed off as true and ancient representations of Jeanne. Many of them I have had the opportunity of seeing.[1176] On the other hand, if they were not so well known, it would give me pleasure to recall certain manuscripts of the fifteenth century, which, like *Le Champion des Dames* and *Les Vigiles de Charles VII*, contain miniatures in which the Maid is portrayed according to the fancy of the illuminator. Such pictures are interesting because they reveal her as she was imagined by those who lived during her lifetime or shortly afterwards. It is not their merit that appeals to us; they possess none; and in no way do they suggest Jean Foucquet.[1177]

While the Maid lived, and especially while she was in captivity, the French hung her picture in churches.[1178] In the Museum of Versailles there is a little painting on wood which is said to be one of those votive pictures. It represents the Virgin with the Child Jesus, having Saint Michael on her right and Jeanne d'Arc on her left.[1179] It is of Italian workmanship and very roughly executed. Jeanne's head, which has disappeared beneath the blows of some hard-pointed instrument, must have been execrably drawn, if we may judge from the others remaining on this panel. All four figures are represented with a scrolled and beaded nimbus, which would have certainly been condemned by the clerics of Paris and Rouen. And indeed others less strict might accuse the painter of idolatry when he exalted to the left hand of the Virgin, to be equal with the Prince of Heavenly Hosts, a mere creature of the Church Militant.

Standing, her head, neck, and shoulders covered with a kind of furred hood and tippet fringed with black, her gauntlets and shoes of mail, girt above her red tunic with a belt of gold, Jeanne may be recognised by her name inscribed over her head, and also by the white banner, embroidered with *fleurs-de-lis*, which she raises in her right hand, and by her silver shield, embossed in the German style; on the shield is a sword bearing on its point a crown. A three-lined inscription in French is on the steps of the throne, whereon sits the Virgin Mary. Although the inscription is three parts effaced and almost unintelligible, with the aid of my learned friend, M. Pierre de Nolhac, Director of the Museum of Versailles, I have succeeded in deciphering a few words. These would convey the idea that the inscription consisted of prayers and wishes for the salvation of Jeanne, who had fallen into the hands of the enemy. It would appear therefore that we have here one of those *ex voto* hung in the churches of France during the captivity of the Maid. In such a case the nimbus round the head of a living person and the isolated position of Jeanne would be easily explained; it is possible that certain excellent Frenchmen, thinking no evil, adapted to their own use some picture which originally represented the Virgin between two personages of the Church Triumphant. By a few touches they transformed one of these personages into the Maid of God. In so small a panel they could find no place more suitable to her mortal state, none like those generally occupied at the feet of the Virgin and saints by the kneeling donors of pictures. This too might explain perhaps why Saint Michael, the Virgin and the Maid have their names inscribed above them. Over the head of the Maid we read *ane darc*. This form *Darc* may have been used in 1430.[1180] In the inscription on the steps of the throne I discern *Jehane dArc*, with a small *d* and a capital *A* for *dArc*, which is very curious. This causes me to doubt the genuineness of the inscription.

The *bestion* tapestry[1181] in the Orléans Museum,[1182] which represents Jeanne's arrival before the King at Chinon, is of German fifteenth-century workmanship. Coarse of tissue, barbarous in design, and monotonous in colour, it evinces a certain taste for sumptuous adornment but also an absolute disregard for literal truth.

Another German work was exhibited at Ratisbonne in 1429. It represented the Maid fighting in France. But this painting is lost.[1183]

† END OF VOLUME II †

References

[1] *Chronique de la Pucelle*, pp. 323, 324. Perceval de Cagny, pp. 160, 161. *Journal du siège*, p. 115. Jean Chartier, *Chronique*, vol. i, p. 98. Morosini, vol. iii, p. 196.

[2] *Ordonnances des rois de France*, vol. ix, p. 71. H. Martin and Lacroix, *Histoire de la ville de Soissons*, Soissons, 1837, in 8vo, ii, pp. 283 *et seq.*

[3] *Journal d'un bourgeois de Paris*, p. 53, *passim*.

[4] *Ibid.*, p. 103.

[5] *Chronique de la Pucelle*, pp. 323, 324. Perceval de Cagny, p. 160. Monstrelet, vol. iv, p. 339.

[6] *Suret* is sour wine (W.S.).

[7] C. Dormay, *Histoire de la ville de Soissons*, Soissons, 1664, vol. ii, pp. 382 *et seq.* H. Martin and Lacroix, *Histoire de Soissons*, vol. ii, p. 319. Pécheur, *Annales du diocèse de Soissons*, vol. iv, p. 513. Félix Brun, *Jeanne d'Arc et le capitaine de Soissons en 1430*, Soissons, 1904, p. 34.

[8] Berry, in *Trial*, vol. iv, pp. 49, 50. Le P. Daniel, *Histoire de la milice française*, vol. i, p. 356. Félix Brun, *Jeanne d'Arc et le capitaine de Soissons*, pp. 26, 39.

[9] De l'Epinois, *Notes extraites des archives communales de Compiègne*, in *Bibliothèque de l'École des Chartes*, vol. xxix, p. 483. Sorel, *Prise de Jeanne d'Arc*, pp. 101, 102.

[10] Perceval de Cagny, p. 160. Monstrelet, vol. iv, p. 340.

[11] Monstrelet, vol. iv, p. 340. *Chronique de la Pucelle*, p. 323. Félix Bourquelot, *Histoire de Provins*, Provins, vol. iv, pp. 79 *et seq*. Th. Robillard, *Histoire pittoresque topographique et archéologique de Crécy-en-Brie*, 1852, p. 42. L'Abbé C. Poquet, *Histoire de Château-Thierry*, 1839, vol. i, pp. 290 *et seq*.

[12] Perceval de Cagny, pp. 160, 161.

[13] *Chronique de la Pucelle*, pp. 324, 325. *Journal du siège*, p. 115. Jean Chartier, *Chronique*, vol. i, pp. 98, 99. Perceval de Cagny, p. 161. Rymer, *Fœdera*, June to July, 1429. *Proceedings*, vol. iii, pp. 322 *et seq*. Morosini, vol. iv, appendix xvii.

[14] Jean Chartier, *Chronique*, vol. i, p. 98. Varin, *Archives législatives de la ville de Reims*, Statuts, vol. i (annot. according to doc. no. xxi), p. 741. H. Jadart, *Jeanne d'Arc à Reims*, original doc. no. 19, p. 118.

[15] Perceval de Cagny, p. 160.

[16] This place name is not to be found in Rogier's copy.

[17] *Trial*, vol. v, pp. 139, 140, and Varin, *loc. cit. Statuts*, vol. i, p. 603, according to Rogier's copy. H. Jadart, *Jeanne d'Arc à Reims*, proofs and illustrations, vol. xiv, pp. 104, 105, and facsimile of the original copy formerly in the Reims municipal archives, now in the possession of M. le Comte de Maleissye.

[18] *Trial*, vol. i, pp. 233, 234.

[19] Morosini, vol. iii, pp. 202, 203, note 2.

[20] *Chronique de la Pucelle*, p. 325. Jean Chartier, *Chronique*, vol. i, pp. 99, 100. *Journal du siège*, pp. 119, 120. Gilles de Roye, p. 207.

[21] *Trial*, vol. iii, p. 91.

[22] *Guerre de la Hottée de Pommes*, cf. vol. i, p. 92. (W.S.)

[23] *Chronique du doyen de Saint-Thibaut de Metz* in D. Calmet. *Histoire de Lorraine*, vol. v, orig. docs., cols, xli-xlvii. Villeneuve-Bargemont, *Précis historique de la vie du roi René*, Aix, 1820, in 8vo. Lecoy de la Marche, *Le roi René*, Paris, 1875, 2 vols. in 8vo.

Vallet de Viriville, in *Nouvelle biographie générale*, 1866, xli, pp. 1009-1015.

[24] *Trial*, vol. ii, p. 444. S. Luce, *Jeanne d'Arc à Domremy*, p. cxcix. Morosini, vol. iii, p. 156, note 3.

[25] *Trial*, vol. v, pp. 105-111.

[26] *Chronique de la Pucelle*, Jean Chartier. *Journal du siège, loc. cit.*

[27] Monstrelet, vol. iv, pp. 340, 344.

[28] Perceval de Cagny, p. 161. Jean Chartier, *Chronique*, vol. i, p. 100. *Chronique de la Pucelle*, p. 325.

[29] Varin, *Archives législatives de la ville de Reims*, Statuts, vol. i, p. 742.

[30] Perceval de Cagny, p. 161.

[31] *Trial*, vol. iii, pp. 14, 15. *Chronique de la Pucelle*, p. 326.

[32] *Journal d'un bourgeois de Paris*, p. 164.

[33] Thomas Basin, *Histoire de Charles VII*, chap. vi. A. Tuetey, *Les écorcheurs sous Charles VII*, Montbéliard, 1874, 2 vols. in 8vo, *passim*. H. Lepage, *Épisodes de l'histoire des routiers en Lorraine* (1362-1446), in *Journal d'archéologie lorraine*, vol. xv, pp. 161 *et seq.* Le P. Denifle, *La désolation des églises, passim*. H. Martin et Lacroix, *Histoire de Soissons*, p. 318, *passim*. G. Lefèvre-Pontalis, *Épisodes de l'invasion anglaise. La guerre de partisans dans la Haute Normandie* (1424-1429), in *Bibliothèque de l'École des Chartes*, vol. liv, pp. 475-521; vol. lv, pp. 258-305; vol. lvi, pp. 432-508.

[34] Pardon issued by King Henry VI to an inhabitant of Noyant, in Stevenson, *Letters and Papers*, vol. i, pp. 23, 31. F. Brun, *Jeanne d'Arc et le capitaine de Soissons*, note iii, p. 41.

[35] Stevenson, *Letters and Papers*, vol. i, pp. 23, 31.

[36] *Journal d'un bourgeois de Paris*, pp. 170, 171. Monstrelet, vol. iv, p. 96. *Livre des trahisons*, pp. 167, 168.

[37] *Journal d'un bourgeois de Paris*, p. 170. According to Monstrelet (vol. iv, p. 96), Denis de Vauru, the Bastard's cousin, was beheaded in the Market of Paris.

[38] *Trial*, vol. iii, pp. 14, 15. *Chronique de la Pucelle*, p. 326.

[39] Eberhard Windecke, pp. 108, 109, 188, 189.

[40] *Trial*, vol. iii, pp. 14, 15. It is Dunois who is giving evidence, and the text runs: *In custodiendo oves ipsorum, cum sorore et fratribus meis, qui multum gauderent videre me*. But there is reason to believe she had only one sister, whom she had lost before coming into France. As for her brothers, two of them were with her. Dunois' evidence appears to have been written down by a clerk unacquainted with events. The hagiographical character of the passage is obvious.

[41] *Trial*, vol. ii, p. 423.

[42] *Ibid.*, vol. i, pp. 51, 66.

[43] Monstrelet, vol. iv, pp. 340, 344.

[44] Monstrelet, vol. iv, p. 342.

[45] *Ibid.*, pp. 342, 343.

[46] Georges Chastellain, fragments published by J. Quicherat in *La Bibliothèque de l'École des Chartes*, 1st series, vol. iv,. p. 78.

[47] Monstrelet, vol. iv, pp. 341, 342.

[48] *Trial*, vol. ii, p. 324; vol. iii, p. 130. Monstrelet, vol. iv, p. 388.

[49] *Trial*, vol. iii, p. 99.

[50] *Ibid.*, vol. iv, pp. 206, 406, 444, 470, 472. Rymer, *Fœdera*, vol. iv, p. 141. G. Lefèvre-Pontalis, *La panique anglaise*.

[51] *Trial*, vol. i, pp. 246, 298. Letter from Alain Chartier in *Trial*, vol. v, pp. 131 *et seq*.

[52] Monstrelet, vol. iv, pp. 344, 345. Perceval de Cagny, pp. 161, 162.

[53] Flammermont, *Histoire de Senlis pendant la seconds partie de la guerre de cent ans* (1405-1441), in *Mémoires de la Société de l'Histoire de Paris*.

[54] Jean Chartier, *Chronique*, vol. i, pp. 101, 102. *Chronique de la Pucelle*, p. 328. *Journal du siège*, p. 118. Falconbridge, in *Trial*, vol. iv, p. 453. Morosini, vol. iii, pp. 188, 189; vol. iv, appendix xvii. Rymer, *Fœdera*, July, 1429. Raynaldi, *Annales ecclesiastici*, pp. 77, 88. S. Bougenot, *Notices et extraits de manuscrits intéressant l'histoire de France conservés a la Bibliothèque impérial de Vienne*, p. 62.

[55] Now, come forth Beauty (W.S.). *Le Livre des trahisons de France*, ed. Kervyn de Lettenhove, in *La collection des chroniques belges*, 1873, p. 198.

[56] Perceval de Cagny, p. 162. Jean Chartier, *Chronique*, vol. i, p. 102. *Chronique de la Pucelle*, p. 329. *Journal du siège*, pp. 119, 120.

[57] Perceval de Cagny, p. 161.

[58] *Le Jouvencel, passim*.

[59] *Chronique de la Pucelle*, p. 329. *Journal du siège*, p. 121.

[60] *Le Jouvencel*, vol. ii, p. 35.

[61] Monstrelet, vol. iv, p. 346.

[62] Perceval de Cagny, p. 162.

[63] Jean Chartier, *Chronique de la Pucelle*. *Journal du siège*. Monstrelet, *loc. cit*.

[64] *Chronique de la Pucelle*, p. 332. Perceval de Cagny, p. 165. Jean Chartier, *Chronique*, vol. i, p. 106. Cochon, p. 457. G. Lefèvre-Pontalis, *La panique anglaise*, Paris, 1894, in 8vo, pp. 10, 11. Morosini, vol. iii, p. 215, note 3. Ch. de Beaurepaire, *De l'administration de la Normandie sous la domination anglaise aux années 1424, 1425, 1429*, p. 62 (*Mémoires de la Société des Antiquaires de Normandie*, vol. xxiv).

[65] A virelay was a later variation of the lay, differing from it chiefly in the arrangement of the rhymes (W.S.).

[66] Le Roux de Lincy and Tisserand, *Paris et ses historiens*, pp. 426 *et seq.*

[67] A winged stag (*le cerf-volant*) is the symbol of a king. Froissart thus explains its origin. Before setting out for Flanders, in 1382, Charles VI dreamed that his falcon had flown away. "Thē apered sodenly before hym a great hart with wynges whereof he had great joye." And the hart bore him to his lost bird. Froissart, Bk. II, ch. clxiv. [The Chronycle of Syr John Froissart translated by Lord Berners, vol. iii, p. 339, Tudor Translation, 1901.] (W.S.) According to Juvénal des Ursins, Charles VI, in 1380, met in the Forest of Senlis a stag with a golden collar bearing this inscription: *Hoc me Cæsar donavit* (Paillot, *Parfaite science des armoiries*, Paris, 1660, in fo., p. 595). In the works of Eustache Deschamps this same allegory is frequently employed to designate the king. (Eustache Deschamps, *œuvres*, ed. G. Raynaud, vol. ii, p. 57.)

[68] Morosini, vol. iii, pp. 66, 67.

[69] *Trial*, vol. iii, pp. 133, 338, 340 *et seq.*; vol. iv, pp. 305, 480; vol. v, p. 12.

[70] *Trial*, vol. v, pp. 3 *et seq.* R. Thomassy, *Essai sur les écrits politiques de Christine de Pisan, suivi d'une notice littéraire et de pièces inédites*, Paris, 1838, in 8vo.

[71] *Du beau jardin des nobles fleurs de lis.*

[72] M. Pierre Champion has kindly communicated to me the text of this unpublished ballad, which he discovered in a French MS. at Stockholm, LIII, fol. 238. This is the title which the copyist affixed to it about 1472: *Ballade faicte quant le Roy Charles VII*[eme] *fut couronne a Rains du temps de Jehanne daiz dicte la Pucelle.*

[73] P. Meyer, *Ballade contre les Anglais* (1429), in *Romania*, xxi (1892), pp. 50, 52.

[74] *Arrière, Englois coués, arrière!* For Coués see vol. i, p. 22, note 2.

[75]

Par le vouloir dou roy Jésus
Et Jeanne la douce Pucelle.

[76] For the legend cf. *Merlin, roman en prose du XIIIe siècle*, ed. G. Paris and J. Ulrich, 1886, 2 vols. in 8vo, introduction. *Premier volume de Merlin*, Paris, Vérard, 1498, in fol. Hersart de la Villemarqué, *Myrdhin ou l'enchanteur Merlin, son histoire, ses œuvres, son influence*, Paris, 1862, in 12mo. La Borderie, *Les véritables prophéties de Merlin; examen des poèmes bretons attribués à ce barde*, in *Revue de Bretagne*, vol. liii (1883). D'Arbois de Jubainville, *Merlin est il un personnage réel ou les origines de la légende de Merlin*, in *Revue des questions historiques*, vol. v (1868), pp. 559, 568.

[77] *Trial*, vol. iii, p. 340. Lanéry d'Arc, *Mémoires et consultations*, p. 402.

[78] *Trial*, vol. iii, pp. 344, 345.

[79] Philippe de Bergame, in *Trial*, vol. iv, p. 523; vol. v, pp. 108, 120.

[80] *Trial*, vol. iii, p. 100. Philippe de Bergame, *De claris mulieribus*, in *Trial*, vol. iv, p. 323. *Chronique de la Pucelle*, p. 271. Perceval de Boulainvilliers, *Lettre au duc de Milan*, in *Trial*, vol. v, pp. 119, 120.

[81] J. Bréhal, in *Trial*, vol. iii, p. 345.

[82] *Chronique de la Pucelle*, p. 328. *Journal du siège*, p. 18. Jean Chartier, *Chronique*, vol. i, p. 106. Perceval de Cagny, pp. 163, 164. Morosini, pp. 212, 213. Flammermont, *Senlis pendant la seconde période de la guerre cent ans*, in *Mémoires de la Société de l'Histoire de Paris*, vol. v, 1878, p. 241.

[83] Perceval de Cagny, p. 164. Monstrelet, p. 352. De l'Epinois, *Notes extraites des archives communales de Compiègne*, pp. 483, 484. A. Sorel, *Séjours de Jeanne d'Arc à Compiègne, maisons ou elle a logé en 1429 et 1430*, Paris, 1889, in 8vo, 20 pages.

[84] French *attournés*, cf. La Curne, *attournés*, Godefroi, *atornés*, magistrates at Compiègne, elected on St. John the Baptist's Day for three years (W.S.). *Procès*, vol. v, p. 174.

[85] *Chronique de la Pucelle*, p. 331. Jean Chartier, *Chronique*, vol. i, p. 106. A. Sorel, *La prise de Jeanne d'Arc devant Compiègne*, Paris, 1889, in 8vo, pp. 117, 118. Duc de la Trémoïlle, *Les La Trémoïlle pendant cinq siècles*, Nantes, 1890, in 4to, vol. i, pp. 185, 212. P. Champion, *Guillaume de Flavy, capitaine de Compiègne*, Paris, 1906, in 8vo, proofs and illustrations, vol. xiii, p. 137.

[86] *Chronique de la Pucelle*, p. 327. *Journal du siège*, p. 118. Jean Chartier, *Chronique*, vol. i, p. 106. Monstrelet, vol. iv, pp. 353, 354. Morosini, vol. iii, pp. 214, 215.

[87] A. Sarrazin, *Pierre Cauchon, juge de Jeanne d'Arc*, Paris, 1901, in 8vo, pp. 49 *et seq.*

[88] Monstrelet, vol. iv, p. 354.

[89] A. Sorel, *Séjours de Jeanne d'Arc à Compiègne*, p. 6.

[90] Perceval de Cagny, pp. 164, 165. *Chronique de Tournai*, vol. iii, in the *Recueil des chroniques de Flandre*, ed. Smedt, p. 414.

[91] *Trial*, vol. i, pp. 82, 83.

[92] *Ibid.*, pp. 245, 246.

[93] A. Longnon, *Les limites de la France et l'étendue de la domination anglaise à l'époque de la mission de Jeanne d'Arc*, Paris, 1875, in 8vo. Vallet de Viriville, in *Nouvelle biographie générale*, iii, col. 255, 257.

[94] *Chronique de Mathieu d'Escouchy*, vol. i, p. 68, and proofs and illustrations, pp. 126, 128, 139, 140. Dom Vaissette, *Histoire générale du Languedoc*, vol. iv, pp. 469, 470. De Beaucourt, *Histoire de Charles VII*, vol. ii, p. 151. Vallet de Viriville, in *Nouvelle biographie générale*, 1861, vol. iii, pp. 255-257. Le P. Ayroles, *La vierge guerrière*, p. 66.

[95] *Annales juris pontificis* (1872-1875), vii, 385. E. Muntz, *La tiare pontificale du VIIIe au XVIe siècle* in *Mem. Acad. Inscript. et*

Belles Lettres, vol. xxvi, I, pp. 235-324, fig. *Les arts à la cour des papes pendant les XVe et XVIe siècles*, in *Bibl. des Écoles françaises d'Athènes et Rome*, vol. iv.

[96] Baluze, *Vitæ paparum Avenionensium*, 1693, I, pp. 1182 *et seq.* Fabricius, *Bibliotheca medii ævi*, 1734, I, p. 1109.

[97] Cf. vol. i, p. 337 (W.S.).

[98] According to Le Maire, *Histoire et antiquités de la ville et duché d'Orléans*, p. 197, this request is addressed to "Jeanne the Maid, greatly to be honoured and most devout, sent by the King of Heaven for the restoration, and for the extirpation of the English who tyrannize over France." *Trial*, vol. v, p. 253. Vallet de Viriville, *Histoire de Charles VII*, vol. ii, p. 131.

[99] Noël Valois, *La France et le grand schisme d'Occident*, vol. iv (1902), in 8vo, *passim*.

[100] *Trial*, vol. i, p. 82.

[101] *Trial*, vol. iii, pp. 466, 467.

[102] *Ibid.*, vol. i, pp. 245, 246.

[103] *Trial*, vol. i, p. 83.

[104] Perceval de Cagny, p. 165. *Chronique de la Pucelle*, p. 331. Jean Chartier, *Chronique*, vol. i, p. 106. Morosini, vol. iii, pp. 212, 213. The accounts of Hémon Raguier, in the *Trial*, vol. iv, p. 24.

[105] *Trial*, vol. ii, p. 450.

[106] So called because stamped with the picture of the Annunciation and bearing the inscription: *Salus populi suprema lex est*; the coin was worth about £1 of our money (W.S.).

[107] *Trial*, vol. i, p. 104. Extracts from the 13th account of Hémon Raguier, in *Trial*, vol. v, p. 267. E. Dupuis, *Jean Fouquerel, évêque de Senlis*, in *Mémoires du comité archéologique de Senlis*, 1875, vol. i, p. 93. Vatin, *Combat sous Senlis entre Charles VII et les Anglais*, in *Comité archéologique de Senlis, Comptes rendus et mémoires*, 1866, pp. 41, 54.

[108] *Trial*, vol. i, p. 264.

[109] Perceval de Cagny, p. 165. The 25th according to *Le journal d'un bourgeois de Paris*, p. 243.

[110] J. Doublet, *Histoire de l'abbaye de Saint-Denys en France, contenant les antiquités d'icelle, les fondations, prérogatives et privileges*, Paris, 1625, 2 vol. in 4to, vol. i, ch. xx and xxiv. Des Rues, *Les antiquités, fondations et singularités des plus célèbres villes*, pp. 84, 85.

[111] J. Doublet, *Histoire de l'abbaye de Saint-Denys*, vol. i, ch. xxxi, xxxiv.

[112] Cf. vol. i, p. 182 (W.S.).

[113] Thomassin, *Registre Delphinal*, in *Trial*, vol. iv, p. 304. See Du Cange, *Glossaire* under the word *Auriflamme*.

[114] J. Doublet, *Histoire de l'abbaye de Saint-Denys*, vol. i, ch. xxii. D. Michel Félibien, *Histoire de l'abbaye royale de Saint-Denys en France*, Paris, in folio, 1706, pp. 229, 320. Vallet de Viriville, *Notice du manuscrit de P. Cochon*, at the end of *La chronique de la Pucelle*, p. 360. *Chronique de Du Guesclin*, ed. Francisque-Michel, pp. 452 *et seq.*

[115] *Trial*, vol. v, pp. 107, 109.

[116] D. M. Félibien, *op. cit.*, ch. ii, pp. 528 *et seq.* Illustrations. J. Doublet, *op. cit.*, vol. i, ch. xliii, xlvi. *Trial*, vol. iii, p. 301. *Gallia Christiana*, vol. vii, col. 142.

[117] *Religieux de Saint-Denis*, pp. 154, 156, 226.

[118] Estienne Binet, *La vie apostolique de saint Denys l'Aréopagite, patron et apostre de la France*, Paris, 1624, in 12mo. J. Doublet, *Histoire chronologique pour la vérité de Saint Denys l'Aréopagite, apôtre de France et premier évêque de Paris*, Paris, 1646, in 4to, and *Histoire de l'abbaye de Saint-Denys en France*, p. 95. J. Havet, *Les origines de Saint-Denis*, in *Les Questions mérovingiennes*.

[119] *Trial*, vol. i, p. 179.

[120] *Journal d'un bourgeois de Paris*, p. 179, note 5.

[121] *Ibid.*, pp. 101, 209, note 1.

[122] *Ibid.*, pp. 241, 242. Monstrelet, vol. iv, p. 354.

[123] *Trial*, vol. i, p. 103.

[124] *Ibid.*, p. 304. Noël Valois, *Un nouveau témoignage sur Jeanne d'Arc*, in *Annuaire-bulletin de la Société de l'Histoire de France*, Paris, 1907, in 8vo, separate issue, pp. 17, 18.

[125] *Trial*, vol. i, p. 236.

[126] *Le Jouvencel*, vol. ii, p. 281.

[127] *Trial*, vol. iii, p. 81.

[128] Perceval de Cagny, p. 166.

[129] *Ibid.*, p. 166.

[130] Vallet de Viriville, *Histoire de Charles VII*, vol. ii, p. 112. De Beaucourt, *Histoire de Charles VII*, vol. ii, pp. 404, 408. Morosini, vol. iii, p. 192; vol. iv, appendix xviii.

[131] *Trial*, vol. v, p. 140.

[132] *Chronique de la Pucelle*, p. 332. Jean Chartier, *Chronique*, vol. i, p. 106. P. Cochon, p. 457. Perceval de Cagny, p. 165.

[133] Monstrelet, vol. iv, pp. 352, 353. *Journal d'un bourgeois de Paris*, pp. 247, 248. D. Félibien, *Histoire de Paris*, vol. ii, p. 813, and proofs and illustrations, vol. iv, p. 591. Morosini, vol. iii, pp. 208, 209, 224, note 2; vol. iv, appendix xviii, pp. 343, 344.

[134] Cf. vol. i, p. 34, note 3 (W.S.).

[135] De Beaucourt, *Histoire de Charles VII*, vol. ii, ch. vii. *La diplomatie de Charles VII jusqu'au traité d'Arras*.

[136] Perceval de Cagny, p. 166.

[137] Le Roux de Lincy, *Hugues Aubriot, prévôt de Paris sous Charles V*, Paris, 1862, in 8vo, *passim*. *Paris et ses historiens au*

XIVe et XVe siècle by Le Roux de Lincy and Tisserand, Paris, in fol. [*Histoire générale de Paris.*]

[138] Delamare, *Traité de la police*, Paris, 1710, in folio, vol. i, p. 79. A. Bonnardot, *Dissertation archéologique sur les enceintes de Paris, suivie de recherches sur les portes fortifiées qui dépendaient des enceintes de Paris*, 1851, in 4to, with plan. *Études archéologiques sur les anciens plans de Paris*, 1853, in 4to. *Appendice aux études archéologiques sur les anciens plans de Paris et aux dissertations sur les enceintes de Paris*, Paris, 1877, in 4to. *Étude sur Gilles Corrozet, suivie d'une notice sur un manuscrit de la Bibliothèque des ducs de Bourgogne, contenant une description de Paris, en 1432*, par Guillebert de Metz, Paris, 1846, in 8vo, 56 pages. Kausler, *Atlas des plus mémorables batailles*, Carlsruhe, 1831, pl. 34. H. Legrand, *Paris en 1380*, with plan conjecturally reconstructed, Paris in fol. 1868, p. 58. A. Guilaumot, *Les Portes de l'enceinte de Paris sous Charles V*, Paris, 1879. Rigaud, *Chronique de la Pucelle, campagne de Paris, cartes et plans*, Bergerac, 1886, in 8vo.

[139] *Journal d'un bourgeois de Paris*, p. 180.

[140] *Journal d'un bourgeois de Paris*, p. 189.

[141] *Ibid.*, pp. 136, 137.

[142] *Ibid.*, p. 107. *Document inédit relatif à l'état de Paris en 1430*, in *Revue des sociétés savantes*, 1863, p. 203.

[143] Christine de Pisan, in *Trial*, vol. v, stanza 56, p. 20. Le Roux de Lincy and Tisserand, *Paris et ses historiens*, p. 426.

[144] *Journal d'un bourgeois de Paris*, p. 251. A. Longnon, *Paris pendant la domination anglaise (1420-1436), documents extraits des registres de la chancellerie de France*, Paris, 1877, in 8vo, introduction, p. xiij. Vallet de Viriville, *Histoire de Charles VII*, vol. ii, p. 116, note 1.

[145] *Journal d'un bourgeois de Paris*, p. 248. *Chronique de la Pucelle*, p. 297. Morosini, vol. iii, p. 79, note.

[146] *Journal d'un bourgeois de Paris*, p. 257. Falconbridge, in *Trial*, vol. iv, p. 453. Morosini, vol. iii, p. 198.

[147] *Journal du siège*, p. 38. Jean Chartier, *Chronique*, vol. i, pp. 106, 107. Falconbridge, in *Trial*, vol. iv, p. 454.

[148] See vol. i, p. 222, note 2 (W.S.).

[149] *Journal d'un bourgeois de Paris*, p. 239, note 2. Le Roux de Lincy and Tisserand, *Paris et ses historiens*, pp. 340 *et seq.*

[150] 14th July, 1429, *Journal d'un bourgeois de Paris*, pp. 240, 241. Falconbridge, in *Trial*, vol. iv, p. 240. Morosini, vol. iii, p. 186.

[151] *Journal d'un bourgeois de Paris*, p. 241.

[152] Falconbridge, in *Trial*, vol. iv, p. 356.

[153] *Journal d'un bourgeois de Paris*, p. 242.

[154] *Ibid.*, p. 243.

[155] Rymer, *Fœdera*, May. *Chronique de la Pucelle*, p. 332. Monstrelet, vol. iv, p. 355. Jean Chartier, *Chronique*, vol. i, pp. 106, 107. Wallon, *Jeanne d'Arc*, vol. i, p. 290, note 1. G. Lefèvre-Pontalis, *La panique anglaise*, p. 9. Morosini, vol. iii, p. 216, note 5; vol. iv, appendix xviii.

[156] *Journal d'un bourgeois de Paris*, p. 243.

[157] *Journal d'un bourgeois de Paris*, p. 243. Perceval de Cagny, p. 166. *Chronique des cordeliers*, folio, 486 verso.

[158] *Journal d'un bourgeois de Paris*, p. 243.

[159] *Ibid.*, pp. 243, 244.

[160] Cf. *ante*, p. 45, note 2 (W.S.).

[161] Register of the Deliberations of the Chapter of Notre Dame (Arch. Nat., LL, 716, pp. 173, 174), in *Le journal d'un bourgeois de Paris, loc. cit.* Le P. Ayroles, *La vraie Jeanne d'Arc*, vol. iii, pp. 530, 531, proofs and illustrations, J, p. 639. Le P. Denifle and Chatelain, *Le procès de Jeanne d'Arc et l'université de Paris*, Nogent-le-Rotrou, 1898, in 8vo.

[162] Register of the Deliberations of the Chapter of Notre Dame, in Tuetey, notes to *Le Journal d'un bourgeois de Paris*, p. 241, note

1. Falconbridge, in *Trial*, vol. iv, p. 456. Le P. Ayroles, *La vraie Jeanne d'Arc*, vol. iii, proofs and illustrations, p. 640.

[163] Register of the Deliberations of the Chapter of Notre Dame, *loc. cit. Chronique de la Pucelle*, p. 332. *Journal d'un bourgeois de Paris*, p. 244. Monstrelet, vol. iv, p. 354. Martial d'Auvergne, *Vigiles*, ed. Coustelier, vol. i, p. 113. Perceval de Cagny, p. 166. *Chronique des cordeliers*, folio, 486 verso. Le P. Ayroles, *La vrai Jeanne d'Arc*, vol. iii, p. 531.

[164] Voragine, *Legenda Aurea*. Anquetil, *La nativité, miracle extrait de la légende dorée*, in *Mem. Soc. Agr. de Bayeux*, 1883, vol. x, p. 286. Douhet, *Dictionnaire des mystères*, 1854, p. 545.

[165] Perceval de Cagny, pp. 166, 168. *Chronique de la Pucelle*, pp. 333, 334. Jean Chartier, *Chronique*, vol. i, pp. 107, 109. Falconbridge, in *Trial*, vol. iv, pp. 456, 458. *Journal d'un bourgeois de Paris*, pp. 244, 245. *Chronique des cordeliers*, fol. 486 verso. P. Cochon, ed. Beaurepaire, p. 307. Morosini, vol. iii, p. 210.

[166] Gaguin, *Hist. Francorum*, Frankfort, 1577, book viii, chap. ii, p. 158. Tanon, *Histoire des tribunaux de l'inquisition en France*, p. 121. Lea, History of the Inquisition in the Middle Age, vol. ii, p. 126. (The Turlupins were a German sect who called themselves "the Brethren of the Free Spirit." W.S.)

[167] Perceval de Cagny, p. 161. Vallet de Viriville, *Histoire de Charles VII*, vol. ii, p. 120, note 1. G. Lefèvre-Pontalis, *Un détail du siège de Paris, par Jeanne d'Arc*, in *Bibliothèque de l'École des Chartes*, vol. xlvi, 1885, pp. 5 *et seq.*

[168] Deliberation of the Chapter of Notre Dame, *loc. cit. Journal d'un bourgeois de Paris*, p. 245. Falconbridge, in *Trial*, vol. iv, p. 457.

[169] *Trial*, vol. i, pp. 240, 246, 298; vol. iii, pp. 425, 427; vol. v, pp. 97, 107, 130, 140.

[170] *Ibid.*, pp. 57, 146, 168, 250.

[171] *Ibid.*, vol. v, p. 130 (letter of the 17th of July, 1429), vol. i, p. 298. "Et hoc sciebar per revelationem." Cf. vol. i, pp. 57, 260, 288 in contradiction.

[172] *Journal du siège*, p. 89.

[173] *Trial*, vol. i, pp. 147, 148.

[174] In 1254 Saint Louis founded this hospital for three hundred blind knights whose eyes had been put out by the Saracens. (W.S.)

[175] Le Roux de Lincy and Tisserand, *Paris et ses historiens*, pp. 205 and 231, note 4. Adolphe Berty, *Topographie historique du vieux Paris, région du Louvre et des Tuileries*, p. 180, and app. vi, p. ix. E. Eude, *L'attaque de Jeanne d'Arc contre Paris, 1429*, in *Cosmos*, nouv. série, xxix (1894), pp. 241, 244.

[176] *Journal d'un bourgeois de Paris*, p. 246.

[177] *Chronique de la Pucelle*, pp. 332, 333. Jean Chartier, *Chronique*, vol. i, p. 108.

[178] Perceval de Cagny, p. 167.

[179] *Trial*, vol. i, p. 148.

[180] *Journal d'un bourgeois de Paris*, p. 245.

[181] *Le Jouvencel*, vol. i, p. 67.

[182] *Chronique de la Pucelle*, p. 333. Jean Chartier, *Chronique*, vol. i, p. 109. *Journal du siège*, p. 127. Martial d'Auvergne, *Vigiles*, ed. Coustelier, 1724, vol. i, p. 113.

[183] Perceval de Cagny, p. 167. Monstrelet, vol. iv, pp. 355, 356. Morosini, vol. iii, note 3. E. Eude, *L'attaque de Jeanne d'Arc contre Paris*, in *Cosmos*, 22 Sept., 1894, vol. xxix. P. Marin, *Le génie militaire de Jeanne d'Arc*, in *Grande revue de Paris et de Saint-Pétersbourg*, 2nd year, vol. i, 1889, p. 142.

[184] *Trial*, vol. i, pp. 57, 246. *Journal d'un bourgeois de Paris*, p. 245. Deliberations of the Chapter of Notre Dame, *loc. cit.* Falconbridge, in *Trial*, vol. iv, p. 457. Perceval de Cagny, Jean Chartier, *Journal du siège*, Monstrelet, Morosini, *loc. cit.*

[185] *Trial*, vol. i, p. 298.

[186] *Trial*, vol. i, p. 111, 273. Berry, in *Trial*, vol. iv, p. 50. F. Brun, *Jeanne d Arc et le capitaine de Soissons*, pp. 31 *et seq.*

[187] *Trial*, vol. i, p. 57.

[188] The oath "*Par mon martin*" (by my staff) is an invention of the scribe who wrote the *Chronicle* which is attributed to Perceval de Cagny, p. 168.

[189] *Chronique de la Pucelle*, p. 334. *Journal du siège*, p. 128. Jean Chartier, *Chronique*, vol. i, p. 109. Monstrelet, vol. iv, pp. 355, 356.

[190] Deliberation of the Chapter of Notre Dame, *loc. cit.*

[191] *Journal d'un bourgeois de Paris*, p. 245.

[192] *Le Jouvencel*, vol. i, p. 142.

[193] *Journal d'un bourgeois de Paris*, pp. 245, 246.

[194] For the opinions of the townsfolk of Paris, see various acts of Henry VI of the 18th and 25th of Sept., 1429 (MS. Fontanieu, 115). Sauval, *Antiquités de Paris*, vol. iii, p. 586 and *circ.*

[195] A. Longnon, *Paris pendant la domination anglaise*, p. 302.

[196] Falconbridge, in *Trial*, vol. iv, pp. 456, 458.

[197] *Relation du greffier de La Rochelle*, p. 344.

[198] *Chronique de Normandie*, in *Trial*, vol. iv, pp. 342, 343.

[199] Perceval de Cagny, p. 168.

[200] *Ibid. Chronique normande*, in *La chronique de la Pucelle*, p. 465. Vallet de Viriville, *Histoire de Charles VII*, vol. ii, p. 120, note 1.

[201] Duchesne, *Histoire de la maison de Montmorency*, p. 232. Perceval de Cagny, p. 168. Vallet de Viriville, *Histoire de Charles VII*, vol. ii, pp. 118, 119.

[202] G. Lefèvre-Pontalis, *Un détail du siège de Paris*, in *Bibliothèque de l'École des Chartes*, vol. xlvi, 1885, p. 12.

[203] Perceval de Cagny, pp. 168, 169. Morosini, vol. iii, p. 219, note 4. Vallet de Viriville, *Histoire de Charles VII*, vol. ii, p. 120, note 1. G. Lefèvre-Pontalis, *Un détail du siège de Paris, loc. cit.*

[204] Diminutive of *amie* (W.S.).

[205] Eberhard Windecke, pp. 184, 186.

[206] Jean Chartier, *Chronique*, vol. i, p. 90.

[207] *Trial*, vol. iii, p. 73.

[208] *Ibid.*, p. 99.

[209] *Ibid.*, vol. i, p. 76.

[210] Jean Chartier, *Chronique*, vol. i, p. 90.

[211] Jean Chartier, *Chronique*, vol. i, pp. 122, 123.

[212] Perceval de Cagny, p. 169. *Chronique de la Pucelle*, pp. 335 *et seq.* Jean Chartier, *Chronique*, vol. i, pp. 112 *et seq.* Monstrelet, vol. iv, p. 356. *Journal d'un bourgeois de Paris*, p. 246. Berry in *Trial*, vol. iv, p. 48. Gilles de Roye, p. 208.

[213] *Trial*, vol. i, p. 260.

[214] Jean Chartier, *Chronique*, vol. i, p. 109. Perceval de Cagny, p. 170. Martial d'Auvergne, *Vigiles*, vol. i, p. 114. Jacques Doublet, *Histoire de l'abbaye de Saint-Denys*, pp. 13, 14.

[215] La Curne, at the word *Blanc*: white armour was worn by squires, gilded armour by knights. Bouteiller, in his *Somme Rurale*, refers to the "*harnais doré*" (gilded armour) of the knights. Cf. Du Tillet, *Recueil des rois de France*, ch. *Des chevaliers*, p. 431. Du Cange, *Observations sur les établissements de la France*, p. 373.

[216] *Trial*, vol. i, p. 179.

[217] *Journal du siège*, p. 130. Perceval de Cagny, pp. 170, 171. *Journal d'un bourgeois de Paris*, pp. 246, 247. Berry, in *Trial*, vol. iv, p. 79. Morosini, vol. iii, p. 219.

[218] *Trial*, vol. iii, p. 86. De Beaucourt, *Histoire de Charles VII*, vol. ii, p. 265. P. Lanéry d'Arc and L. Jeny, *Jeanne d'Arc en Berry, avec des documents et des éclaircissements inédits*, Paris, 1892, in 12mo, chap. vi.

[219] *Trial*, vol. iii, p. 85, note 1. De Beaucourt, *Histoire de Charles VII*, vol. i, p. 418, note 7.

[220] *Trial*, vol. iii, p. 85.

[221] *Ibid.*, pp. 81, 86.

[222] Lanéry d'Arc and L. Jeny, *Jeanne d'Arc en Berry*, pp. 72, 73.

[223] "*In balneo et stuphis.*" *Trial*, vol. iii, p. 88.

[224] *L'amant rendu cordelier à l'observance d'amour*; poem attributed to Martial d'Auvergne, A. de Montaiglon, Paris, 1881, in 8vo, lines 1761-1776 and note p. 184. A. Franklin, *La vie privée d'autrefois*, vol. ii, *Les soins de la toilette*, Paris, 1887, in 18mo, pp. 20 *et seq.* A. Lecoy de la Marche, *Le bain au moyen âge*, in *Revue du monde catholique*, vol. xiv, pp. 870-881.

[225] *Livre des métiers*, by Étienne Boileau, edited by De Lespinasse and F. Bonnardot, Paris, 1879, pp. 154, 155, and note. G. Bayle, *Notes pour servir à l'histoire de la prostitution au moyen âge*, in *Mémoires de l'Académie de Vauctuse*, 1887, pp. 241, 242. Dr. P. Pansier, *Histoire des prétendus statuts de la reine Jeanne*, in *Le Janus*, 1902, p. 14.

[226] Lanéry d'Arc and L. Jeny, *Jeanne d'Arc en Berry*, pp. 76, 77.

[227] *Trial*, vol. iii, p. 100.

[228] *Ibid.*, p. 88.

[229] *Trial*, vol. iii, p. 87. Lanéry d'Arc and L. Jeny, *Jeanne d'Arc en Berry*, pp. 73, 74.

[230] *Trial*, vol. iii, pp. 86, 87.

[231] *Ibid.*, pp. 86, 88.

[232] *Trial*, vol. iii, p. 88.

[233] *Ibid.*, p. 87.

[234] *Ibid.*, pp. 87, 88.

[235] Noël Valois, *Un nouveau témoignage sur Jeanne d'Arc*, in *Annuaire bulletin de la Société de l'Histoire de France*, Paris, 1907, in 8vo, pp. 8 and 18 (separate issue).

[236] *Trial*, vol. iii, p. 217. De Beaucourt, *Histoire de Charles VII*, vol. ii, p. 265. A. Buhot de Kersers, *Histoire et statistique du département du Cher, canton de Mehun*, Bourges, 1891, in 4to, pp. 261 *et seq.* A. de Champeaux and P. Gauchery, *Les travaux d'art exécutés pour Jean de France, duc de Berry*, Paris, 1894, in 4to, pp. 7, 9, and the miniature in *Les grandes heures* of Duke Jean of Berry at Chantilly.

[237] Perceval de Cagny, pp. 170, 171. Berry, in *Trial*, vol. iv, p. 48. Letter from the Sire d'Albret to the people of Riom, in *Trial*, vol. v, pp. 148, 149. Martin Le Franc, *Champion des dames*, in *Trial*, vol. v, p. 71.

[238] *Chronique de la Pucelle*, p. 310. *Journal du siège*, p. 107. Morosini, vol. ii, p. 229, note 4. Perceval de Cagny, p. 172.

[239] *Trial*, vol. iii, p. 217. Jaladon de la Barre, *Jeanne d'Arc à Saint-Pierre-le-Moustier et deux juges nivernais à Rouen*, Nevers, 1868, in 8vo, chaps. ix *et seq.*

[240] *Trial*, vol. v, p. 356. Lanéry d'Arc and L. Jeny, *Jeanne d'Arc en Berry*, p. 89.

[241] *Trial*, vol. iii, p. 217.

[242] *Ibid.*, p. 218.

[243] *Ibid.*, vol. i, p. 106. *Journal d'un bourgeois de Paris*, pp. 259, 260, 271, 272. Nider, *Formicarium*, in *Trial*, vol. iv, pp. 503, 504. J. Quicherat, *Aperçus nouveaux*, pp. 74 *et seq.* N. Quellien, *Perrinaïc, une compagne de Jeanne d'Arc*, Paris, 1891, in 8vo. Mme. Pascal-Estienne, *Perrinaïk*, Paris, 1893, in 8vo. J. Trévedy, *Histoire du roman de Perrinaïc*, Saint-Brieuc, 1894, in 8vo. *Le roman de Perrinaïc*, Vannes, 1894, in 8vo. A. de la Borderie, *Pierronne et Perrinaïc*, Paris, 1894, in 8vo.

[244] *Trial*, vol. v, index at the words *Catherine, Michel, Marguerite.*

[245] *Ibid.*, vol. i, p. 106.

[246] *Journal d'un bourgeois de Paris*, pp. 271, 272.

[247] *Trial*, vol. iii, pp. 104 *et seq.*

[248] *Ibid.*, vol. ii, p. 450. *Journal d'un bourgeois de Paris*, pp. 271, 272.

[249] *Journal d'un bourgeois de Paris*, p. 235.

[250] *Trial*, vol. i, p. 106.

[251] *Ibid.*, p. 107.

[252] Arcère, *Histoire de La Rochelle*, 1756, in 4to, vol. i, p. 271. *Trial*, vol. v, p. 104, note. Vallet de Viriville, *Histoire de Charles VII*, vol. ii, pp. 24, 75 *et seq.*, 219, 279.

[253] *Trial*, vol. i, pp. 107, 108.

[254] *Trial*, vol. i, p. 107.

[255] *Trial*, vol. i, pp. 108, 109.

[256] *Ibid.*, p. 107.

[257] *Ibid.*, p. 108.

[258] *Ibid.*

[259] "Perrinet Crasset, mason and captain of men-at-arms." *Chronique des cordeliers*, fol. 446 verso. Jean Chartier, *Chronique*, vol. i, p. 117. Monstrelet, vol. iv, p. 174. Vallet de Viriville, *Histoire de Charles VII*, vol. i, p. 328.

[260] S. Luce, *Jeanne d'Arc à Domremy*, p. cclxxviii. A. de Villaret, *Campagne des Anglais*, p. 109. Le P. Ayroles, *La vraie Jeanne d'Arc*, vol. iii, pp. 20, 21, 373 *et seq.* J. de Fréminville, *Les écorcheurs en Bourgogne* (1435-1445); *Étude sur les compagnies franches au XVe siècle*, Dijon, 1888, in 8vo. P. Champion, *Guillaume de Flavy.* Proofs and illustrations, xxx.

[261] Sainte-Marthe, *Histoire généalogique de la maison de la Trémoïlle*, 1668, in 12mo, pp. 149 *et seq*. L. de La Trémoïlle, *Les La Trémoïlle pendant cinq siècles*, Nantes, 1890, vol. i, p. 165.

[262] *Trial*, vol. v, p. 149. Jean Chartier, *Chronique*, vol. iii. *Journal du siège*, p. 129. Monstrelet, vol. v, chap, lxxii. A. de Villaret, *Campagne des Anglais*, p. 108.

[263] *Trial*, vol. v, p. 146. F. Perot, *Un document inédit sur Jeanne d'Arc*, in *Bulletin de la Société archéologique de l'Orléanais*, vol. xii, 1898-1901, p. 231.

[264] *Trial*, vol. v, pp. 147-150. Lanéry d'Arc and L. Jeny, *Jeanne d'Arc en Berry*, ch. viii.

[265] S. Luce, *Jeanne d'Arc à Domremy*, p. cclxxix.

[266] Acta Sanctorum, March, i, 554, col. 2, no. 61. Abbé Bizouard, *Histoire de sainte Colette*, pp. 35, 37. S[ilvere], *Histoire chronologique de la bienheureuse Colette*, Paris, 1628, in 8vo.

[267] *The Maid* (W.S.).

[268] *Servant*. Cf. Godefroy, *Lexique de l'ancien Français* (W.S.).

[269] *Histoire chronologique de la bienheureuse Colette*, pp. 168-200.

[270] S. Luce, *Jeanne d'Arc et les ordres mendiants*, in *Revue des deux mondes*, 1881, vol. xlv, p. 90. L. de Kerval, *Jeanne d'Arc et les Franciscains*, Vanves, 1893, pp. 49, 51. S. Luce, *Jeanne d'Arc à Domremy*, pp. cclxxviii *et seq*. F. Perot, *Jeanne d'Arc en Bourbonnais*, Orléans, in 8vo, 26 pp., 1889. F. André, *La vérité sur Jeanne d'Arc*, in 8vo, 1895, pp. 308 *et seq*.

[271] *Trial*, vol. v, pp. 146-148.

[272] *Ibid*., pp. 146, 148. Facsimile in *Le Musée des archives départementales*, p. 124.

[273] F. Perot (*Bulletin de la Société archéologique de l'Orléanais*, vol. xii, p. 231).

[274] A. de Villaret, *Campagne des Anglais*, p. 107, proofs and illustrations, xvii, pp. 159, 168. *Trial*, vol. v, pp. 268, 270, according to the original documents in the Orléans Library.

[275] La Thaumassière, *Histoire du Berry*, p. 161. *Trial*, vol. v, pp. 356, 357. Lanéry d'Arc and L. Jeny, *Jeanne d'Arc en Berry*, pp. 105 *et seq.* A. de Villaret, *Campagne des Anglais*, pp. 111, 112.

[276] *Mémoires de la Société des Antiquaires du Centre*, vol. iv, 1870-1872, pp. 211, 239.

[277] Vallet de Viriville, *Histoire de Charles VII*, vol. ii, p. 126. Lanéry d'Arc and L. Jeny, *Jeanne d'Arc en Berry*, p. 89.

[278] Perceval de Cagny, p. 172.

[279] *Le Jouvencel*, vol. ii, pp. 216, 217.

[280] Extract from the Book of Accounts of the town of Périgueux, in *Bulletin de la Société historique et archéologique du Périgord*, vol. xiv, January to February, 1887. S. Luce, *Jeanne d'Arc à Domremy*, proofs and illustrations, ccxvii, p. 252. Le P. Chapotin, *La guerre de cent ans et les dominicains*, pp. 74 *et seq.*

[281] *Trial*, vol. i, p. 106.

[282] *Journal d'un bourgeois de Paris*, p. 271.

[283] Morosini, vol. iii, pp. 232, 233. Le P. Denifle and Chatelain, *Cartularium Univ. Paris*, vol. iv, p. 515.

[284] Noël Valois, *Un nouveau témoignage sur Jeanne d'Arc*, Paris, 1907, in 8vo, 19 pages.

[285] Morosini, vol. iii, p. 232.

[286] *Journal d'un bourgeois de Paris*, pp. 354, 355.

[287] *Sentent la persinée*: literally, smell of roast parsley. Cf. Godefroy, *Lexique de l'ancien français* at the word *persinée*. *Sentir la persinée*: to be suspected of heresy (W.S.).

[288] Pardon granted to Le Sourd and Jehannin Daix, in *Trial*, vol. v, pp. 142-145.

[289] *Trial*, vol. i, p. 107.

[290] *Ibid.*, vol. iii, p. 84; vol. iv, pp. 312 *et passim*. A. de Villaret, *loc. cit.* Proofs and illustrations.

[291] *Trial*, vol. v, pp. 150-153. J. Hordal, *Heroinae nobilissimae Joannae Darc, lotharingœ, vulgo aurelianensis puellae historia....* Ponti-Mussi, 1612, small 4to. C. du Lys, *Traité sommaire tant du nom et des armes que de la naissance et parenté de la Pucelle, justifié par plusieurs patentes et arrêts, enquêtes et informations....* Paris, 1633, in 4to. De la Roque, *Traité de la noblesse*, Paris, 1678, in 4to, ch. xliii. Lanéry d'Arc, *Jeanne d'Arc en Berry*, ch. x.

[292] See analytical index, in *Trial*, vol. v, at the word *Pucelle*.

[293] *Trial*, vol. v, p. 270.

[294] *Ibid.*, vol. iii, pp. 19, 74, 203. H. Daniel Lacombe, *L'hôte de Jeanne d'Arc à Poitiers, Maître Jean Rabateau, président du parlement de Paris*, in *Revue du Bas-Poitou*, 1891, pp. 48, 66.

[295] *Trial*, vol. iii, pp. 88 *et seq*.

[296] Extract from the Accounts of the town of Orléans, in *Trial*, vol. v, p. 331.

[297] Vallet de Viriville, *Un épisode de la vie de Jeanne d'Arc*, in *Bibliothèque de l'École des Chartes*, vol. iv (1st series), p. 488. *Trial*, vol. v, pp. 154-156.

[298] Jules Doinel, *Note sur une maison de Jeanne d'Arc*, in *Mémoires de la Société archéologique et historique de l'Orléanais*, vol. xv, pp. 491-500.

[299] *Journal du siège*, pp. 15, 16.

[300] Jules Doinel, *Note sur une maison de Jeanne d'Arc, loc. cit.*

[301] S. Luce, *Jeanne d'Arc à Domremy*, p. 360.

[302] *Trial*, vol. i, p. 295.

[303] Accounts of the fortress, in *Trial*, vol. v, pp. 259, 260.

[304] *Trial*, vol. v, p. 159.

[305] Perceval de Cagny, p. 173. *Chronique de la Pucelle*, p. 258. *Berry*, in Godefroy, p. 376. Morosini, vol. iii, p. 294, notes 4, 5. Vallet de Viriville, *Histoire de Charles VII*, vol. i, pp. 139, 163. De Beaucourt, *Histoire de Charles VII*, vol. ii, p. 144.

[306] Monstrelet, vol. iv, p. 378. D. Plancher, *Histoire de Bourgogne*, vol. iv, p. 137. Morosini, vol. iii, p. 268.

[307] Du Tillet, *Recueil des rois de France*, vol. ii, p. 39 (ed. 1601-1602). Rymer, *Fœdera*, March, 1430.

[308] P. Champion, *Guillaume de Flavy*, pp. 35, 152.

[309] De Beaucourt, *Histoire de Charles VII*, vol. ii, pp. 351, 389.

[310] *Trial*, vol. v, p. 160, according to Rogier's copy. H. Jadart, *Jeanne d'Arc à Reims*, proofs and illustrations xv. Facsimile in Wallon, 1876 edition, p. 200. The original of this letter exists, likewise the original of the letter addressed on the 9th of November, 1429, to the citizens of Riom. These two letters, about one hundred and twenty-six days apart, are not written by the same scribe. The signature of neither one nor the other can be attributed to the hand which indited the rest of the letter. The seven letters of the name *Jehanne* seem to have been written by some one whose hand was being held, which is not surprising, seeing that the Maid did not know how to write. But a comparison of the two signatures reveals their close similarity. In both the stem of the J slopes in the same direction and is of identical length; the first *n* through one letter being written on the top of another has three pothooks instead of two; the second pothook of the second *n* obviously written in two strokes is too long, in short the two signatures correspond exactly. We must conclude therefore that having once obtained the Maid's signature by guiding her hand, an impression was taken to serve as a model for all her other letters. To judge from the two missives of the 9th of November, 1429 and the 16th of March, 1430, this impression was most faithfully reproduced. Cf. *post*, p. 117, note 2.

[311] *Trial*, vol. iii, p. 11.

[312] Perceval de Cagny, p. 172.

[313] *Trial*, vol. i, p. 83.

[314] *Ibid.*, vol. v, p. 156.

[315] Monstrelet, vol. iv, pp. 24, 86, 87. J. Zeller, *Histoire d'Allemagne*, vol. vii, *La réforme*, Paris, 1891, pp. 78 *et seq.* E. Denis, *Jean Hus et la guerre des Hussites* (1879); *Les origines de l'Unité des Frères Bohêmes*, Angers, 1885, in 8vo, pp. 5 *et seq.*

[316] Two of the great leaders of the Hussites who held large parts of central Germany in terror from 1419-1434 (W.S.).

[317] L. Paris, *Cabinet historique*, vol. i, 1855, pp. 74, 76. Rogier, in *Trial*, vol. iv, p. 294. Morosini, vol. iii, pp. 132, 133, 136, 137, 168, 169, 188, 189; vol. iv, supplement, xvii.

[318] *Trial*, vol. i, p. 240; vol. v, p. 126.

[319] Morosini, vol. iii, pp. 82-85. Christine de Pisan, in *Trial*, vol. v, p. 416. Eberhard Windecke, pp. 60-63.

[320] Eberhard Windecke, pp. 108, 115, 188.

[321] Lea, *A History of the Inquisition in the Middle Ages*, vol. ii, p. 481 (1906).

[322] Th. de Sickel, *Lettre de Jeanne d'Arc aux Hussites*, in *Bibliothèque de l'École des Chartes*, 3rd series, vol. ii, p. 81. A wrong date is given in the German translation used by Quicherat, *Trial*, vol. v, pp. 156-159.

[323] *Trial*, vol. i, p. 246.

[324] *Ibid.*, vol. v, p. 95.

[325] Another of the Hussite leaders (W.S.).

[326] J. Nider, *Formicarium* in *Trial*, vol. iv, pp. 502-504.

[327] *Trial*, vol. v, pp. 161, 162.

[328] *Ibid.*, vol. iv, p. 299, and H. Jadart, *Jeanne d'Arc à Reims*, pp. 60 *et seq.* Mémoires de Pierre Coquault, *ibid.*, pp. 109 *et seq.*

[329] This letter was published by J. Quicherat, in *Trial*, vol. v, pp. 161, 162, and by M. H. Jadart, *Jeanne d'Arc à Reims*, pp. 106, 107

and document XVI, according to Rogier's inaccurate copy. The original which had disappeared from the municipal archives at Reims was considered to be lost; but it has been found in the possession of the Count de Maleissye. Cf. the reproduction by A. Marty and M. Lepet, *L'histoire de Jeanne d'Arc.... Cent facsimilés de manuscrits, de miniatures*, Paris, 1907, in large 4to. Here for the first time is to be found a text correct according to the original document.

[330] The signature appears to be autograph. It differs from the two identical signatures of the letters from Riom and Reims (see *ante*, p. 108, note 1); and it bears trace of the resistance of a hand which was being guided.

[331] *Trial*, vol. v, pp. 161, 162. Varin, *Archives législatives de la ville de Reims*, vol. i, p. 596. H. Jadart, *Jeanne d'Arc à Reims*, pp. 106, 107.

[332] Perceval de Cagny, who was in the pay of the Duke of Alençon, is the only chronicler to suggest it, p. 173.

[333] "In the year 1430, Jeanne the Maid started from the country of Berry accompanied by divers fighting men...." Jean Chartier, *Chronique*, vol. i, p. 120.

[334] Jean Chartier, *Chronique*, vol. i, p. 120. Martial d'Auvergne, *Vigiles*, ed. Coustellier, vol. i, p. 117. Note concerning G. de Flavy, in *Trial*, vol. v, p. 177. P. Champion, *Guillaume de Flavy*, p. 36, note 2.

[335] *Journal du siège*, p. 12.

[336] De Beaucourt, *Histoire de Charles VII*, vol. ii, p. 293, note 3. True, the loan was made later; none the less the dependence of Jean d'Aulon on the Sire de la Trémouille existed at this time.

[337] *Trial*, vol. i, p. 99, note. *Journal du siège*, pp. 235, 238.

[338] This comes from the *Journal d'un bourgeois de Paris*, p. 271.

[339] *Trial*, vol. v, pp. 159, 160.

[340] The Pardon of Jean de Calais in A. Longnon, *Paris sous la domination anglaise*, pp. 301-309. Stevenson, *Letters and Papers*, vol. i, pp. 34-50.

[341] So it appears from Morosini, vol. iii, pp. 274-275.

[342] Morosini, vol. iii, pp. 228-231. Concerning Perrinet Gressart see vol. i, p. 389.

[343] May 3, 1430.

[344] G. Lefèvre-Pontalis, *La panique anglaise*. Le P. Ayroles, *La vraie Jeanne d'Arc*, vol. iii, pp. 572-574.

[345] *Trial*, vol. i, pp. 115, 253, April 17-23. Perceval de Cagny, p. 173. *Chronique des cordeliers*, fol. 502 recto. P. Champion, *Guillaume de Flavy*, p. 158, note 2.

[346] Monstrelet, vol. iv, p. 363 (April 16).

[347] Jean Chartier, *Chronique*, vol. i, p. 125. Monstrelet, vol. iv, p. 378. Chastellain, vol. ii, p. 28. Melun certainly belonged to the French on the 23rd of April, 1430.

[348] *Trial*, vol. i, pp. 114-116. G. Leroy, *Histoire de Melun*, Melun, 1887, in 8vo, ch. xvi ... x ... *Jeanne d'Arc à Melun, mi-avril*, 1430, Melun, 1896, 32 pp.

[349] *Trial*, vol. i, p. 147.

[350] *Journal d'un bourgeois de Paris*, p. 259.

[351] *Chronique de la Pucelle*, pp. 334, 335. Jean Chartier, *Chronique*, vol. i, pp. 110, 111. F.A. Denis, *Le séjour de Jeanne d'Arc à Lagny*, Lagny, 1894, in 8vo, pp. 3 *et seq.*

[352] Monstrelet, vol. iv, p. 384. Jean Chartier, *Chronique*, vol. i, pp. 120, 121. Perceval de Cagny, p. 173.

[353] Jean Chartier, *loc. cit.* Martial d'Auvergne, *Vigiles*, vol. i, p. 117. P. Champion, *Guillaume de Flavy*, p. 38, note.

[354] Jean Chartier, *Chronique*, vol. i, p. 121.

[355] Monstrelet, vol. iv, p. 384.

[356] H. Jadart, *Jeanne d'Arc à Reims*, p. 61.

[357] *Trial*, vol. i, p. 158.

[358] *Ibid.*, pp. 158, 159.

[359] *Journal d'un bourgeois de Paris*, pp. 71, 72. Sauval, *Antiquités de Paris*, vol. i, p. 104. A. Longnon, *Paris pendant la domination anglaise*, p. 118. H. Legrand, *Paris en 1380*, Paris, 1868, in 4to, p. 65.

[360] *Piquette*, a sour wine or cider, made from the residue of grapes or apples. A kind of second brewing (W.S.). *Journal d'un bourgeois de Paris*, pp. 150, 154, 156, 187. Francisque-Michel and Edouard Fournier, *Histoire des hôtelleries, cabarets, hôtels garnis*, Paris, 1851 (2 vols. in 8vo), vol. ii, p. 5.

[361] A. Longnon, *Paris pendant la domination anglaise*, p. 117.

[362] *Journal d'un bourgeois de Paris*, pp. 71, 72. A. Longnon, *Paris pendant la domination anglaise*, p. 118, note 1.

[363] A. Longnon, *Paris pendant la domination anglaise*, pp. 119-123.

[364] *Journal d'un bourgeois de Paris*, pp. 251, 253. Falconbridge, in A. Longnon, *Paris pendant la domination anglaise*, p. 302, note 1. Sauval, *Antiquités de Paris*, vol. iii, p. 536. Vallet de Viriville, *Histoire de Charles VII*, vol. ii, p. 140. Morosini, vol. iii, pp. 274 *et seq.*

[365] *Trial*, vol. i, pp. 158, 159.

[366] *Ibid.*, p. 159.

[367] *Ibid.*, p. 254. Monstrelet, vol. iv, p. 385. E. Richer, *Histoire manuscrite de la Pucelle*, book i, folio 82.

[368] *Le Jouvencel*, vol. ii, pp. 210, 211.

[369] *Trial*, vol. i, p. 105.

[370] A. Denis, *Jeanne d'Arc à Lagny*, Lagny, 1896, in 8vo, pp. 4 *et seq.* J.A. Lepaire, *Jeanne d'Arc à Lagny*, Lagny, 1880, in 8vo, 38 pages.

[371] *Trial,* vol. i, p. 105.

[372] *Religieux de Saint-Denis,* vol. ii, p. 82. Jean Juvénal des Ursins, in *Coll. Michaud et Poujoulat,* p. 395, col. 2.

[373] *Acta Sanctorum,* 6th of March, pp. 381 and 617. Abbé Bizouard, *Histoire de Sainte Colette,* pp. 35, 37. Abbé Douillet, *Sainte Colette, sa vie, ses œuvres,* 1884, pp. 150-154.

[374] Le Curé de Saint-Sulpice, *Notre-Dame de France,* Paris, in 8vo, vol. vi, 1860, p. 57.

[375] For the etymology of Avioth see C. Bonnabelle, *Petite étude sur Avioth et son église,* in *Annuaire de la Meuse,* 1883, in 18mo, p. 14.

[376] Le Curé de Saint-Sulpice, *loc. cit.,* vol. v, pp. 107 *et seq.* Bonnabelle, *loc. cit.,* pp. 13 *et seq.* Jacquemain, *Notre-Dame d'Avioth et son église monumentale,* Sedan, 1876, in 8vo.

[377] *Trial,* vol. i, pp. 105, 106.

[378] Arch. mun. of Senlis in *Musé des archives départementales,* pp. 304, 305. J. Flammermont, *Histoire de Senlis pendant la seconds partie de la guerre de cent ans,* p. 245. Perceval de Cagny, p. 173. Morosini, vol. iii, p. 294, note 5.

[379] Manuscript History of Beauvais by Hermant, in *Trial,* vol. v, p. 165. G. Lecocq, *Étude historique sur le séjour de Jeanne d'Arc à Elincourt-Sainte-Marguerite,* Amiens, 1879, in 8vo, 13 pages. A. Peyrecave, *Notes sur le séjour de Jeanne d'Arc à Elincourt-Sainte-Marguerite,* Paris, 1875, in 8vo. *Elincourt-Sainte-Marguerite, notice historique et archéologique,* Compiègne, 1888. Ch. vii, pp. 113, 123.

[380] *Trial,* vol. v, pp. 164, 165. *Les miracles de Madame Sainte Katerine de Fierboys,* pp. 16, 62, 63.

[381] P. Champion, *Guillaume de Flavy.* Proofs and illustrations, pp. 150, 154. Morosini, vol. iii, p. 276, note 3. Note concerning G. de Flavy, in *Trial,* vol. v, p. 176.

[382] Monstrelet, ch. xxx. Note concerning G. de Flavy, in *Trial*, vol. v, p. 175. P. Champion, *Guillaume de Flavy*. Proofs and illustrations, xliv, xlv.

[383] "In this country the Emperor [of Constantinople] has a city called Capha, which is a seaport belonging to the Genoese and whence is obtained wood for the making of bows and cross-bows, likewise wine called Rommenie." *Le Livre de description des pays de Gilles le Bouvier*. Ed. E.T. Hamy, Paris, 1908, p. 90.

[384] De La Fons-Mélicocq, *Documents inédits sur le siège de Compiègne de 1430* in *La Picardie*, vol. iii, 1857, pp. 22, 23. P. Champion, *Guillaume de Flavy*. Proofs and illustrations, p. 176.

[385] Lefèvre de Saint-Rémy, vol. ii, p. 178. H. de Lépinois, *Notes extraites des archives communales de Compiègne*, in *Bibliothèque de l'École des Chartes*, 1863, vol. xxiv, p. 486. A. Sorel, *La prise de Jeanne d'Arc devant Compiègne et l'histoire des sièges de la même ville sous Charles VI et Charles VII, d'après des documents inédits avec vues et plans*, Paris, 1889, in 8vo, p. 268.

[386] Jacques Duclercq, *Mémoires*, ed. Reiffenberg, vol. i, p. 419. *Le Temple de Bocace* in *Les œuvres de Georges Chastellain*, ed. Kervyn de Lettenhove, vol. vii, p. 95. P. Champion, *Guillaume de Flavy, capitaine de Compiègne, contribution à l'histoire de Jeanne d'Arc et à l'étude de la vie militaire et privée au XVième siècle*, Paris, 1906, in 8vo, *passim*.

[387] Jean Chartier, *Chronique*, vol. i, p. 125. *Chronique des cordeliers*, fol. 495 recto. Rogier, in Varin, *Arch. de la ville de Reims*, 11th part, Statuts, vol. i, p. 604. A. Sorel, *loc. cit.*, p. 167. P. Champion, *loc. cit.*, p. 33.

[388] Monstrelet, vol. iv, pp. 379, 381. *Chronique des cordeliers*, fol. 495 recto. *Livre des trahisons*, p. 202.

[389] Monstrelet, vol. iv, pp. 382, 383. Berry, in *Trial*, vol. iv, p. 49.

[390] According to a note by Dom Bertheau, in A. Sorel, *Séjours de Jeanne d'Arc à Compiègne, maisons où elle a logé en 1429 et 1430*, with view and plans, Paris, 1888, in 8vo, pp. 11, 12.

[391] Magistrates of the town. Cf. *ante*, p. 34, note 3.

[392] *Accounts of the town of Compiègne*, CC 13, folio 291. Dom Gillesson, *Antiquités de Compiègne*, vol. v, p. 95. A. Sorel, *La prise de Jeanne d'Arc*, p. 145, note 3.

[393] Choisy surrendered on the 16th of May. *Chronique des cordeliers*, fol. 497, verso. *Livre des trahisons*, p. 201. Monstrelet, vol. iv, p. 382. Berry, in *Trial*, vol. iv, p. 49. A. Sorel, *La prise de Jeanne d'Arc*, pp. 145, 146. P. Champion, *Guillaume de Flavy*, pp. 40-41, 162-163.

[394] Berry, in *Trial*, vol. iv, pp. 49, 50.

[395] F. Brun, *Jeanne d'Arc et le capitaine de Soissons en 1430*, Soissons, 1904, p. 5 (extract from *l'Argus Soissonnais*). P. Champion, *loc. cit.*, p. 41.

[396] Berry, in *Trial*, vol. iv, p. 50. P. Champion, *loc. cit.*, p. 168. Proofs and illustrations, xxxv, p. 168. F. Brun, *Nouvelles recherches sur le fait de Soissons (Jeanne d'Arc et Bournel en 1430) à propos d'un livre récent*, Meulan, 1907, in 8vo.

[397] *Trial*, vol. i, p. 273.

[398] I have rejected the story told by Alain Bouchard of Jeanne's meeting with the little children in the Church of Saint Jacques. (*Les grandes croniques de Bretaigne*, Paris, Galliot Du Pré, 1514, fol. cclxxxi.) M. Pierre Champion (*Guillaume de Flavy*, p. 283) has irrefutably demonstrated its unauthenticity.

[399] Monstrelet, vol. iv, p. 382. Lefèvre de Saint-Rémy, vol. ii, p. 178. *Chronique des cordeliers*, fol. 498 verso.

[400] *Trial*, vol. i, p. 114. Perceval de Cagny, p. 174. Extract from a note concerning G. de Flavy, in *Trial*, vol. v, p. 176. Morosini, vol. iii, p. 296, note 1.

[401] Manuscript map of Compiègne in 1509, in Debout, *Jeanne d'Arc*, vol. ii, p. 293. Plan of the town of Compiègne, engraved by Aveline in the 17th century, reduction published by *La Société historique de Compiègne*, May, 1877. Lambert de Ballyhier, *Compiègne historique et monumental*, 1842, 2 vols. in 8vo, engravings. Plan of the restitution of the town of Compiègne in

1430, in A. Sorel, *La prise de Jeanne d'Arc*. P. Champion, *Guillaume de Flavy*, p. 43.

[402] Monstrelet, vol. iv, pp. 383, 384.

[403] *Le Jouvencel*, vol. ii, p. 196.

[404] *Trial*, vol. i, p. 116. Letter from Philippe le Bon to the inhabitants of Saint-Quentin, *Trial*, vol. v, p. 166. Letter from Philippe le Bon to Amédée, Duke of Savoy in P. Champion, *loc. cit.* Proofs and illustrations, xxxvii. Falconbridge, in *Trial*, vol. iv, p. 458. William Worcester, in *Trial*, vol. iv, p. 475, and *Le Journal d'un bourgeois de Paris*, p. 255.

[405] *Trial*, vol. i, pp. 78, 223, 224. Chastellain, vol. ii, p. 49. The Clerk of the Brabant *Chambre des Comptes*, in *Trial*, vol. iv, p. 428.

[406] Notes concerning G. de Flavy, in *Trial*, vol. v, p. 177. *Chronique de Tournai*, in *Recueil des Chroniques de Flandre*, 1856, vol. iii, pp. 415, 416.

[407] Chastellain, vol. ii, p. 49.

[408] *Le Jouvencel*, vol. i, p. 91.

[409] Monstrelet, vol. iv, p. 387. Lefèvre de Saint-Rémy, vol. ii, p. 179. Chastellain, vol. ii, p. 48. Note concerning G. de Flavy, in *Trial*, vol. v, p. 176.

[410] Letter from the Duke of Burgundy to the inhabitants of Saint-Quentin, in *Trial*, vol. v, p. 166. Monstrelet, Lefèvre de Saint-Rémy, Chastellain. Notes concerning G. de Flavy, *loc. cit.*

[411] Perceval de Cagny, p. 176. Falconbridge, in *Trial*, vol. iv, p. 458. Monstrelet. Note concerning G. de Flavy; Lefèvre de Saint-Rémy, Chastellain, *loc. cit.*

[412] Note concerning G. de Flavy, *loc. cit.* Du Fresne de Beaucourt, *Jeanne d'Arc et Guillaume de Flavy* in *Bulletin de la Société de l'Histoire de France*, vol. iii, 1861, pp. 173 *et seq.* Z. Rendu, *Jeanne d'Arc et G. de Flavy*, Compiègne, 1865, in 8vo, 32

pp. A. Sorel, *La prise de Jeanne d'Arc*, p. 209. P. Champion, *Guillaume de Flavy*, appendix i, pp. 282, 286.

[413] Perceval de Cagny, p. 175.

[414] Perceval de Cagny, p. 175. Chastellain, vol. ii, p. 49. Jean Chartier, *Chronique*, vol. i, p. 122; vol. iii, p. 207. Quicherat, *Aperçus nouveaux*, p. 87.

[415] Perceval de Cagny, p. 176.

[416] Letter from the Duke of Burgundy in *Trial*, vol. v, p. 166. Perceval de Cagny, p. 175. Monstrelet, vol. iv, p. 400. Lefèvre de Saint-Rémy, p. 175. Chastellain, vol. ii, p. 49. Note concerning G. de Flavy, in *Trial*, vol. v, p. 174. Martial d'Auvergne, *Vigiles*, vol. i, p. 118. P. Champion, *loc. cit.*, pp. 46, 49. Lanéry d'Arc, *Livre d'Or*, pp. 513-518.

[417] Richer, *Histoire manuscrite de la Pucelle*, book iv, fol. 188 *et seq.* P. Champion, *loc. cit.* Proofs and illustrations, xxxiii. Monstrelet, vol. iv, p. 388. Note concerning G. de Flavy, *loc. cit.* Letter from the Duke of Burgundy to the inhabitants of Saint-Quentin, *loc. cit.* *Journal d'un bourgeois de Paris*, p. 255. Falconbridge, in *Trial*, vol. iv, p. 459.

[418] According to *Le Journal d'un bourgeois de Paris*, p. 255, four hundred French were killed or drowned.

[419] Note concerning G. de Flavy, in *Trial*, vol. v, p. 176. Perceval de Cagny, p. 175.

[420] Letter from the Duke of Burgundy to the inhabitants of Saint-Quentin, in *Trial*, vol. v, p. 166.

[421] Monstrelet, vol. iv, p. 388. Chastellain, vol. ii, p. 50. A. Sorel, *La prise de Jeanne d'Arc*, pp. 253 *et seq.*

[422] Jean Jouffroy, in d'Achery, *Spicilegium*, iii, pp. 823 *et seq.*

[423] Monstrelet, vol. iv, p. 388.

[424] *Ibid.*, p. 389. P. Champion, *loc. cit.*, p. 168.

[425] *La Chronique des cordeliers*, and Monstrelet, *passim*. Vallet de Viriville, *Histoire de Charles VII*, vol. ii, pp. 165, 166.

[426] *Trial*, vol. v, p. 167. J. Quicherat, *Aperçus nouveaux*, p. 95.

[427] *Trial*, vol. v, p. 358. Le P. Ayroles, *La vraie Jeanne d'Arc*, vol. iii, p. 534. P. Champion, *Guillaume de Flavy*, pp. 169-171.

[428] Note concerning Guillaume de Flavy in *Trial*, vol. v, p. 177. A. Sorel, *La prise de Jeanne d'Arc*, p. 333.

[429] Falconbridge, in *Trial*, vol. iv, p. 458. *Journal d'un bourgeois de Paris*, p. 255. J. Quicherat, *Aperçus nouveaux*, p. 96. U. Chevalier, *L'abjuration de Jeanne d'Arc au cimetière de Saint-Ouen et l'authenticité de sa formule*, Paris, 1902, in 8vo, p. 18.

[430] *Trial*, vol. i, pp. 8-10. E. O'Reilly, *Les deux procès*, vol. ii, pp. 13, 14. P. Denifle and Chatelain, *Chartularium Universitatis Parisiensis*, vol. iv, p. 516, no. 2372.

[431] *Trial*, vol. i, p. 12. E. O'Reilly, *Les deux procès*.

[432] *Trial*, vol. i, pp. 3, 12; vol. iii, p. 378; vol. v, p. 392.

[433] *Domini canes*. Thus they are represented in the frescoes of the Capella degli Spagnuoli in Santa-Maria-Novella at Florence.

[434] Tanon, *Histoire des tribuneaux de l'inquisition en France*, ch. ii.

[435] Le P. Denifle and Chatelain, *Chartularium universitatis Parisiensis*, vol. iv, p. 510; *Le procès de Jeanne d'Arc et l'université de Paris*, Paris, 1897, in 8vo, 32 pp.

[436] *Journal d'un bourgeois de Paris, passim*. Falconbridge, in *Trial*, vol. iv, p. 450.

[437] *Journal d'un bourgeois de Paris*, p. 237. T. Basin, *Histoire de Charles VII et de Louis XI*, vol. iv, pp. 103, 104. Monstrelet, vol. iv, ch. lxiii. Bougenot, *Deux documents inédits relatifs à Jeanne d'Arc*, in *Revue bleue*, 13 Feb., 1892, pp. 203, 204.

[438] Le P. Denifle and Chatelain, *Chartularium Universitatis Parisiensis*, vol. iv, p. 515, no. 2370; *Le procès de Jeanne d'Arc et l'université de Paris*.

[439] Monstrelet, vol. iv, p. 389. Perceval de Cagny, p. 176. Morosini, vol. iii, pp. 300-302; vol. iv, pp. 254-355. De La Fons-Mélicocq, *Une cité picarde au moyen âge ou Noyon et les Noyonnais aux XIVe et XVe siècles*, Noyon, 1841, vol. ii, pp. 100-105. In 1441 Lyonnel de Wandomme, who was governor of this town, was driven out by the inhabitants on the death of Jean de Luxembourg (Monstrelet, vol. v, p. 456).

[440] Perceval de Cagny, p. 177, very doubtful.

[441] *Trial*, vol. i, pp. 163-164, 249.

[442] *Ibid.*, p. 151.

[443] Vallet de Viriville, *Note sur deux médailles de plomb relatives à Jeanne d'Arc*, Paris, 1861, in 8vo, 30 pages. Forgeais, *Notice sur les plombs historiés trouvés dans la Seine*, Paris, 1860, in 8vo. J. Quicherat, *Médaille frappée en l'honneur de la Pucelle, Six dessins sur Jeanne d'Arc tirés d'un manuscrit du XVe siècle*, in *L'autographe*, No. 24, 15 Nov., 1864.

[444] P. Lanéry d'Arc, *Le culte de Jeanne d'Arc au XVe siècle*, Paris, 1887, in 8vo, 29 pages.

[445] *Trial*, vol. i, p. 290.

[446] Carreau, *Histoire manuscrite de Touraine*, in *Procès*, vol. v, pp. 253, 254.

[447] *Trial*, vol. v, p. 104. E. Maignien, *Oraisons latines pour la délivrance de Jeanne d'Arc*. Grenoble, 1867, in 8vo (*Revue des Sociétés savantes*, vol. iv, pp. 412-414). G. de Braux, *Trois oraisons pour la délivrance de Jeanne d'Arc*, in *Journal de la Société d'Archéologie Lorraine*, June, 1887, pp. 125, 127.

[448] *Vita Jacobi Gelu ab ipso conscripta*, in *Bulletin de la Société archéologique de Touraine*, iii, 1867, pp. 266 *et seq*. The Rev. Father Marcellin Fornier, *Histoire des Alpes Maritimes ou Cottiennes*, vol. ii, pp. 313 *et seq*.

[449] *Ibid.*, pp. 319, 320.

[450] Thomassin, in *Trial*, vol. iv, p. 312. *Chronique du doyen de Saint-Thibaud*, in *Trial*, vol. iv, p. 323. *Chronique de Tournai*, in *Recueil des chroniques de Flandre*, vol. iii, p. 415. *Chronique de Normandie*, ed. A. Hellot, Rouen, 1881, in 8vo, pp. 77, 78. *Chronique de Lorraine*, ed. Abbé Marchal (*Recueil de documents sur l'histoire de Lorraine*, vol. v).

[451] Summary of a letter from Regnault de Chartres to the inhabitants of Reims, *Trial*, vol. v, p. 168.

[452] *Journal d'un bourgeois de Paris*, p. 272. Lefèvre de Saint-Rémy, vol. ii, p. 263. Martial d'Auvergne, *Vigiles*, vol. i, p. 124.

[453] A. Maury, *La stigmatisation et les stigmates*, in *Revue des Deux Mondes*, 1854, ch. viii, pp. 454-482. Dr. Subled, *Les stigmates selon la science*, in *Science catholique*, 1894, vol. viii, pp. 1073 *et seq.*; vol. ix, pp. 2 *et seq.*

[454] Letter from Regnault de Chartres, in *Trial*, vol. v, p. 168.

[455] *Trial*, vol. i, pp. 295 *et seq.*

[456] Letter from Regnault de Chartres, in *Ibid.*, vol. v, p. 168.

[457] *Ibid.*, p. 168.

[458] This point was not called in question at the time; but what might be discussed is whether the Bishop of Beauvais could exercise ordinary jurisdiction over the Maid. On this subject see: Abbé Ph. H. Dunand, *Histoire complète de Jeanne d'Arc*, Paris, 1899, vol. ii, pp. 412, 413.

[459] Robillard de Beaurepaire, *Notes sur les juges et assesseurs du procès de Jeanne d'Arc*, Rouen, 1890, p. 12. Douet d'Arcq, *Choix de pièces inédites relatives au règne de Charles VI*, vol. i, pp. 356, 357. Chanoine Cerf, *Pierre Cauchon de Sommièvre, chanoine de Reims et de Beauvais, évêque de Beauvais et de Lisieux; son origine, ses dignités, sa mort et ses sépultures*, in *Travaux de l'Académie de Reims*, CI (1898), pp. 363 *et seq.*, A. Sarrazin, *Pierre Cauchon, juge de Jeanne d'Arc*, Paris, 1901, in 8vo, pp. 26 *et seq.*

[460] Le P. Ayroles, *La vraie Jeanne d'Arc*, vol. i, p. 116. A. Sarrazin, *P. Cauchon*, pp. 36, 37.

[461] Du Boulay, *Historia Universitatis Parisiensis*, 1670, vol. v, p. 912. The Abbé Delettre, *Histoire du diocèse de Beauvais*, Beauvais, 1842, vol. ii, p. 348.

[462] Robillard de Beaurepaire, *Notes sur les juges*, p. 13.

[463] A. Sarrazin, *P. Cauchon*, pp. 58 *et seq.*

[464] Rymer, *Fœdera*, vol. x, p. 408, *passim*.

[465] *Trial*, vol. i, p. 13. Vallet de Viriville, *Procès de condamnation*, pp. 10 *et seq.* A. Sarrazin, *P. Cauchon*, pp. 108 *et seq.*

[466] *Trial*, vol. i, pp. 10, 11. M. Fournier, *La faculté de décret*, vol. i, p. 353, note.

[467] *Trial*, vol. i, pp. 13, 14.

[468] *Trial*, vol. i, p. 14.

[469] Du Boulay, *Historia Universitatis Parisiensis*, vol. v, pp. 393-408. *Monumenta conciliorum generalium seculi decimi quinti*, vol. i, pp. 70 *et seq.* Le P. Denifle and Chatelain, *Le procès de Jeanne d'Arc et l'Université de Paris*.

[470] Valeran Varanius, ed. Prarond, Paris, 1889, book iv, p. 100.

[471] *Trial*, vol. i, pp. 109, 110; vol. ii, p. 298; vol. iii, p. 121. Monstrelet, vol. iv, p. 389. E. Gomart, *Jeanne d'Arc au château de Beaurevoir*, Cambrai, 1865, in 8vo, 47 pages (*Mem. de la Société d'émulation de Cambrai*, xxxviii, 2, pp. 305-348). L. Sambier, *Jeanne d'Arc et la région du Nord*, Lille, 1901, in 8vo, 63 pages. Cf. Morosini, vol. iii, p. 300, notes 3 and 4, vol. iv, supplement xxi.

[472] *Trial*, vol. i, pp. 95, 231. Monstrelet, vol. iv, p. 402. Vallet de Viriville, *Histoire de Charles VII*, vol. i, p. 2; vol. ii, pp. 72, 73.

[473] A. Duchêne, *Histoire de la maison de Béthune*, ch. iii, and proofs and illustrations, p. 33. Vallet de Viriville, *loc. cit.*, and Morosini, vol. iv, pp. 352, 354.

[474] *Trial,* vol. i, pp. 95, 231.

[475] *Ibid.*, vol. ii, pp. 438, 457; vol. iii, p. 121.

[476] *Trial,* vol. iii, pp. 120, 121.

[477] *Ibid.*, vol. i, p. 150.

[478] *Trial,* vol. i, pp. 150, 151.

[479] *Ibid.*, p. 13; vol. v, p. 194.

[480] *Ibid.*, vol. i, pp. 110, 151, 152.

[481] *Trial,* vol. i, p. 166. *Journal d'un bourgeois de Paris,* p. 268. J. Quicherat, *Aperçus nouveaux*, pp. 53, 58.

[482] *Chronique des cordeliers,* fol. 507, recto. Morosini, vol. iii, pp. 301-303. *Chronique de Tournai,* ed. Smedt, in *Recueil des Chroniques de Flandre,* vol. iii, pp. 416, 417.

[483] Lottin, *Recherches sur la ville d'Orléans,* vol. i, p. 252. *Trial,* vol. i, p. 99, note 1. *Journal du siège,* pp. 235-238. S. Luce, *Jeanne d'Arc à Domremy,* p. cclxiii, note 2.

[484] *Trial,* vol. i, pp. 296, 297.

[485] Register of the Accounts of the town of Tours for the year 1430, in *Trial,* vol. iv, p. 473, note 1.

[486] *Trial,* vol. iv, p. 473.

[487] *Ibid.*, p. 473.

[488] *Ibid.*, vol. i, p. 295.

[489] *Trial,* vol. i, p. 106, note. *Journal d'un bourgeois de Paris,* p. 271. Vallet de Viriville, *Procès de condamnation de Jeanne d'Arc,* pp. lxi-lxv.

[490] *Journal d'un bourgeois de Paris,* p. 271.

[491] *Journal d'un bourgeois de Paris,* pp. 271, 272.

[492] Voltaire, *Dictionnaire philosophique,* article, Arc.

[493] *Journal d'un bourgeois de Paris,* pp. 259, 260.

[494] *Journal d'un bourgeois de Paris*, pp. 259-260, 271-272. Jean Nider, *Formicarium*, in *Trial*, vol. iv, p. 504. A. de la Borderie, *Pierronne et Perrinaïc*, pp. 7 *et seq.*

[495] H. Vandenbroeck, *Extraits des anciens registres des consaux de la ville de Tournai*, vol. ii (1422-1430), and Morosini, vol. iii, pp. 185, 186.

[496] H. Vandenbroeck, *Extraits analytiques des anciens registres des consaux de la ville de Tournai*, vol. ii, pp. 338, 371-373. Canon H. Debout, *Jeanne d'Arc et les villes d'Arras et de Tournai*, Paris, n.d., p. 24.

[497] Le P. Anselme, *Histoire généalogique de la maison de France*, vol. iii, pp. 723, 724. Vallet de Viriville, *Histoire de Charles VII*, vol. ii, pp. 175, 176. Morosini, vol. iv, supplement xix.

[498] *Trial*, vol. i, pp. 95, 231.

[499] *Ibid.*, pp. 13, 14.

[500] *Les miracles de madame Sainte Katerine*, Bourassé, *passim.*

[501] "Was waited on in prison like a lady," says *Le Journal d'un bourgeois de Paris*, p. 271, concerning the Rouen prison.

[502] *Trial*, vol. i, p. 100.

[503] *Ibid.*, pp. 101, 206, 291; vol. iii, p. 87; vol. v, pp. 104, 305. Chastellain, ed. Kervyn de Lettenhove, vol. ii, p. 46. P. Lanéry d'Arc, *Le culte de Jeanne d'Arc au XVe siècle*, Orléans, 1887, in 8vo. Noël Valois, *Un nouveau témoignage sur Jeanne d'Arc*, pp. 8, 13, 18.

[504] *Trial*, vol. i, pp. 95, 96, 231. Canon Henri Debout, *Jeanne d'Arc prisonnière à Arras*, Arras, 1894, in 16mo; *Jeanne d'Arc et les villes d'Arras et de Tournai*, Paris, 1904, in 8vo; *Jeanne d'Arc*, vol. ii, pp. 394 *et seq.*

[505] On the 7th of November, 1430, a messenger from the town of Arras received forty shillings for having taken two sealed letters to the Duke of Burgundy, one from Jean de Luxembourg, the other from David de Brimeu, Governor of the Bailiwick of

Arras; we know nothing of the tenor of these letters written concerning "the case of the Maid." P. Champion, *Notes sur Jeanne d'Arc, II; Jeanne d'Arc à Arras*, in *Le Moyen Âge*, July-August, 1907, pp. 200, 201.

[506] H. de Lépinois, *Notes extraites des archives communales de Compiègne*, in *Bibliothèque de l'École des Chartes*, 1863, vol. xxiv, p. 486. A. Sorel, *Prise de Jeanne d'Arc*, p. 268. P. Champion, *Guillaume de Flavy*, pp. 38, 48 *et seq.*

[507] *Chronique des cordeliers*, fol. 500 verso.

[508] Chastellain, vol. ii, p. 53.

[509] Monstrelet, vol. iv, p. 390.

[510] Monstrelet, vol. iv, pp. 390, 391. Lefèvre de Saint-Rémy, vol. ii, p. 180. Morosini, vol. iii, pp. 306, 307. Chastellain, vol. ii, pp. 51, 54. A. Sorel, *La prise de Jeanne d'Arc*, pp. 233 *et seq.* P. Champion. *Guillaume de Flavy*, p. 50.

[511] *Le Jouvencel*, vol. i, pp. 49 *et seq.*

[512] *Chronique des cordeliers*, fol. 502 verso. P. Champion, *Guillaume de Flavy*, proofs and illustrations, xli, xlii, xliii.

[513] *Livre des trahisons*, p. 202.

[514] Monstrelet, vol. iii, pp. 410-415. Lefèvre de Saint-Rémy, vol. ii, p. 185. *Livre des trahisons*, p. 202. A. Sorel, *La prise de Jeanne d'Arc*, proofs and illustrations, xiii, p. 341. P. Champion, *loc. cit.*, p. 176.

[515] Monstrelet, vol. iv, p. 418. De La Fons-Mélicocq, *Documents inédits sur le siège de Compiègne*, in *La Picardie*, vol. iii, 1857, pp. 22, 23. Stevenson, *Letters and Papers*, vol. ii, part i, p. 156.

[516] Monstrelet, vol. iv, p. 419. P. Champion, *Guillaume de Flavy*, p. 57.

[517] Sorel, *La prise de Jeanne d'Arc*, proofs and illustrations, p. 343.

[518] *Trial*, vol. i, p. 9. Vallet de Viriville, *Histoire de Charles VII*, vol. ii, p. 175.

[519] Morosini, vol. iii, p. 236. U. Chevalier, *L'abjuration de Jeanne d'Arc*, p. 18, note.

[520] Morosini, vol. iii, p. 276, note.

[521] Chronicle of Jean de la Chapelle, in *Trial*, vol. v, pp. 358-360. Lefils, *Histoire de la ville du Crotoy et de son château*, pp. 111-118. G. Lefèvre-Pontalis, *La panique anglaise*, p. 8, note 5. L'Abbé Bouthors, *Histoire de Saint-Riquier*, Abbeville, 1902, pp. 185, 215, 220.

[522] Perceval de Cagny, pp. 22, 137.

[523] *Trial*, vol. iii, p. 121. A. Sarrazin, *Jeanne d'Arc et la Normandie*, pp. 63 *et seq.*; Lanéry d'Arc, *Livre d'or*, p. 521.

[524] *Trial*, vol. i, p. 89; vol. iii, p. 121. Le P. Ignace de Jésus Maria, *Histoire généalogique des comtes de Ponthieu et maïeurs d'Abbeville*, Paris, 1657, p. 490. *Trial*, vol. v, p. 361.

[525] Monstrelet, vol. iv, pp. 353, 354. *Trial*, vol. v, p. 143.

[526] *Trial*, vol. i, pp. 15, 16. M. Fournier, *La Faculté de décret et l'Université de Paris*, vol. i, p. 353.

[527] *Trial*, vol. i, p. 21. Le P. Ignace de Jésus Maria, in *Trial*, vol. v, p. 363. F. Poulaine, *Jeanne d'Arc à Rouen*, Paris, 1899, in 16mo. Ch. Lemire, *Jeanne d'Arc en Picardie et en Normandie*, Paris, 1903, p. 10, *passim*. Lanéry d'Arc, *Livre d'or*, pp. 524, 549.

[528] A. Sarrazin, *Jeanne d'Arc et la Normandie au XVe siècle*, Rouen, 1896, in 4to, ch. v.

[529] *Trial*, vol. iii, pp. 136-137. Vallet de Viriville, *Histoire de Charles VII*, vol. ii, p. 198.

[530] L. de Duranville, *Le château de Bouvreuil*, in *La Revue de Rouen*, 1852, p. 387. A. Deville, *La tour de la Pucelle du château de Rouen*, in *Précis des travaux de l'Académie de Rouen*, 1865-1866, pp. 236-268. Bouquet, *Notice sur le donjon du château de Philippe-Auguste*, Rouen, 1877, pp. 7 *et seq.*

[531] *Trial*, vol. ii, pp. 317, 345; vol. iii, p. 121.

[532] *Ibid.*, p. 154. A. Sarrazin, *Jeanne d'Arc et la Normandie*, p. 190, note 1. L. Delisle, *Revue des Sociétés savantes*, 1867, 4th series, vol. v, p. 440. F. Bouquet, *Jeanne d'Arc au donjon de Rouen*, in *Revue de Normandie*, 1867, vol. vi, pp. 873-883. L. Delisle, *Revue des Sociétés savantes*, vol. v (1867). Lanéry d'Arc, pp. 528-533.

[533] Ballin, *Renseignements sur le Vieux-Château de Rouen*, in *Revue de Rouen*, 1842, p. 35. A. Sarrazin, *Jeanne d'Arc et la Normandie*, p. 188.

[534] *Trial*, vol. ii, p. 7.

[535] *Ibid.*, vol. iii, p. 155.

[536] *Ibid.*, vol. iii, p. 180. A. Sarrazin, pp. 191, 192.

[537] Vallet de Viriville, *Histoire de Charles VII*, vol. ii, pp. 240, 241.

[538] *Trial*, vol. i, p. 47.

[539] *Ibid.*, vol. ii, p. 322.

[540] *Ibid.*, vol. ii, pp. 216, 217. J. Quicherat, *Aperçus nouveaux*, p. 112.

[541] *Trial*, vol. ii, p. 18.

[542] Lea, *A History of the Inquisition in the Middle Ages* (1906), vol. iii, p. 359.

[543] *Trial*, vol. iii, p. 154.

[544] *Ibid.*, vol. ii, pp. 318, 319; vol. iii, pp. 131, 140, 148, 161. A. Sarrazin, *P. Cauchon*, p. 200.

[545] *Trial*, vol. iii, pp. 186, 187.

[546] *Ibid.*, pp. 199, 200.

[547] *Ibid.*, p. 200.

[548] *Trial*, vol. iii, p. 179.

[549] Morosini, vol. iii, p. 236.

[550] *Trial*, vol. iii, pp. 121, 123.

[551] *Ibid.*, p. 140.

[552] C. de Beaurepaire, *Recherches sur le procès de condamnation de Jeanne d'Arc*, in *Précis des travaux de l'Académie de Rouen*, 1867-1868, pp. 470-479. U. Chevalier, *L'abjuration de Jeanne d'Arc*, p. 29.

[553] De Beaurepaire, *Notes sur les juges*, p. 17.

[554] *Gallia Christiana*, vol. ii, p. 732. Vallet de Viriville, *Histoire de Charles VII*, vol. ii, pp. 213, 214. S. Luce, *Jeanne d'Arc à Domremy*, p. ccxcv.

[555] C. de Beaurepaire, *Recherches sur le procès de condamnation de Jeanne d'Arc, loc. cit.* A. Sarrazin, *Jeanne d'Arc et la Normandie*, pp. 168, 171.

[556] 28 December, 1430. *Trial*, vol. i, pp. 20, 23. De Beaurepaire, *Notes sur les juges*, p. 46.

[557] *Trial*, vol. i, pp. 18, 19.

[558] A. Sarrazin, *Jeanne d'Arc et la Normandie*, pp. 1771, 1778.

[559] J. Quicherat, *Aperçus nouveaux*, p. 147. De Beaurepaire, *Notes sur les juges*, p. 9.

[560] *Trial*, vol. i, p. 24; vol. iii, p. 162. De Beaurepaire, *Notes sur les juges*, p. 26. A. Sarrazin, *Jeanne d'Arc et la Normandie*, p. 220.

[561] *Trial*, vol. i, p. 25.

[562] *Trial*, vol. i, p. 25; vol. iii, p. 137. A. Sarrazin, *loc. cit.*, pp. 221, 222.

[563] L. Tanon, *Histoire des tribunaux de l'inquisition en France*, pp. 550, 551.

[564] De Beaurepaire, *Recherches sur le procès de condamnation*, p. 320.

[565] *Trial*, vol. i, p. 25; vol. iii, p. 137. De Beaurepaire, *Recherches....* p. 103. A. Sarrazin, *loc. cit.*, pp. 222, 223.

[566] *Trial*, vol. i, p. 26. De Beaurepaire, *Recherches....* p. 115. A. Sarrazin, *loc. cit.*, pp. 223, 224.

[567] Eymeric, *Directorium Inquisitorium*, quest. 85. J. Quicherat, *Aperçus nouveaux*, p. 109. De Beaurepaire, *Notes sur les juges*, p. 9.

[568] De Beaurepaire, *Recherches....* pp. 321 *et seq.*

[569] De Beaurepaire, *Notes sur les juges*, pp. 27-114. J. Quicherat, *Aperçus nouveaux*, pp. 103, 104. Boucher de Molandon, *Guillaume Erard l'un des juges de la Pucelle*, in *Bulletin du comité hist. and phil.*, 1892, pp. 3-10.

[570] *Trial*, vol. i, p. 30, note. Du Boulay, *Historia Universitatis, Paris*, vol. v, pp. 912, 920. J. Quicherat, *Aperçus nouveaux*, p. 105. De Beaurepaire, *Notes*, pp. 30, 31. A. Sarrazin, *loc. cit.*, pp. 226, 227.

[571] *Trial*, vol. ii, pp. 5, 6. De Beaurepaire, *Notes*, pp. 121-125. A. Sarrazin, *loc. cit.*, pp. 308-310.

[572] De Beaurepaire, *Recherches*, pp. 321 *et seq.*

[573] J. Quicherat, *Aperçus nouveaux*, p. 101.

[574] *Trial*, vol. i, pp. 5-8.

[575] A notary or secretary in France under the old monarchy (W.S.).

[576] *Trial*, vol. ii, p. 463.

[577] *Ibid.*, p. 453.

[578] *Trial*, vol. iii, pp. 192, 193.

[579] *Ibid.*, vol. i, pp. 105, 146, 234.

[580] *Ibid.*, pp. 208, 209, 213.

[581] J. Quicherat, *Aperçus nouveaux*, p. 117.

[582] *Trial*, vol. i, pp. 245, 246.

[583] *Ibid.*, vol. ii, p. 200.

[584] De Beaurepaire, *Recherches, loc. cit.* J. Quicherat, *Aperçus nouveaux,* pp. 122-124. L. Tanon, *Histoire des tribunaux de l'inquisition,* pp. 389-395.

[585] *Trial,* vol. i, pp. 117, 300.

[586] *Trial,* vol. ii, p. 362.

[587] *Ibid.*, vol. iii, p. 63.

[588] De Beaurepaire, *Notes sur les juges,* pp. 72-82. A. Sorel, *loc. cit.*, pp. 243, 247.

[589] *Trial,* vol. ii, pp. 10, 342; vol. iii, pp. 140, 141, 156, 160 *et seq.*

[590] *Ibid.*, vol. iii, p. 181.

[591] *Ibid.*, p. 141.

[592] *Tractatus de hæresi pauperum de Lugduno,* apud Martene, *Thesaurus anecd.*, vol. v, col. 1787. J. Quicherat, *Aperçus nouveaux,* pp. 131, 132.

[593] Eymeric, *Directorium,* part iii, *Cautelæ inquisitorum contra hæreticorum cavilationes et fraudes.*

[594] L. Tanon, *Histoire des tribunaux de l'inquisition en France,* p. 394.

[595] *Trial,* vol. ii, pp. 10, 342.

[596] Vallet de Viriville, *Nouvelles recherches sur Agnès Sorel,* pp. 33 *et seq.* Du Cange, *Glossaire,* at the word *Matrimonium.*

[597] *Trial,* vol. iii, pp. 102, 209.

[598] *Trial,* vol. iii, pp. 155, 163.

[599] A. Sarrazin, *Jeanne d'Arc et la Normandie,* p. 40.

[600] *Trial,* vol. iii, p. 175.

[601] *Ibid.*, vol. i, pp. 217, 218.

[602] *Trial,* vol. i, pp. 27, 28.

[603] *Ibid.*, pp. 28, 29.

[604] *Ibid.*, pp. 29, 31.

[605] *Trial*, vol. i, pp. 31-33.

[606] *Ibid.*, p. 32. J. Quicherat, *Aperçus nouveaux*, p. 102. De Beaurepaire, *Notes sur les juges*, pp. 24-27. Le P. Chapotin, *La guerre de cent ans, Jeanne d'Arc et les dominicains*, pp. 141-143. A. Sarrazin, *P. Cauchon*, p. 124.

[607] *Trial*, vol. i, p. 33.

[608] *Trial*, vol. i, p. 35. De Beaurepaire, *Notes sur les juges*, p. 394. Doinel, *Mémoire de la Société archéologique-historique de l'Orléanais*, 1892, vol. xxiv, p. 403. Le P. Chapotin, *La guerre de cent ans, Jeanne d'Arc et les dominicains*, p. 141. U. Chevalier, *L'abjuration de Jeanne d'Arc*, p. 32.

[609] *Trial*, vol. i, p. 35.

[610] *Ibid.*, pp. 40-42.

[611] *Trial*, vol. i, pp. 38, 39.

[612] *Ibid.*, pp. 42-43.

[613] *Ibid.*, p. 43.

[614] *Ibid.*, p. 43.

[615] Le P. Denifle and Chatelain, *Le procès de Jeanne d'Arc et l'Université de Paris*.

[616] *Trial*, vol. i, pp. 88, 94, 151, 155, *passim*.

[617] *Trial*, vol. i, p. 45.

[618] *Ibid.*, p. 46.

[619] *Ibid.*, pp. 46-47.

[620] *Trial*, vol. i, p. 47.

[621] *Ibid.*, pp. 47, 48.

[622] *Trial*, vol. i, p. 48.

[623] *Trial*, vol. iii, pp. 131-136.

[624] *Ibid.*, p. 135.

[625] *Trial*, vol. i, p. 48. A. Sarrazin, *Jeanne d'Arc et la Normandie*, pp. 323, 324.

[626] L. Tanon, *Histoire des tribunaux de l'inquisition*, p. 420.

[627] *Trial*, vol. i, pp. 48-50.

[628] *Ibid.*, p. 50.

[629] Du Boulay, *Historia Universitatis Paris.*, vol. v, p. 919. De Beaurepaire, *Notes sur les juges*, pp. 27-30.

[630] *Trial*, vol. i, p. 51.

[631] *Ibid.*

[632] *Ibid.*, pp. 51, 52.

[633] *Trial*, vol. i, p. 52.

[634] Bréhal, *Mémoires et consultations en faveur de Jeanne d'Arc*, ed. Lanéry d'Arc, p. 409.

[635] See Appendix I, Letter from Doctor G. Dumas.

[636] *Trial*, vol. i, p. 52.

[637] *Ibid.*, pp. 53, 54.

[638] *Ibid.*, p. 54.

[639] *Ibid.*, pp. 55, 56; vol. v, p. 95.

[640] *Trial*, vol. ii, p. 456; vol. iii, pp. 91, 92. Morosini, vol. iii, p. 104. Eberhard Windecke, pp. 152, 153. J. Quicherat, *Aperçus nouveaux*, pp. 131-133. Le P. Ayroles, *La vraie Jeanne d'Arc*, vol. iv, p. 440, ch. i, *La royauté de Jésus Christ*.

[641] *Trial*, vol. iii, pp. 89, 142, 161, 176, 178, 201.

[642] *Ibid.*, p. 4.

[643] *Ibid.*, vol. i, p. 56.

[644] *Ibid.*, p. 56.

[645] We find it impossible to agree with Quicherat (*Aperçus nouveaux*) and admit that Jeanne gradually invented the fable of the crown during her examination and while her judges were questioning her as to "the sign." The manner in which the judges conducted this part of their examination proves that they were acquainted with the whole of the extraordinary story.

[646] *Legenda Aurea*, ed. 1846, pp. 789 *et seq.*

[647] *Trial*, vol. i, pp. 120-122.

[648] *Ibid.*, p. 90.

[649] *Ibid.*, p. 56.

[650] *Ibid.*, vol. iii, p. 57.

[651] Jean Bréhal, *Mémoires et consultations en faveur de Jeanne d'Arc*, ed. Lanéry d'Arc, p. 409.

[652] *Trial*, vol. iii, p. 57.

[653] *Ibid.*, p. 48.

[654] *Ibid.*, vol. i, p. 57.

[655] *Ibid.*, pp. 61, 70.

[656] *Trial*, vol. i, p. 62.

[657] *Ibid.*, pp. 61-64.

[658] *Ibid.*, p. 279.

[659] *Ibid.*, pp. 58-60.

[660] *Ibid.*, pp. 60, 61.

[661] *Grandes chroniques*, ed. P. Paris, vol. v, p. 188.

[662] *Trial*, vol. i, p. 64.

[663] E. Hinzelin, *Chez Jeanne d'Arc*, pp. 37, 177.

[664] *Trial*, vol. i, pp. 64, 65.

[665] *Ibid.*, p. 65. "*Souvent on est blâmé de trop parler,*" a proverb common in the 15th century. Cf. Le Roux de Lincy, *Les proverbes français*, vol. ii, p. 417.

[666] *Trial*, vol. i, p. 65.

[667] *Ibid.*, vol. ii, pp. 21, 358.

[668] *Ibid.*, vol. i, pp. 65-68.

[669] *Ibid.*, p. 68.

[670] The French expression runs, "*se resemblent comme deux sœurs.*"

[671] *Trial*, vol. i, p. 68.

[672] *Ibid.*, vol. iii, pp. 48, 49.

[673] *Trial*, vol. iii, p. 51.

[674] *Ibid.*, p. 49.

[675] *Ibid.*, pp. 51, 52.

[676] What induces me to fix this illness on the 25th of February is Jean Beaupère's question at the sitting of the 27th, "How have you been?" and Jeanne's ironical reply. This indisposition must not be confused, as it generally has been, with Jeanne's serious illness, which occurred after Easter. The shad and the herrings belong naturally to Lent; and Maître Delachambre says explicitly that Jeanne recovered after the bleeding.

[677] *Trial*, vol. i, p. 70.

[678] *Ibid.*, pp. 68, 69.

[679] *Ibid.*, vol. ii, pp. 332, 362; vol. iii, pp. 60, 133, 141, 156, 162, 173, 181.

[680] *Ibid.*, vol. i, p. 70.

[681] *Ibid.*, p. 71.

[682] *Trial*, vol. i, p. 72.

[683] Lanéry d'Arc, *Mémoires et consultations en faveur de Jeanne d'Arc*, p. 406.

[684] *Trial*, vol. i, p. 72.

[685] *Ibid.*, pp. 72, 73.

[686] *Trial*, vol. i, p. 73.

[687] *Ibid.*, pp. 74, 75.

[688] *Ibid.*, p. 75. I have re-inserted "my fine lord" according to *Trial*, vol. iii, p. 80.

[689] *Trial*, vol. i, pp. 75-77.

[690] *Ibid.*, pp. 77, 78.

[691] *Ibid.*, p. 78.

[692] *Ibid.*, p. 34; vol. ii, p. 318.

[693] *Trial*, vol. ii, pp. 350, 365.

[694] *Ibid.*, vol. i, pp. 79, 80.

[695] *Trial*, vol. ii, pp. 11, 341.

[696] See the evidence of Thomas de Courcelles in *Trial*, vol. iii, p. 38.

[697] *Trial*, vol. ii, pp. 12, 300, 341; vol. iii, p. 138.

[698] *Ibid.*, vol. ii, pp. 12, 203, 252, 300; vol. iii, pp. 50, 138.

[699] *Ibid.*, vol. i, pp. 252, 326, 354, 356; vol. iii, pp. 171, 172.

[700] *Trial*, vol. ii, pp. 356, 359.

[701] *Ibid.*, vol. i, pp. 80, 81.

[702] *Ibid.*, p. 82.

[703] *Analecta juris Pontif.*, vol. xiv, p. 117.

[704] *Trial*, vol. i, pp. 82, 84.

[705] The expression, "*À Dieu vous recommande, Dieu soit garde de vous*," occurs in the letters to the people of Tournai, to those

of Troyes and of Reims, and in the letter to the Duke of Burgundy. And what is still more significant, in two of these letters, one to the people of Troyes, the other to the Duke of Burgundy, are the words: "*Le Roi du ciel, mon droiturier et souverain seigneur*." *Trial*, vol. i, p. 246.

[706] *Ibid.*, pp. 82, 83.

[707] De Beaurepaire, *Notes sur les juges*, pp. 27, 32, 75, 82.

[708] *Trial*, vol. i, pp. 84, 85.

[709] *Trial*, vol. i, p. 86.

[710] Le Loyer, iv, *Livres des Spectres*, Angers, 1605, in 4to.

[711] *Trial*, vol. i, p. 86.

[712] *Ibid.*, pp. 86, 87. Vallet de Viriville, *Les anneaux de Jeanne d'Arc*, in *Mémoires de la Société des Antiquaires de France*, vol. xxx, 1868, pp. 82, 97.

[713] *Trial*, vol. i, p. 86.

[714] *Ibid.*, p. 89.

[715] A. Maury, *Croyances et légendes du moyen âge*, pp. 171 *et seq.*

[716] *Trial*, vol. i, p. 90.

[717] *Trial*, vol. i, pp. 90, 91.

[718] *Ibid.*, vol. ii, p. 16.

[719] De Beaurepaire, *Recherches sur le procès de condamnation*, p. 115.

[720] *Trial*, vol. ii, p. 16.

[721] *Ibid.*, vol. i, pp. 91, 92.

[722] *Trial*, vol. i, p. 93.

[723] *Ibid.*, p. 94.

[724] *Ibid.*, pp. 95-97.

[725] *Ibid.*, p. 99.

[726] *Chronique de la Pucelle*, p. 301. *Journal du siège*, pp. 98, 99.

[727] *Trial*, vol. i, p. 101.

[728] *Ibid.*, p. 89.

[729] *Trial*, vol. i, p. 102.

[730] *Ibid.*, p. 103.

[731] Lea (1906), vol. iii, p. 456.

[732] *Le Jouvencel*, vol. ii, p. 237.

[733] *Trial*, vol. i, p. 104.

[734] *Trial*, vol. i, p. 111.

[735] *Ibid.*, pp. 111, 112.

[736] *Ibid.*, p. 113.

[737] Gélu, *Questio quinta*, in *Mémoires et consultations en faveur de Jeanne d'Arc*, ed. Lanéry d'Arc, pp. 593 *et seq.*

[738] *Trial*, vol. iii, pp. 299 *et seq.*

[739] *Ibid.*, vol. i, p. 117.

[740] *Ibid.*, pp. 117, 119.

[741] On the contrary it was then that they began to argue against her or that they began to argue most effectively. She seems to forget that the interview at Chinon preceded the examination at Poitiers. It is interesting to notice that Brother Pasquerel, who was informed of these matters by her, makes the same error in his evidence.

[742] *Trial*, vol. i, pp. 120, 122.

[743] *Trial*, vol. i, pp. 122-124.

[744] *Ibid.*, p. 125.

[745] *Trial*, vol. i, p. 126.

[746] *Ibid.*

[747] *Ibid.*

[748] Lanéry d'Arc, *Mémoires et consultations*, pp. 224, 434, 435. Le P. Ayroles, *La vraie Jeanne d'Arc*, vol. i, pp. 351 *et seq.*, 481 *et seq.*

[749] *Trial*, vol. i, p. 128.

[750] *Ibid.*

[751] *Chronique des quatre premiers Valois*, p. 47.

[752] II Corinthians, iv.

[753] Galatians v, 18. Lanéry d'Arc, *Mémoires et consultations*, p. 275.

[754] *Trial*, vol. i, p. 130.

[755] *Trial*, vol. i, pp. 130, 131.

[756] *Ibid.*, pp. 131, 132.

[757] *Ibid.*, vol. v, p. 252. E. de Bouteiller and G. de Braux, *Nouvelles recherches sur la famille de Jeanne d'Arc*, pp. 14, 15. S. Luce, *Jeanne d'Arc à Domremy*, pp. xlvi *et seq.*

[758] *Trial*, vol. i, p. 133.

[759] *Trial*, vol. i, p. 134.

[760] *Ibid.*, pp. 134, 138.

[761] *Ibid.*, p. 139.

[762] *Trial*, vol. i, pp. 140, 141.

[763] About ten feet (W.S.).

[764] *Trial*, vol. i, pp. 141-142.

[765] "*Fleure bon et fleurera bon, pourvu qu'elle soit bien gardée.*"

[766] Lanéry d'Arc, *Mémoires et consultations*, p. 212. Le P. Ayroles, *La vraie Jeanne d'Arc*, vol. i, p. 346.

[767] *Trial*, vol. i, p. 144.

[768] *Trial*, vol. i, p. 145.

[769] *Ibid.*, p. 146.

[770] Eberhard Windecke, pp. 184, 186.

[771] *Trial*, vol. i, pp. 147, 148.

[772] *Ibid.*, pp. 150, 152.

[773] *Ibid.*, p. 157.

[774] *Trial*, vol. i, pp. 154, 156.

[775] *Trial*, vol. i, p. 156.

[776] *Ibid.*, p. 157.

[777] See *ante*, pp. 124 *et seq.* (W.S.).

[778] *Trial*, vol. i, pp. 158, 159.

[779] *Ibid.*, pp. 159, 161.

[780] *Trial*, vol. i, p. 162.

[781] *Ayde-toy, Dieu te aidera. Le Jouvencel*, vol. ii, p. 33.

[782] *Trial*, vol. i, pp. 163, 164.

[783] *Trial*, vol. i, pp. 165, 166.

[784] *Ibid.*, pp. 166-169.

[785] *Trial*, vol. i, pp. 170, 171.

[786] *Ibid.*, p. 173.

[787] *Ibid.*

[788] S. Luce, *Jeanne d'Arc à Domremy*. Proofs and illustrations, pp. 74, 75.

[789] *Trial*, vol. i, p. 174.

[790] *Trial*, vol. i, pp. 174, 176.

[791] *Trial*, vol. i, p. 178.

[792] *Ibid.*, p. 180.

[793] *Ibid.*, p. 181.

[794] *Ibid.*, pp. 182-183.

[795] Martène and Durand, *Thesaurus novus anecdotorum*, vol. v, col. 1760 *et seq.*

[796] *Trial*, vol. i, p. 183.

[797] *Ibid.*, p. 184.

[798] *Ibid.*, pp. 184, 185.

[799] *Trial*, vol. i, p. 185.

[800] *Trial*, vol. i, p. 187.

[801] *Ibid.*

[802] *Ibid.*, p. 194.

[803] *Ibid.*, p. 195.

[804] J. Quicherat, *Aperçus nouveaux*, pp. 130, 131. E. Méru, *Directorium Inquisitorium*, Romæ, 1578, p. 295.

[805] *Trial*, vol. i, pp. 200, 201. J. Quicherat, *Aperçus nouveaux*, pp. 129, 130.

[806] L. Tanon, *Histoire des tribunaux de l'inquisition*, pp. 400 *et seq.* U. Chevalier, *L'abjuration de Jeanne d'Arc*, p. 34.

[807] Méru, *Directorium Inquisitorium*, p. 147.

[808] *Trial*, vol. i, p. 201.

[809] *Trial*, vol. i, pp. 202-323.

[810] *Ibid.*, p. 202.

[811] *Ibid.*, pp. 324, 325.

[812] *Ibid.*, p. 327; vol. iii, p. 143.

[813] *Ibid.*, vol. iii, p. 60. U. Chevalier, *L'abjuration de Jeanne d'Arc*, p. 38.

[814] *Trial*, vol. iii, p. 232. J. Quicherat, *Aperçus nouveaux*, pp. 124, 129.

[815] *Trial*, vol. ii, pp. 22, 212; vol. iii, p. 306; vol. v, p. 461.

[816] *Ibid.*, vol. i, pp. 328, 336.

[817] *Ibid.*, p. 337.

[818] *Trial*, vol. i, pp. 337, 374.

[819] *Ibid.*, vol. iii, p. 51.

[820] *Ibid.*, vol. i, pp. 374-375.

[821] *Trial*, vol. i, pp. 376, 378.

[822] *Ibid.*, p. 379.

[823] *Ibid.*, pp. 380, 381.

[824] *Trial*, vol. i, p. 381.

[825] *Ibid.*, pp. 381, 382.

[826] De Beaurepaire, *Notes sur les juges*, pp. 114, 117.

[827] *Trial*, vol. i, pp. 383, 399.

[828] *Trial*, vol. i, pp. 400, 401.

[829] Nicolas Eymeric, *Directorium inquisitorium....* Rome, 1586, in fol. p. 24, col. 1. Ludovicus a Paramo, *De origine et progressu officii sanctœ inquisitionis*, MDXCIIX, in fol., lib. III, questio 5, p. 709.

[830] *Trial*, vol. i, p. 399.

[831] *Ibid.*, pp. 399, 400.

[832] *Ibid.*, pp. 401, 402.

[833] *Trial*, vol. i, pp. 402, 404.

[834] *Recueil des historiens de la France*, vol. xx, p. 601; vol. xxi, p. 34. *Histoire littéraire de la France*, vol. xxvii, p. 70.

[835] *Trial*, vol. i, pp. 407, 413, 420. M. Fournier, *La faculté de décret de l'Université de Paris*, p. 353. Le P. Denifle and Chatelain, *Chartularium Universitatis Parisiensis*, vol. iv, pp. 510 *et seq.*

[836] *Trial*, vol. i, pp. 407, 408. U. Chevalier, *L'abjuration de Jeanne d'Arc*, p. 42.

[837] The University of Paris (W.S.).

[838] *Trial*, vol. i, pp. 414, 419.

[839] *Ibid.*, p. 414. Migne, *Dictionnaire des sciences occultes.*

[840] *Trial*, vol. i, pp. 417, 420.

[841] From a theological point of view the record of the Poitiers trial may have been insignificant; but at any rate it contained the arguments presented to the King and the memoranda of Gélu and of Gerson.

[842] *Trial*, vol. i, pp. 404, 429.

[843] *Ibid.*, vol. i, pp. 429, 430.

[844] De Beaurepaire, *Notes sur les juges*, pp. 126-127.

[845] *Trial*, vol. i, p. 430.

[846] *Trial*, vol. i, pp. 430, 437.

[847] Du Boulay, *Historia Universitatis Parisiensis*, vol. v, p. 929.

[848] De Beaurepaire, *Notes sur les juges*, p. 88.

[849] *Trial*, vol. i, pp. 437, 441.

[850] *Ibid.*, pp. 441, 442.

[851] *Trial*, vol. ii, p. 21.

[852] *Ibid.*, vol. iii, p. 146. De Beaurepaire, *Notes sur les juges*, pp. 445 *et seq.*

[853] Old name for a cemetery close to a church. Godefroy, *Lexique de l'ancien français* (W.S.).

[854] *Trial*, vol. ii, p. 351.

[855] *Trial,* vol. iii, p. 54.

[856] De Beaurepaire, *Notes sur le cimetière de Saint-Ouen de Rouen,* in *Précis analytique des travaux de l'Académie de Rouen* 1875-1876, pp. 211, 230, plan. U. Chevalier, *L'abjuration de Jeanne d'Arc et l'authenticité de sa formule,* p. 44. A. Sarrazin, *Jeanne d'Arc et la Normandie,* p. 351.

[857] *Trial,* vol. i, pp. 442, 444. O'Reilly, *Les deux procès,* vol. i, pp. 70-93.

[858] De Beaurepaire, *Notes sur les juges,* pp. 402, 408.

[859] *Trial,* vol. iii, p. 113.

[860] *Ibid.*, vol. i, pp. 469, 470.

[861] *Ibid.*, p. 444. E. Richer, *Histoire manuscrite de la Pucelle d'Orléans,* bk. i, fol. 8; bk. ii, fol. 198, v°.

[862] *Trial,* vol. iii, p. 61.

[863] *Ibid.*, vol. ii, pp. 15, 17.

[864] *Ibid.*, vol. i, pp. 456, 457. U. Chevalier, *L'abjuration de Jeanne d'Arc,* pp. 46, 47.

[865] *Trial,* vol. ii, pp. 15, 17, 335, 345, 353, 367.

[866] *Ibid.*, p. 17.

[867] *Ibid.*, vol. i, pp. 444, 445.

[868] *Ibid.*, p. 445.

[869] *Ibid.*, vol. ii, p. 358.

[870] *Ibid.*, vol. i, p. 445.

[871] *Trial,* vol. i, pp. 445, 446.

[872] *Ibid.*, p. 446.

[873] *Ibid.*, vol. iii, p. 146.

[874] *Ibid.*, vol. i, p. 473.

[875] *Trial,* vol. iii, p. 146.

[876] *Ibid.*, vol. ii, pp. 17, 331; vol. iii, pp. 52, 156.

[877] *Ibid.*, p. 123.

[878] *Ibid.*, vol. i, pp. 474, 475.

[879] *Ibid.*, p. 473 note.

[880] *Ibid.*, vol. iii, pp. 65, 147, 149, 273. De Beaurepaire, *Recherches sur le procès*, p. 358.

[881] *Trial*, vol. ii, p. 323.

[882] *Ibid.*, pp. 137, 376.

[883] *Ibid.*, p. 356; vol. iii, pp. 157, 178.

[884] *Ibid.*, p. 55.

[885] *Trial*, vol. iii, pp. 90, 147, 156.

[886] *Ibid.*, pp. 52, 65, 132, 156, 197. U. Chevalier, *L'Abjuration de Jeanne d'Arc*.

[887] *Trial*, vol. iii, pp. 156, 157 (evidence of Jean Massieu, Usher of the court).

[888] *Ibid.*, vol. ii, p. 323.

[889] *Trial*, vol. iii, p. 157.

[890] *Ibid.*, vol. ii, p. 331; vol. iii, p. 157. This deed, written in a large hand and containing but a few lines, appears to be an abridgment of that contained in the *Trial*, vol. i, pp. 447, 448 (cf. vol. iii, pp. 156, 197).

[891] *Trial*, vol. iii, pp. 156, 197.

[892] *Trial*, vol. ii, p. 338; vol. iii, p. 147.

[893] *Ibid.*, pp. 55, 143.

[894] *Ibid.*, p. 123.

[895] *Trial*, vol. ii, p. 361. J. Quicherat, *Aperçus nouveaux*, p. 135.

[896] *Trial*, vol. iii, pp. 147, 156.

[897] *Ibid.*, vol. ii, p. 376.

[898] *Ibid.*, p. 17; vol. iii, p. 164.

[899] *Trial*, vol. i, pp. 450, 452.

[900] *Ibid.*, p. 452.

[901] L. Tanon, *Tribunaux de l'inquisition*, p. 454.

[902] *Trial*, vol. ii, p. 14.

[903] *Ibid.*, vol. iii, pp. 52, 149.

[904] *Ibid.*, vol. i, p. 19.

[905] *Ibid.*, vol. ii, p. 14.

[906] *Ibid.*, p. 376.

[907] *Ibid.*, vol. i, pp. 452-453.

[908] *Trial*, vol. iii, p. 155.

[909] *Ibid.*, p. 89.

[910] *Trial*, vol. iii, p. 148.

[911] *Trial*, vol. ii, p. 14; vol. iii, p. 148.

[912] De Beaurepaire, *Notes sur les juges*, pp. 82 *et seq.*

[913] *Trial*, vol. ii, p. 354.

[914] *Ibid.*, vol. iii, pp. 158, 180.

[915] *Ibid.*, vol. i, p. 454; vol. iii, p. 148.

[916] *Ibid.*, vol. ii, p. 5. Isambart's evidence refers to this day, the 28th.

[917] *Trial*, vol. i, pp. 455-457.

[918] *Ibid.*, vol. ii, pp. 5, 8, 365; vol. iii, pp. 148, 149.

[919] *Ibid.*, vol. ii, p. 18.

[920] *Trial*, vol. ii, p. 18.

[921] "*Responsio mortifera,*" wrote the notary Boisguillaume in the margin of his minutes. *Trial*, vol. i, pp. 456, 457.

[922] *Trial*, vol. i, pp. 456-458.

[923] *Ibid.*, vol. ii, pp. 5, 8, 305.

[924] *Ibid.*, vol. i, pp. 459, 467.

[925] Bernard Gui, *Pratique*, part iii, p. 144. L. Tanon, *Tribunaux de l'inquisition*, pp. 464 *et seq.*

[926] *Trial*, vol. i, pp. 462, 463.

[927] *Ibid.*, p. 463.

[928] L. Tanon, *Tribunaux de l'inquisition*, pp. 472, 473.

[929] *Trial*, vol. i, pp. 463, 467.

[930] *Trial*, vol. i, p. 466.

[931] *Ibid.*, pp. 467, 469.

[932] *Ibid.*, vol. ii, pp. 3, 4 (evidence of Brother Isambart de la Pierre). *Ibid.*, p. 8 (evidence of Brother Martin Ladvenu).

[933] *Trial*, vol. i, p. 481. (In the Introduction I have given my reasons for regarding the information given after the death of the Maid as possessing great historical significance.)

[934] *Trial*, vol. i, pp. 462-467.

[935] *Ibid.*, p. 479. Or "to such of you as are churchmen." *Ibid.*, p. 482 (information furnished after her death).

[936] Robillard de Beaurepaire, *Notes sur les juges*.

[937] *Trial*, vol. i, p. 480.

[938] *Ibid.*, pp. 480, 481 (information furnished after her death).

[939] *Ibid.*, pp. 482, 483.

[940] *Ibid.*, vol. ii, p. 114 (evidence of Brother Jehan Toutmouillé).

[941] *Trial*, vol. i, pp. 481, 482 (information given after Jeanne's death).

[942] *Textus decretalium*, lib. v, ch. iv.

[943] Ignace de Doellinger, *La Papauté*, traduit par A. Giraud-Teulon, Paris, 1904, in 8vo, p. 105.

[944] *Trial*, vol. iii, p. 158.

[945] *Trial*, vol. ii, p. 334.

[946] *Ibid.*, vol. ii, pp. 19, 334. De Beaurepaire, *Recherches sur le procès*, pp. 116, 117.

[947] *Trial*, vol. i, pp. 482, 483 (information procured after Jeanne's death).

[948] *Ibid.*, vol. ii, pp. 19, 308, 320; vol. iii, pp. 114, 158, 183, 197.

[949] For Jeanne's communion see also De Beaurepaire, *Recherches sur le procès*, pp. 116-117.

[950] *Trial*, vol. iii, p. 191.

[951] *Ibid.*, vol. i, p. 485. Maître N. Taquel would lead us to believe that the interrogatories took place after Jeanne's communion, but this can hardly be admitted.

[952] *Trial*, vol. ii, p. 320; vol. iii, p. 162.

[953] A. Sarrazin, *Jeanne d'Arc et la Normandie*, p. 369.

[954] Bouquet, *Rouen aux différentes époques de son histoire*, pp. 25 *et seq.* A. Sarrazin, *Jeanne d'Arc et la Normandie*, pp. 374, 375. De Beaurepaire, *Mémoires sur le lieu du supplice de Jeanne d'Arc*, with plan of the Old Market Square of Rouen according to the *Livre de fontaine de 1525*, Rouen, 1867, in 8vo.

[955] De Beaurepaire, *Note sur la prise du château de Rouen, par Ricarville*, Rouen, 1857, in 8vo, p. 5.

[956] Bouquet, *Jeanne d'Arc au château de Rouen*, p. 25. De Beaurepaire, *Mémoire sur le lieu du supplice de Jeanne d'Arc*, p. 32. A. Sarrazin, *Jeanne d'Arc et la Normandie*, pp. 376 *et seq.*

[957] *Trial*, vol. iv, p. 459.

[958] *Trial,* vol. i, pp. 470; vol. ii, pp. 14, 303, 328; vol. iii, pp. 159, 173.

[959] *Ibid.*, vol. i, p. 470; vol. ii, p. 334; vol. iii, pp. 53, 114, 159.

[960] Chapter xii, 26 (W.S.).

[961] *Trial,* vol. iii, p. 194.

[962] *Ibid.*, p. 159.

[963] L. Tanon, *Histoire des tribunaux de l'inquisition,* p. 374.

[964] *Trial,* vol. ii, p. 19; vol. iii, p. 177.

[965] *Ibid.*, vol. ii, pp. 19, 351.

[966] *Ibid.*, vol. iii, p. 56.

[967] *Trial,* vol. ii, pp. 6, 20; vol. iii, pp. 53, 177, 186.

[968] *Ibid.*, vol. iii, p. 188. A. Sarrazin, *Jeanne d'Arc et la Normandie,* p. 386. Guedon and Ladvenu added to their evidence that not long afterwards a certain Georges Folenfant was also given up to the secular arm. But the Archbishop and the Inquisitor sent Ladvenu to the Bailie "in order to warn him that the said Georges was not to be treated like the Maid who was burned without the pronouncement of any definite and final sentence." *Trial,* vol. ii, p. 9.

[969] *Ibid.*, p. 344.

[970] Falconbridge, in *Trial,* vol. iv, p. 459. Yet Martin Ladvenu says "until the last hour," etc., which is obviously false.

[971] *Trial,* vol. iii, p. 53.

[972] Shakespeare, Henry VI, part 1, act i, scene 1.

[973] *Trial,* vol. ii, p. 6; vol. iii, pp. 53, 191, 375.

[974] *Missel Romain, Office des morts.* Cf. Le P. C. Clair, *Le Dies irœ, histoire, traduction et commentaire,* Paris, in 8vo, 1881, pp. 38-142.

[975] *Trial,* vol. ii, pp. 6, 20.

[976] *Ibid.*, vol. iii, p. 170.

[977] *Ibid.*, p. 186.

[978] *Ibid.*, vol. ii, p. 8; vol. iii, pp. 169, 194.

[979] *Ibid.*, vol. ii, p. 7.

[980] *Ibid.*, vol. iii, p. 186.

[981] *Trial*, vol. iii, p. 191. *Journal d'un bourgeois de Paris*, pp. 269, 270.

[982] L. Tanon, *Histoire des tribunaux de l'inquisition*, p. 478.

[983] *Chronique des cordeliers*, fol. 507 verso. *Journal d'un bourgeois de Paris*, p. 269.

[984] *Trial*, vol. iii, pp. 159, 160, 185; vol. iv, p. 518. Th. Basin, *Histoire de Charles VII et de Louis XI*, vol. i, p. 83. Th. Cochard, *Existe-t-il des reliques de Jeanne d'Arc?* Orléans, 1891, in 8vo.

[985] *Trial*, vol. ii, pp. 7, 352, 366.

[986] *Trial*, vol. i, pp. 493, 495.

[987] Le P. Denifle and Chatelain, *Cartularium Universitatis Parisiensis*, vol. iv, p. 527.

[988] *Trial*, vol. iii, pp. 240, 243.

[989] *Trial*, vol. i, pp. 485, 496; vol. iv, p. 403. Monstrelet, vol. iv, ch. cv.

[990] *Trial*, vol. i, pp. 496, 500.

[991] *Journal d'un bourgeois de Paris*, pp. 270, 272. This sermon contains curious inaccuracies. Are they the fault of the Inquisitor or of the author of *Le Journal*?

[992] *Trial*, vol. iv, p. 473.

[993] Th. Basin, *Histoire de Charles VII et de Louis XI*, vol. iv, pp. 103, 104. Monstrelet, ch. lxiii. Bougenot, *Deux documents inédits relatifs à Jeanne d'Arc*, in *Revue bleue*, 13 Feb., 1892, pp. 203, 204.

[994] *Trial*, vol. ii, pp. 3, 344, 348, 373; vol. iii, p. 189; vol. v, pp. 169, 179, 181. Dibon, *Essai sur Louviers*, Rouen, 1836, in 8vo, pp. 33 *et seq.* Vallet de Viriville, *Histoire de Charles VII*, vol. ii, pp. 246 *et seq.*

[995] Le P. Denifle, *La désolation des églises de France vers le milieu du XVe siècle*, vol. i, p. xvi.

[996] Jean Chartier, *Chronique*, vol. i, p. 132. Monstrelet, vol. iv, p. 433. Lefèvre de Saint-Rémy, vol. ii, p. 265.

[997] *Journal d'un bourgeois de Paris*, p. 272.

[998] *Journal d'un bourgeois de Paris*, p. 272.

[999] Vallet de Viriville, *Histoire de Charles VII*, vol. ii, p. 248. De Beaurepaire, *Recherches sur les juges*, p. 43.

[1000] Lea, *History of the Inquisition*, vol. iii, 377 (ed. 1905).

[1001] Lefèvre de Saint-Rémy, vol. ii, pp. 263, 264.

[1002] *Journal d'un bourgeois de Paris*, p. 274.

[1003] Lefèvre de Saint-Rémy, vol. ii, p. 264.

[1004] Martial d'Auvergne, *Vigiles*, ed. Coustelier, vol. i.

[1005] Gruel, *Chronique d'Arthur de Richemont*, p. 81. Vallet de Viriville, in *Nouvelle biographie générale*. De Beaucourt, *Histoire de Charles VII*, vol. ii, p. 297. E. Cosneau, *Le connétable de Richemont*, pp. 200, 201.

[1006] Perceval de Cagny, pp. 170, 173, *passim*.

[1007] Carlier, *Histoire des Valois*, 1764, in 4to, vol. ii, p. 442. Vallet de Viriville, *Histoire de Charles VII*, vol. i, p. 307. The Regent also believed in astrology (B.N. MS. 1352).

[1008] Gruel, *Chronique d'Arthur de Richemont*, pp. 120, 121. Dom Félibien, *Histoire de Paris*, vol. iv, p. 597.

[1009] *Chronique du doyen de Saint-Thibaud de Metz*, in *Trial*, vol. v, pp. 321, 324. Jacomin Husson, *Chronique de Metz*, ed. Michelant, Metz, 1870, pp. 64, 65. Cf. Lecoy de la Marche, *Une fausse Jeanne d'Arc*, in *Revue des questions historiques*, October, 1871, pp. 562 *et seq.* Vergniaud-Romagnési, *Des portraits de Jeanne d'Arc et de la fausse Jeanne d'Arc*, in *Mémoires de la Société d'Agriculture d'Orléans*, vol. i (1853), pp. 250, 253. De Puymaigre, *La fausse Jeanne d'Arc*, in *Revue nouvelle d'Alsace-Lorraine*, vol. v (1885), pp. 533 *et seq.* A. France, *Une fausse Jeanne d'Arc*, in *Revue des familles*, 15 February, 1891.

[1010] Varanius alone says that Jacques d'Arc died of sorrow at the loss of his daughter. *Trial*, vol. v, p. 85.

[1011] *Ibid.*, p. 280.

[1012] *Ibid.*, pp. 279, 280. G. Lefèvre-Pontalis, *La fausse Jeanne d'Arc*, p. 6, note 1.

[1013] *Trial*, vol. v, p. 210. Lefèvre de Saint-Rémy, vol. ii, p. 176.

[1014] *Trial*, vol. v, pp. 321, 324.

[1015] *Le Metz ancien* (Metz, 1856, 2 vol. in folio) by the Baron d'Hannoncelles, which contains the genealogy of Nicole Lowe.

[1016] "And was recognised by divers tokens" (*enseignes*) (*Trial*, vol. v, p. 322). M. Lecoy de la Marche (*Une fausse Jeanne d'Arc*, in *Revue des questions historiques*, October, 1871, p. 565), and M. Gaston Save (*Jehanne des Armoises, Pucelle d'Orléans*, Nancy, 1893, p. 11) understand that she was recognised by several officers or ensigns (*enseignes*). I have interpreted *enseignes* in the ordinary sense of marks on the skin, birth-marks. (Cf. La Curne.)

[1017] *Chronique du doyen de Saint-Thibaud*, in *Trial*, vol. v, p. 322.

[1018] *Journal d'un bourgeois de Paris*, p. 354.

[1019] Nevertheless see on this subject M. Germain Lefèvre-Pontalis, who is our authority for this prophecy (Eberhard Windecke, pp. 108-111).

[1020] The republic of Metz (W.S.)

[1021] *Chronique du doyen de Saint-Thibaud*, in *Trial*, vol. v, p. 322. Chronique de Philippe de Vigneulles, in *Les chroniques Messines* of Huguenin, p. 198.

[1022] *Trial,* vol. ii, p. 457. L. Champion, *Jeanne d'Arc écuyère,* ch. ii, ch. vi.

[1023] Variant of *La chronique du doyen de Saint-Thibaud* sent from Metz to Pierre du Puy, in *Trial,* vol. v, pp. 322, 324.

[1024] *Ibid.*, pp. 322, 324.

[1025] D. Calmet, *Histoire de Lorraine,* vol. vii. Proofs and illustrations, col. vi.

[1026] *Trial,* vol. v, pp. 322, 324. Eberhard Windecke, p. 108. Morosini, vol. iii, p. 62, note.

[1027] M. le Baron de Braux was kind enough to write to me from Boucq near Foug, Meurthe-et-Moselle, on the 28th of June, 1896, explaining that Bacquillon (*Trial,* vol. v, p. 322) is an erroneous reading of one of the manuscripts of the Doyen of Saint-Thibaud. "By comparing," he added, "the various versions (V. Quicherat and *Les chroniques Messines*) we may ascertain that it is really Vaucouleurs, Valquelou," mistaken for Bacquillon.

[1028] *Trial,* vol. ii, pp. 406, 408, 445, 449.

[1029] The *Chronique de Tournai* says of the true Jeanne that she came from Mareville, a small town between Metz and Pont-à-Mousson. "This Jeanne had long dwelt and served in a *métairie* [a kind of farm] of this place."

[1030] *Chronique du doyen Saint-Thibaud,* in *Trial,* vol. v, pp. 322, 324. Lecoy de la Marche, *Jeanne des Armoises,* p. 566. G. Save, *Jehanne des Armoises, pucelle d'Orléans,* p. 14.

[1031] *Trial,* vol. v, pp. 352 *et seq.*

[1032] *Chronique du doyen de Saint-Thibaud,* in *Trial,* vol. v, pp. 322, 324. Dom Lelong, *Histoire du diocèse de Laon,* 1783, p. 371. Abbé Ledouble, *Les origines de Liesse et du pèlerinage de Notre-Dame,* Soissons, 1885, pp. 6 *et seq.*

[1033] *Trial,* vol. v, p. 322, note 2. G. Lefèvre-Pontalis, *La fausse Jeanne d'Arc,* p. 21, note 1.

[1034] *Chronique normande* (MS. in the British Museum), in *Trial*, vol. iv, p. 344. Symphorien Champier, *Nef des Dames*, Lyon, 1503, *ibid.*

[1035] *Journal d'un bourgeois de Paris*, p. 272. *Chronique normande*, in *Bibliothèque de l'École des Chartes*, second series, vol. iii, p. 116. D. Calmet, *Histoire de Lorraine*, p. vi, proofs and illustrations. G. Save, *Jehanne des Armoises*, pp. 6, 7. It is well known that Gabriel Naudé maintained the paradox that Jeanne was only burned in effigy. *Considérations politiques sur les coups d'état*, Rome, 1639, in 4to. G. Lefèvre-Pontalis, *La fausse Jeanne d'Arc*, p. 8.

[1036] Lanéry d'Arc, *Le culte de Jeanne d'Arc*, Orléans, 1887, in 8vo. *Revue du Midi.*

[1037] *Trial*, vol. v, p. 275. Lottin, *Recherches*, vol. ii, p. 286.

[1038] *Trial*, vol. v, p. 262. Lecoy de la Marche, *Jeanne des Armoises*, p. 568.

[1039] He died at the age of one hundred and eighteen. *Trial*, iii, p. 29.

[1040] *Trial*, vol. v, p. 326. Vallet de Viriville, *Histoire de Charles VII*, vol. ii, p. 376, note. G. Lefèvre-Pontalis, *La fausse Jeanne d'Arc*, p. 23, note 5.

[1041] *Trial*, vol. v, p. 327.

[1042] *Trial*, vol. v, p. 326. Lottin, *Recherches*, vol. i, pp. 284-285.

[1043] Since 1432. But there is no evidence of any anniversary service having been held in 1433 and 1434. It was reinstituted in 1439.

[1044] *Trial*, vol. v, pp. 274, 275. Lottin, *Recherches*, vol. i, p. 286.

[1045] *Chronique du doyen de Saint-Thibaud*, in *Trial*, vol. v, p. 323. Jean Nider, *Formicarium*, in *Trial*, vol. iv, p. 325. Lecoy de la Marche, *loc. cit.*, p. 566.

[1046] *Art de vérifier les dates*, vol. xv, pp. 236 *et seq. Gallia Christiana*, vol. xiii, pp. 970 *et seq.*; Gams, *Series Episcoporum* (1873), pp. 317, 319.

[1047] Quicherat, in *Trial*, vol. iv, p. 502, note, erroneously states that the contest for the Archbishopric of Trèves was between Raban of Helmstat and Jacques of Syrck. Concerning Jacques of Syrck or Sierck, see de Beaucourt, *Histoire de Charles VII*, vol. iv, p. 264.

[1048] Jean Nider, *Formicarium*, book v, ch. viii. D. Calmet, *Histoire de Lorraine*, vol. ii, p. 906.

[1049] *Trial*, vol. i, pp. 245-246.

[1050] Jean Nider, *Formicarium*, in *Trial*, vol. iv, p. 502; vol. v, p. 324.

[1051] H. Vincent, *La maison des Armoises, originaire de Champagne*, in *Mémoires de la Société d'Archéologie Lorraine*, 3rd series, vol. v (1877), p. 324. G. Lefèvre-Pontalis, *La fausse Jeanne d'Arc*, p. 2, note 4.

[1052] In his *Histoire de Lorraine* (vol. v, pp. clxiv *et seq.*), Dom Calmet says that the contract of marriage between Robert des Armoises and the Maid of France, which had long been preserved in the family, was lost in his day. There is no need to regret it, for it is now known that this contract was forged by Father Jérôme Vignier. Le Comte de Marsy (*La fausse Jeanne d'Arc, Claude des Armoises; du degré de confiance à accorder aux découvertes de Jérôme Vignier*, Compiègne, 1890) and M. Tamizey de Larroque (*Revue critique*, the 20th October, 1890). For Vignier's other forgeries cf. Julien Havet, *Questions Mérovingiennes*, ii.

[1053] Jean Nider, *Formicarium*, bk. v, ch. viii. *Trial*, vol. iv, pp. 503, 504.

[1054] The preceding deed, by which "*Robert des Harmoises et la Pucelle Jehanne d'Arc, sa femme*," acquired the estate of Fléville, is very doubtful (D. Calmet, 2nd edition, vol. v, p. clxiv, note).

[1055] *Chronique du doyen de Saint-Thibaud*, in *Trial*, vol. v, p. 323. *Journal d'un bourgeois de Paris*, pp. 354-355.

[1056] *Trial*, vol. iii, p. 206, note 2.

[1057] *Ibid.*, p. 219.

[1058] Jean Nider, *Formicarium*, in *Trial*, vol. v, p. 325.

[1059] *Chronique du doyen de Saint-Thibaud*, in *Trial*, vol. v, pp. 323-324.

[1060] *Trial*, vol. i, p. 183.

[1061] *Ibid.*, vol. i, pp. 106, 108, 119, 296. *Journal d'un bourgeois de Paris.*

[1062] Extracts from the accounts of the town of Orléans, in *Trial*, vol. v, pp. 331-332. Lecoy de la Marche, *Une fausse Jeanne d'Arc*, pp. 570-571.

[1063] Original documents of Orléans, in *Trial*, vol. v, p. 270.

[1064] *Trial*, vol. v, p. 274. Lottin, *Recherches*, vol. i, p. 286.

[1065] Extracts from the accounts of the town of Orléans, in *Trial*, vol. v, pp. 331-332. Lottin, *Recherches*, vol. i, p. 287.

[1066] *Trial*, vol. v, p. 260.

[1067] *Ibid.*, pp. 112-113.

[1068] *Trial*, vol. iii, p. 17; vol. v, p. 327.

[1069] *Ibid.*, vol. v, p. 332. G. Lefèvre-Pontalis, *La fausse Jeanne d'Arc*, pp. 23-24.

[1070] *Trial*, vol. v, p. 332.

[1071] Vallet de Viriville, *Notices et extraits de chartes et de manuscrits appartenant au British Museum*, in *Bibliothèque de l'École des Chartes*, vol. viii, 1846, p. 116.

[1072] Abbé Bossard, *Gille de Rais*, p. 174.

[1073] Pardon, in *Trial*, vol. v, pp. 332-334.

[1074] *Journal d'un bourgeois de Paris*, p. 335. Lecoy de la Marche, *Une fausse Jeanne d'Arc*, p. 574.

[1075] *Journal d'un bourgeois de Paris*, pp. 338 *et seq*. De Beaucourt, *Histoire de Charles VII*, vol. iii, pp. 384 *et seq.*

[1076] *Journal d'un bourgeois de Paris*, p. 270.

[1077] De Beaucourt, *Histoire de Charles VII*, vol. iii, ch. xvi.

[1078] *Journal d'un bourgeois de Paris*, pp. 354, 355. Lecoy de la Marche, *Une fausse Jeanne d'Arc*, p. 574.

[1079] *Journal d'un bourgeois de Paris, loc. cit.*

[1080] *Journal d'un bourgeois de Paris*, pp. 354, 355. Lecoy de la Marche, *Une fausse Jeanne d'Arc*, p. 574. G. Lefèvre-Pontalis, *La fausse Jeanne d'Arc*, p. 27.

[1081] Vergnaud-Romagnési, *Des portraits de Jeanne d'Arc et de la fausse Jeanne d'Arc* and *Mémoire sur les fausses Jeanne d'Arc*, in *Les Mémoires de la Société d'Agriculture d'Orléans*, 1854, in 8vo.

[1082] *Trial*, vol. v, pp. 210, 213.

[1083] *Trial*, vol. v, p. 279.

[1084] *Trial*, vol. v, pp. 212, 214. Lottin, *Recherches*, vol. i, p. 287. Duleau, *Vidimus d'une charte de Charles VII, concédant à Pierre du Lys la possession de l'Isle-aux-Bœufs*, Orléans, 1860, in 8vo. 6. G. Lefèvre-Pontalis, *La fausse Jeanne d'Arc*, p. 28, note 1.

[1085] I have not made use of the very late evidence given by Pierre Sala (*Trial*, vol. iv, p. 281). It is vague and somewhat legendary, and cannot possibly be introduced into the Life of La Dame des Armoises. For the bibliography of this interesting subject, see Lanéry d'Arc, *Le livre d'or de Jeanne d'Arc*, pp. 573, 580, and G. Lefèvre-Pontalis, *La fausse Jeanne d'Arc*, Paris, 1895, in 8vo, concerning the account given by M. Gaston Save.

There are those who have supposed, without adducing any proof, that this pseudo-Jeanne was a sister of the Maid (Lebrun de Charmettes, *Histoire de Jeanne d'Arc*, vol. iv, pp. 291 *et seq.*).

Francis André, *La vérité sur Jeanne d'Arc*, Paris, 1895, in 18mo, pp. 75 *et seq.*

[1086] De Beaucourt, *Histoire de Charles VII*, vol. iii, p. 335.

[1087] Le P. Ayroles, *La Pucelle devant l'église de son temps*, p. 10.

[1088] *Trial*, vol. iii, p. 565.

[1089] *Ibid.*, vol. i, p. 403.

[1090] *Ordonnances*, vol. xiii, pp. 267, 291. *Preuves des libertés de l'église gallicane*, edited by Lenglet-Dufresnoy, second part, p. 6. De Beaucourt, *Histoire de Charles VII*, vol. iii, pp. 353, 361. N. Arlos, *Histoire de la pragmatique sanction, etc.*

[1091] Hefelé, *Histoire de l'Église gallicane*, vol. xx, p. 357. De Beaucourt, *Histoire de Charles VII*, vol. iii, p. 363. De Beaurepaire, *Les états de Normandie sous la domination anglaise*, pp. 66, 67, 185, 188.

[1092] Du Boulay, *Hist. Universitatis*, vol. v, p. 431. De Beaurepaire, *Notes sur les juges*, p. 28.

[1093] *Trial*, vol. ii, pp. 10, 12, 332, 362; vol. iii, pp. 60, 133, 141, 145, 156, 162, 173, 181.

[1094] De Beaurepaire, *Notes sur les juges et assesseurs du procès de condamnation*, pp. 78, 82.

[1095] J. Quicherat, *Aperçus nouveaux*, p. 106.

[1096] De Beaucourt, *Histoire de Charles VII*, vol. iii, p. 372.

[1097] De Beaurepaire, *Les états de Normandie sous la domination anglaise*, pp. 66, 67, 185, 188. De Beaucourt, *loc. cit.* p. 362.

[1098] De Beaurepaire, *loc. cit.*, p. 17. *Notes sur les juges et assesseurs du procès de condamnation*, p. 117. *Recherches sur le procès*, p. 124.

[1099] De Beaucourt, *Histoire de Charles VII*, vol. v, ch. i.

[1100] Lanéry d'Arc, *Mémoires et consultations en faveur de Jeanne d'Arc*, p. 249.

[1101] *Trial*, vol. ii, pp. 1, 22.

[1102] *Gallia Christiana*, vol. iii, col. 1129 and vol. xi, col. 90. De Beaucourt, *Histoire de Charles VII*, vol. v, p. 219. Le P. Ayroles, *La Pucelle devant l'église de son temps*, ch. vi.

[1103] De Beaurepaire, *Les états de Normandie sous la domination anglaise*, pp. 185, 188.

[1104] *Trial*, vol. v, p. 276.

[1105] *Ibid.*, vol. ii, pp. 108, 112.

[1106] *Ibid.*, p. 95. Le P. Ayroles, *La Pucelle devant l'église de son temps*, p. 607. J. Belon and F. Balme, *Jean Bréhal, grand inquisiteur de France et la réhabilitation de Jeanne d'Arc*, Paris, 1893, in 4to.

[1107] *Trial*, vol. ii, pp. 82, 92.

[1108] *Ibid.*, pp. 92, 112.

[1109] *Ibid.*, pp. 193, 196.

[1110] *Ibid.*, pp. 291, 463; vol. iii, pp. 1, 202.

[1111] *Trial*, vol. ii, pp. 378, 463.

[1112] *Ibid.*, vol. v, pp. 112, 113, 331.

[1113] *Ibid.*, vol. ii, pp. 23, 35.

[1114] *Ibid.*, pp. 1, 19.

[1115] *Ibid.*, vol. iii, p. 202.

[1116] *Ibid.*, pp. 2 *et seq.*

[1117] *Ibid.*, p. 16.

[1118] De Beaucourt, *Histoire de Charles VII*, vol. vi, p. 43. P. Dupuy, *Histoire des Templiers*, 1658, in 4to. Cimber and Danjou, *Archives curieuses de l'histoire de France*, vol. i, pp. 137-157. (See also, Michelet, History of France, translated by G.H. Smith, vol. ii, p. 206.) Note – Alençon says to his English valet: "If I could have a powder that I wot of and put it in the vessel in which the King's sheets are washed, he should sleep sound enough [*dormir tout sec*]." *Trial of Alençon* (W.S.).

[1119] *Trial*, vol. iii, p. 90.

[1120] *Ibid.*, p. 209.

[1121] *Ibid.*, p. 65.

[1122] *Ibid.*, p. 100.

[1123] *Ibid.*, p. 85.

[1124] *Ibid.*, vol. ii, pp. 20, 21, 161; vol. iii, pp. 43, 53, *passim*.

[1125] *Trial*, vol. iii, pp. 44, 56. J. Quicherat, *Aperçus nouveaux*, p. 106.

[1126] *Ibid.*, vol. ii, pp. 161; vol. iii, pp. 41, 42, 195.

[1127] De Beaurepaire, *Notes sur les juges*.

[1128] *Trial*, vol. ii, pp. 329 *et seq.*

[1129] *Trial*, vol. ii, pp. 363 *et seq.*, 434 *et seq.*

[1130] Lanéry d'Arc, *Mémoires et consultations en faveur de Jeanne d'Arc*, p. 576.

[1131] *Trial*, vol. iii, pp. 32, 87, 100, 116, 119, 120, 126, 128 *et passim*.

[1132] Lanéry d'Arc, *Mémoires et consultations*, p. 402.

[1133] *Trial*, vol. iii, p. 398.

[1134] *Trial*, vol. iii, p. 355.

[1135] *Ibid.*, p. 162.

[1136] *Gallia Christiana*, vol. xi, col. 793.

[1137] *Histoire ecclésiastique et politique de la ville et du diocèse de Toul*, 1707, p. 529.

[1138] Abbé Bossard, *Gilles de Rais*, pp. 333 *et seq.*

[1139] De Beaucourt, *Histoire de Charles VII*, vol. vi, p. 197.

[1140] Inquiry of 1476, in G. de Braux and E. de Bouteiller, *Nouvelles recherches*, p. 10.

[1141] Or Chaumussay. Lecoy de la Marche, *Une fausse Jeanne d'Arc*, Paris, 1871, in 8vo, p. 19.

[1142] Lecoy de la Marche, *Une fausse Jeanne d'Arc*, in *Revue des questions historiques*, October, 1871, p. 576. *Le roi René*, Paris, 1875, vol. i, pp. 308-327; vol. ii, pp. 281-283.

[1143] *Trial*, vol. iii, p. 314, note 1. *Gallia Christiana*, vol. ii, fol. 518. Du Boulay, *Hist. Univ. Paris*, vol. v, p. 905. Le P. Ayroles, *La Pucelle devant l'église de son temps*, pp. 403, 404.

[1144] Lanéry d'Arc, *Mémoires et consultations*, p. 247.

[1145] Du Clercq, *Mémoires*, ed. Reiffenberg, Brussels, 1823, vol. iii, pp. 98 *et seq.* Jean de Roye, *Chronique scandaleuse*, ed. Bernard de Mandrot, 1894, vol. i, pp. 13, 14. *Chronique de Bourdigné*, ed. Quatrebarbes, vol. ii, p. 212. Dom Piolin, *Histoire de l'église du Mans*, vol. v, p. 163.

[1146] Chastellain, ed. Kervyn de Lettenhove, vol. iii, p. 444.

[1147] Jacques du Clercq, *Mémoires*, vol. iii, pp. 107 *et seq.*

[1148] Antoine du Faur, *Livre des femmes célèbres*, in *Trial*, vol. v, p. 336.

[1149] De Beaucourt, *Histoire de Charles VII*, vol. vi, pp. 442, 451. *Chronique Martiniane*, ed. P. Champion, p. 110.

[1150] Mathieu d'Escouchy, vol. ii, p. 422. Jean Chartier, *Chronique*, vol. iii, pp. 114-121.

[1151] *Gallia Christiana*, vol. vii, col. 151 and 214. Hardouin, *Acta Conciliorum*, vol. ix, col. 1423. De Beaucourt, *Histoire de Charles VII*, vol. vi, p. 444.

[1152] *Trial*, vol. iii. p. 219.

[1153] *Trial*, vol. i, p. 52 and *passim*.

[1154] A famous French alienist (1825-1893). – W.S.

[1155] *Progrès medical*, January 19, 1878.

[1156] The existence of patches devoid of feeling was considered in the Middle Ages to prove that the subject was a witch. Hence needles were run into the supposed witch. And if she felt them in every part of her body she was acquitted. - W.S.

[1157] *Trial*, vol. i, p. 52.

[1158] *Trial*, vol. i, p. 53.

[1159] *Trial*, vol. i, p. 186.

[1160] According to the evidence of Maître Pierre Maurice, at the condemnation trial (vol. i. p. 480), Jeanne must have seen the angels "in the form of certain infinitesimal things" (*sub specie quarumdam rerum minimarum*). This was also the character of the hallucinations experienced by Saint Rose of Lima ("Vie de Sainte Rose de Lima," by P. Léonard Hansen, p. 179).

[1161] *Trial*, vol. i, p. 144.

[1162] *Trial*, vol. i, p. 110.

[1163] *Trial*, vol. i, p. 279 and *passim*.

[1164] Michel de Nostre-Dame, called Nostradamus (1503-1566), a Provençal astrologer, whose prophecies were published under the title of "Centuries." He was invited to the French court by Catherine de' Medici, and became the doctor of Charles IX. - W.S.

[1165] The last syllable but one of the surname of the Prophet will Diane take for her day and her rest. Far shall wander that inspired one delivering a great nation from the burden of taxes.

[1166] Marc René Marquis d'Argenson (1652-1721), after being Lieutenant Général de la Police at Paris, became, from 1718-1720, Président du Conseil des Finances and Garde des Sceaux. - W.S.

[1167] *Gazette d'Amsterdam*, March-May, 1697; *Annales de la cour et de Paris* (vol. ii. pp. 204, 219); *Theatrum Europœum* (vol. xv. pp. 359-360); *Mémoires de Sourches* (vol. v. pp. 260, 263); *Lettres de Madame Dunoyer* (Letter xxvi); *Saint Simon, Mémoires*, ed.

Régnier (*Collection des Grands Ecrivains de la France*), vol. vi. pp. 222, 228, 231; Appendix X, p. 545; *Mémoires du duc de Luynes*, vol. x. pp. 410, 412 - Abbé Proyart, *Vie du duc de Bourgogne* (ed. 1782), vol. i. pp. 978, 981.

[1168] Antoine Marie Chamans, Comte de La Valette (1769-1830), was a French general during the first empire. Having been arrested in 1815 and condemned to death, he was saved by his wife. - W.S.

[1169] *Rapport adressé à S. Ex. le Ministre de la Police Générale sur l'état du nommé Martin, envoyé par son ordre à la maison royale de Charenton, le 13 Mars, 1816, par MM. Pinel, médecin en chef de l'hôpital de la Salpêtriere, et Royer-Collard, médecin en chef de la maison royale de Charenton, et l'un et l'autre professeurs à la faculté de médecine de Paris.* Inscribed at the end with the date - Paris, 6 May, 1816 - 39 pages in 4° MS. in the library of the author. Le Capitaine Paul Marin, *Thomas Martin de Gallardon Les Médecins et les thaumaturges du XIXe siècle*, Paris, s.d. in 18°. *Mémoires de la Comtesse de Boignes*, edited by Charles Nicoullaud, Paris, 1907, vol. iii. pp. 355 and *passim*.

[1170] *Trial*, vol. i, pp. 100, 292.

[1171] There is a wood engraving of this figure in Wallon, *Jeanne d'Arc*, p. 95.

[1172] E. de Bouteiller and G. de Braux, *Notes iconographiques sur Jeanne d'Arc*, Paris and Orléans, 1879, in 18° royal paper.

[1173] Reproduced in many works, notably opposite p. 17 in the book of E. de Bouteiller and G. de Braux, referred to above.

[1174] *Ibid.*, see woodcut opposite p. 8.

[1175] In the Orléans Museum. A copper-plate engraving by M. Georges Lavalley, in the *Jeanne d'Arc*, of M. Raoul Bergot, Tours, s.d. large 8°.

[1176] Of this class of so-called portrait, I will merely mention the miniature which serves as frontispiece to vol. iv. of *La Vrai Jeanne d'Arc*, of P. Ayroles, Paris, 1898, in large 8°, and the miniature of the Spetz Collection, reproduced in the *Jeanne d'Arc* of Canon Henri Debout, vol. ii. p. 103 (also in *The Maid of France* by Andrew Lang, 1908. W.S.).

[1177] *Le champion des dames*, MS. of the fifteenth century; *Bibl. nat.*, fonds français, No. 841; Martial d'Auvergne, MS. of the end of the fifteenth century, fonds français, No. 5054. An initial of a fifteenth-century Latin MS., *Bibl. nat.*, No. 14665.

[1178] *Trial*, vol. i, p. 100. N. Valois, *Un nouveau témoignage sur Jeanne d'Arc*, pp. 8, 13.

[1179] Reproduced in chromo in Wallon's *Jeanne d'Arc*.

[1180] The form *Darc* occurs in the condemnation trial (*Trial*, vol. i, p. 191, vol. ii, p. 82). But side by side we find also *Dars* (document dated March 31, 1427), *Day* (patent of nobility), *Daiz* (communicated to me by M. Pierre Champion) and *Daix* (*Chronique de la Pucelle*).

[1181] Tapestry representing small animals. - W.S.

[1182] Reproduced in chromo in Wallon's *Jeanne d'Arc, cf.* J. Quicherat, *Histoire du costume en France depuis les temps les plus reculés, jusqu' la fin du XVIIIe siècle*, Paris, 1875, large octavo, p. 271.

[1183] *Trial*, vol. v, p. 270.

Have you read the first part of this story? Also from Benediction Classics:

Large format paperback, ISBN: 9781849024914

Also from Benediction Books ...
Wandering Between Two Worlds: Essays on Faith and Art
Anita Mathias
Benediction Books, 2007
152 pages
ISBN: 0955373700

Available from www.amazon.com, www.amazon.co.uk

In these wide-ranging lyrical essays, Anita Mathias writes, in lush, lovely prose, of her naughty Catholic childhood in Jamshedpur, India; her large, eccentric family in Mangalore, a seacoast town converted by the Portuguese in the sixteenth century; her rebellion and atheism as a teenager in her Himalayan boarding school, run by German missionary nuns, St. Mary's Convent, Nainital; and her abrupt religious conversion after which she entered Mother Teresa's convent in Calcutta as a novice. Later rich, elegant essays explore the dualities of her life as a writer, mother, and Christian in the United States-- Domesticity and Art, Writing and Prayer, and the experience of being "an alien and stranger" as an immigrant in America, sensing the need for roots.

About the Author

Anita Mathias is the author of Wandering Between Two Worlds: Essays on Faith and Art. She has a B.A. and M.A. in English from Somerville College, Oxford University, and an M.A. in Creative Writing from the Ohio State University, USA. Anita won a National Endowment of the Arts fellowship in Creative Nonfiction in 1997. She lives in Oxford, England with her husband, Roy, and her daughters, Zoe and Irene.

Visit Anita at http://www.anitamathias.com, and on
http://theoxfordchristian.blogspot.com, her Christian blog;
http://wanderingbetweentwoworlds.blogspot.com/, her personal blog, and
http://thegoodbooksblog.blogspot.com, her literary and writing blog.

The Church That Had Too Much
Anita Mathias
Benediction Books, 2010
52 pages
ISBN: 9781849026567

Available from www.amazon.com, www.amazon.co.uk

The Church That Had Too Much was very well-intentioned. She wanted to love God, she wanted to love people, but she was both hampered by her muchness and the abundance of her possessions, and beset by ambition, power struggles and snobbery. Read about the surprising way The Church That Had Too Much began to resolve her problems in this deceptively simple and enchanting fable.

About the Author

Anita Mathias is the author of Wandering Between Two Worlds: Essays on Faith and Art. She has a B.A. and M.A. in English from Somerville College, Oxford University, and an M.A. in Creative Writing from the Ohio State University, USA. Anita won a National Endowment of the Arts fellowship in Creative Nonfiction in 1997. She lives in Oxford, England with her husband, Roy, and her daughters, Zoe and Irene.

Visit Anita at http://www.anitamathias.com, and on http://theoxfordchristian.blogspot.com, her Christian blog; http://wanderingbetweentwoworlds.blogspot.com/, her personal blog, and http://thegoodbooksblog.blogspot.com, her literary and writing blog.

www.ingramcontent.com/pod-product-compliance
Lightning Source LLC
LaVergne TN
LVHW050919080826
845145LV00001B/134

* 9 7 8 1 8 4 9 0 2 4 9 2 1 *